RED&W PHOE.NIA

THE ADVENTURES OF A HESSLE ROAD LAD

KEITH POLLARD

Published by Tablo

Jason with his niece Libby
and sister Tracy

This book is dedicated to my son,
Jason Wilson Pollard
who passed away in 2011
after a short illness

Copyright © 2018, 2021 Keith Pollard

All rights reserved.
No part of this publication may be reproduced,
stored in a retrieval system, or transmitted, in any form or
by any means, without the prior written permission of the
publisher, nor be otherwise circulated in any form of
binding or cover other than that in which it is published
and without a similar condition being imposed on the
subsequent publisher.

Keith Pollard has asserted his right to be identified
as the author of this work under the Copyright, Designs
and Patents Act 1988.

Published by Tablo Publishing
Publisher and wholesale enquiries: orders@tablo.io

Published 2021.
First edition published 2018. Second edition 2021.

ISBN 978-1-6496955-0-5

CONTENTS

Keith Pollard

FOREWORD

In sport, as in life, being in the right place at the right time is so important. Prop forwards mature in the later part of their rugby lives, and Keith Pollard was no exception.

His career at Hull Kingston Rovers probably faltered because the time was not right.

During his time as a young player with the Robins, there were a number of other forwards competing for the prop positions, and Keith's face perhaps just did not fit.

After learning more about his trade from Mick Clarke at Keighley, he went on to play his best rugby on the other side of the world, where he was truly appreciated.

But despite the fact that his time at Craven Park was not as successful as he would have hoped, he has retained his love for the club and has remained loyal to it. He cares deeply for the club and for the game in general, and has forthright opinions on both.

Keith is now a valued member of the Rovers' Heritage Group, where he is always prepared to give his time to its varied activities, sharing his knowledge, views and memories across its audiences. Through this group, I have been privileged to enjoy his friendship and company over the last few years.

Roger Pugh
Hull KR historian and author of 'The Robins'

INTRODUCTION

I have never been a famous superstar or celebrity. I was quite well known in the relatively small world of local rugby league in Kingston upon Hull in the 1960s, but I have never been rich, handsome or slim! Those who have known me may think I was not too bad a player or a mate, whilst one never knows what those that pretend to be friends really think. Whatever, I have enjoyed my life to the full, and have always wanted to tell my story. My memories not only from rugby, but a life working and living in both England and abroad.

Now I am retired, with not a great deal to take up my spare time and every day is a Saturday, I have found time to put together my story, and some of the tales I have gathered during my chequered career. To be honest, when you have stopped working you are at least at the age when you have had a life and a story to tell.

As a keen reader with an interest in biographies, I have read those of famous actors and sportsmen, including some from my own sport of rugby league, and I've often been disappointed as some of them have been quite boring, based only on facts and statistics and with sycophantic quotes from people who knew them.

I want my story to reflect my life as it was, and to be an account that most of us ordinary people can identify with. It is based on true experiences, as far as my memory allows but I have altered some names, to protect the innocent as it were! Of course, life has not all been a bed of roses. As with us all, there have been 'ups and downs' and even some very dark days at times.

If you are wondering about the title of the book, the phoenix as most of you will know is a bird from Greek mythology that is associated with the sun, that obtains new life by arising from the ashes of its predecessor. According to some sources, the phoenix dies in a show of flames and combustion, although there are other sources that claim that the legendary bird dies and simply decomposes before being born again. According to some texts, the phoenix could 'live' over 1,400 years before rebirth. Anyway, the phoenix was the emblem of Boulevard school that I attended over sixty years ago. It was a strong rugby league area and most of the boys were Hull FC supporters, or the 'Black and Whites' as they were called. Their main rivals, on the other side of the city, were Hull Kingston Rovers – the 'Red and Whites' – but they were never mentioned in this part of Hull, not by schoolboys anyway. Well, I did not die, but I rebelled and was 'reborn' as a Red and White, and Hull Kingston Rovers play a very big part in my story.

Keith Pollard

I hope you enjoy my book and perhaps at the end you might feel encouraged to do the same and to tell your own story. I know there are many other people out there who have great stories to tell. Reliving moments that are embedded in your memory is a wonderful journey, one that often brings a smile to your lips and a tear to your eye as you think back of days gone by. I hope this story might stir some memories for you, and I thank you for taking the time to read it.

I am releasing my book as a second edition after selling out my first one to people far and wide.

As with my first edition, all net proceeds will be going to the Alpha-1UK Support Group helping them to bring awareness to this terrible disease which took the life of our son Jason.

Unfortunately not enough is known about this disease.

Keith Pollard
February 2021

ACKNOWLEDGEMENTS

I would like to thank Roger Pugh, the Hull KR historian and author of 'The Robins' the history of Hull Kingston Rovers, and Mike Sterriker of Riverhead, for their assistance in writing and producing this book, without their invaluable help it would never have happened.

I also must thank my wonderful wife Jacqueline for putting up with me over the two years it has taken me to finish it.

DISCLAIMER
Due to my story being based on my life over 70 years and having some historical content included, I would like to point out that I have searched the internet looking for relevant information, to give the reader an accurate picture of Hull's history and where I was brought up. Having collected this information from various websites I have not, as far as I am aware, used any copyright material.

CHAPTER 1
HULL, HESSLE ROAD
& THE FISHING INDUSTRY

Before I start my story, I would like to give you a brief background about the city of Kingston upon Hull, and particularly the famous Hessle Road area of the city where I grew up.

Hull was granted a Royal charter in 1229, and thus became known as Kingstown upon Hull – the river upon which it stands – and its' history goes back as far as Anglo-Saxon times. What we now call Hessle Road was in the 19th century called Patrick Ground Lane, in the then Pottery District of Hull. Maps of the time show how the lane was in open countryside, with only a small concentration of buildings located around the still standing *Vauxhall Tavern*.

By then, it was becoming evident that Patrick Ground Lane, and the rough track from it that led to the village of Hessle, was quite unsuitable as an effective thoroughfare. By the early 19th century, many wealthy influential merchants had begun to move away from the town centre to new large mansions in the rapidly-developing villages to the west of the city, such as Hessle and its neighbour North Ferriby. The construction of a good road between the business centre of Hull and the merchants' new mansions was essential.

Charles Frost, a Hull solicitor, was the main instigator of the building of the new turnpike road from Hull to Hessle. He received strong support from the majority of the local estate owners, with opposition coming from the competition-fearing trustees of the Hull-Anlaby-Kirk Ella turnpike, now Anlaby Road.

An Act was passed that enabled the turnpike to be built, and the first tolls were collected on July 28th 1825. For some twenty years, the road was identified on maps as Hessle New Road, being shortened to Hessle Road by the 1840s, and Patrick Ground Lane was no more. A toll bar was erected on the town and county boundary two miles to the west of the city centre, at Galley Clough Lane, roughly where Division Road stands today, and the road remained a turnpike or toll road until 1873.

During the 1870s, Hessle Road really began to expand westwards towards the neighbouring village of Dairycoates, which was also growing rapidly. 1872 and 1873 trade directories show that the Hull end of the road was becoming a busy commercial centre with grocers, butchers, fishmongers and more public houses competing for trade. The *Vauxhall Tavern*, the *Alexandra Inn* (formerly the *Hessle Road Inn*), four unnamed beer-houses and

7

Keith Pollard

several coffee houses are also listed. However, in the area between Coltman Street and Dairycoates village, housing remained fairly sporadic and rural in nature. In Dairycoates, a Wesleyan Chapel had been erected, having been opened in December 1865, and the *Dairycoates Inn* was popular.

By the mid-1870s, building on the north side of Hessle Road had spread nearly a mile from Coltman Street up to Glasgow Street, whilst the south side was even more built-up. The commercial development of Dairycoates had continued with a post office, grocer, cobbler and butcher all flourishing – not to mention the *Locomotive Hotel* and the *Temperance Hotel*. The growth of the Hessle Road community saw several new churches being consecrated, including St Barnabas Church (1874), on the junction with South Boulevard, and a Congregational Church (1877) near Coltman Street. The growth in trade and improvements in transport were primarily responsible for this expansion, whilst the opening of West Dock (later Albert Dock) added to the boom and an influx of workers led to more and more housing development in the area.

The growth and importance of the railway system led to Dairycoates becoming a major railway junction, and when Hessle Road ceased to be a turnpike, the new freedom from tolls encouraged the introduction of the horse-drawn tram system across the city between 1875 and 1877. This service meant that it was now possible for people to commute even greater distances to work, further encouraging the growth of the suburbs.

Whaling was a big part of the history of Hull, with vessels sailing to the Scandinavian Peninsula in the latter part of the 1500s; and by 1618 vessels from Hull, along with those from Holland, were using the Norwegian island of Jan Mayen as a fishing station. Due to the English Civil War and the London-based Muscovy Company's constant claims that the Hull whalers were 'interlopers,' the Dutch began to dominate whaling in the late 1600s, but, during the following century, government bounties and subsidies, along with the duty placed on imported oil and bone, helped the whaling business to grow in England.

In 1766, Samuel Standidge began the investment that laid the foundations of Hull as a major whaling port. War with England, and a blockade during the war with France, meant that the Dutch involvement in whaling was effectively dead by the beginning of the 1800s. By this time, the Hull fleet made up about 40% of the British whaling fleet, and peaked around 1820, when 62 vessels returned with the produce from 688 whales, worth approximately £250,000. This amount of trade in the city resulted in the expansion of other manufacturing.

1821, however, was a disaster for the whaling industry, with nine vessels crushed in ice. Many investors withdrew their money

8

and the fleet was reduced by almost a third. In 1822, another six vessels were lost and eight others failed to catch a single whale. The industry declined to the extent that, by 1869, the *Diana* was the sole remaining vessel sailing from Hull. After this was wrecked off Donna Nook on the Lincolnshire coast, the whaling industry moved to Scotland. But by this time, the fishing industry had become of primary importance to Hull's economy, and by the later part of the nineteenth century, it dominated the Hessle Road area of the city. Most of the families in this area lived in predominantly 'two up, two down' terrace houses in an area of about four square miles, bordered by Anlaby Road to the north, Coltman Street to the east, Goulton Street to the south and Hawthorn Avenue to the west.

We 'Hessle Roaders' liked to think of the area as a small village on its own, proud that we were from Hull and yet living in a close, friendly community, whose residents were honoured to say that they 'come off Hessle Road.' At its' peak, the fishing industry sustained an estimated 50,000 local lives. There were more than 160 long-distance trawlers based in the port, several of them built locally in shipyards at Beverley and Selby.

The way that the owners of the ships named their vessels is very interesting. Hamblings' trawlers all were all named after Saints, such as the *St Romulus;* all trawlers owned by Lord Line were 'Lords', such as the *Lord Nelson*; Kingston's trawlers were named after jewels, like the *Kingston Topaz;* the names of Boyd Line ships began with 'Arctic;' and Ross Group trawlers' names started with 'Ross'.

Sadly, there were all-too-many dark days of tragedy over the years, deeply affecting the Hessle Road community, when Hull trawlermen were lost to the cruel seas. The words of skipper Philip Gay of the *Ross Cleveland* on March 5th 1968 leave a lasting memory. He called over the radio, "I am going over. We are laying over. Help us, Len, she's going. Give my love and the crew's love to the wives and families." She was the third Hull trawler to be lost within 26 days. In modern times it was an unparalleled blow, even for a community well used to sacrificing its men folk who fished the unforgiving northern seas.

It fell to the workers of the Fishermen's Bethel to tell families of their losses. It must have been an awful job breaking the bad news to relatives in days when large families were quite normal, and there were around 50 families for each ship. Firstly, they had to inform them that the company had lost contact with the ships and later, after no radio contact or sightings by other trawlers, they had to impart the tragic news.

The earliest losses were recorded in 1862, when three men died, and the last in 2000, when Michael Lambert, aged 59, died result of an accident on the *Westella*. In all, the list of Hull's lost

Keith Pollard

trawlermen has over six thousand names on it. The youngest were boys aged 14, lost or killed in accidents between 1862 and 1895, when children left school at an early age. One of my own uncles started work at 14, as clerk to an engineering company on St Andrews Dock. At the other end of the spectrum, James Coull, the cook on the *Alonso*, was the oldest trawlerman to die at sea, aged 71, when his ship was presumed to have hit a mine in 1944. Two Pollards are on the list, Joseph, who was killed in an accident on board the *Achilles* in 1863, and Thomas, who was lost overboard on the *Tubal Cain* in 1884, but I have been unable to find out if either were directly related to my family.

I have traced my own family history back to 1690 on my father's side, to a gentleman named Adenego in Bradford West Riding and to 1690 on my Grandmothers side Levi Gibbs from Fingest, a small village in Buckinghamshire. Funnily enough there was a Mesheck and Shadrach also on the Pollards side. But on my mother's side, I have been able to go back only as far as 1841. Her mother, Louisa, was one of eight children whose maiden name was Boynton, from the South Shields area. But my grandfather on my mother's side came from a seafaring family in Hull. My mother's father was killed in an accident at sea, not on a trawler, but on a merchant ship. Apparently, he slipped, fell down the engine room steps, and died from his injuries. After that, my grandmother was unable to cope with five children, who were taken into the Sailors' Childrens' Society orphanage on Cottingham Road in Hull, where they stayed until they were able to be returned to their mother.

My mother's cousin, Ray Mearns, was aged 34 when he was a mate on the *St Romanus,* which went down with all hands on the January 11th 1968 on its way to fish off Norway. Not unusually at the time, the *St Romanus* had gone to sea without a radio operator. Many radio operators refused to sail on some ships because accommodation was so limited that they had to sleep in the tiny chart room. Trawlermen were very suspicious people, and some trawlers had 'a bit of a shadow' hanging over them – the *St Romanus* was one of these. There were stories about a crewman jumping overboard, saying he had decided to go home to see his girlfriend, and being drowned, along with a shipmate who had jumped over to try and save him. Another lad, who had previously sailed on her, had a premonition about going down with the ship and signed off before she sailed on her last trip. It was a feeling he could not explain, and he never went to sea again.

Bill Weightman, my uncle's brother-in-law, was skipper of the *St Sebastian*. At the age of 27, he was lost with all hands when the ship sank on the 29th September 1938, and left a wife and two children.

Several times, lads with whom I went to school or worked with, lost relations. When I was nine, the *Lorrella* and *Roderigo* went down on January 26th 1955. I can still hear the women crying as they ran through the streets, knocking at doors and calling out with the news of the sinkings – there were few televisions in those days and no local radio stations, so it was all word of mouth. Johnny Rose, the brother of my friend Colin, lived on Newton Street, only 100 yards from our terrace, was only 19 and was on the *Roderigo.* Tom Sutton, the father of my good friend Steve, who lived very nearby on Division Road, was on the *Lorrella.*

A Facebook group entitled 'Hull's Fishermens History' contains a letter from the owners of the *Lorrella*, J Marr & Son, sent to the wife of one of the men who was lost, that shows the approach of the trawler owners towards their workforce, who were effectively casual labour – something that fishermen have fought for years to put right. I think the letter illustrates the stark reality of life for the men and their families who put the fish on our tables, and a look at this group's Facebook page is well worth the time spent. The letter reads as follows:

Dear 'Mrs Smith'

It is with very great regret that we have had to abandon all hope for the Lorrella or her crew. We wish to offer to you our deepest sympathy in your bereavement.

Nothing can be done to recompense you for your loss of your husband but we are very anxious that you should suffer no financial hardship until such time as your affairs are put in order and we are therefore making an ex gratia payment to you of £6. 11. 3d per week for the next eight weeks. Our cheque for the first week's payment is enclosed.

Yours faithfully,

J. Marr and Son Limited

Another trawler to be lost was the *Kingston Peridot,* which went down with all hands when she capsized off Norway in 1968. One of the crew was Kenny Swain, who was on his first trip as a 'decky learner.' I had been to school with Kenny, and although he was two years older than me, I knew him quite well. He had been finished at the Langham Picture Theatre, where he worked as a projectionist, and so he decided to go to sea. I was chatting to him a couple of days before he joined the ship and wished him the best of luck on his new venture. That gives you a very sobering sense of mortality and even thinking about it now gives me shivers up my spine.

Accidents were numerous. My Uncle Jim got washed overboard and swears that he must have gone underneath the ship, as he saw the hull. Whilst the crew were looking over the side for him he was washed back on board behind those searching for him. All he sustained was a broken leg which was set and placed in a splint on board – so he completed the 19-day trip with a permanent limp.

Some fourteen poor souls never even got to sea or died when returning home in St Andrews Dock. One trawler, the *Lady Jeannette,* foundered off the dock, or 'turned turtle,' in the river, with the loss of nine lives. These unfortunate souls would probably have been in the accommodation area, getting their kit bags ready to go ashore at the time. The youngest was only 18.

What the trawlers used to do was to reverse into the lock to make it easier when they were leaving – it allowed them to merely sail straight out into the river and head for Spurn Point and north to the fishing grounds. Depending on which way the tide was running, they could come in four hours either side of high tide. The *Lady Jeanette* must have been coming in on the outgoing tide, as she had gone inland towards Hessle to turn round in the river, then used the tide to bring her back down towards St Andrews dock, whilst using the engines as a brake to ensure she did not come into the lock head too quickly. Apparently however, the tide was nearly at its lowest and she hit a sand bank, but with the river still running fast it pushed her over and off the bank in to deeper water. According to my father, who saw the tragedy, quite few men managed to swim ashore, but those inside the ship had no chance.

One of the most well-known, or infamous, disasters was that of the 'super trawler' the *Gaul.* Modern and supposedly watertight, the Gaul was only eighteen months old when she disappeared with the loss of her entire 36-man crew in the Barents Sea, 70 miles off Norway, during a fierce storm in February 1974. It was described as the 'worst ever single trawler disaster.' In the absence of any trace of the ship or its crew in the aftermath, it was alleged that the *Gaul* was engaged in 'cold war' espionage activities – claims repeated in a TV documentary the following year. After the examination of a wreck that was confirmed as the *Gaul* over 20 years later, a re-opened formal investigation concluded that an attempted emergency manoeuvre by the *Gaul's* watch officer (a perfectly logical move to try to turn 'into the sea') caused 100 tonnes of floodwater to surge across to the starboard side of the ship, leading to a catastrophic loss of stability. Flooding took place through open doors, waste chutes and hatches and, losing her buoyancy, the *Gaul* sank very rapidly, stern first. The RFI report dismissed the idea that Gaul was involved in espionage or that she was in a collision, but relatives of the crew were still not satisfied and claimed that the 'truth was still to be told.'

The list of trawlermen lost or killed just within a mile of where I lived was quite staggering:

Bean Street-36, Boulevard-28, Division Road-36, Edinburgh Street-16, Eton Street-46, Flinton Street-39, Harrow Street-39,

RED & WHITE PHOENIX

Havelock Street-30, Liverpool Street-38, Regent Street-13, Rosamond Street-30, Rugby Street-32, Scarborough Street-37, Somerset Street-23, Strickland Street-37, Subway Street-24, Walcott Street-70 and Wassand Street-61.

Those from the Boulevard were either skippers, mates, chief engineers or engineers. As they were the 'upper class' of the fishing industry they were the best paid, and this was a street with big grand houses, many of which survive today, even if many are somewhat run down. Most of the others who died were 'rank and file' crew hands. Not that the upper classes were in any way protected from tragedy. In all, 282 skippers alone failed to return home – 187 went down with their ships whilst the rest were either lost overboard or died whilst at sea. Everyone, whether the companies that owned the trawlers, the families of the crews, and the community as a whole, sustained significant losses – no-one who lived in the Hessle road area would have been unaffected by trawler tragedies. But more men did come home than did not, and for them there were both good times and bad. A particularly good 'catch' would result in the trawlermen receiving a very favourable amount of 'settlings' at the end of the trip, whilst on a less good trip it was not uncommon for them to 'settle in debt' after the deduction of allowances sent to wives and partners whilst they were at sea. It was well known that the trawlermens' wives would frequently pawn their husband's suits the minute they set sail. Then, a couple of days before the owner was due home, the suit would be taken back out, ready for use over the owner's two days 'recreation' in the many 'watering holes' of the area. Such was the decline of the fishing industry that, by 1954, only three of these pawnbrokers remained – all of whom were making up their income with a second business. William Leighton added carpet dealing to his business plan and a Leighton's carpet shop survived on Hessle Road until 2001. Issadore Turner, or "Izzy" as he was known to his clients, added gentlemens' outfitting to his pawnbroking activities.

It was a very hard life for the trawlermen and their families, but for the Hessle Road area of Hull the fishing industry was its lifeblood. When the industry was thriving, the area thrived too; and now that the fishing industry in Hull is no more, the character of the whole area has changed beyond recognition.

Keith Pollard

Clive Rutter's Fish Merchant workers, my Dad on the left

Clive Rutter's workforce on St Andrews Dock

CHAPTER 2
EARLY YEARS

My Uncle Scrat walked in through the back door.

"Is Eddie in, Lou?" he said.

"In the living room," replied my mam, pointing to the door. "He's looking after the young un." Calling it the 'living room' made it seem grander than it was but that was typical of my mother. It was a 'two up, two down' terrace house, with no hot running water, no bathroom (there was a tin bath hung outside on a nail) and an outside toilet.

"Nah then Ed, how's things?" Scrat said to my old man. "And how long you 'ad the pup?" he added when he saw me laid naked on the rug in front of the fireplace. Dad laughed and said, "Cheeky bastard – meet my son Keith."

"Oh, I thought he was a bull terrier," Scrat replied, "No matter, I'd still enter him for Crufts. But by the look of those legs, he'll play for the black and whites one day." How disappointed he was to be.

Then in walked my Uncle Tom, "Ready then?" he said.

"Seen the new pup?" asked Scrat.

"Bloody hell, he's a beauty," said Tom. I was about a month old at this time and they were seeing me for the first time. Tom, a trawler skipper, was home from sea – two days at home then 19 days at sea. My dad was a fish-filleter all his life – 'the best on the dock,' he always said, modestly. The three of them were getting together to go to *Rayners* for 'an afternoon session'.

I was born on June 27th in Clarence Avenue, Rosamond Street, off Hessle Road, to proud parents Cyril and Louisa. I must have been a bit of a surprise, as they had been married about seven years and they were not really trying for a baby. My old man had lost his first wife and baby in childbirth. But I just turned up unannounced as I have continued to do for seventy years now – all three and a half pounds of bouncing baby, six weeks premature. I was born by caesarean section, and I was told that it was a difficult birth for both my mother and I. The doctor said that it could have been very traumatic for me and could have left me with some mental scars. But apart from the occasional urge to get out of a car through the sun roof, rather than the door, I haven't noticed any ill effects.

My memories are of a great childhood down Clarence Avenue, which had only eight houses in the terrace but had a great set of people and a real community spirit. Sadly, Clarence Avenue is no longer there, it was pulled down to be replaced by some slums under the guise of redevelopment.

Keith Pollard

My Dad working on Fish Dock

My Mother aged 30

Granddad Pollard

Me and my friend 'Basher Bell'

RED & WHITE PHOENIX

At one of the houses were Mr and Mrs Johnson, who had a son that everyone called Bimy. I have no idea how he got that name or what his real name was. He was a lot older than me but he used to invite me in to his bedroom when I was about 10 to show me the toy soldiers he used to paint, and he gave me little presents. Thinking back, he was a bit odd, but quite harmless and was always alright with me. Nowadays, he would have been given some label or other, but these had not been thought of then – not on Hessle Road anyway. Bimy's dad was my old man's best mate. They used to go to the *Albert* club in Somerset Street together – until they started allowing women in, and my old man never went again.

"Women shouldn't be allowed in clubs," my old man said, and he stuck by it. He was very stubborn and self-centred at times.

Denise and Gloria Day lived at number 3, opposite, and the Carrigans at number 4 had a daughter Rita, who was my childhood sweetheart. Ted and Joyce Newton moved in next door when I was about 14 or 15 and I vividly remember having a schoolboy crush on Joyce, whom I thought the sexiest woman in the world – albeit in my then limited experience. Mr and Mrs Hardy lived at number 7, but I do not remember who lived at number 8, presumably they must not have made a big impression on a young lad.

Rosamond Street itself was about a quarter of a mile long, in the heart of 'black and white' country, with Hull FC's Boulevard rugby ground at the end. In those days you only seemed to know the people around your 'end' of the street – perhaps reflecting the smaller world that it seemed to be then. At the corner of the next street, Redbourne Street, there was a police station, with a great bakers' shop, *Ray's Bakery* (my stop-off point for breakfast on my way to school every morning), on the opposite side. There was also the *Red Lion* pub, where I enjoyed many a fine night in later years.

Nearly opposite our terrace was Conway Street, where the Shakesby family lived. Kenny was one of my best mates and he had three older sisters, Pat, Val and Cynthia, as well as a younger brother. Sadly, Sylvia passed away a few years back. Not long ago, I met Val and her husband one Sunday dinner time in *Rayners* on Hessle Road – the only time I have seen her in over 50 years. Pat lost her husband in a tragic accident when he was drowned in the river Humber whilst out fishing. At the time, they were landlord and landlady of the *Albion* near the City Centre.

The Sach family lived further down the street – if the Shakesby family would be thought large today, the Sachs dwarfed them. They seemed to come in twos – Barry and Brian, Mike and Malcolm, Denise and a sister whose name I cannot remember, and at least another brother and sister. As I was an only child, it used to mesmerise me whenever I went in their house. There were bodies everywhere and it was not a big house either. I think the younger

17

Keith Pollard

Louise, my Dad's first wife

Me with John and Elaine Broberg

Mam, front row second from right, on a bus trip to Wembley

boys all slept in the same bed, 'topped and tailed.' When I asked Mally which end of the bed he slept at, he said 'the shallow end.' They moved across the city to the Longhill council estate when that was built in the late 'fifties – it was only about five and half miles away but it might as well have been in Australia in those days, and I never saw them again.

Nearby was Sefton Street, where the Cutsforths lived. The old man had a haulage company that served the fishing industry, and his stinking lorries were always down the street. His son, Leslie, was a bit younger than we were but he knocked about with us anyway, along with Allan 'Smiler' Baldwin and Robert Mawer, who lived in the terrace at the bottom of the cul-de-sac. Robert Mawer was the speedster of our gang, and could he run! He was the fastest kid on the block and always won all the races we had – especially 'fagging out' races.

My cousins lived at the corner of the next terrace, Sefton Terrace; Uncle Jim Shepherd, Aunt Mary, Jimmy junior, Carol and Susan. Uncle Jim was a skipper with Kingston Line. On the opposite corner of the terrace lived the Dyble family, who they owned the *Dee Street club* and a bookmaker's shop. They were the affluent residents of Rosamond Street, and I can remember taxis pulling up outside their house, as even they did not own a car. They always used nearby Subway Cars who had an Austin Princess, which was like a Rolls Royce to us. Opposite our terrace lived June Gibbs. We were all in love with June, who was a stunner, and we drooled over her from 11 onwards. She eventually married a lad from the other side of Hessle Road, Eton Street, called Keith Sanderson, whose dad had a beer off-licence – so we had no chance! After that she moved to another part of the city and is another one who might as well have gone to the moon.

Now, of course, the internet has made the world smaller and I have joined Facebook. Since I started writing these memoirs I have been in touch with a few of the people I have mentioned. Facebook attracts more than its' share of bad press, but for me it is wonderful, particularly for contacting old friends you have lost touch with. I do not want to tell the world about what I had for dinner or that my piles are playing up but being able to chat to people 12,000 miles away at the click of a button is great for me.

In those days, with no phones at all, we seemed to have extra sensory perception about when we were going to meet up to have a game of 'touch'. I would wander round the corner towards the *Lion* pub and sure enough the teams were gathering as I walked up.

"Fancy a game, Pol" someone would call out, and I would always reply, "Yeah, count me in." We played 'touch rugby' down the street with a rolled up newspaper held together with pieces of *Elastoplast* off discarded roll ends from Smith and Nephew that were dumped at Hessle tip. Our pitch was invariably down Newton

Me with my first bus, I've been collecting them ever since

My first cowboy outfit   My Mam's father, seated on left

RED & WHITE PHOENIX

Street between Redbourne Street and Boulevard. In those days you did not need to worry about cars, because no one had one. There we learned to play rugby the 'right way,' letting the ball do the work of beating a man with a pass, not like so much modern rugby – all brawn and no brain. We had one lad who had one leg longer than the other – his left leg was longer so he always played on the right wing. He was quite fast but could only run in the gutter. Once we tried him on the left wing but he kept falling over.

I remember that I went to Constable Street Junior School from the age of five up to eleven, although my memories of those days are very hazy. But I do know that I had a great upbringing. I had a few good hidings along the way – my old man was very serious and a disciplinarian – he gave me a few 'back-handers' over the years, but it certainly did me no harm.

One clear memory from my younger days was when we went to a party at my Uncle Tom's house. As a trawler skipper, he was pretty rich and had a television long before we did. He lived on the north side of the railway line at 1, Arthur Street, and to get there we had to walk down Division Road and cross over the footbridge. This was a real adventure, because if you timed it right and were lucky enough to be on the bridge when a steam train passed underneath, you got engulfed in clouds of smoke – which really appealed to me as a young boy. Sadly, kids do not get this simple pleasure now unless they are lucky enough to go to a preserved steam railway. Anyway, I think it was my cousin Lawrence's birthday and all we kids were there, but the one thing that sticks in my memory is a guy called Donald Peers on the television singing, '*In a Shady Nook by a Babbling Brook*' – amazing what strange things get etched in your brain!

Another memory is that of the train set. My old man bought me a lot of toys, in fact you could say I was spoiled rotten; nearly every Saturday lunchtime he took me and bought me a *Dinky toys* car, truck or bus – I blame him for my passion for cars. When I was about four, he bought me a train set for Christmas. It was a Hornby OO set, and the engine was *Sir Nigel Gresley*, the same type as the world famous *Mallard*, with the blue livery and streamlining. I had it going round and round on a circular track and until I decided that this was not exciting enough. To a four-year old a rail crash is a bit of fun, and the catastrophe duly happened. *Sir Nigel Gresley* was derailed, I think by a police car, the black type used by the flying squad in London, or perhaps a fire engine, I am not sure – but what I do know is that my dad went berserk when he saw that the pistons on the engine were broken.

"You little bastard," was the last thing I heard as I disappeared through the back kitchen and up the stairs. I was always rather quick but when someone is trying to rip your head off, it is

Keith Pollard

Mam and Dad's wedding-1939

Withernsea donkey rides

My first car ride

Me, Mam and Dad at Withernsea

surprising how quickly you can go. Looking back this helped me a lot in my rugby career. I heard my mother calling from upstairs, "What the fuck is going on?" People on Hessle Road did not pull punches and their language was often quite colourful to say the least. Anyway the old man eventually calmed down and after a while all was rosy, but it cost him a fortune to send the engine back to Hornby for repair.

I knocked about with my cousins, the Brobergs, quite a bit in those early days and I was often round at their house. There was John, Elaine, Thomas, and Victor, John and Elaine both being older than me. They had my grandmother living with them, along with my mother's sister Frances, so it was quite a house full. My uncle's real name was John, but he was usually known as Jack, or 'Scrat' to us kids. He was a real character to say the least. He had a bad accident working on the docks as a 'bobber', whose job was to unload the fish from the trawlers, ready for the early morning market. He was working in the hold, filling the baskets that were lowered down on a winch, when his glove got caught in the hook and he was winched up to about twenty feet in the air. The winches used were steam driven and did not react that quickly to the controls, so by the time the operator realised what had happened, Scrat was hanging above the deck of the ship. Unfortunately, at that point his glove ripped, he fell on to the dockside fracturing his skull, pelvis and arm. The arm was never the same again and he used to call his other arm his 'one wing' after that.

My mother's sister Olive was the matriarch of the family – the one who held it all together. We had some great parties at their house – it was a big house, which it had to be for that lot. One thing that always sticks in my memory is that they did not have carpets – either just lino or bare boards, but not like the polished wood floors of today, just bare wooden ones. But Scrat was given about three thousand pounds in compensation for his accident – a fortune in those days – and a guaranteed job for life. With some of the money they decorated and carpeted every room in the house – as well as buying a new three-piece suite.

When looking back, as most of us do, I associate specific things with particular people. In Scrat's case, of all the mad things he used to do, the party piece I recall (and he had a few) is the old poem by J. Milton Hayes which I believe was written in the early 1900's – '*The Green Eye of the Little Yellow God.*'

I remember the first lines:

There's a one-eyed yellow idol to the north of Kathmandu,
There's a little marble cross below the town;
There's a broken-hearted woman tends the grave of Mad Carew,
And the Yellow God forever gazes down.

Keith Pollard

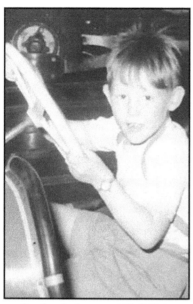

On the dodgems at Hull Fair

Me and my cousin, Carol Shepherd

Climbing the cliffs at Withernsea

Dad - he loved that bike

RED & WHITE PHOENIX

Apparently, the poem was written specially for an actor called Bransby Williams, christened Bransby William Pharez, who was born in 1870 and died in 1961 – not a bad innings in anyone's language. Anyway, Scrat used to put on an act like he was on the music hall stage; it was an age when people only had the radio or music halls for entertainment, so they often provided their own at parties. My father used to quote poems from Rudyard Kipling but I will stop there before I put you to sleep.

Uncle Jim, the trawler skipper, was big mates with Scrat, much to the displeasure of his wife, Aunt Mary. Mary detested Scrat due to his outspoken nature and very colourful language – in addition to which, whenever Jim was home from sea and he went 'on the pop' with Scrat, he always finished up legless, which was not well received when he was only home for two or three days and spent most of it either asleep or the worse for wear. Mary always had a go at Scrat about getting Jim drunk, which was like a red rag to a bull with Scrat, and it was great entertainment when they 'went off at each other' – invariably in the street, as Mary would not let Scrat in the house.

My cousin Carol reminded me a while back about how we used to play with my *Bayco* Building Set – which would now be a collector's item. In 1960, the company was bought by *Meccano*, who tried to improve the *Bayco* set, but by then *Lego* was on the market. *Lego* was much easier for kids to use, and manufacture of the *Bayco* sets ended in the 1967. I also had an early *Meccano* set, which I handed down to my son Jason in a wooden box that his grandad, George, made. Whilst in Liverpool for few days recently, I saw that a museum there had a *Meccano* set on display, as apparently they were manufactured in that city.

My old man had a good job but often he did a 'bit on the side,' not all of which was quite above board. No-one ever asked questions, and I will not elaborate. I will just say that we had a TV before anyone else in the street, and my Mam was never short of money. My dad was also very strong-willed, to say the least. He smoked about 60 woodbines a day until an x-ray showed a shadow on his lung – he stopped that same day and never smoked again.

He came from a very strict upbringing. His father, who was born in 1867, was an engineer on trawlers and merchant ships. The old man told me that he was a bit of an oddball; he was apparently psychic and was known as 'Mad Pollard'. On one voyage around the world, he was shipwrecked and subsequently taken into hospital in India, from where he wrote a letter back home. It took the letter two weeks to arrive in Hull from India, and of course when it arrived it was quite a big event. The family sat around my grandma, whilst she read it to them – there was no TV then, of course! According to my dad, part of the letter said that, 'whilst you

Keith Pollard

A pensive Mam

Me and Mam at Cleethorpes

Mam, Me, John Broberg and Aunt Frances

RED & WHITE PHOENIX

are reading this letter, Laurie will come into the house and tell you that your cousin Annie has died'. Dad said that, very spookily, this is exactly what happened.

The old man also told me that once, during the school holidays and when his father was home from sea, dad was going to go to Madeley Street swimming baths as usual, but his father told him not to go as there was going to be an accident and someone would die. There were no arguments or trantrums in those days, and dad just did not go. He later learned that one of his friends had dived in to the pool from the top platform that day and had not come up. Although no one actually witnessed the accident, it seems he hit his head on the bottom of the pool, and his body was found floating in the water.

Whilst in the Indian hospital, in the next bed to my grandfather was a South African. Grandfather apparently spoke in detailed terms about Pretoria, but subsequently admitting, to this man's amazement, that he had, 'never been to South Africa, but have seen it in my visions.' He then went on to tell the South African that he knew where the 'Kruger Millions' were hidden. In 1900, the then South African President, Paul Kruger, fled from the British army with a huge amount of gold bullion at the end of the Boer War. The gold was alleged to have been buried, but has never been found. Grandfather later told dad that he knew where it was and would return after his death to tell him. Unfortunately, though, this never happened! Dad also said that his father's visions had foretold that his grandchildren and great-grandchildren 'will all own their own homes, drive cars, and will never want for anything.' Some statement for the early 1900s, but it turned out to be pretty much true.

My dad turned out to be a keen gardener and had an allotment near to the old railway sidings at Dairycoates. Tom, a docks policeman who was a good mate of his, had a few pigs there and I used to go and help look after them when I was about ten years old. I can still remember their stink and the way that they literally ate anything you gave them. A lot of the men with allotments gave all their rubbish to Tom, and it all went to the pigs, along with anything else Tom could get his hands on. When those allotments were closed, dad got one in Gypsyville, about a mile and a half away. He got it when I was about eleven, and I never seemed to see him again until I was eighteen. He worked from about four o'clock in the morning, when he went down to St Andrews dock to buy fish then fillet it, then get it packed into boxes and transferred to lorries. He was finished by lunchtime, after which he came home on his bike and was away to the allotment. In the summer I was always out playing, and by the time I got in he was in bed, as he had to be up so early.

Keith Pollard

Dad, Mam and Me at Withernsea   Jacky's Mam and Dad's wedding

My mother hardly ever went out with him to the pub or club, witness the *Albert* Club incident I mentioned earlier, but went out on her own a few nights a week playing bingo, or darts for the *Rosamond* Club. The last time they went out together might have been my wedding day, but even then they did not travel together. My mother went in a wedding car and the old man went on the bus halfway and walked the rest – he hated cars.

They used to argue a lot, and then did not talk to each other for ages after. I remember once they had not spoken for quite literally nearly three months and I ended up being their 'go between.' Mam would say 'tell your dad this' and he would say 'tell her to fuck off.' The worst incident I can remember and there were quite a few (no wonder I like my own company – particularly as I was an only child), was when my mother had ordered a picture of her lovely baby – yes, me! It was based on a photo, which had been painted to look like an oil painting, and I think it cost about £15 – which in those days was a fortune. When my old man found out he went berserk. They actually got to blows and he had her by the throat on the floor. I stood there, like the referee at an all-in wresting session, shouting at them to stop it. Eventually they did, but after that, they did not speak for about four months. It all ended when one night I had finally had enough of passing on messages and not trying to side with one or the other. Dad had given me a message to pass to Mam and I exploded.

"For fuck's sake will you two stupid bastards give it up," I said. In unison, they both said, "Don't you swear in this house!!" You two are great to talk, I thought, but all of a sudden they were talking again as if nothing had happened. Looking back, it was a long while before the arguments started again. Deep down they loved each other and the marriage lasted until the old man passed away.

Mam and I used to go on trips run by a Mrs Armstrong who ran the 'open all hours' shop on the corner of Conway Street. 15 to 20 *Grey De Luxe* coaches used to take residents from all the surrounding streets on these eagerly awaited trips to Bridlington or Scarborough. The old man never went – just me and Mam – but it was a real highlight of the year for us. We would gather down the street on the appointed Sunday morning, all packed up with egg sandwiches, buckets and spades, and crates of beer for the grown-ups (especially Guinness for the women). I remember all the kids running down the street with the buses as they took positions to take on borders, shouting and yelling with excitement. Off we would go with the passengers split between the coaches depending on what part of the street they lived in. Mrs Armstrong was always on our bus, the front one; she was a real character who would always start the singsongs on the bus with, "I want to go a wandering along the mountain track, val deree valderah!" Oh, such simple joy!

We might as well have just gone round the corner for when we got to wherever the destination was, the script was always the same – on the beach for an hour, the egg sandwiches ending up with sand sprinkled on them and ending up thrown away as they were inedible, then into the beer garden of some pub or other, for the adults an afternoon 'on the sauce,' a cafe for a fish and chip tea, and then catching the bus home again. The end of perfect day for working class families in those days. They were more friendly days, there was more of a community spirit, and you could go out and leave your house unlocked.

It was a totally different childhood from that of today. No earphones or mobile phones; simple entertainment like sing-songs and buckets and spades; hardly any cars or traffic. There were just some great times that I will never forget.

CHAPTER 3
SCHOOLDAYS

It was September 5th 1957. I stood lost in a sea of faces, 400 boys brought together from four different schools in the Hessle Road area. A varied bunch indeed, but some had talents that would enable them to achieve great heights in their own fields.

The school building itself was used originally for Riley High School, which had moved to a new location further up Anlaby Road. The new school was one of the new 'secondary moderns,' known as Boulevard High, into which boys from Constable Street, Chiltern Street, Daltry Street and Wheeler Street schools transferred at the age of ten. Looking back, although it was an old building it was in a way quite modern, with decent sized classrooms, a gymnasium, a large assembly hall, woodwork and metalwork workshops, and a good science laboratory. It was supposed to be ahead of its time, and it was certainly better than we had been used to.

The deputy headmaster, a Mr Stan Adams, addressed the assembled throng. 'The Beak,' as he was known, was a living legend and terrified everyone in the school. He was a rugged looking character with a big bent nose protruding from his bald head rather like the bald eagle in American comics and pictures. The broken nose was from playing professional rugby, which he had also refereed and coached. In fact, Stan was Rovers' first team coach upon their return to action after the end of World War II. Later, he became my last rugby coach at school, and an excellent one at that. When we played another school, no matter what reputation they had, we daren't lose when we put on the red, black and yellow hooped jersey – the same colours as the old traditional Dewsbury RLFC shirts. An additional incentive to come away victorious was that he gave us each an old three-penny bit for our bus fares home if we won. But most times we ended up trekking the long way back from Anlaby Park Road South, where the playing fields were, because we had spent the money on 'goodies'.

On that first morning, as Mr Adams introduced the teachers and staff to the new boys, a worried voice behind me said, "Christ, who the hell is that?"

I would not have wanted to meet him down a dark alley anyway. After welcoming us all to the school, Stan, as I came to know him much later, introduced himself and asked the headmaster, Mr Gillies, to step forward and say a few words. Looking back, I realise that Mr Gillies was something special, a real leader, with a charisma that produced in us such awe that there was a deathly hush, in which you could hear the proverbial pin drop. Welcoming us, he described how honoured he was to be given the job of headmaster at the new school and told us a bit about his history. It felt as if you were being greeted individually. He was a rather red-faced and quiet man, but he commanded great respect throughout the school.

Mr Gillies sat down to rapturous applause and Stan called for silence once again. He then explained what was to happen next in more detail, before closing the proceedings. The new arrivals then left the assembly and followed Stan and our new teachers to the gym, a place I came to hate. We jostled and pushed as young boys do, walking along the corridor behind these men we had never set eyes on before. We congregated there in little groups predicated by our original schools, and stood there like lambs awaiting the slaughter. As the garbled chattering continued amongst the boys, Stan shouted, "Okay, shut up you lot! Now listen up." I thought, God he's been watching too many American war films. I had only ever heard John Wayne come out with that phrase, and Stan was no silver screen hero type, no Cary Grant or Gary Cooper look-alike.

The teachers were to become our tutors and mentors for the next few years. In many ways they helped to shape us into what we are today, and in retrospect, they did a pretty good job. Each one stood with a card, showing which form he was taking, and the first of them started to call out the names of the boys that would be in his class. Mine was a small red- faced, ginger-haired man called Mr Johnston. He was the double of Charlie Drake, his hair perhaps not as curly, but with the same features and funny eyes. He wore a sports jacket that matched his hair and grey flannel trousers. His class was 1A, which was the highest class in the first year. Each boy was called in alphabetical order, and as Mr Johnston worked his way down his list you could see the expressions on some of the boys' faces change as they realised they were not in the top class of the year. As he got to the Ps, "… Paterson, Pearson, Plummer…" I held my breath acting all nonchalant (I could speak French, for heaven's sake) and trying to appear as if I did not care if I was in his class or not, whilst deep down my bowels lurched, "… Pollard"

After each one, he looked around to see which boy he had inherited, and as I put my hand up, he looked straight at me and I swear the cheeky bugger shook his head. We were all secretly quite chuffed to be in the top class as we followed Mr Johnston to our classroom on the second floor, directly above the gym and just down the corridor from Stan Adams' office. The latter became a bit of a 'no go' area, because if you were spotted running past it, it was the Spanish inquisition all over again.

'What you doing out of class?' 'Why are you in the corridor?'

Keith Pollard

'Why were you running?' The tirade descended like a thunderstorm.

As we left the gym that morning, I looked back with a bit of sadness at some of the lads I had been with at Constable Street who had not been put in the new 'elite'. They were mates who had been with me since I was five. John Harvey, Judda Maltby, 'Gina' Peacham, Johnny Lyons, Gary Douse and Willie Allan, were all left standing waiting for their names to be called. Another was Billy Connelly, who was the only black kid I had ever seen at the time. It was so unusual to see black people in Hull that I can remember all the early ones I met, Keith Barnwell and Clive Sullivan at Hull FC, another pal, Mike 'Tweedy' Bram and later Bak Diabira, a half-back from Bradford whom I played against several times.

That morning represented a new beginning, a new era, for us. We actually wore uniforms with the school emblem, the Phoenix, on it, and a tie in the school colours of black with red and yellow stripes. The phoenix represented the school having arisen 'from the ashes' of the four dissolved schools. To our Mams this was just another expense and mine got a club cheque from Mr Tadman, the 'tally man,' so that I could be duly kitted out. My blazer was a black suit jacket with lapels that would not have looked out of place against *Concorde*, had that been thought of then. They kept curling over and I suppose looked quite ridiculous, but to me the jacket was the bee's knees. I had my first pair of long trousers, grey flannels from *Boyes* at the top of Constable Street, along with a school cap. Now school caps were not the 'in thing' on Hessle Road, the only caps I had ever seen were the flat ones every bloke on the road wore, and the only school cap I had ever seen was on Billy Bunter on telly. I put mine on in the house, looked in the mirror and thought, I look a right prat, I'm not wearing that.

"You effing well are," I was informed, "I'm not wasting 9/6d." I left the house wearing it but it soon disappeared into my satchel. I say satchel, but it was actually an ex-Army, khaki gas-mask holder, which was later replaced with a 'state of the art' duffel bag. But at least I had the uniform, whilst some kids had council clothes on and the '*Tuff*' boots that had just been introduced to the nation. They were guaranteed for twelve months not to wear out, until, that is, a group of dockers wore them every shift for three months, swapping them between each other irrespective of size, three shifts a day. *Tuff* kept replacing them every six months as they inevitably wore out. I do not believe they ever discovered the scam, but the guarantee was quietly dropped.

We settled down in our desks on that first day, some boys next to complete strangers and luckier ones next to lifelong mates, and listened to our new mentor Mr Johnston as he set out the 'curriculum' for the year.

RED & WHITE PHOENIX

"What's a curriculum?' was the whisper round the room. I thought it was a new model of Ford car, like a Cortina. After I'd nearly nodded off a couple of times, the bell went for play time and we went out into the yard to meet up with our old mates. We really did meet round the back of the bike shed, where some had already lit up their Park Drives or Woodbines and were happily sucking away. Judda said he'd had enough already and was packing it in.

"Bugger this," he said, "they want us to do homework." You couldn't get Judda to do anything in school, never mind at home.

"Whose class you in, Judda?" I asked.

"Mr Harpham" he said, "that old music teacher who's as mad as a hatter." Mr Harpham was allocated the lowest class in the year, 1D, and they were in a hall across the road from the main school, which is now a chemist's shop, I think.

"They have even put us out in the sticks so no one can hear him howling," 'Gina' Peacham lamented. For some reason, they had nicknamed him 'Daddy' and that is how he was always known. We all gave thanks for not being put in his class, as he used to be at Constable Street, from whence his reputation preceded him. For me, after settling down, it was not too bad. I met a lot of new mates both in the classroom and in the rugby team, some that were to become lifelong friends.

That year, I made my first visit to Wembley. It was the 1958 Rugby League Challenge Cup final between Wigan and Workington. We went on the train, meeting at Paragon Station at around 6am, with a 'pack-up' for lunch, which had gone by 8.30. After arriving at Kings Cross we transferred to the underground, where we were jammed like sardines into a carriage, before catching another train to the stadium itself. There were 90,000 people crammed into the stadium to watch a game that no one from Hull really gave a damn about who won, and for the first time I witnessed Wigan lift the cup. After the game, we were back on the cattle train again to return to the West End where we had tea at The London Polytechnic Institute on Regent Street. After that we were taken to the *Palladium Theatre* to see Johnny Ray. (EDIT?)

Standing with the Workington supporters earlier, I thought I had seen enough of people crying that afternoon, but here was another bugger howling. I thought he was pretty crap to be quite honest, but I suppose it is all a matter of opinion.

Back at school, we were invited to meet the coaches of the rugby and football teams, as school teams had to be chosen to be entered in the new season's competitions. As I was rather portly, although some people put it less politely, I was sent to meet Mr Jim Watts, a maths teacher and my first rugby league coach. He was a tall, rather arrogant man, who looked like Cary Grant with glasses. He was a glory hunter and I never really got on with him as he

Keith Pollard

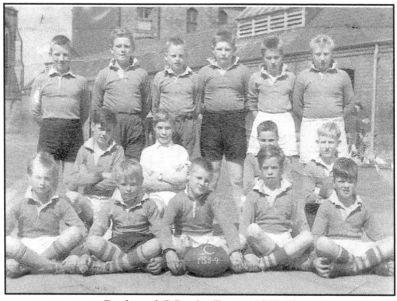

Boulevard C Rugby Team - 1958-59

Boulevard High School B Team - 1959-60

34

always favoured the stars of the team like Billy Halsey, Tommy Ball, Melvyn Rollinson and Vic Gay, four players who were a little older than me and were in the 'B' Team when I was in the 'C' team. But despite being one of the mere mortals, I did manage to get into the team, much to the amazement of some of the other kids in the squad!

Billy Halsey, who scored 44 tries in 15 games, and Vic Gay, who scored 39 tries and kicked 60 goals, were something special. Apart from being a good rugby player, Bill was an excellent athlete. He represented the city at both athletics and rugby, and at 11.3 seconds, was the record holder for the hundred yards sprint for the 13/14 age group. Vic also held an athletics record in the same age group, 10.78 metres for the hop, step and jump, which was pretty good by any standard. I think it is worth mentioning that, like the great Roger Millward at Castleford some years later, both Bill and Vic played for the 'A' team as well as the 'B', which was really unheard of in those far off days.

It was different for me though. When the two best players picked their teams for our impromptu games, I was always the last to be picked. No one wanted 'Fatty Pollard' in their team, and I doubt even if they could have foreseen the future that it would have made any difference! The same happened during my 14 years as a professional rugby league player. I had one or two coaches over the years that must have been the best players at their schools, because they would not pick me either! But I digress.

In the 1958-59 season, I managed to get into the Boulevard 'C' team in the Hull schools competition that was played on a Saturday morning. Amongst the players in that team were lads I was to play with and against for the next twenty or more years. We were quite a formidable team. Robert Mawer, a mate for many years, who could run like the wind; Mike and Mally Sach were another two 'Rossy' (Rosamond Street) lads; Colin Angel was at full-back; big Steve Richardson and I were the two biggest lads in the team and therefore the prop forwards; Walter Woodhouse, the tallest hooker in the world and Gary Douse shared the hooking spot. Gary lived opposite Constable Street school and his older brother 'Sonny', whose real name I never knew was to become very big in the trade union movement in Hull. John Usher did not stop long with us, he would have been a good player but, like others before and after, he 'emigrated' to Longhill, along with Johnny Harvey our loose-forward. The lad who always stood out in all the school teams was Willie Allen, the scrum half. He really was brilliant and if he had taken life more seriously he could have been a professional. We finished top of our league, losing only once at home and reaching our cup semi-final, so we were quite pleased with ourselves in our first season.

Keith Pollard

Boulevard High School 7 a-side team - Hull Schools Champions 1960-61
Stan Adams was Hull KR's first coach after World War II

Some of our teachers were soon forgotten, but Mr Parkinson had actually taught my father at the old Scarborough Street school and must have been about 70 by then. Alan Teasdale, the woodwork teacher, was hated by everyone and used an implement best described as a slim wooden cricket bat, that really stung when used to smack many an unfortunate pupil across the buttocks. Jack Goulding, the other woodwork teacher, was also the boxing club trainer and was always helpful and fun to be around. I joined the boxing club and the first time I was ever punched in the mouth – the first of many over the years – he told me something I never forgot.

"You don't feel the one that knocks you out," he said.

He was right, I have been in the land of nod a few times, never knowing what had hit me.

I was a big Hull FC supporter in those days. Their Boulevard ground was at the top of our street and we used to get our sweets, or 'goodies' as we call them in Hull, from a little sweet shop called Goldbergs on the way to the game. We used to call old Goldberg 'Jewie'. Looking back I can see he hated it, but to us it was just a nickname like with everyone else. There was nothing malicious or racist about it, we did not know any different in those days.

Like goodies, there were quite a few things that had different

36

RED & WHITE PHOENIX

names in Hull. Patties were like fishcakes, but were made of potato and herbs; teacakes were bread cakes without fruit in them; when it rained very hard, it was silin' down; a ten-foot was an alley or ginnel – and there were many more. And you never, ever pronounced an 'h' at the beginning of a word or a 'g' at the end.

It was around that time that they started to demolish the houses around the area for 'redevelopment', and I 'lost' a few mates to the new council estates that were being built on the outskirts of the city. Greatfield and Longhill were two bus rides away from us, and apart from finding the bus fare it was a full day out to visit them. You needed a 'pack up' to go that far away from home. I never went over North Bridge into East Hull until I was about eleven years old and I started playing rugby at school. I certainly would not have believed that this alien area would play a big part in my life in the future. But most of the other schools in Hull that played rugby league were to the east of the city. I also ventured over a few times to see some of my mates in their new houses. They seemed very posh with their bathrooms and mod cons, we never had a house with a bathroom until I was twenty.

At school, we stayed with 'old Johnno' as we called him, for that first year and my end-of-year report could be summed up in that old familiar phrase, 'could do better'. In the second year, we were with Mr Houlton in form 2A. He was a rather sour-faced disciplinarian; he did not like me and I sure as hell did not like him. Much to my delight, but unfortunately for him, he hurt his back and was off school for a long time. That year was a struggle for me; every day was a chore and I came to hate school and all it stood for. Mostly we stayed in the same classroom and just the teachers changed. But the school was growing rapidly due to the 'war baby syndrome' and was not physically big enough to hold all its pupils, so we were sent to Francis Askew school a couple of days a week. By this time, Judda and some of the others with whom I had been at junior school, had moved into higher classes and were also travelling to 'Franny Askew' as everyone called it.

We had quite a few adventures on our days out there and coming back home on the number 73 trolley bus from Dairycoates. There used to be some allotments opposite the Regis Cinema in Gypsyville, and we used to go in there to get some flowers for our Mams, and the odd basket of vegetables. It was very thoughtful of us, but whilst the blokes that had the allotments were very generous, they did not know that we were just helping ourselves. We did this every week until Judda threw a cabbage through someone's greenhouse window so that we could get some tomatoes, not knowing that the owner was in his shed having forty winks at the time. He chased us all the way down Hessle Road, until he could run no further. I can make a clean breast of this now, as most of those blokes will now be pushing up daisies, not growing them. Looking back, we were a bunch of minor delinquents, nothing major, just the usual 'boys will be boys' stupidity, and we were very lucky not to get caught at times. Most of us went 'apple chudding' in Hessle during the school holidays, but the apples were crap and I really do not know why we ever pinched them in the first place.

When Mr Houlton was off sick, we 'obtained the services' of a Mr 'Dick' Barker, PE teacher and self-proclaimed former England ABA boxer, and a big-headed, little bastard – until one memorable day. Steve Wilkinson was excused PE due to some burns injuries he sustained one bonfire night when a spark from a bonfire ignited a consignment of bangers that were stored in his back pocket. I thought Steve was rather lucky, not only to survive the incident, but also to be excused PE. I hated exercise in the gym. In fact, apart from playing rugby, I hated exercise full stop. I was not built for jumping over horses and climbing ropes; to me it was pointless. As Judda said, the ropes were not even long enough to get over the borstal wall. However, on the day in question, Mr Barker told 'Wilky' that he had to do PE and started pushing him towards the changing room. Steve told him that he was excused and was not doing it and asked Barker not to push him. Now Steve, although only twelve, was nearly six feet tall and about twelve and a half stones. He looked like Buddy Holly with his dark rimmed glasses. Barker took no notice and the inevitable happened. Steve lost his temper, punched him, and old Dicky went flying straight on his back on top of the piled-up coconut mats. Needless to say, he never bothered Steve again and was overheard later to say that he had never been hit so hard in his life.

A couple of memorable teachers came in to our lives in that second year. Mr 'Neddy' Hood was our Science teacher and swimming instructor, a blond-haired guy with a great Jimmy Hill type jaw. We used to go to Madeley Street baths every Thursday morning, walking there and back, and stopping at the 'cob shop' in Wellsted Street for a couple of dry bread cakes for our dinner. We all thought it was great, learning to swim and taking our swimming certificate exams. There was a bloke at the baths called Jack Hale, who was as fit as the proverbial butcher's dog. Someone said he had invented the butterfly stroke, and we twelve-year olds all believed that. Jack got us through the first class certificate exam, where we had to swim a length, save one of our mates and dive off the top platform. Now all the swimming and saving I could manage easy, but diving off that top platform – bugger that! We all lined up at the bottom of the steps and I was pushed to the front of the line. Jack was standing on the balcony that ran round the pool where all the changing cubicles were, and up I went, legs trembling and

RED & WHITE PHOENIX

nearly messing myself.

"Don't worry," he said, "it's just like falling off a log."

Now I know I'm not the sharpest, but I had never ever seen a ten-foot thick log.

He said quite softly, "Put your arms out in front of you, bend your back a bit and close your eyes." I thought he's all right this bloke, no agro, just nice and relaxed.

"If you don't want to do it, don't. It's entirely up to you."

I thought, if he's not bothered, I am certainly not. Then just as I was about to chicken out, the bastard pushed me. Well it was all over in a flash and, to be honest, apart from the big red mark on my belly where I hit the water, it was not too bad. All the lads cheered and clapped as I emerged from the pool like a drowning walrus, and then everyone else followed me up the steps. If 'Fatty Pollard' could do it, they could, and after that diving was no problem.

I liked swimming but I have never been able to tread water. Apparently everyone has a buoyancy level but it seems that mine is just above the eyes. Anyway, I even joined a swimming club that we attended every Friday night and really enjoyed – they even had sex lessons. Not officially of course, but one of the older girls who attended used to swim up to the boys and feel them under the water. Now at twelve-years-old and never having even been kissed, this was worth far more than the subs we paid. I remember the first time it happened to me. My mate told me that the girl would masturbate you if you asked her. She was about sixteen I think, and quite good looking, although at twelve almost any girl was good looking. He told her that I fancied her and that I wanted to see her after the swimming club. You may well ask what she was doing with twelve-year old boys, but then I did not know about such things and certainly did not care.

The next week, I was resting against the side of the pool in the deep end, hanging on to the wall and keeping out of the way of the non-swimmers and learners in the shallow end, when I spotted this yellow swimsuit coming towards me. When she raised her head and said "Hello," I melted. And when she slipped her hand inside my trunks I thought all my Christmases had come at once. I can still taste the sweet kiss she gave me as she hung on to me around my neck and slowly, well not really slowly, brought me to a climax. It was the first time for several things, not least having a science lesson as well as a sex lesson, as I immediately found out that semen does not mix with water. Then off she went and said she would meet me outside after getting changed. I was love-struck. A fat twelve-year-old in love with a sixteen-year-old goddess who had kissed me and deflowered me in front of the whole swimming club - if only they had known it.

We met after the club and when I walked home along Hessle

39

Keith Pollard

Road later I was as high as a kite. I did not hear a word that any of the other lads were saying, I only could hear her. This happened on several Friday nights and I could not wait for Fridays to come round, until I found out she was also providing her services quite freely to other club members. This ended my first romance and a harsh lesson was learned. But sex had started to be part of my life, albeit for a while thereafter, a more solitary part.

We used to go to the baths a lot, especially during the six-week school holidays, when we had no money and few other places to go. Madeley Street had two baths; a big pool and a small one. On Saturdays, you could go in the small bath only for a penny and you did not have to wear a costume. This they called 'penny buff morning' and was for the poor sods that couldn't afford a costume – but I might as well not have had one anyway, as it was one of those woollen ones with a snake belt that used to absorb water when you went in and it finished up round your ankles. If you dived in, especially off the diving platform, as you hit the water it peeled off like a used condom. The best part was when you came out you could use the hairdryer on the wall and get a pennyworth of *Brylcream* out of a machine.

We also used to go for rugby and football training on the bus to Anlaby Park Road South, using the playing fields that are now housing estates. During the summer months, we used to have athletics training, but by now you will have gathered I was not built for athletics. In fact, I was not built for anything but rugby league, but we just had to do it anyway.

We sat the eleven plus that year, but I made sure I failed. I did not want to go to a grammar or high school, as they were known. But my Mam and Dad wanted me to, so I had to go to Wheeler Street school on a Saturday morning would you believe, to sit the exam. When we were told to turn the paper over, I only wrote two words on mine, and they were guaranteed to ensure I did not pass. For the rest of the morning, I carved my name in the top of the desk, where I am sure it remained for many years to come, along with the others, as my small mark in history. We had to go back the next Saturday as well, which was becoming more than a joke. I had better things to do with my time than waste it at exams. I had found what girls were and after my experience in the swimming club I knew what was more important.

In the 1959-60 season, I was a member of the school rugby 'B' team, which won six out of ten league games, finishing second in the league. In the top-four play-offs (yes, they had them in those days too) we lost 27-8 to Craven Street, and were well beaten, 35-2, by Mersey Street in the first round of the cup. Another new team, Greatfield, had emerged and they took great pleasure in beating us at their place by two points, rubbing salt into the wounds by using

RED & WHITE PHOENIX

some of our own former players. On the positive side, four of our team, Willy Allen, Roy Foster, Walter Woodhouse and Pete Walker were good enough to be picked for the Hull Intermediates team.

The school year came and went largely uneventfully, which was in keeping with my life as a whole at that time. During the winter they used to put a wooden floor over the swimming pool at Madeley Street and on Friday night we went roller-skating. For Christmas, my old man bought me some boots with skates attached, from *Asbestos & Co* in town, and I even used to go to skating early for (don't laugh) dance lessons. I'm not entirely sure how I got into that, but I did and actually quite enjoyed it. You had to be there for the lessons an hour before the general public, to ensure there was enough room to practice the basic movements. It was a bit like ice figure skating but on wheels. It was run by a couple, the guy's name was Tony and although I cannot remember what his wife was called, I do remember that she was very attractive, which might have accounted for my enthusiasm.

The best part of the night was when they played all the rock n' roll records and everyone took their skates off and started bopping. They were great nights! I went skating for a couple of years and surprisingly became quite proficient at it. I enjoyed the dance instruction but that was probably to do with having to put my arm round Tony's wife and hold each other close. I remember it was all done by numbers and beats. You had to count the beats of the music and then perform a numbered move. They had funny names for moves like Chasse; LFO meant left foot out and the women would do LBO, left foot out going backwards. It was really confusing at times trying to remember the moves whilst counting the beats of the music, but it was good fun. I have some idea what the '*Strictly*' contestants are going through!

When I was about fourteen, I was standing outside Madeley Street baths after skating one night, when a black lad of about sixteen came up to me. Black people were really rare in Hull then. He grabbed me by the collar and tried to take my skates.

"Give me those skates or I'll belt you," he said. They were tied together by the laces and hung round my shoulders. I told him to go away and tried to jerk away from him, but he grabbed me again. He was about a foot taller than me and bigger. I was still short and fat then, but I was also both frightened and annoyed at the same time. The skates had steel soles with wooden wheels with ball bearings in them and had solid leather boots attached to them, so they were quite heavy. To try and lull him into a false sense of security, I said, "Okay, but please don't hit me," and cowered back as if I was going to hand them to him. Stooping forwards, I must have looked like Quasimodo, but when I had the laces in my hand I swung them upwards and hit him as hard as I could in the face

41

with both skates.

As he gave a cry of pain and put his hands to his face in agony, I took off down Hessle Road like the proverbial bat out of hell, not looking back, but running as fast as I could. Instead of heading straight home I ran down Coltman Street, through Cholmley Street and Constable Street, across Boulevard and into Newton Street and the safety of home. I did not go to skating for a couple of weeks just in case he was there but I never saw him again. Some of the lads had seen what happened and they said I had made a right mess of his face. There was blood everywhere and apparently he ran off in the opposite direction to me. Perhaps my actions meant that he did not pick on any little fat kids again.

I had got used to rejection by girls around this stage. We used to ask if we could take them home but got knocked back more times than not. Just now and again, when a girl was perhaps feeling a bit 'horny' we would get a bit of encouragement that culminated in what I think was politely called a 'heavy petting' session in the romantic location that was Division Road Cemetery. One girl in particular was good fun to be with, to put it politely, and generous with her favours. I remember waiting my turn and hoping I did not achieve happiness before at least I had a chance for her to help me with it.

On Monday nights at the baths there was all-in wrestling. I was a great fan of this 'sport' and used to go every week without fail, well before Kent Walton's programme made it so popular on ITV. I used to sneak into the back where the dressing rooms were and meet the wrestlers. My favourite was a big Scottish guy called Ian Campbell, who was a giant of a man, about twenty-stone and six-feet four inches tall and with a great big beard. I remember one night him fighting 'The Mask'. It was said that whoever beat 'The Mask' could remove the mask and divulge his identity. Well Campbell did win. He nutted 'The Mask', the blood oozed through the holes in his mask and it came off. I remember Campbell holding it up like he had won the World Cup itself, and the crowd went barmy. People said it was all show and called them actors, but there was no acting in these fights, I assure you.

I remember another bloodthirsty fight between Campbell and Jack Pye. I think Jack was a nightclub owner from Blackpool but he was a dirty fighter and it was billed as a big grudge fight. Campbell hit Pye over the head with a big enamel bowl that they used in the corner, splitting his head open so that there was blood everywhere. Then whilst he was laid on the floor, Campbell dragged him over to the ropes and tied Pye's long black hair to the bottom rope and started stamping on him. The referee and corner men were trying to pull him off, but eventually they abandoned the bout and the MC announced that, as Jack Pye was unable to defend himself and Ian Campbell was disqualified, the result did not stand.

I know some people thought it was all fixed, but I saw quite a lot of fights back in those days, and for my money they certainly were not. There were some great characters around and they had fantastic names; Billy Two Rivers, an American Red Indian; Rene Ben Chemoul, who was allegedly French; Johnny Kwango, who used to come into the ring wearing a leopard skin headdress; and Ricky Starr, an ex-ballet dancer who used to skip round the ring on his toes.

Once, I broke my arm playing rugby and Billy Two Rivers autographed the pot for me. It was my pride and joy, but when I went to get the plaster off at the Infirmary, the nurse would not give me the old cast, saying it was not allowed.

Occasionally, they had wresting at the '*Langham*', the picture house at the top of our street, and I managed to save up to go. Once, after the show I went in Curtis's fish shop opposite Rosamond Street and some of the wrestlers came in, including Chick Purvey and my hero Ian Campbell. Campbell stood alongside me. He was massive. I was just looking up at him in awe, when he said, 'Hello,' to me and asked if I had been to the show. His voice sounded like thunder and he ordered three large haddocks and chips. In those days 'large' really was large. He fed one into his mouth like feeding a stingray and he chomped away until it had gone. I was mesmerised, but he just looked down at me and said, "Great, I needed that," and walked out of the shop. No one said a word, they just stood there amazed at what they had seen.

We went to Wembley again in 1959, this time to see the Hull FC against Wigan final. Our music teacher even taught us the Hull FC song, '*Old Faithful*.' That was something of a waste of time; we did not get to sing much as Wigan won easily. I was beginning to dislike those cherry and white shirts, and seeing the great Wigan winger Billy Boston charging down the flank with Ivor Watts hanging on to him like a bush baby, will live in my memory for ever. I could never have dreamed then that I would later play against Boston. It was much the same itinerary as before, but this time when we ended up at the Palladium, where Frankie Vaughan topped the bill.

At school, we were being divided up into streams based on ability, in line with the then new secondary modern organisation. It made little difference to me, I had very little enthusiasm for schoolwork and again my school report read 'could do better'. In the third year I was put in Mr Adamson's class, 3A. Alan, as we used to call him, was big Hull FC supporter and still is. I met him years later at the Boulevard when I was stood on Bunkers Hill at the Gordon Street end, watching Hull FC v Fulham. He asked if we were from Fulham, because my wife Jacky was supporting them (she is rank 'red and white' and would support anyone against Hull

FC). I recognised him and said, "You used to teach me at school." When he realised who I was he turned to his son and said, "It's Fatty Pollard!" When he repeated the statement a couple of times, I said, "Say that again and I'll twat you, ex-teacher or not!"

Our classes were focused around what we wanted to do in the future. There was a seamanship course, a building course, a commercial course, and, the one I picked, a technical course. This is where we met 'Jock' Russell, the technical drawing teacher with ginger hair and a bad attitude, I could not stand the man. On reflection, I have always had a problem with discipline. I inherited from my mother the 'Frank Sinatra syndrome' and always had to do it 'my way.' Part of the course was the choice between woodwork and metalwork. There was no way I was going in Mr Teasdale's class and I was not going to give Jack Goulding the chance to smack me in the mouth for cutting the wood too short, so I decided to take metalwork under Mr Houlder, who was okay. I think he was ex-RAF; he was a great teacher who was really helpful to the boys. Another teacher we met in this year was Mr Shaw, the art teacher. He was a shortish guy with a scruffy moustache and patches on the elbows of his jacket. I think he was one of the first hippies, really laid back and one of the lads. It was always a pleasure to go to his classes. I even took an interest in maths, where the teacher, a Mr Brain, put a different slant on things and even made maths interesting. I was actually starting to like school, was I getting old?

We also had to pick a foreign language. I ask you, half of us could not speak English – only "'Ull' – but we had to choose, so for some reason I chose German. After our first lesson I realised I had chosen the right subject. The teacher, Frau Ashworth, was a wonderful looking woman, a tall, elegant blonde and what I thought an archetypal German Fraulein. You could hear a pin drop as she first entered the class, followed by stifled exclamations all round. Frau Ashworth had a profound influence on me, changing my life completely, not that I learned to speak German, but it started my attraction for tall, well-built women. I only learnt one sentence in German, "Haben sie eine cigarette bitter, mien Herr," which at least came in handy when we were on the docks and trying to tap seamen up for some free cigs. Thank you, Frau Ashworth, wherever you are, you lived in my dreams for many years.

In the 1960/61 season, I played in the school 'A' team that was run by Stan Adams. We had a good year, winning the league with an unbeaten record in all our fourteen league games. We also won the seven-a-side tournament and the Hull and District Challenge Cup, beating our old foes Mersey Street, who had earlier beaten us in the league play-offs again. This time, however, we came out on top 19-5. I was picked, much to the surprise of many in the squad, for a seven-a side competition that was held on the Boulevard, to us then the holy grail of rugby grounds. As I was still a Hull FC supporter then, I thought it would be great to play on the sacred turf, and went off with the squad that Wednesday evening after school with great anticipation. But although we won the competition, I never got a game. Stan promised me a game if we got to the final, but we got to the final and he did not pick me. He told the lads that it was through me we won, for if I had played we would not have won the last game. I am still trying to work that one out, possibly the best bit of bullshitting I have ever heard, and my first lesson in coaching skills, lie and make them believe you. Bill Halsey (again) and Tommy Ball were picked for Hull Boys and Yorkshire, and Gordon Storr for Hull Boys. Bill Halsey was also chosen as Hull and District Player of the Year, with Tommy Ball coming second by only one vote. This was a great honour for both the lads, as well as for the team and the school.

I made the acquaintance in my final year at school of a Mr Moody, who was to be my last form teacher. His class was 4A – the crème de la crème – the top class in the school. He was a very big man who looked like Jerry Lee Lewis, with a great shock of brushed back, blonde hair, and who always wore a bow tie. He was an excellent teacher who was respected by all in his class. He somehow managed to make us work hard but enjoy it at the same time. Mr Moody gave me one of the best compliments I had at school. We had been given the task of writing a technical essay and once we were finished we had to draw a picture of the subject and talk about it to the class. I picked on the German U2 bomb or 'doodle bug', as it was known. I learned about it from a book I found in the library and was well prepared. The talk went down a bomb, if you will excuse the pun, and I felt as if I had the class in the palm of my hand. Mr Moody was very impressed and praised the talk in front of the whole class. I was as proud as hell and it was one of my best moments at school. The choice of subject reflected my belief at the time that the Germans were the best at everything that they did.

That year, I was even made a prefect and given a badge. I was starting to think I was a pillar of society! My duties included sorting the milk out whilst the assembly was going on first thing in the morning. This was heaven to an overweight kid that could eat and drink for England. They were only little bottles, and for some strange reason we were always short when we finished putting the milk into the crates according to the respective class numbers. Obviously, unlike me, the milkman had not had a good maths teacher.

My friends at the time included Tommy Ball, who later signed

Keith Pollard

for Hull FC. We remain friends but I have not seen him for a while as he emigrated to the USA after living in Canada for a few years. Pete Walker, who was one of the 'house captains', who signed for Hull KR, and later played for Bradford Northern and Salford. Both played with me in the team at Constable Street Youth Club. Mel Rollinson was another, a great all round athlete at cricket, gymnastics, rugby and swimming, whatever he did he was good at and why he did not become a professional sportsman I do not understand. When Constable YC played against Castleford Juniors in the Yorkshire Cup semi-final, Mel played stand-off against future rugby league great, Roger Millward. Mel played him off the park and in later years Roger asked me several times, 'whatever happened to that bastard Rollinson?'

Others I remember from that class included Jimmy Hornsby, who became a policeman. Willie Allan, who was captain of the school and youth club rugby teams, and a really talented player but a bit of a 'Jack the Lad,' who died a few years ago after he had a heart attack helping a friend move some furniture. Billy Halsey, the star of the Yorkshire schools' rugby league and Yorkshire sprint champion, who later signed for Hull KR from Constable YC for a record fee for a junior but sadly did not make it as a pro. Dave Hawkins, or 'Hawkeye' as we called him, who became a welder. I met him in the *Silver Cod* pub on Anlaby Road twenty-five years later and he greeted me like a long lost brother. We talked for an hour or so and I have never seen him since! Sadly, others, like Ian Wilson, who sat next to me, Graham Huggins, who was a fellow prefect, and Head Boy Fred Fenton, I have never seen or heard of since.

I have not seen Roy and 'Buddy' Foster either, whose uncle Brian Hambling played for Hull FC in the 1960s, since we left school, but I believe Buddy finished up in the Gulf as skipper of supply boats. I recently got in touch with him on Facebook. The Foster boys had been in my class right from our first year and we had some great laughs. They came from Daltry Street School along with Norman Plummer, who became one of the biggest fish merchants in Hull. I remember Norman taking the exams to go to nautical school, but he failed due to his eyesight. They told him he could go for a radio operator's job and he declined, so his poor eyesight turned out to be a blessing! Norman and I were big mates in that last year and went everywhere together.

I even made the school athletics team that year as a discus thrower. I was entered in the selection trials for the Hull City athletics team (no other boy in the school had even put in for it) but I came next to last. When the PE teacher was looking for a discus thrower, he said, "Pollard, you'll do – throw this!" I naturally thought my physique had grabbed his attention – the Greek athlete thing you see – but then again, perhaps not. Anyway, I threw it and it sailed straight over the school playground wall and through a window in the church next door. I think the teacher's words were 'fucking hell,' but I was most impressed, as I had never thrown a discus before. The teacher had a hell of a job trying to convince the vicar of the church that he had found an Olympic champion discus thrower and that a stained glass window was not that important. The vicar did not go along with this and duly sent the school a bill for the repair. It did not cost me anything but there was no more discus practice in the school playground after that.

I was defrocked as a prefect after being caught at the City Sports meeting at the Hull Cricket Club ground, the Circle, where the KC Stadium now stands, fighting with our deadly enemies, the nautical school boys. Whilst six of us were scrapping with the sailors behind the main stand, Stan Adams had to come round the corner. The following morning, I was doing my milk duties when one of the younger lads came out of assembly and told me I was wanted. The other five lads from the 'Battle of The Circle' were already at the front of the assembled school. I had to join them, where my prefect's badge was ripped from my lapel. I was later given 'six of the best' by Mr Gillies, who said very little throughout the whole proceedings.

There was another Wembley trip, this time for the 1959-60 final between Hull FC and Wakefield Trinity. Again, the Black and Whites were on the wrong end of a thrashing and the only consolation was that Hull FC hooker Tommy Harris was awarded the Lance Todd trophy for the man of the match, having played with concussion after being knocked from pillar-to-post in an injury-riddled Hull side. We went to the *'Chicken Inn'* for tea in Baker Street and I had chicken for the second time that day as my old lady had bought me one from the *Rotary Spit* on Hessle Road to take with me. But again I had eaten that by half past eight on the train down to London, well we did leave at 5.45 in the morning! After tea we went to the *Palladium* again, this time someone who I had always wanted see was top of the bill – Liberace and the Beverley Sisters. They were real stars at the time. The train home left Kings Cross Station at 12.30am and arrived back in Hull just before six o'clock in the morning. It was a real 24-hour shift and I was absolutely knackered.

One thing that came out of that trip to London was an indication of how we were brought up in those days. A gentleman called Mr Russell Feeney of Southampton was in London that day and whilst on the underground was really impressed with the behaviour and manners of some of the lads from Boulevard school in Hull. So much so that he sent a letter to a national newspaper. The letter read as follows:

Keith Pollard

Dear Sir,

Hull may have lost the Rugby League Cup Final. But they possess some young supporters whose courtesy cannot be beaten. Travelling by underground from Liverpool Street, I entered a coach filled with schoolboy fans, each well adorned with black and white favours. They did not seem to be accompanied by adults. As I entered the coach, I was immediately offered a seat by a Yorkshire Galahad. At subsequent stops all adults - male and female - were likewise given seats as they entered. My curiosity was aroused and I inquired from a boy regarding the team they were supporting, and to which school did they belong. I was told that the school was Boulevard, Hull.

Apparently the age of chivalry is not dead in Yorkshire, neither need we despair for the youth of Britain

Yours, Russell C. Feeney, Southampton

You can tell by the prose that he was not off Hessle Road! It was a very fine gesture from Mr Feeney.

We sat the Secondary Modern Schools Certificate at the end of term that year and I passed with flying colours – seven passes and two credits. Mr Gillies gave me my certificates and final leaving reference; he was kind enough not to include the fact I had been demoted from prefect and gave me a glowing reference.

Looking back, it seems funny that we all just seemed to lose contact after school. Perhaps my becoming a 'red & white' had something to do with it! Even now, I still see people who have a go about me signing for Rovers over fifty years since it happened. The TV commentators talk about the derbies between Leeds and Bradford or Wigan and St Helens, but to me there is no question, the only true derby in rugby league is Hull v Rovers. It is the only city with two top-class rugby league teams within the city limits. The feeling I used to get when running out on the old Craven Park and Boulevard was like nothing else I have ever experienced. To hear the Hull supporters baying for my blood, having given a penalty away for some indiscretion, gave me an incredible feeling and without doubt made me play better. We will talk about this later, but I still get a tingle down my spine when I think about it.

CHAPTER 4
INTO THE BIG WIDE WORLD

After leaving school in August 1961 at the age of 15, I went straight to being an apprentice sheet metal worker at *George Clarke's* on Hawthorn Avenue. I also joined Constable Youth Club and played in their under 17s under coach Ron Everett. We played 'friendly' games that season, not entering the league till 1962.

Clarke's was an old coppersmith engineering company that had been in Hull for many years. On my first day, I was put to work with a lad called Latus, John was his first name, I think; he was a senior apprentice, so was actually given jobs to do by himself. He was making some aluminium pipe clips and he gave me the job of cutting off the bits of pipe that the bolts went through. With a feeble old hack-saw it was a bastard of a job. They had a brand new saw and I said to John, "Why don't we use that?" But he said I needed the practice. I took a few lengths of this aluminium pipe and cut about 50 of these bits, but he was not impressed and went to the foreman, who gave me a telling off on my first day for not doing as I was told.

I can still remember a few of the coppersmiths I worked with even 55 years later. Stan Clark, who had crooked foot because apparently he got caught up in an old drive shaft which twisted his leg really badly; Bernard Brown, who also sold goldfish at Hull fair every year; Bob Sanders, who was probably one of the oldest tradesmen in the world and always had a cold; 'Geordie,' who cleaned the aluminium filler rods with emery cloth and degreased them with methylated spirits, which he used to drink – especially on Saturday mornings when we worked overtime and he had been on the pop the night before; another Ray Ward, who had a bad leg and only relief he got was if he had it raised, so he used to stand next to a bench with his leg on it and fall asleep standing up.

But I wasn't really interested in the copper-works and did not really learn much there. I was much more interested in rugby. Constable under 17s at the time were one of the best teams in Hull, with players that we looked up to as kids with admiration. Big Ritchie Wilds was the captain – a great leader and prop forward; Arty Glentworth, like his old man, Harry, he became a bit of a legend in and around Hull – a real 'one off'; Laurie Rawlings was at loose forward and later coach of West Hull ARLFC and Yorkshire; Paddy McGee was a real hard man; Tommy Smith was a strong hard winger who should have made it as a pro – he was a bit like Jason Robinson in stature but had more of a nasty side.

Keith Pollard

Several players did turn professional, like Keith Barnwell, Cliff Stark, Maurice 'Bim' Fletcher, Richie Wilds and Dave Robson, who was later to be on the board of directors at Rovers; all these signed for Hull FC and were just a few of those we associated with and learned our trade from.

They were great times down at the youth club. We were a bit of a raggedy bunch but we never got into anything more serious than a few scuffles. There were no drugs in those days – only drink, and we were daft enough on that!

I had my first drink at about 15 when I started work, in the *Red Lion* on Redbourne Street. I didn't have a lot – just enjoyed myself. The *Kevin* ballroom in Market Place and the *Locarno* on a Monday night were places you just had to go. I remember standing on the fringes watching the girls dancing in a ring round their handbags, trying to drum up courage to go and 'split them,' hoping you did not get 'knocked back' and have to make the long walk back to the side with your head held low and your tail between your legs. We waited for the last dance to 'move in for the kill' hoping you could take a girl home – but more often than not it was a slow walk home alone or with the lads, saying there was no-one there you fancied anyway.

My time at the youth club, 'Cunny' we called it, always brings back pleasant memories. The club leader was called Mr Johnston – a rather straight-laced man that you would never have dreamt would be involved with a youth club on Hessle Road, but he kept a tight ship and was really good at his job. He was also in charge of youth employment in Hull. Come to think of it, not many of our lads were out of work and we all had decent apprenticeships – I would not be so impertinent as to say he favoured our club but I am it sure it helped. Alongside Ron Everett our coach, was the former Hull KR hooker and captain, Jim Tong. Jim was a smashing bloke who took to coaching kids like a duck to water. They were not just coaches but like uncles or father figures to us, and they helped us in more ways than just rugby. Ron later was employed by Hull KR as their first academy coach, which was a very clever move by them, as he was Mr Rugby League at the time in Hull. He travelled all over the town on his *Lambretta* scooter, watching players and persuading them to join Rovers rather than the Black & Whites at the Boulevard. He had done the same thing in reverse whilst at Cunny, when he got the likes of Tony McGowan, Ron Martin, Chris Davidson and Dennis Oaten, to move across the river from East Hull. It was a big move for them, but at the end of the day, I am sure it worked out to be a good one.

We did not play 'out of town' a lot in those days, as the local league was very strong and the road system was not what it is today. The M62 was not even dreamed of and few people had cars.

RED & WHITE PHOENIX

One time we did play away was in the Yorkshire Cup competition. When they announced the draw at the beginning of the season we hoped we would be drawn away from home because it meant a trip away and a night on the beer. There was an apocryphal story that the Cunny under 19s team, the lads who moved up to this age group the year we joined the under 17's, went away to play in the West Riding on one occasion and on the way home stopped at *Buckles Inn* near York on the A64. As the Cunny coach was about to leave, a coach from Wakefield arrived, and 'pleasantries' were passed between the rival groups. Allegedly Tommy Smith and Allan Kirkby went onto the Wakefield bus 'to say hello,' and when they staggered off they were covered in blood and in a partial state of undress. Apparently they had taken on all comers before being overwhelmed by sheer weight of numbers and thrown off the coach. Fun times!

I met my first real girlfriend whilst at Cunny. Maggie Berry was her name. She was a smashing lass and still is a good friend. We still share a laugh about old times when I see her. Maggie used to sing on the working mens' club circuit with her brother Alf, who became a big clubland turn – a country and western singer off Hessle Road, that is culture for you! Alf now lives in the posh part of the city at Kirk Ella, but in those days they lived in a terrace off Redbourne Street behind where another mate, Howard Laybourne, lived above his dad's shop. Whilst Maggie and I were going out together we had a few 'snogging sessions' down the back passage and his old man, Fred, would often shout out of the bedroom window, "Hey Pol, eff off home – I want to get some sleep, you fat bastard." Our relationship did not last long, I cannot remember exactly why – I think I was one for being with the lads and too young to start courting on a regular basis. Or perhaps it was just the exotic places I took her to.

Maggie married a real character off Hessle Road, Jimmy Hicks. Jimmy used to play for the now defunct Dee Street Recs Amateur Rugby League Club. One year they got to the Yorkshire Cup final, where they were losing with two minutes to go, when the ball was moved out to the wing and Jim took it in full stride. He flew down the touchline with only the full-back to beat, and being Jim, did not take into consideration that the rain had made the ball like a piece of soap, so he went for the big finale and dived full length for the corner – a bit like the South African winger who played for Hull FC, Wilf Rosenberg. When poor Jim landed, the ball shot out of his hands and into the crowd, whereupon the whistle blew and Dee Street had lost.

Some of the lads did get 'hooked' very early though and quite a few met their wives at the Cunny. Three former team mates who did were Willie Allan, who married Joanne Platten; Joe Kelsey,

Constable Youth Club Under 17 - 1960-61

Constable Youth Club Under 17 Squad - 1962-63

52

RED & WHITE PHOENIX

who married Carol Bilton; and Pete Walker, who married Irene Oakes. It was a really close family club and a great time in my life. There was a real friendship amongst us, and other girls that come to mind are Anne Rex, who married a fisherman, Jimmy Crellin; Sue Sharp, who was a real bonny girl whose brother Jon used to knock about with us; and Denise Dunn, who was part of our gang. I had not seen Denise since we were 1963 until one day in the mid 1980s when I was in the *Spread Eagle* in Withernsea with my dog Mac. It was a Sunday afternoon and when Denise came in, the dog snarled at her, which was unusual for him, but some people are frightened of dogs, who can smell fear. When I realised who it was and told him she was okay, he stopped and I told her that he was only protecting me. She said that she could not ever remember me needing protection, we had a good laugh and both she and Mac relaxed. It was great to see her again after all that time. I had a thing for her then – I thought she was 'really nice,' which was how you described a girl you fancied in those days. Mac loved going in the *Spread Eagle,* and even when I was working away, he used to try and take my wife Jacky in there when she took him for walks down the beach. She said, "Every time we walk past the beer garden entrance, he turns left to go in." I replied that I could not understand that – knowing full well that we always called in for a pint when I took him out.

In the summer of 1962, I had my first holiday away 'on my own.' Mike Lunn, Pete Walker, Howard Laybourne and I rented a chalet at the Golden Sands Chalet Park in Withernsea. Mike Lunn thought he was God's gift to women that he could pull 'anywhere, anytime, any-place.' He played for Cunny on the wing and later signed for Hull FC; he was an all-round athlete who also swam for England schools, but if making love was an Olympic sport, he would have been a gold medallist. Pete was madly in love with his then girlfriend, Irene, and Howard had an obsession for a girl from Cunny called Linda Hookem, but we left all the girls behind and went off on the train to 'With.' Withernsea was to Hull what Southend was to London – a place where working class people took their holidays before the aeroplane opened up travel to places like Majorca. I had been there lots of times in my younger years staying in places like converted railway carriages and double-decker buses. We had a great holiday – drinking in the *Spread Eagle* and the *Butterfly* and dancing at Withernsea pavilion. It was the 'Swinging Sixties,' with the young girls in their summer frocks and miniskirts.

One night after a good drink – well for 16-year olds it was a good drink anyway – Howard and I met a couple of girls at the pavilion and took them down onto the sands. They were staying at the north end of the town on Nettleton's Field, a well-known part

53

Keith Pollard

Constable Youth Club Under 19

of the resort at the time. The girl I was with and I were minding our own business when 'Lab' started calling to me out of the gloom. Apparently, he was having problems with his girl. Now I did not need to know this anyway, but when I heard the girl cry and him march off I jumped up and went to find out what was going on. I started running after him with my jeans falling down my knees and doing a good impression of a penguin. But he was out of sight, so I went back to my girl – only to find her consoling her friend, so all our evenings were spoiled. I never did find out what had happened with 'Lab' and the girl but I arranged to meet my girl again the following day. We met near the lighthouse before going back to her caravan on Nettleton's Field whilst all her family were out. I know it was well worth the wait, but all I can remember of her was that she was from North Hull – an area I never really frequented.

Inevitably, Mike Lunn had got together with a girl from Manchester on the first night and that was him taken care of for the week – she must have been really something because he was well and truly knackered by the time we went home – so much for the Olympic champion! As I said, 'Lab' had a thing about Linda, and we were walking back to the chalet one night after a few drinks, when I realised I could no longer hear him behind me. I could not see him anywhere, and thought he had fallen over the cliff edge, so

54

RED & WHITE PHOENIX

I shouted for the others to come and help me look for him. By the time we heard a voice somewhere in the distance I had sobered up somewhat, and we eventually found him in a gully laying on his back pulling petals out of a flower and saying 'she loves me, she loves me not.'

It was around this time that I first started getting interested in pop music, along with country music, which at that time was not the typical sound that you heard a lot on Hessle Road – although my old man was a big fan of Jim Reeves. I was into the Stones; blues; Long Jon Baldry, who sang with Alexis Korner's *Incorporated*; the Beatles to some extent; Billy Fury, who was my favourite Liverpool singer; and the Hollies. I remember Billy Fury being on at the *Kevin* ballroom when all hell broke loose, which was not unusual at that establishment. There were fights going everywhere and the band had stopped playing, whilst Billy Fury was watching through a gap in the curtains until someone took a swing at him and he quickly disappeared off stage.

Later in Australia I got into country music; Glen Campbell, John Denver, Merle Haggard and Charlie Pride were my favourites. I remember even when I was back home Glen Campbell was always on the radio singing *Wichita Lineman*, which was his big break. He was massive in the states and I understand that 52 million people a week used to watch his TV show. Someone once said to me that he looked like someone you would want your daughter to go out with. He was born in 1936, one of 12 children, in a small town called Delight in Arkansas, and learned to play the guitar without being able to read music. It certainly worked for him because after becoming a session musician and playing for many well-known singers he sold 45 million records of his own. There are many other artists that I admire from the sixties and going forward to present times, my music appreciation covers numerous forms. I only wish that I had learned to play a musical instrument.

Around this time, Peter Walker and I saw an advert in the *Hull Daily Mail* about an open trial being held at Rovers old Craven Park ground and decided to go along on our bikes and have a go. At the time I had only been in East Hull twice – practically a full day trip with two buses each way required to make the journey. The trials consisted of four half-hour games and we played in all four. Afterwards, Rovers' legendary coach Colin Hutton asked to see us, and noted down our addresses and other details. When it emerged that we were still only 15, he spluttered and said he should not even be speaking to us. Nevertheless, he told us that the club would get in touch with us later if we were interested. Later, I got a message through Ron Everett, asking if I would like to play for Rovers 'B' as well as Cunny.

I had certainly improved on the rugby front, because I signed

Keith Pollard

K Sanderson, R Davis, P Walker, Me, D Stockman, T Ingram, J Milner,
M Rollinson and J Walker on a night out at the Continental Club in Hull

A family night out at Skyline in 1965

RED & WHITE PHOENIX

professional forms for Hull KR on October 12th 1962, aged 16 years and five months, along with Johnny Moore, Cliff Wallis, Eric Palmer, Chris Young, Peter Fox, Les Chamberlain and Brian Mennell – all of whom made their mark on the club in various ways. The deal was that Rovers let players finish off their seasons with their amateur clubs before joining them on a more regular basis.

So I played out the season with Cunny and we won the Yorkshire Cup that year, the first time ever for a Hull team. We beat Thornhill Boys Club from Dewsbury in the final at Castleford's Wheldon Road ground. After returning to Hull with the cup, we set off, cup in hand, to our local, '*The Engineers Arms*'. The landlady, Maud, duly took the silver chalice from our captain, Willie Allan, and offered to fill it up with amber nectar. Only on handing it back to Willie did she read the inscription on the cup – 'Yorkshire County Continuation Cup Under 17s.'

"Bloody hell!" she said. "You bastards have been coming in here for two years!" But no more was said as we drank our fill of the Worthington E best bitter.

We also won the Hull and District Cup that season – it was a good season all round. My life had changed completely now. I was a professional sportsman, training two nights a week and playing at weekends for either Rovers 'B' team, eventually to became the Colts, or for Cunny. I made my debut for Rovers 'A,' the reserve team, against Bramley at the old Barley Mow ground on a dark winter's day. It was a depressing place. The old dressing rooms were at the back of the pub with old rickety wooden stairs that were as steep as the north face of the Matterhorn. The visiting players' bath was not much bigger than a normal bath and looked like a watering trough for animal. Brian Gill was the A team captain, and former long-serving first team full-back Wilf McWatt was the coach. Wilf's only words of wisdom were, "If you make a break and pass the ball keep your eye on their full-back, he is right dirty bastard and will take your head off."

As the runner in the forwards, with quite a turn of speed for a prop, I made a few breaks during the game. On one occasion as I ran through the defence I passed the ball to my left for Brian Burwell to score and I spotted out of my right eye the full-back lining me up for a stiff arm tackle. Just as he came near, I stepped off my left foot, raised my right elbow, which him right between the eyes, and he dropped like the proverbial stone. The referee did not penalise me, and I swear that he had a slight smile on his face as he pointed to the spot for Brian's try. As I looked back to see the fullback face down in the mud, Brian Gill murmured in my ear, "Welcome to professional rugby league." Then, as we lined up for the restart my fellow prop forward, Ken Grice, an experienced old

57

Keith Pollard

Me, 'Spider', Billy Walster and Colin Smith in Ferry Boat Inn

Me and 'Spider' with some of the Hessle Road beauties

hand, looked at me and said, "Well done, young 'un!" I felt quite chuffed to be honest, and I turned out for quite a few games in the reserve team in that 1962/63 season.

During the summer close season, Rovers ran coaching clinics for their 'up-and-coming stars' – and me. Jim Drake, a former Hull FC legend who was by then with Rovers, looked after the forwards and a Rovers legend, 'The Cornish Express,' Graham Paul, took the backs. We trained one night a week and Jim gave us many words of wisdom on tactics and what would be expected of us as professional rugby players. Jim and his brother Bill played in Hull FC's great forward packs of the late nineteen-fifties and early 'sixties. FC then had a great side under the man many believe was the instigator of modern coaching, Roy Francis. What Roy did not know about rugby league was not worth knowing. Amongst Jim's words of wisdom was his theory about forwards that is still applicable to this day. "You have three types of forward," he said, "runners, ball-players and crunchers." The latter did all the tackling, 'taking ball up' (driving into the first line of defence) and enforcing – exactly what Jim himself did.

"The average player can do one of these things,' he used to say. "A good player can do two of the things and the great players can do everything." When I think back over the years about the great forwards, going back to the 1960's, I realise that he was absolutely right. In those days, we had forwards like Derek Turner, Vince Karalius, Frank Foster and Laurie Gilfedder, who could fulfil all three roles. In the modern era, their counterparts are Sam Burgess, James Graham, Gareth Hock and Sonny Bill Williams.

Jim used to tell a story about when the Black and Whites were in their pomp. In those days, of course, they played throughout the winter, and over Christmas they had the traditional Christmas Day fixture at home to Rovers, who were not then a very strong side, and were away to Bramley at Barley Mow on Boxing Day. Roy Francis decided that as these were two reasonably easy games he would rest half of his forwards for each game and give a few reserves a 'run out.' In modern times, many players do not drink alcohol from the start of pre-season right through to the end of the season – but it was very different then. Roy told Jim that he would play against Rovers and would be rested for the away fixture, when Bill would play. Roy asked that those who played in the first game abstained from drinking on Christmas Eve and could have a drink afterwards, and those who had the Rovers game off should not drink on Christmas Day.

It was a plan they all agreed to. Bill decided to go and see his mother in York between the two games, but was to be back to travel on the team bus to Bramley. All the players arrived at the Boulevard in good time for the bus except for Bill. There were no mobile phones then, of course, and very few people even had landlines, so Bill could not be contacted. Roy decided that they would leave Hull and hope that Bill could get to the café near Boothferry Bridge, that both Hull and Rovers used for a meal en route – usually steak and eggs.

When the bus arrived at the café the owner informed Roy that someone had rung, saying they were on their way and not to worry. He had not left a name but it was assumed that it was Bill Drake. Jim, meanwhile, was on the bus, albeit feeling a bit under the weather due to his having imbibed more than a few drops of the amber nectar the night before.

After eating, the players were about to start their ritual walk towards Goole to stretch their legs and 'walk off the meal' they had just eaten, when a taxi arrived, out of which emerged Bill Drake, covered in bunting, wearing a coned hat and blowing a Christmas horn. He walked up to Roy, blew the horn in his face and wished a happy Christmas – all of which went down as well as you would imagine. Roy told him to get back in the taxi and that he would deal with him at training next week. As he turned to get back on the bus, Jim was chuckling away, as a twin brother would, when Roy turned to him and said, "I don't know what you're bloody laughing at Jim, you are playing today now."

Roy was something of a disciplinarian, and when he said 'jump' the only question was 'how high?' – so there was no point in Jim arguing. So he played, and as it transpired, he was not the only one who had been 'on the pop.' What should have been a straightforward game was won only by a slender margin. Even the part-time professionals went off the rails now and again, and some things will never change. Rugby players will always be rugby players, and most of all human beings.

As you will have gathered, I was not very interested in work – and by then playing rugby was my main priority. I may not have been the brightest, but even I could work out that I was better off playing rugby at £7 for a win and £3 ten shillings for a loss, rather than working a basic 42 hours a week (including two hours on a Saturday morning) for £2 6s 5d a week. Added to this was my belief that Clarks only used apprentices as cheap labour and that the foreman hated me as a rebel without a cause. We were supposed to go to night school three nights a week to pass exams that then allowed you day release to go to college, but needless to say I did not go. I used to go out of the back door with all my gear, put it all in the shed and instead take my training gear and go to the Cunny and go training. My old man used to go barmy when he found out – usually from his mate, Jimmy Lloyd. Jimmy always reminds me of this when I see him whilst watching West Hull, where he is on the committee.

RED & WHITE PHOENIX

By this time, I was a regular in Rovers 'A,' playing every Saturday. Playing for Rovers opened up lots of other possibilities for me, especially with the girls. I was a bit of a 'Jack the lad' around town in those days. We used to meet in city centre at a pub called the *King Edward* opposite the old *Gainsborough* fish restaurant. It was a Darley's pub and the beer was awful. At 16, I was an expert in beers – after all I had been drinking for two years at least! But it was a central place and the upstairs was the place to be seen at the time. We also met there on Mondays before going to the *Locarno* ballroom – we could not get a drink in there because they only had a members' club and you had to produce your birth certificate to join. We met at the *King Edward* if we were going 'around town' or up to the *Ferry Boat Inn* on Hessle Haven. This was a great pub at the time, with live bands on most nights of the week. There were plenty of girls there too, and I knew quite a few of the regulars. Another good pub was the *Halfway* on Spring Bank, which also had live bands on, and the place really rocked.

I met my second regular girlfriend, Silvia Crickmore, at a dance in Hessle Town Hall. She was a lovely girl, whose brother was Charlie Crickmore, who at the time played for Hull City in their great team of the early sixties with players like Chris Chilton and Ken Wagstaff. One day, I went to pick Silvia up at their house in Havelock Street. I was very keen on her and had taken her out a few times but had never met her parents before then. She answered the door and took me into the lounge where her old man was sitting, reading the *Hull Daily Mail*'s 'Sports Green'. He lowered the paper for a second to say 'hello,' and then carried on reading. The room was full of Tigers memorabilia and photographs – and Charlie was everywhere you looked. Silvia's father lowered the paper again and said, "City did well – did you go?" When I said that I had not, he appeared aghast and looked me up and down. I said that I preferred rugby, upon which he asked if I was a Hull FC supporter. I said that I used to be, but that I was better now, and laughing nervously, told him that I played for Rovers. He looked at me as if the cat had just dragged me in, stood up without saying a word, and walked out of the door with his sports mail under his arm. I never set eyes on or spoke to him again all the time I was going out with Silvy – which was not really all that long. I was too young to settle down, we split by mutual agreement, and I do not remember ever seeing her again.

Hessle Road had quite a few pubs running its length, in fact there was an old saying you couldn't drink half a pint in each pub without getting drunk – I made a few attempts and can confirm this is true. Our pub crawl started at the *Vauxhall Tavern*, built around 1809 and one of the oldest pubs in Hull, and then on to the *Inkerman Tavern* and the *Barrel*, both down side streets, but pubs

Keith Pollard

The 1966 Christmas Party at the Railway Club, Capper Pass

you just had to visit. Back then onto 'the Road' to the *Rose, Lilly, Alexandra Hotel* (still there today), and the *Adelaide Club*. The latter was a great venue and one of my favourite places for a night out – and it used to have real top line entertainment in those days. Freddie Star was on one night when he first started off, whilst Freddy 'Parrot Face' Davies – a great comedian – and Kenny Ball and his Jazz Men were two more who appeared there and became international artists. Unfortunately, the *Adelaide* was demolished to build the flyover at Daltry Street and the licence was transferred to the *Phoenix Club*.

The next stop on the pub crawl, was the *Strickland Arms*, then the *Wassand Arms*, both off the main road and both still standing, before returning to the main road to the *Criterion* and then the *Red Lion* down Redbourne Street. This pub it was a great little place – right on the corner of Redbourne Street and Sefton Street. It was a bit like the Rovers Return on *Coronation Street*. It had a great atmosphere and had been in the Mellors' family for years. Maude Mellors was a really typical pub landlady and we had some great times in that pub. One of our pals, Lennie Lloyd, who was a great practical joker, organised a bus trip to Bridlington and everyone in the pub put their names down to go and paid him their money every week.

RED & WHITE PHOENIX

On the appointed morning at 9.30, Maud opened up early to accommodate the throng – I remember that one grown man even had a bucket and spade, would you believe. We were sitting there waiting patiently when, quite casually, in walked Lenny. "Where are you lot going?" he said, looking amazed. "What!? The Bridlington bus trip – remember!!" the whole pub reverberated. "Who organised that without asking me if I wanted to go?" was his reply. There was a deathly silence in the room. "What about the money we have been giving you every week, you fat bastard?" someone asked.

"That was for the Christmas 'diddlum', I told you that when I started collecting" he replied. I started to see the funny side, but I was the only one at first, and my cousin demanded to know what the hell I was laughing at. He was sitting there with a handkerchief on his head, tied with a knot at each corner, with his wife June who was dressed up to the nines, as she usually did – a good looking girl our June. In the end, Maud put some food on at short notice and we all had a day in the pub – and probably had just as much fun there.

Back to the pub crawl, there was then one of Hull's most famous pubs – the *Star and Garter* – better known as 'Rayners' after one of its' most famous landlords. This was the pub used by most of the fishermen and was always heaving when I was a kid. It was supposed to be the longest saloon bar in the north of England, and had four pump stations, each with three or four barmaids on a busy day, which in those days was just about every day. It was a real 'drinker's pub', which also had a back room, which I am led to believe a lot of ladies of the night used – not that I frequented that, of course.

St Andrews Club was opposite *Rayners* down West Dock Avenue. Sunday dinner times were a great session there. The father of Hull FC player, Tony Dukes, was compere there for years. Across the road and down the next street was *Dee Street Club*, notable for its' great open age rugby team, Dee St Recs, who were very strong in the 1950s and early 1960s.

Of course, pubs were only open 12 until 3pm and 6pm until 10.30 then, and I do believe that was better than today's unlimited opening. There did not seem to be as much trouble with drunks as there is now. After *Dee Street*, there was the *Subway Club*, then, back on the main road, the next pub was the *Halfway* – supposedly halfway along the road but I always thought it was rather more than that, especially after a few drinks! The last pub was 'Millers', another pub named after one of its old landlords. Its' proper name is the *Dairycoates Inn* and it is also still there. Believe me, it was quite a journey, which I never made without being three sheets to the wind, as the old fishermen used to say.

The people who lived on the road were very superstitious,

Keith Pollard

particularly the 'three day millionaires' as the seamen used to be called, as they were very flush with money for a few days after returning home from sea. One of the things they did not like was going back on board ship with what they called 'shrapnel' or pockets full of loose change, so they would often literally throw it away before they got in their taxis to go down to the dock. Often, as a young kid, I profited when a fisherman who was going away threw his loose change in the air amongst us.

There was everything you needed on Hessle Road. We used to go in Burton's Snooker and Billiard Hall, which was above a furniture shop, and we used to go in Tommy Hollome's barber shop because he gave a great crew cut which was all the fashion in those days. Tommy's son Keith was a lead singer in a local Rock n' Roll band. He was quite good too, I remember seeing him quite a few times at the *Half Way* on Spring Bank in Hull.

Another character was Sammy Wolfe, who had a barber shop at the town end of the Road, near Daltry Street, that was very popular amongst the fishermen. They always had a cut, or their ears lowered, as we said, before going away on a 19-day trip and it was a dead giveaway when you saw a fisherman with a fresh haircut that he'd be going back to sea the following day.

On the subject of pub crawls, the 'Old Town' of Hull is a really good place to go, with some of the finest pubs in the entire county of Yorkshire, reflecting centuries of history. We used to meet at the *Kingston,* which is in the Market Place near Trinity House Lane, a really old pub with big Italian-style windows and hand-crafted wooden carvings which decorate the bar. After leaving there, we turned right where, just a few yards down the road, there is the *Bonny Boat.* This is a small pub, but it has a long history, its name reflecting the great days when Hull was one of the world's biggest whaling ports. One of my mother's cousins was the landlord here and, as a teenager, when we went in town, Mam used to say, 'go and see your Uncle Toby.' I always used to say 'hello' and although it was never much more than that, it was a good bragging right to have an uncle with a pub. Reportedly, one sea captain returned with an Eskimo he had captured during a sea skirmish. The Eskimo, complete with his kayak, was kept in the city, but pined for his homeland and his freedom until he died. His boat, now kept in Trinity House, was his memorial – a 'bonny boat'. From there we would across the bottom end of Whitefriargate and into the quaintly-named Land of Green Ginger – the longest street name in Yorkshire. Down this street is *The George*, one of the oldest pubs in the city which has a truly great bar – a typical English pub.

The *George*'s claim to fame is as having the smallest window in the world. The unusual street name attracts speculation. Some believe it arose from the ginger trade but the more romantic prefer a very different story. It is said the street is called after a lady of the night who walked the area in the 18th Century. A red-head, it is claimed she was hailed with cries of 'gie us a grin, Ginger.' From there it was on to the *Burlington Tavern*, a popular and long established Bass house. After the *Burlington*, it was down a narrow passage and the entrance to *Ye Olde White Harte* – surely one of the most remarkable public houses in Hull. It was the venue of a critical meeting that saw the beginnings of the English Civil War, when Sir John Hotham refused entry through the gates of Hull to the Royalist forces. The room where the decision was taken, aptly named the Plotting Room, was for several years a restaurant and is now available for private bookings. The carving in the Plotting Room is original and dates back to the Jacobean Period – the 17th Century. It really is an 'olde worlde' pub – it even has a carefully preserved skull retained behind the bar. The story goes that the skull, which has been examined by doctors on several occasions, was found in the attic during renovation work in 1881 and is that of a poor serving girl. Others have claimed it is the skull of a young man who may have died from a blow to the head. Either way, the *George* is an essential place to visit.

One of the places we used to go to was the old *Palace* Theatre on Anlaby Road. It was built in 1897 and was one of 23 theatres that have existed in the city over the years, only a couple of which are still in existence. The *New Theatre*, opened in 1939, is a reconstruction of the *Assembly Rooms* and the *Hull Truck* theatre, which is now housed in a brand new building on Ferensway in the City Centre.

The *Palace* had been turned into a variety show establishment, with the stalls area housing tables and chairs in cabaret style. It seems old-fashioned now, in the modern day era of discos and night clubs, but the *Palace* was a great night out. It was under the same ownership as another old theatre, the *Tivoli*, which opened in 1902 as the *Alexandria Theatre*, before changing its name to Tivoli in 1912, and then the *New Tivoli* in 1914. An artiste called Arthur Lucan used to play an old women called 'Old Mother Riley' at the Tivoli. He used his wife as his daughter in his sketches and made quite a lot of black and white films that were quite funny at the time. I suppose he was the first 'Mrs Brown'. Lucan actually died backstage at the Tivoli in May 1954, midway through performing his act. Drag artist Danny La Rue unveiled a bronze statue of Arthur Lucan years later in 1986 to mark the place where he died, which is now at the back of a café in what is now Tivoli House.

One act that sticks in my memory is a stand-up comedian called Joe Church. He used to walk out on the stage with a plank of wood under his arm and rested his arm on it whilst he held the microphone in the other hand. Towards the end of his act he used

Keith Pollard

to say, "I suppose you are wondering why I take this plank of wood with me, and keep turning it over?" Of course, the audience usually shouted a few ribald comments, after which he said "It is my lucky plank – apart from which, it has all my jokes on the back." He turned it round and sure enough there were postcards the full length of the plank. He then took a bow and walked off, the crowd giving him a rousing ovation. I later spoke to him at the bar and he told me he could never remember jokes, so he took the plank on with him.

We had some great nights at the *Palace*. In 1958, it took the name of '*The Hull Continental*' but sadly, some seven years later, it closed its doors for the last time in 1965. One of the comperes there was Duggie Brown, whose sister Lynne Perrie played Ivy Tilsley on 'the Street' and who later became famous through *The Comedians* on television. The resident dancers, some of whom lived in a caravan at the back of the building, were the J W Jackson Girls, who each week performed a routine that appeared to the regulars to be little different from the previous week – it was just the music that had changed. The entertainment was varied to say the least, with jugglers, magicians, singers, comedians, even the occasional stripper, but it was all good clean fun and in the best possible taste. I still love live acts and club life.

A couple of years ago, I went to a 'Hessle Road reunion' at *West Park Club* down Walton Street, where the famous Hull Fair is held. It was the first time I had been in a working mens' club for years and it was still same routine, with a couple of acts and the bingo. The bingo was the part of the evening I really could not stand – in the old days at the *Phoenix,* we used to go downstairs for a few quick ones and leave the women in the concert room to play.

Until quite recently, a few of my mates and I still went 'down road' to visit some of the old haunts. It is not quite the same these days, as most of the houses have been pulled down and new ones rebuilt, or the land turned into factory units. But it is still a great place to shop and visit.

Back to my rugby career. At the end of the 1962 season I went to Bisham Abbey to attend the coaching course set up by the rugby football league, along with team-mates Cliff Wallis, Billy Halsey and Chris Young. Two of us went by train – not a journey I'd want to repeat – and came back with Colin Hutton in his car. The other two went with Colin and came back on train. It was a cost-cutting measure – not much has changed over time!

We did not know it then, but there were some of the all-time greats of the game on that course. Dougie Laughton of St Helens became an established international and later a coach, winning pretty much everything; Terry Fogerty of Halifax, a great forward who sadly passed away a few years back; Tony Karalius, who

66

played for St Helens for many years; Colin Clarke of Wigan, who went on to play for Great Britain and fathered Phil, who followed in his footsteps and is now a Sky TV pundit; the late, great Leeds half-back Mick Shoebottom; and Derek Robinson of Swinton, another to become a Great Britain tourist. There were too many to mention. Our coaches were Colin Hutton, Bert Cook, Laurie Gant and Albert Fearnley, who trained us hard every day. Albert was one of the famous Halifax pack of the late 50's and early 60's who terrorised the game, and he certainly commanded our respect.

There was a pub more or less outside the Abbey Gates, the *Bull Inn,* a typical little country Inn that we went into nearly every night – unless we went down the road to Marlow or Cookham. It was all new to us – I had never really been out of Hull or travelled 'down south,' apart from going to Wembley for the final. We had a great week that I will remember forever.

One incident will always live with me. In a pub we visited, the *Ferry* I think it was, there were quite a few girls, and a lot of the lads were happily chatting away with them. I was sitting at the bar when I was approached by a woman. I was only 16 and she might have been about 30 – she was tallish but very slightly built and her hair was cut short, the Mary Quant look, if you remember that; she had the shortest mini-skirt I had seen and a real low-cut top. She started talking to me, asking me what we were all doing in the area as she had heard the mixture of strange accents. I thought what a friendly sort, and at just 16 I was soon in love with this beautiful creature. I was under no illusions that she was in my league, and why she had picked me out from the mob that had invaded Cookham this evening I did not know, but I went along with the flow anyway. She asked me my name and told me hers was Simone, I had never heard such an exotic name – it all added to her attraction and I was hooked, 'line and sinker' as they say. As we sat on the bar stools, her with her back to the wall in the corner, her skirt started to ride up and I could not help but look down. I was definitely getting turned on and she knew it, whispering something about liking younger boys, and asking me my age. As you have to be 18 to legally drink in pubs, but only 16 to have sex, and as there were no bar staff in earshot, I said sixteen.

"Mmmm, that's a wonderful age," she said, "and you are a big boy for your age." We continued to talk and I could not quite believe what we going on. Then she asked me if I fancied going somewhere quieter with her. Did I!? She went to the toilets, returned to finish her drink and said, "Let's go outside, away from the crowd." As she slipped off the bar stool I lowered my eyes, hoping for a glimpse of what was beneath her skirt and saw she was not wearing any panties. She looked right in to my eyes, giving me the most sensuous smile I had ever seen, then said to me, "It's all

Keith Pollard

yours if you want it."

Coming off Hessle Road, the only time I had mixed with ladies of this age was in pubs and clubs, and most were either married to fishermen or worked in fish houses – being seduced by an older woman was totally a new experience for me, the sort of thing I could only read or fantasise about. We went out into the beer garden, where darkness was falling, and she led me round the back of an outbuilding into a short and narrow dead end. She put her arms around my neck and her lips met mine, her tongue exploring the inside of my mouth, whilst my hands slid down from her waist onto her firm bottom and her breasts were pushing into my chest so hard I could feel her erect nipples. I let my hand explore between her legs and felt her wetness as she gave a little moan. If there had been a lottery then, I would have thought I had won it.

We feverishly undid our clothing and I lifted her on to me, I could lift her quite easily, she put her arms around my neck again her legs wrapped around me as I slid inside her. It was the best feeling of my short life. Alas, it was not a prolonged one, and as I approached the point of no return I moved to pull out, but she whispered, "No, it's okay, leave it there." I did as I was told and just enjoyed my sensational finale. We stayed joined, still kissing, after it was over – I was still in heaven. When I put her down and she fished a pair of the skimpiest knickers out of her handbag, put them under my nose and I automatically sniffed them, the mixture of fragrance from her perfume and her love juices were beyond belief. She laughed and said, "Come on, we must get back inside." We went back into the pub and I ordered a drink, whilst a few of the lads were grinning and looking my way, with 'we know what you were doing' looks on their faces.

I was still under the foolish impression I was going to finish the day in cuddled up in bed with her for the night, but ten minutes or so later an older bloke walked up, about 60 I reckon, a real country gent, all Harris tweed and corduroy trousers. He gave her a peck on the cheek and she introduced her husband. He asked her if she was ready, whereupon they both said it was nice to meet me, and as she walked out the pub arm-in-arm with him she turned and mouthed, 'I'm sorry.'

My jaw was on the floor when one of the younger local girls came up to me and whispered in my ear, "Don't worry you are not the first, and you most certainly won't be the last." She said that the woman was a local and well known for her fetish for young boys. It seemed that her hubby was impotent, and knew what was going on. She would go out find someone, he would then pick her up and she would tell him the story of what she had just done. I asked her how she knew.

"I used to work for her and she used to talk about her conquests quite openly," she said. All the locals in the pub knew what was going on and that I was this week's or day's victim – but I must be honest, I didn't really mind too much. I did enjoy it – oh yes, I most certainly did.

In the 1963/64 season, I played every game in Rovers 'A' team and enjoyed it. But work was another matter. I had hated working at Clarks pretty well from the first day. I was hauled up in front of the manager, a Mr Collins, who started to chastise me about not going to night school and said that if I did not enrol that year they would sack me. I told him that there was no point as they did not have an evening painting and decorating course – all I ever seemed to do at work was to paint pipes, I never got the chance to do what I thought was supposed to be my job. At nearly 18, I couldn't even weld properly. It was three years of my working life wasted.

The foreman, Jack Gledhill, put his two penneth in and, firing on all cylinders by now, I told him what to do as he had never given me any help, and I gave him a few other home truths for good measure. So it was no surprise that a few days later I was summoned to the MD's office. Mr Peter Smythe, so the story went, had married Sir Thomas Ferens' daughter, which had moved him up the ranks – he had never been on the shop floor and had not a clue how the other half lived. I was escorted in by Jack Gledhill again and told to sit down in front of this big oak desk. Mr Smythe read me my rights, so to speak, telling me once again that if I did not enrol I was out of the door. I told him exactly what he could do with his job in what might be termed industrial language.

Jack said, "You can't talk to Mr Smythe like that," so he got a taste too. I had never seen eye-to-eye with Jack, overtime being a big bone of contention. I was never offered Saturday mornings, which I could do, only evenings, when I was training – which, of course, I could not.

Fortunately, though, I had organised another job through a friend of mine who worked at Capper Pass, a big smelting plant on the outskirts of Hull, at Melton. The maintenance manager there was a chap called Harry Collinson, who happened to be a big Rovers supporter. He told my mate Tony that if they sacked me I had to go and see him and they would take me on as an apprentice to finish my time. I had already been to see Harry and told him they had sacked me, which was a bit of a white lie at the time, but I needed to get away, so it was all set up for me to start at Cappers as soon as I got clearance or my P45, whichever came first.

I was later called in and given another chance to redeem myself by Mr Smythe, who told me that as I was nearly 18, I did not have to go to night school. I panicked then, but gave him another mouthful in the hope that he would sack me. It worked that time, and I was marched out – free at last! I felt like a condemned man who has been given a pardon – a great feeling anyway. My old man fumed as only he could, almost frothing at the mouth like a rabid dog. But once he had come down off the ceiling and I could tell him about Capper Pass he was okay. I had a week off and started work at Cappers the following Monday morning. It was one of the best things I ever did.

At the time, I was knocking about with a few lads – 'Spider' Davies, Trevor Ingram, 'Bull' Milner and Colin Smith, who eventually became my best man at my wedding. We drank together and 'hung out' a lot at each other houses. Spider, as his name suggests, was a tall lanky bloke but who could pull women like there was no tomorrow – some of them absolutely gorgeous too! Spider, Colin, Trevor and I went on holiday in the summer of '64 to the Norfolk Broads. We hired a boat for a week, despite the fact that you had to be 21 to do so, but my old man signed all the forms and we never let on how old we were. We paid a mate from work to take us in his car, and it was a horrendous journey across country to get there. But the boat was duly handed over to us, and after a quick lesson in how to handle it, off we went. It was a Captain class boat, like a caravan on water, with two cabins, each with two separate bunks, to use the nautical vernacular. We set off for Great Yarmouth, stopping at as many hostelries as we could on the way. We reached a vast stretch called Breydon Water, where very shallow boats must keep to the marked channels, and it really felt like going out to sea. From there, we kind of turned a corner and crossed the expanse of water to Great Yarmouth, at the mouth of the river Yare – amazing what you remember from all those years ago!

We had a great holiday with lots of drink and girls. Of course, Spider met a girl one night in Great Yarmouth and fell in love as usual. I never knew anyone fall in and out of love like him. When we moved on, he actually got a bus back to meet this girl – Colin also going with him to see a girl he had met. I'm afraid that in those days, love never entered my head. Most of the pubs we stopped at on the Broads were out of the way and often with young ladies with their parents, bored looking for some fun – so we felt obliged whenever we could help out. We used to take it in turns to take girls back to the boat – do not rock the boat certainly never came into it!

One day, I decided not to visit the alehouse that we had moored up near to, as I had over-indulged in the amber nectar the evening before. When the lads went off for a session, I stayed behind for an easy day doing what I did best then – bugger all. Whilst I was sat up in the aptly-named cockpit area, contemplating going to the pub to meet the lads, a young lady walked up the towpath. Apparently she was staying on a caravan park not far from where we were moored and had gone for a walk along the tow path. As she walked up I could see that she had a wonderful figure and I smiled at her. We exchanged a few pleasantries before I asked her if she fancied a cool drink, as it was a quite warm that day. She said, "Yes please," so I told her to come aboard, trying to impress her with the nautical speak.

Anyway, whilst she had her drink, she was looking about as if she had never been on a boat before, so I offered to show her around. There was not really that much to see, but I caught a twinkle in her eye when she said she would like to see everything. Perhaps it was just that, but there was something about this girl that seemed to get to me in a very short time. We came to the main cabin, with single beds either side, and she sat on one and said, "Mmmm, these are comfy." She then handed her drink to me and lay down on it, kicking off her sandals off as she did. She must have been nearly six feet tall because her head was at one end whilst her feet were nearly over the end at the other. As she lay there, her tee-shirt had moved up, showing her midriff, and she said, "Ooh, I could sleep in these no problem – they're great." I put the drinks down and sat on the edge of the bunk, still not 100% sure if she wanted some fun.

"I'd love to share it with you," I said, looking straight into her eyes. She looked straight back at me, but I picked up no real emotion. Her hand was on the bunk beside her, her long slender fingers quite gorgeous in their own right, so I put my hand on hers. She then rolled it over and, entwining our fingers, lifted them both together to her mouth, first kissing, then licking my fingers, and then taking them in her mouth one at a time and slowly sucking each one. I bent over to kiss her lips and she responded with her tongue that parted my lips and entered my mouth. She then pulled my tee-shirt over my head and started to lick my nipples. I responded in kind, removing a rather sexy lace bra and making sure that I gave her equal attention. That did it, and she moaned, "Ooh yes, I love that, suck them!" As she arched her back her stomach muscles hardened, and I thought she was definitely the sporty type who worked out.

As she kicked her shorts off and I stood up to remove my jeans she smiled and then slipped her panties off. I'd never seen a shaved girl before, and as I looked she started to play with herself. She then grabbed me, pulled me to the side of the bunk and took me in her mouth, whilst I took over from her with my hand. When I got on top of her she wrapped her legs round me, I entered her and we worked our bodies together slowly. She then whispered, "I want it doggy, okay?" Ever the gentleman, I always try to oblige, and as she got on her knees with her head in the pillow, I entered her from behind. It was the best sex I'd had in my short career – this girl left them all for dead! As far as I was concerned at the time, she was an expert.

We lay together afterwards, just exploring each other's bodies, stroking and touching, and eventually we did it all over again. We stayed together most of the afternoon before she had to go, as her parents were returning in the late afternoon. I asked could we meet again, but she was going home to Bristol the following day, which was just a bit too far away! I really had fallen for this girl – she had something that certainly turned me on.

I went to see the lads in the pub about four hours late, by which time it was closing time. I say closing time but the landlord there did not bother – there was no chance of the police being around there unless they were lost, the road was nothing more than a track. The lads were on the way out as I walked up, "Where the hell have you been?" they said, but I just said I'd fallen asleep. That night we went back in the pub, and guess who walked in with her parents. She smiled when she spotted me, but gave me a 'please don't come over' look. Later, she came to the bar and we had a few words before she returned to parents. Spider said, "I think you're in there, Pol."

"Nah, not my type," I replied. I've often wondered whatever happened to her, I will never forget her and that wonderful afternoon we spent wrapped in each other's arms.

Spider and I were mates for a few years until he started working away and he hitched up with a girl down south. He later emigrated to South Africa and currently lives in Fish Hoek, which is now part of Cape Town. Bull Milner and Trevor Ingram drifted away too, and that left Colin and I, who remained friends for years.

Me, Trevor Ingram and John Milner in the Ferry Boat Inn

CHAPTER 5
FIRST TEAM BREAKTHROUGH

I had a very decent injury-free rugby season in 1963/64 – not really outstanding, but serving my apprenticeship in Rovers 'A' team – and my real breakthrough came the following season. I made my first team debut at the tender age of 18 years six months – very young for a prop forward in those days. It was on December 28th 1964 when I came on as a substitute for Jim Drake against Castleford. Jim was my hero when I was a kid and regularly went to the Boulevard, so to even be on the same team sheet as him was one of the greatest feelings I have had. When I told him this, he just told me to 'fuck off' in his gruff Cumbrian accent, but he had a glint in his eye when he said it. I actually think he was a bit moved, but he was too much of a man to openly show it.

Rovers trainer Johnny Williams told me later that Jim had mentioned it to him and had seemed pleased, as no-one had said that to him before. We had played a few games together in the reserves – he was such a hard man he frightened us to death, never mind the opposition. I remember him clipping our scrum half, Norman Gillard, behind the ear on one occasion because he had missed a tackle and the opposition had scored a try.

I must have done okay that day because I was given a starting place in the team for the next match, away at Doncaster. Rovers were riding high in the league at the time though, and I remained mostly in the reserve team. By the end of the season I had made four first team appearances – although I was still only 18 and a baby for a prop forward. The following season, 1965/66, was my best at Rovers and I appeared regularly for the first team squad, making 17 appearances, including one as substitute. It did not count as an appearance unless you actually went on the field, and my total was now 22 since joining the club.

The last two games of the season stand out in my memory. I started in the first round of the top 16 play-offs, against Oldham on 24th April 1965. Oldham had one of the hardest packs in the league, containing the likes of Charlie Bott, Harry Major, and Bobby Irving. They finished just one place below us in the league that season in ninth place. I scored a try as we beat them 26-14, earning the right to travel to play St Helens in the next round. Saints had finished top that season and were a team full of household names – Alex Murphy, one of the greatest there has ever been (if you ask him, he will tell you); Tom Van Vollenhoven, the great South African winger; Great Britain prop Cliff Watson, a rugged forward whom I got to know personally when I emigrated to Australia; and John Tembey, a giant of a man from Cumbria – tackling him was like trying to pull an oak tree down. But we had a decent side with Harry Poole, Frank Foster, Bill Holliday, and 'Flash' Flanagan all international forwards. It was an experience I will never forget. St Helens always went out first and went to the other end of the ground, which meant you were coming out of the tunnel and seeing thirteen giants waiting for you and the crowd baying for your blood. I thought what the hell am I doing here? Frank Foster and Mervin Hicks were sent off for fighting in the first half, Frank went through with the ball and as someone tackled him on his way down Mervin hit him right between the eyes with a punch that would have felled a bull, but Frank got up and just shook his head. That started a brawl and my thought was, who do I hit first? Cliff Watson was nearest to me and as I looked at him, he looked at me and said in his Brummy accent, "Aah, leave 'em to it, son." Talk about relief. I was just about to crack him, well that's my version of it anyway. I remember chasing Alex Murphy along the best stand touchline and thinking that he was not that bloody quick, and as I dived to tackle him he just accelerated and left me like a duck that had been shot in full flight landing face first in the Knowsley Road mud. Some embarrassment, but a lesson learned. It was a game where we weren't quite good enough and we lost 24-6.

My first 'motorised transport' was a Vespa scooter that I bought from a shop on Spring Bank for £20 as soon as I could get a licence. When I signed on at Rovers, I traded this in and bought a Honda 50 with part of my signing on fee – a brand new and red and white one of course! The Honda 50 was a cheap and practical motorcycle with a 50cc motor and three-speed transmission that literally anyone could use – it was so easy to ride that even novices could use it as easily as a pushbike. It became known as a scooterette and set a new fashion in commuter motorcycling. But I was flogging it to death going back and forth to Cappers.

One day, over lunch in the canteen, when I was moaning about its' lack of power, one of the lads who was into bikes asked why I didn't buy combi. I didn't even know what a combi was, and he had to explain that it was a motorbike and side car, which you could not only ride on 'L plates,' but you could also carry passengers in it. I gave this some thought and looked around a few of the bike shops before alighting on one down Brazil Street, off Holderness Road. The man there confirmed what I'd been told and asked if I wanted to try one. Well, upgrading from a 50cc scooter to a 650cc motorbike was hell of an increase and I was a bit daunted at first. But I thought what the hell, and after he showed me how to use the clutch and gear change I took it, rather timidly at first, down the street. There were not many cars about and I got to the end, turned round and came back with no problems. I got a surge of confidence, the power felt great compared to the Honda, and I thought, 'I'm having this!'

I cannot remember how much it was now, I didn't need a loan, and I arranged my insurance and picked it up on the Friday after work. It was great riding a big powerful bike, but I took my first left hand corner too fast and the sidecar went up in the air like a fairground ride. It was then that I remembered what the man at the garage told me – 'don't take left hand corners too fast.' Too late! But I slowed down, not braking and making it flip over, and thankfully it landed okay. It was a close shave and it was a good job there were no policemen about. I concentrated on the task in hand, set off again and both the bike and I got home in one piece. Over the weekend, I went for a couple of decent spins on it and had no problems. I was quite pleased with myself – a real big 'Hairy Biker'!

On the Monday morning, it was cold and damp as I set off to work on my new wheels. Passing through Hessle Square I noticed Allan, one of the lads I worked with, near the bus stop. I pulled over and asked him if he wanted a lift. He looked rather apprehensive as he got in and closed the door, but he gave me the 'thumbs up' through the small side window and off we went. I went along the then new Ferriby bypass – now part of the A63 – where I opened it up and was enjoying myself. Then I came to the turning down Brickyard Lane and took the left too fast again.

Up came the sidecar again and it seemed as if I went 50 yards on the two wheels. I was desperately trying to get it down again as I glanced at the window could see Allan screaming with fear. The sidecar hit the ground with a thud and we just kept going, right in at the works gate and pulling up at the clocking on station.

"You fucking stupid bastard," Allan shouted as he got out, his face grey, "You're fucking mental! Never, ever again!" He seemed a bit upset, so I tried to keep a straight face and said, "You don't want lift home then?"

"What!? No chance!! I'd rather walk home than come with you!" But he did, and I picked him up on a regular basis after that. It seemed funny to me that he had been in the army as a marine and I had frightened him – I wondered what he would have been like on the front line if someone was firing bullets at him.

But by the start of the 1965 season, I had been learning to drive a car, and was booked to take my first driving test in Hessle. At that time, I had not played the twenty first team games for Rovers that warranted you being awarded a blazer with the red badge of courage on it – the Hull KR emblem with the three crowns of the city on it. You had to earn the right to wear a badge in those days.

Keith Pollard

I had been told that if you had the blazer on for the test, you were guaranteed to pass, so I borrowed a blazer from Pete Murphy. The advice was good. I had an inauspicious start to the test when an old lady stepped off the kerb right in front of me as I set off, and I had to do a real and unscheduled emergency stop. The examiner nearly went through the windscreen – there were no seat belts in those days – and said, "That will do for the emergency stop!" We got back to the office in Hessle Square and he handed me the slip of paper to say I was proficient enough to drive solo. The BSM instructor dropped me back home and I went back to work on my motor bike, chuffed as hell that I had passed.

When I got back to work, I bought an old Bedford Dormobile from a guy called Terry for the princely sum of £25. It was idyllic. It had seats in the back that folded down to make a bed perfect for my extra-curricular activities, and even a wash basin in the corner that was ideal for emergency use. What more could a 19-year old ask for! My old motorbike and sidecar were left outside the house down the terrace, and my old man kept saying to me, "When are you getting rid of that bloody coffin out there?" He always called it a coffin, which I suppose was not unfair. It was double adult side car in all black with a Triumph Tiger 210 bike attached.

In May 1966, I was sent once again to Bisham Abbey and I decided to go in my mobile den of vice. There were five of us from Rovers this time – Phil Lowe, Mick Stevenson, John Hickson, a big Geordie lad called Alan Burns and myself – who set off down the A1 to Buckinghamshire. There were some decent players on the course, but two I remember particularly were a young John Crossley, an off-half who played for Widnes, and Brian Atherton – with whom I remain in contact. Brian now lives in Taree in Australia and is President of the North Coast Division Men of League organisation. He had talks at my old club, Maitland, when he emigrated, but it did not work out for him there.

We had a great time again, but there were a couple of significant incidents during the week. The first took place one night when we went into Marlow for a quiet pint and a potter round. There was a fair on and we were walking across the fairground when I heard a voice screaming. I turned and saw Allan Burns holding some bloke by the throat with his legs off the ground. I ran across to find out what was going on and saw a second bloke lying on the ground. Apparently, Alan was talking to a girl when these two came over and started making some smart remarks, thinking he was on his own. They must have either have been stupid or drunk – you would not say anything untoward to Burnsy on the phone, never mind stood next to him. All he needed was a bolt through his neck and he could have been in the Adams family. I told Alan to put the poor bugger down as he was looking blue and decidedly unwell. Alan gave him a crack, dropped him alongside his mate, and we set off to walk back to the van pretty sharpish.

We were just about to cross the Marlow bridge when a police car pulled up alongside us and we were told to get in. I stupidly decided to be clever and the next thing I knew we were sat in the back of the car and with a copper glowering at us from the front seat.

"What's going on?" I asked politely – learning quickly.

"Wait till we get to the station," was the reply. There, the duty sergeant asked our names, and then Allan told them his, the sergeant looked at me and said, "what nationality is he?" When I said "a Geordie," he asked him again for his name, but the only thing I picked up was 'ya'nah' at the end of the sentence. We finally explained who were and that we were at Bisham Abbey. I asked why we were there and was told that two blokes had been found crawling down a street near the fair in rather a distressed state, complaining that they had been beaten up by a gang of men.

Now I have always been on the big side and Burnsy was certainly no midget, but to call us a gang was a bit over the top. I said to the copper that round our way, if you pick a fight with someone and you unfortunately come off second best, then that's your hard luck. But he was a southerner and obviously did not go along with this logic. I was started to get a bit worried by now about how I would talk us out of this – I certainly was not going to get any help from Burnsy on that one! We were left on our own for a while and I saw the two men going into another room – they certainly did not look too good and I fleetingly wondered why they had not been taken to hospital, but without much concern.

Shortly after, another copper came in, and I started to tell him the same story, commenting that southern wimps were all the same, when he interrupted to say that he was from Whitehaven. He went in to say that, when questioned, the two had admitted that they had approached Allan with less than honourable intentions, and that we were free to go with no charges. I asked if they would give us a lift back to the Abbey and was politely told what to do. I failed to mention that my van was parked in a pub car park on the other side of the bridge!

The other occasion was rather more serious. About twelve of us went to Windsor in the van for a night out. I took it easy driving as it was a long way and even I realised that I needed my wits about me driving that far on country roads at night – and it was a bloody good job I did. We had gone to a dance joint called the *Ricky Tick* – a famous Rhythm & Blues club where the Rolling Stones, The Who, Jimmy Hendrix, Pink Floyd had performed. Locally, it was **the** place to go.

We had a couple of pints in a pub and set off to the dance hall.

77

Keith Pollard

It was really dark inside, with blue lights that make everything very bright, it was okay but a bit futuristic for me. We had a good time chatting to the local girls, even though as soon as we opened our mouths and they realised we were from north of Watford we were out of our depth.

At the appointed time, I and a couple of others started to walk the half mile or so back to the car park where I had left the van. We had not gone far when a police car pulled up. I thought, 'not again,' this was twice in a week. But we were asked to get into their car and taken to Windsor Police Station. I was thankful that I was sober when I got there, as we were separated and put into different rooms. I was told that we could be charged with indecent assault and possibly rape, which really shook me up and I told the copper I had no idea what he was on about. I was not actually cautioned, but there was no mistaking his seriousness. After I told him my story, he took a statement from me and asked if I had any objections to being put in a line-up. Knowing I was innocent, I said that was no problem. Shortly after, the five of us that were rounded up were put in to a room and lined up with some soldiers from the nearby barracks – although by this time it was the middle of the night! The two girls who had allegedly been molested, picked a couple of guys out. Thankfully, I was not one of them, and I shall not name those who were – quite literally to protect the innocent.

By this time, Colin Hutton and Albert Fearnley had arrived – far from amused about being dragged out of their beds and summoned to Windsor police station in the middle of the night. They gave us a grilling as well as right bollocking. The next morning, we were all summoned to the swimming baths, everyone from the course, whether they had been with us on the night before or not. None of us were in doubt about the seriousness of the situation. Once again, we were lined up and the two girls who were at the line-up the previous night walked up and down the line a few times – but they couldn't even pick out the same two that they had the night before. By this time, I was starting to realise that something was not right. As the girls were taken to a police car, Albert Fearnley collared one of the policeman and asked him what was going on. I later learned that upon being told that the girls were not sure who it was, Albert came out with a gem, "If someone had grabbed my balls, I would have known them for a fucking month never mind a day."

Apparently the girls later admitted to a policewoman that they had been with a couple of local lads round the back of some houses, when a resident had heard their activities and called the police. The lads scarpered quickly when the police arrived, and the girls made up a story about being assaulted by some northern boys – they had heard us talking in the dance hall. When the girls' parents became involved the girls did not want to tell them that they were having

RED & WHITE PHOENIX

sexual relations with these two lads, so they carried on with their tale. It was only after they messed up at the identity parade that they broke down and told the truth. We were sent away with neither explanation or apology, but then we were only northern country bumpkins.

That summer, four of us decided to go to Blackpool on tour in my bus – two sleeping in the bus and the other two in a tent. Col Smith, John Milner, Tony Milner and I met at the *Barrel* on Hessle Road at lunch time to set off for Blackpool in the afternoon. By the time we had had sunk a few pints it was late afternoon, but the drink and drive laws had not come in by then, so off we went. By then, the old bus used more oil than petrol and the starter motor used to drop off, as there was only one bolt holding it to the crank case. I used to open the cover to the engine, which was inside between the two front seats, and put my foot on the starter motor when I pressed the starter button, which was on the floor – there were no keys then! But I had wheels and this was a big advantage over other guys in 1966. Somehow we missed Blackpool and finished up in North Wales, I have no idea how, but when you are 19 and half-pissed you are very lucky to find yourself anywhere near your destination.

We stopped that night at a pub somewhere in the wilds and pitched the tent in a farmer's field – not that he knew about it – but we did not care, we were off to the pub! Later that evening, with our senses considerably dulled and our bladders stretched to bursting point we were trying to find our way back the van. Just hop over this fence, I said. Tony Milner went first, followed by a loud sloshing sound and a loud 'fucking hell!' It transpired that he had jumped straight into a large pile of pig dung. When he reappeared, he was covered up to his waist in pig shit. His shoes were full of it, his jeans were sodden and stuck to him, and the stink was unbelievable. We were all helpless with laughter – but needless to say he was far from impressed! We told him to strip off and leave the gear there on the fence and pick it up in the morning. Fortunately, there was no one around to witness the spectacle of him walking down the road, half-naked and half-covered in shit. We managed to find barrel of water behind a shed near the farm and washed him down in it – much to his annoyance – but no way was he sleeping in the tent or my van in the state he was in. His shoes were ruined and all he had with him was a pair of ex- army sandshoes, which he wore the rest of the holiday. He was not about to waste good beer tokens buying new shoes, so he earned the nickname of 'brown sannies,' which, like the cause of his problems, stuck.

The next day we set of on our adventures, finishing up in Colwyn Bay. After further deliberations we decided to head for

Keith Pollard

Aberystwyth – that being a university town, and universities mean young ladies, which was logical thinking for 19-year olds with rampant hormones. On arrival in the town we headed for the beach, but I think the water must have been on holiday in Ireland – not that this mattered to us, we were not there for the swimming anyway. There were some guys playing touch rugby on the sands, so we offered to play them, with the winners buying a round. However, Bull and I played and the other two did not – and the four lads that we thought we were going to turn over easily were quick to say the least. After we had each bought these four a pint each, and had a couple more for good measure, we set off to find a place to park and pitch the tent. Well, have you ever tried pitching a tent with six pints in you? Do not bother. Anyway, we did it in the end and had a well-earned rest.

By nine o'clock we were changed and ready for the fray again. This time we went to the university quarter to size up the local talent. In the first pub, when we walked in, everyone was chatting away, but as soon as we opened our mouths they all became aliens and started talking a funny language – it was like another world. I had heard of this happening to other people when they had been to the Principality, but it was my first encounter with the Welsh and it came as quite a shock. We finished off our drinks and left to look for a more amiable pub.

We then came across a pub with lots of girls outside in the beer garden – this will do us we thought. There we saw the lads we had already met on the beach. Apparently they had told us to meet them there but as usual we were not really taking notice. After a few pints, one of them invited us to a party, so we quickly bought some crates of ale – no four-packs in those days, just wooden crates containing bottles of warm beer – and followed them up the street to a block of flats. There were lots of girls there but there must be something about the Hull accent that turns girls deaf, because we couldn't get anywhere with any of them. I have never professed to be the best looking guy in the world but, at 20, I was as fit as anyone and had what I believed to be a decent 'chat up' patter – maybe the fact that we had not washed for a few days had a bit to do with it, but we never thought about that.

The nearest I came to pulling anyone was later in the night when I was sat with a guy in his mid-thirties, discussing the respective merits of rugby union and rugby league, when he placed his hand on my knee and asked me if I would like to go back to his place for coffee – just the two of us. I had never met a gay man then, and I was quite taken aback, to put it mildly. I told him what I would do if he put his hand on me again and called him a bent bastard. I know this would not be politically correct now, but this was 1965 and things have changed a lot over the years. Now, you see guys getting suspended for making homophobic remarks on the rugby field, but when I played you called them what you liked – it was all part of the game and what was said on the pitch stayed on the pitch. It was all part of the 'winding up' process and trying to get the upper hand.

After the frustrating experience of Aberystwyth, we decided to head inland to see some of the beautiful Welsh countryside and headed for Swallow Falls and Betws-y-Coed. But seeing water falling over some rock in the middle of nowhere was not really four young drinking mens' thing and we found the inevitable pub, had more beer, a fish supper (which is about the only thing I remember eating on that trip) and camped for the night. The following day we set off to Weston–super-Mare, which I know seems odd, given that we had originally meant to go to Blackpool, and if you can see the logic you are smarter than me. By the time we arrived late in the afternoon, the old bus was smoking like the Hessle Road Smoke House fish factory, but it was still going.

Somerset must be a wonderful place to visit when you are sober, but when you are full of Watney's Red Barrel mixed with local cider, it does not make much impression. The only thing I can remember about the two days we spent in that wonderful place was that we finally had some success with some young local girls. We met them in a pub one night and went back to the camp site, if you could call it that. A good night finished up as a great night, and we even cooked breakfast for the girls in the morning. I remember thinking that it was kind of sexy seeing the girls sitting around the camp fire in our shirts and their knickers, with the mist and dew on the grass. We knocked around with them most of the day but I cannot remember their names now. I hope their memories of their encounter with northern men that night are fond ones anyway.

Pre-season training for the new 1966/67 season was harder than usual. We trained on East Park under Rovers' trainer Johnny Williams, who was a real hard task master. The drink made it worse for me and looking back I was drinking too much in those days. I should have cut down, but of course that did not happen. Some things never change with rugby players and now even some of the superstars now drink too much, but they do have more time on their hands as they no longer have jobs outside rugby like we did.

I replaced the van with an old E class Ford – the ones where you could have any colour you wanted as long as it was black. I paid £10 for it to a Welsh bloke at Cappers – I should have known better, because it lasted a whole week. Mike Stephenson and I went to watch Rovers in a Yorkshire Cup game one Tuesday night at Hunslet's old Parkside ground in south Leeds. We never saw the game because the car broke down on the way and I left it at a garage on York Road, where it cost me £5 to pay the owner to get

Keith Pollard

rid of it. Mick and I had to thumb a lift to Selby to meet the team in a pub where they were celebrating their win, and we came home on the team bus.

I did manage a few games in the first team that season, but it never felt right. Towards the end of the season, one of our wingers, Mike Blackmore, broke his jaw and, being a bit light in that department, Rovers swapped me with York winger Stan Flannery for the last few games of the season. I enjoyed it there as another hero of mine from my Hull FC-following days was there. Tommy Harris was one of the best Welsh players and hookers ever to have put on a Great Britain shirt. That year Leeds won the championship and my debut for York was against them at Headingley. In fact, we played them twice in our last four games, another of which was against Rovers at Craven Park. I had been asked by York if I would be willing to go there on a permanent move, so I asked Rovers vice-chairman Ron Chester if they would let me go.

"No, you have a big future here at Rovers," he said – and what a load of shite that was. I told Tommy Harris at the last game at Doncaster that I would not be joining the 'Minstermen' and he said he was disappointed, but that he understood. So I went back to Rovers on April 8th 1967, ready for the 1967-68 season. From being a regular in the first team the previous season, I had not even been getting many runs in the reserves. I still do not really know why and have often thought that I got the blame for the problems we had at Bisham Abbey. As I was the elder statesman of the group, I think the directors blamed me, but being brutally honest, they were a rather spineless crew and no one said anything. The A team coach at the time was an ex-player called Ronnie Mills and I asked him what was going on. He just shrugged his shoulders and rolled his eyes. No one ever gave me a straight answer. I'd had enough and asked for a transfer. I put in a request every Tuesday for about a month until they called me in to see the board of directors.

Wilf Spaven was the chairman at the time, and he asked why I wanted to get away from Craven Park. I said, rather bluntly I suppose, that in my opinion I was not getting a fair crack of the whip. I mentioned the Bisham Abbey fiasco but they said this had no reflection on my ability as a rugby player and that they were not blaming me for what happened. Anyway we had had a clear the air meeting and all seemed well. They agreed to put me on the transfer list at the price of £1,250 – not a lot you may think, but when the world record at the time was about £13k paid for Brian Shaw from Hunslet to Leeds, it was a reasonable fee.

I always thought that Rugby League, especially in my day, was the only professional sport in which a nobody could be a somebody by becoming a director of a club. Some of those that I have been

RED & WHITE PHOENIX

involved with and met at other clubs were beyond belief. Most of them knew bugger all about the game, had never played or had anything to do with the amateur game. All they had was a few quid, and that give them the right to run a professional sporting club, which was unbelievable! I think it is a bit better now in Super League, which it is a full-time business, but I am sure that a few still nip in under the net, so to speak – none more so than at the Rugby Football League itself. It is a great pity, because there is a danger that those running the RFL will spoil what is still the greatest game.

After my meeting with the directors, I got back in the A team and started to enjoy my rugby again. I played against Featherstone Rovers away, which was always a hard game – they did not take prisoners at Post Office Road. Even if I say so myself, it was one of my better games – in fact I took on the 'Colliers' pack on my own and battered them. I had something to prove. But it was an all-round good game that I think we won, and I left feeling rather pleased with myself. The next week, I was substitute in the first team, so I must have impressed somebody, but on the down side I was called in and informed my transfer fee had been upped to £1,500. I was told I had a good game at Featherstone, hence my being chosen for the first team. I asked if every time I had a good game were they going to raise the fee, because if so I had no chance of getting away. But they did as they liked then. They also raised Terry Major's fee from £5,000 to £6,000 because Leeds were showing an interest.

As a forward, I was well down in the pecking order at Rovers. I had played with what in my opinion was the best ever back-row Rovers ever had – Bill Holliday, Frank Foster and Harry Poole. In fact, at one time I was the only forward in the pack who was not an international, as the other two were 'Flash' Flanagan and Brian Tyson. They were a great set of blokes. The reserves were a great side too. The experienced Arthur Mullins at full-back; Chris Young, who went on to play for Great Britain, on one wing; and Danny Raper, a giant of a centre who had great hands and pace, and who could kick goals, but who unfortunately, in his own words, was not that bothered whether he played or not. He was a docker in the days when, for a Hull lad, getting a job on the docks was the next best thing to winning the lottery.

One of my uncles, Ted 'Nagger' Boynton, was a foreman docker, and being a foreman was in a really influential position for a working man. He promised me he would get me a 'book' when I reached 21 – you had to be 21 to get on the docks in those days. He got my cousin Jim on when he came out the navy, but unfortunately for me they stopped taking names and closed the book a week before I was 21. I have often wondered what direction my life

83

would have taken if I had gone on the docks. Would I have earned or been given a nickname like so many of the characters there? The Judge was always sitting on a case, the Destroyer was always looking for a sub, the Balloon was always saying 'don't let me down boys,' or the Candle, who was always saying to the foremen, 'don't blow me out.' The place was full of men who were 'one offs,' no two alike, and it was great just to mix with them in the pubs and clubs in Hull.

I remember one day being on a bus going down Hedon Road and coming up to the Marfleet Lane junction. The bus stop was on the other side of the traffic lights and some of the lads were eager to jump off as the bus slowed down for the lights. But there was a little old man at the front of the open platform holding them up, he had a hump on his back, and all the lads were shouting at him hurry up and get off.

"Come on, fucking jump," one shouted and he turned round and, pointing to his back, said, "What the hell do you think this is, a fucking parachute?" Absolute classic.

But we had a great camaraderie at Rovers at the time too, especially in the reserve team, and we used to knock about a lot together. They were mostly local guys, some of whom would have got regular first team football if they had bothered to move away. But with no M62 then, Hull was something of an outpost. We would often go off for nights out, especially if the first team were in some cup game. One I remember, well most of it, was when Rovers were in the Yorkshire Cup final and we went to Leeds to see game in my car. There was Colin Cooper, Mike Stephenson, John Crawley, who was nicknamed 'the Length,' and was great friend of Rovers legendary hooker 'Flash' Flanagan. John had signed for the 'black and whites' but had struggled to get into their first team due to the crop of stars already there. He was a back row forward, but with the likes of John Whiteley, Bill Drake, Harry Markham and Cyril Sykes he had no chance – even the reserves were overloaded with good players at the time.

Anyway, after the game we decided to head for Wakefield and the *Blue Dolphin* Pub, a strange name for a pub nearly 60 miles from the sea. There was a comedian on in there, and the Length had been giving him a hell of a time every time he told a gag – just as he got to his punchline 'the length' shouted it out. Of course, the crowd were loving it and John was playing to the gallery, but a few blokes were telling him to keep quiet. Being told what to do egged him on and things started to get a bit spicy. Colin Cooper was getting a bit agitated and, not for the first time, I could see the red mist coming down in his eyes. As usual, it erupted and outside we went with the help of a couple of bouncers who thought they had heard enough from the non-resident comedian. After going to another couple of boozers we decided to go back to Hull. I couldn't remember driving home – all I could remember was waking the lads up in the car outside Colin's house near the *East Riding* Pub down Cannon Street. Of course, they had sobered up by then and wanted to kick on, but it was after midnight so we couldn't get another drink then in those days, so it was 'night, night.'

As we get older the list of people no longer with us grows. John Crawley and his old mate 'Flash' Flanagan are on the list, as are old Keighley mates Terry Hollindrake, Mick Clarke, the best coach I ever played for, and Chris Forster, the ex-Hull FC and Huddersfield forward. I could write another book just about the players I have known as team mates and opponents who have gone to the great playing fields in the sky. So many seem to be taken before their time, like Danny Jones of Keighley, who actually died on the field of play, leaving a wife and young twins. As the old saying goes, two things in life are certain in life, taxation and death, and it's such a shame we have to have either.

I made my final first team appearance for Rovers on March 25th 1966, by which time I had been picked for the first team around 35 times, actually making 22 appearances, including two as substitute. One of the highlights was on January 8th 1966 – the day we beat Wigan 16-2 at the old Craven Park. Wigan used to have a defensive move where Eric Ashton used to shoot the line and take out the opposing centre, and the great Billy Boston used to come in and crash tackle his opposite winger. This time the centre was Rovers' Terry Major, who passed the ball to Mike Blackmore, who ran for the gap, and as Boston closed in on his prey, Mike squeezed through, passing Boston by a mere fraction. But Boston could not stop himself and took out both Eric and Terry in one perfect crash tackle, whilst Mike duly scored under the posts. As I went over to congratulate him he was grey.

"Great try, Mike! You okay?" I said.

"All I saw was this cherry and white wall coming at me out of the corner of my eyes so I shut them and felt the slipstream off Billy's charge as I went through," was his rather shaky reply.

I was propping against Wigan's international prop Brian McTigue – one of the best front row forwards ever to play the game. In fact, he was the only man I ever heard Frank Foster pay any respect to. Before the game, whilst sitting next to Frank in the dressing room, he said to me, "You know who you are up against today?"

"Of course – Brian McTigue," I replied

"Leave him alone and he will be okay," Frank advised, "but try anything on with him and he will fucking kill you." Well that shattered any confidence I might have felt! If Foster was wary of him, what chance did an 18-year old have!? Anyway, the game

Keith Pollard

Gordon Young on the attack during Rovers' 1965-66 victory against Wigan

Pre-season training session 1963

started off according to plan and everything was honky dory. My job in those days was to run off Frank Foster, Bill Holliday and Harry Poole – Harry used to say to me, "When I tell thee to run, thee run or I'll fucking belt thee, never mind them bastards."

I was quite quick despite my portly build - some used less kind terms - and I had made a couple of breaks and was doing okay, when it happened. I went short off a ball from Frank and I saw a Wigan shirt coming in from my right, so I lifted my elbow, cracked whoever it was on the nose and we hit the floor together with me on top. I looked down and saw to my horror that it was McTigue. He growled something at me but I wasn't hanging about. I got up double-quick and played the ball. At the next scrum, he put my head where he wanted it and I saw his fist in front of me. I am in deep shit here, I thought – he had me set up and I could not move. The fist travelled only six inches and hit me straight between the eyes.

"Keep your elbows to yourself, young'un, or there will be more," he growled. I did not answer because I did not want him to see that I was afraid, but deep down I was terrified. But I had no more trouble from him afterwards and I even hit him really hard, man and ball, putting him right on his arse. When he stood up to play the ball and said, "Good tackle, son," I felt as if I had been knighted.

As I walked off at the end of the game, McTigue came up to me, put his arm round my shoulders and said, "Well played son – keep it going and you will do well in the game." To think that a player of Brian McTigue's stature thought I was good made me feel another six inches tall. Then, when I got home my old man said he had been listening to the game on BBC radio and that the commentator, Keith Macklin, had said that, "Rovers win was due to them having the best three players on the field – Frank Foster, Bill Holliday and a young prop called Keith Pollard." It was one of the proudest days of my career.

I only recently found out that the reason Frank thought so highly of Brian McTigue was that when he was an up-and-coming youngster at Workington he stiff arm tackled Brian, who did not retaliate at the time, but a bit later on in the game he flattened Frank with a cool left hook when no-one was watching. Frank was carried off on a stretcher. Even the mighty meet their match sometimes!

Rovers had good players in the backs too. Cyril Kellett at full back was a great player and man; centres Johnny Moore and Terry Major were two strong and talented centres; and at half-back they had a pool of talent in Colin Cooper, Norman Gillard, Davie Elliott, Arthur Bunting, Alan Burwell, Brian Hatch, Brian Brook and Mike Stephenson – and that was before they went and bought the daddy of them all in Roger Millward. It is sad to think that today most

Frank Foster congratulates Peter Flanagan on his selection for Great Britain

My last game for Rovers in 1967 - Back row: David Wainwright,
Brian Tyson, Bill Holliday, Frank Fox, Mike Blackmore, Terry Major,
Cyril Kellett and Me. Front row: Peter Flanagan, Alan Burwell,
Roger Millward, Frank Foster, John Moore, Dave Elliott, Chris Young

RED & WHITE PHOENIX

British clubs struggle to find a decent locally-born half-back. But, in those days, every club had a sprinkling of great players, even the lower teams, and without being disrespectful, I am talking about the likes of Keighley, Bramley, Dewsbury, Batley – whoever you played, it was always a hard game, especially away from home.

Rovers had several good backs in the reserves too – apart from the half-backs there were Ted McNamara, father of Steve, wingers Bob Harris and Chris Young, and centre Brian Wrigglesworth, who was bought from Bramley and went on to play for Featherstone Rovers. There was also George McDonald Kennedy, a Scottish winger who came down from Scottish Rugby Union club Leith Academicals and won the reserve team player of the year in successive seasons, but never got a real chance in the first team for some reason. George was a canny bloke. He wrote to Rovers for a trial, and they sent him a fixture list and told him to pick dates that he could come down for a couple of trial games. George thought he would look at the first team league standings because if the first team was in the lower levels of the league, the reserves had a good chance of being not much cop either. He picked York, Batley Bramley and Keighley, scored nine tries in those four games, and Rovers snapped him up. He went on to score 27 tries in his first season, whilst I scored one. George later went on to become a high flyer in the City and I met him several years later when I was working on the channel tunnel.

The A team finished top of their competition that year, but the old enemy beat us in the play-offs and went on to play Castleford in the final, losing 9-0. In the forwards with me were Eric Palmer and Brian Mennell, both of whom played for Rovers at Wembley in the 1964 Challenge Cup final. There were also loose-forward Ted Bonner; local men Peter Murphy and Gordon Young; hooker Peter Walker; the experienced Frank Fox; and ex-Rugby Union prop John Bath. Along with the established first teamers such as Poole, Foster, Holliday, Tyson, Flanagan and the young Phil Lowe, who became one of the finest running back-rowers the game has ever seen, this represented a great depth of forward strength.

The big games to look forward to were the local derbies against Hull FC. The first I played in was the Eva Hardaker Cup game at home in 1965/66 season at Craven Park. It was supposed to be a friendly, but it was a hard fought game as all derbies should be and usually are. Hearing the opposition supporters slagging you off, and in my case calling me a 'fat bastard traitor' because I left Hessle Road and became a 'red and white,' was always music to my ears. Supporters tend not to realise that when they are abuse the opposition or the referee, they actually make them play better, or in the referees' case, give the opposition more penalties. A well-known referee once told me as long as they kept abusing him, the

Keith Pollard

Rovers A team at the Boulevard
Back row: D Raper, Me, C Wallis, P Murphy, T Bonner, B Burnett, C Cooper, A Mullir
Front row: T McNamara, R Coverdale, A Holdstock, R Morrell, C Young

The Rovers' pack that played at Hunslet in the 1964-65 season:
Harry Poole, Len Clark, Bill Holliday, Me, Alan Holdstock and John Bath

team got penalised for any split decision. As Nobby Stiles, the great Manchester United and England footballer, used to say, "When they are calling me names, I know I am having a good game."

That day I was playing no 10 with Foster, Holliday and Poole in the back row and Flanagan and Frank Fox in the front row with me. My abiding memory is that after we had scored a try, the kick off back to us was short and went straight at me on the 10-yard line, just in from touch. I took the ball on the full and three of them came at me, one of them being the great Clive Sullivan. I managed to duck under a couple of head high shots, bumped off Clive as he went low for me, and was off in the open up the best stand side, with the Rovers supporters urging me on from the Well. I had got to just over the 25-yard line and Sully got back to tackle me just as Arthur Keegan hit me. It was like being hit with a truck when Arthur tackled you, and I was bundled into touch. As I got up, Sully said to me in his Welsh accent, "Bloody hell, Keith I did not realise you were so bloody fast!" Arthur added, "well done, son." They were two gentlemen of the game, two fantastic blokes who are sadly missed. Later on in the game, I made a break and ran straight at Arthur in front of the posts. I heard Arthur Bunting screaming for the ball, but as I turned to pass it, Keegan wrapped his arms round me and it was like being in a clamp – I could not move never mind pass the ball. Bunting was still screaming for the ball as Keegan whispered in my ear, "no chance, mate."

It was during this game that the infamous incident occurred between the late Eric Broom and Frank Foster. It all started with a scrum flare-up after Frank's fist had flattened Alan McGlone, who was out cold as a maggot. Eric was mouthing off at Frank about what he was going to do to him but ensuring he did not get anywhere near, and believe me that was the right choice. The quote that really wound Frank up, and a wound-up Frank Foster was not good news, was Eric's, "I'll have you after the game." The Dad's Army expression, 'you stupid boy' came to mind, and even the Hull FC players looked at him with amazed 'are you crazy' looks. Frank went right over the top of me to get at Eric, who went down alongside the still-asleep Alan McGlone.

Whilst getting changed after the game, I asked Frank if he was going for a pint. He looked straight at me with those eyes of steel and said, "No, there is only one place I am going. Mr Broom wants to see me." Colin Hutton had to take Frank up into the stand to calm him down whilst they got Eric Broom out of the ground. From that day, Eric Broome never again played against Frank Foster. He had injuries, car breakdowns, relations who died, you name it. Even the Hull FC players joked about it. If Eric had just played in one game, even if he got flattened by Frank, no one would have said anything, but his behaviour was unprofessional. It

The Rovers A team that defeated Hull A 21-5 at Craven Park

was a pity because Eric was not a bad second row on his day.

Derby games were like no others. Ted Bonner told a story about his first derby, when Bill Drake punched Jim Jenkins for no apparent reason, other than that it was the thing to do in a derby. Ted, being an ex-rugby union player actually asked Bill, "What was that for?" Bill just said, 'We have to start some fucking time don't we?"

Rovers' A team coach at that time by Bob Coverdale, a man of mature years who had joined Rovers from Wakefield in 1959. He had previously played for Hull FC and played in the first World Cup in 1954. He was a great bloke and knew more about prop forward play than any man I ever met. One of my first A team games for Rovers was away to Keighley when I was about 17. The prop opposite me was giving me a bit of a hard time in the scrums, and I gave him a few cracks but to no avail.

"At the next scrum we'll swap over and I'll sort him out," Bob said to me. We duly did, and I heard Bob tell him to leave me alone, followed by the unmistakable sound of fist on bone and a loud 'uugh' from the other side of the scrum. When the pack broke up this guy was face down in the mud and I had no more problem from him for rest of the game. That is what I call looking after your young players! It is something that is missing from modern day rugby league – reserve teams where young players can learn their trade from seasoned professionals.

At Batley, a young prop thought he was a bit of a hard case and was giving 'the old man' a hard time. It was the biggest mistake he made – Bob hit him on the inside as he lowered his head into the scrum, a straight upper cut which no-one saw, and as the scrum broke up this guy fell to the floor. When his eyes opened he reminded me of Marty Feldman, both popping out and looking towards his nose.

92

RED & WHITE PHOENIX

Also in the reserves at that time was a lad called John 'Slick Hic' Hickson. John was not the brightest bunny in the warren and you could have written a book of stories about him alone. I remember us playing away at St Helens in the cup when the game was called off on the Saturday and rearranged for the Monday night. We stayed over at Cleveleys, near Blackpool, and Colin Hutton told us we could have some free time in the evening as long as we did not go over the top with drink and were back for 10pm. Frank Foster and Bill Holliday said that they were going to take the tram into Blackpool and go to the pictures.

"That's a good idea," chipped in Slick, and Frank and Bill exchanged looks. On the tram, Slick said, "What we going to see?" and was told he could go and see what he wanted, just to tell them about it when they met up later. At the appointed rendezvous the three met and Frank asked, "Okay Slick, what did we go and see?" Only Slick could have replied, "I don't know – I fell asleep."

When they got back, Colin was standing on the steps of the hotel, ensuring that everyone was back on time, and of course he asked where they had been. What story they told him is not clear – but he would not have expected much sense from Slick anyway.

Once, at Bradford, Rovers were attacking Bradford's line when John made a great break and was tackled just short of the line. If he had reached over he could have scored a try, and later Colin asked him why he had not done. "We had a move on," he replied quite seriously.

For those who do not know the ground, the changing rooms at Bradford's Odsal stadium are at the top of the bowl that forms the stadium, and the teams walk down at the beginning and back up again at the end. Slick was a substitute there one day and was in charge of the water bucket used by the 'sponge man' or trainer. At the end of the game, we were making the long trek back up the hill and Slick was complaining to Colin about the bucket of water being heavy.

"For fuck's sake John!" Colin said. "Stop moaning – just empty the fucking thing!" To be fair to Slick though, whenever he put a Rovers shirt on, he gave 100%. He was not the best player at the club, but he was a real trier.

Sadly, many of those great players have since passed on, men like Cyril Kellett, Terry Major, Johnny Moore, Davy Elliott, Mike Blackmore, Bob Harris, Frank Fox and Jim Drake. The world is a poorer place for that, and I certainly go to more funerals now than I do christenings.

We always played Hull FC on Christmas Day morning in those days, and on one such occasion I was on the team sheet as 18th man for the away game at Boulevard. Not thinking I would be playing, I was out on the ale the night before. I was in the old 'Blue Heaven'

Keith Pollard

pub on Southcoates Lane until after midnight then at a party down Buckingham Street until the early hours. We had to be at the ground for 10 o'clock at the latest and as I walked in, feeling far from well, Frank Foster stopped me and told me I was substitute.

"Bugger off," I said, "I'm still half pissed."

"Don't let Hutton see your eyes, or you will never play for him again," he replied. I went and got a coffee in the tea hut before going into the dressing room where I tried not to make eye contact with anyone. I did not need a jersey – my eyes were red enough! Cyril Kellett had cried off, so Arthur Mullins went full-back and I took his place on the bench. We got into the lead and all was going well until Gordon Young suffered a hand injury. He played on until half time, when we went in for the break still ahead. But Gordon was in so much pain that he had to come off.

"Keith you're on, go no 10," said Colin. Bloody hell, I thought, but I said, "Okay, great." We ran out and to be honest I was feeling quite good. At the first scrum I packed down opposite their number 10, a rugged Cumbrian forward, Jim Neale, who was a decent guy. He said to me, "Bloody hell, Keith you stink! What have you been drinking?" I replied, "If you hit me, Jim, you're going to find out." He just laughed and said something about Christmas spirit, but he never roughed it up, just played the game as it is supposed to be played hard but fair. He was another hard man who was ok if you left him alone. I had quite a good game and we won, which was always the main thing, especially against Hull FC, so my drinking never came up. I never ever did it again – I had learned my lesson that day. I must have done okay because I was in the starting line-up for the game against Castleford the following day, so I laid off the booze and had another decent game.

CHAPTER 6
A TIME OF CHANGE

Two great things happened to me in 1967. Firstly, we moved to a house with a bath, in Park View, Gypsyville. My old man had said, "When we get the chance to move, you had better be stopping and help pay the rent, or we aren't going." He was not particularly happy with the way things turned out. I remember going to look at the new house with Mam and we went upstairs to look at the bathroom. We could not believe it – a bathroom! I remember just standing there with her looking down at the bath, neither of us saying a word, just looking it. It seems surreal now, but it was a complete novelty for us then.

Secondly, I met my lovely wife Jacky. I had not done any serious courting, but had been seeing a couple of girls on a pretty regular basis over the previous few years. One was June, a nurse I met at the Hull Royal Infirmary Christmas dance and went out with for about six months. She worked on the same ward as my mother, who was a ward orderly, which is how I got tickets to the dance – they were only sold to people who actually worked at the hospital. Presumably this was to keep our people like me who had a thing about nurses in uniform. I had got on quite well with June, who told my Mam she had met me and hoped to see me again – or so my mother said.

I sent message to her via Mam and managed to get her phone number – they must be posh bastards up in Bilton Grange I thought. We duly met in town and went for a drink. I did not have car at the time so it was awkward, to say the least, travelling up to Bilton Grange, which was about eight miles and two buses each way. One night we went to Hornsea with Howard Laybourne and his girlfriend, Hilary, in his car. I end up dropping him and Hilary off and taking June home in his car. By then, I had been welcomed in to the fold and was allowed into the house, although whenever we sat canoodling on the sofa, a voice kept coming from the room above saying, "Isn't it about time Keith went?" We used to laugh, but I was thinking, bugger off for Christ's sake I'm trying to score here! This particular night, after another frustration, we said our goodnights and I went back to the car. But I could not get it to start, and unable to call for assistance, I thought bugger it – we'll worry about it tomorrow.

The following day, Howard turned up at our house to collect his car. When I said that it was at Bilton Grange, he was not a happy bunny, and when I told him it would not start, he was even less

The Keighley first team in 1967

My debut for Keighley against Bradford in 1967

happy. We set off in my motorbike and side car – which was the ultimate insult to Mr Laybourne, who would be mortified if anyone saw him travelling in a mobile hearse. When we got up to Bilton Grange he managed to get the car going, but another problem had arisen. It had a puncture, and, sure enough, there was no spare wheel. But there was a jack and a spanner so we managed to get wheel off and away we went to try and get puncture mended.

Four hours later we arrived back with said tyre repaired, not so much repaired as with a new inner tube, as they did then. We put the wheel back on, Howard got in the car and I was about to set off when I heard the car giving that familiar sound that we've all heard on a cold morning when trying to start the car – yes, the battery was flat. I have no idea why, but I had a length of rope in my sidecar, so with the help of a tow, we finally got the car started. I laugh at it now but Howard never ever forgave me for making him travel in sidecar, especially with a car tyre in his lap – it totally ruined the image of the dandy he thought he was, and the bastard never let me use his car again.

The other girl I saw for quite a while was Anne. She was about 20 when we met and a single mum, who lived in a flat off Beverley Road. She was a great looking girl and how and why she fell for me I will never know. My mates and I went out together in Hessle quite a lot and often ended up at the *Ferryboat*. Nine times out of ten, Anne and her mates came in too, and we would finish up going home together. This went on for quite a while but again I was not ready for a relationship. As we sat snogging on the settee one night, and Matt Munroe was on the record player singing *Walk away, please go*, I thought to myself how apt, and that I should tell her. Soon after, though, I did tell her that I did not want to go on seeing her so regularly. She had a flatmate who was not there the night we split, but a couple of days later she spotted me in the street and flew at me, giving me hell of a verbal pounding, calling me all the bastards and saying how I had broken Anne's heart. Anne eventually married a guy who used to hang around the same places as us and they have been happily together for a long time now, and I am pleased that we sometimes meet and can say hello as friends.

By this time, I had bought a new set of wheels, a Ford Anglia in blue and white – it was the one with the sloping back window that was very trendy in those swinging sixties times. Little did I know when I bought it, that whilst it might have looked good, that was as far as it went. We were at training one night and had decided to go in to town to the *King Edward VII* – one of our favourite haunts. Pete Walker got in the back and I heard him say, "Fuck me, I'm on the floor!"

"What are you on about, Whack?" I replied.

"My feet have gone through the floor! I am stood on the car

Keith Pollard

The Keighley first team in 1968

Me and Jacky in 1966

Me at Scarborough

park," he said. I got out and went round to his side of the car – sure enough the floor had collapsed and he was stood in a puddle.

"You useless bastard," I said to him. "How the hell did you manage to do that?"

"Don't have go at me because your car's a load of crap, it's not my fault!" He pulled his feet back through the hole and we put a blanket over it before setting off to town. Next morning at work, I ripped up the carpet – not such a good idea as it was actually holding the floor together. Before the MoT test came in, all that was required was that the brakes and steering had to be okay – the bodywork was not examined. I had a word with the foreman and got some thin plate cut to size and repaired the floor in the back with pop rivets. With a fibre glass coat of red lead paint it was good as new.

I had left Capper Pass and gone to work for a company in East Hull called Steel Fabrications, where I was given the task of manufacturing Generator Bodies from rolled steel drums. It turned out to be a really boring job, doing the same thing day after day, and I lasted only about 12 months before I could not stand it any longer. At least the Ford Anglia was still going though.

Around this time, I briefly went out with Miss Hull Kingston Rovers. Although she was a great girl, it was not to be for us. I went to her parents' one night, a posh house in the Heads Lane area of Hessle. I think her father was a bank manager and I felt totally out of place. That was the beginning of the end and we were just about finished when I met Jacky.

By then, I had changed jobs again and was now with an old established company called Abba's, on Goulton Street off Hessle Road. As I was working as a welder, one of the stipulations was that I had to join the plumbers trade union. The manager was a real old fashioned gentleman called Jack Hutchcroft, who asked if I fancied working in the shop and learning how to 'fire bend' pipes – the old-fashioned way of bending them that not many people could do. Pete Thomas, an old guy called Jack Stephenson, who had left Abba's to go to Broady's, and myself were amongst the very few in Hull. Winter was coming on and I thought that working on a big coke fire, and being nice and warm would be a welcome change to being out on site and up to my ears in mud. I was working with a couple of experienced lads, Syd Matfin and Charlie Musared, and it was really interesting and enjoyable work.

One day, I was in the old tin hut, as they used to call Rovers supporters club on the Craven Park ground. Jacky and her mate Beryl were in there and, although I didn't really know them, I got chatting to them as you do. But it seemed as if I was getting the cold shoulder from Jacky. Now without sounding big-headed I was not used to this treatment from the fairer sex – by then I'd was not having any difficulty in getting girlfriends. So I was a bit taken aback and I started to see Jacky Wilson as a bit of a challenge – there was just something about her that attracted me. I persevered and started seeing her on a regular basis. I was taken home to meet mum and dad – her dad, George was as sound as a pound – a Rovers supporter and off Hessle Road like me. But her mum was a different kettle of fish – she did not like me from the first and the feeling was mutual. She thought I was not good enough for her beloved Jacky, and you could see 'it will never last' written across her face, even when we had been going out for a few months. I think I proved her wrong.

We used to go in the *Maybury* pub on Marfleet Lane with Danny Raper and his girlfriend-to-become-wife Pam, Arthur and Joan Mullins, and Colin and Pat Cooper. It was the place to be in East Hull, with music and live bands always on. It was a great night – you had to be in there at six o'clock, or you did not get a table. We then went back to Pam's house just off Portobello Street, taking fish and chips or a Chinese with us – or we went into town for a Chinese meal. Breathalysers had not come in then, so everyone did drink and drive, and not until they introduced the Evidential Breath Testing laws in 1967 did people start to take notice. It took me quite a few years to get used to it, but now I only have one pint if I am driving. Looking back, I realise I had been both very foolish and very lucky.

In the September of 1967, my former team-mate, Eric Palmer, who was then playing at Keighley, got in touch and asked me if I fancied going to Lawkholme Lane, as they called their ground then. The directors there had asked him to ask me before they put in an offer to Rovers. I said, "Yes, I would love the opportunity for regular first team football." I was only 21 and I was not really getting anywhere with Rovers. Funnily enough, I was then picked as substitute for Rovers' first team at against Dewsbury and one of the club directors, Frank Parkinson, stopped me as I was leaving the dressing room afterwards, and said, "You had better take your boots with you."

"What are you on about, Frank?" I replied.

"You are off to Keighley – you will get a letter tomorrow to confirm it," he said. So I went round to see Eric and he confirmed that Keighley had got me on a month's trial loan, and I was to go through with him on Tuesday for training.

We duly went on the Tuesday, and what a journey. There was no M62 then and it took over two hours to go through Selby, Leeds, Shipley and Bingley before you got there. I do not know how I kept doing it, but I did. The coach at the time was a bloke from Wakefield called Don Metcalfe. From the first time we met, he did not like me and I certainly did not like him. I think it was the first

RED & WHITE PHOENIX

training session that did it.

"You are late," was the first thing he ever said to me. I thought fuck you mate and gave him mouthful about travelling two hours in traffic, and from that moment we just did not hit it off. He was the first player/coach I had been involved with and he thought he was 'king of the castle' – a real big head. A week or so before I joined Keighley, he had told the board to get rid of Arthur Render – and actually said that in his programme notes. Arthur was a 'no nonsense' type of player with a heart as big as a lion and the same killer instincts, who had a long career that had started with Hunslet. As it happened, Arthur came back to the club after Metcalfe had gone, and finished up as A team coach.

In those days, the directors picked the team, which was the same as at most clubs, so I was picked to play in the first team local derby with Bradford on Saturday 30th September 1967. At the time Northern were the unbeaten league leaders and we lost 14-2, but we gave them a really good shake up. They had a very good team at the time, with people like Terry Clawson, Alan Kellett, Bak Diabira, Tony Fisher, and the ex-rugby union full-back Terry Price. I had a blinder, even if I say it myself, one of the best games I ever played, and afterwards the chairman, Norman Mitchell, asked me if I was willing to sign there and then – never mind the four trial games agreed with Rovers. I was quite pleased to agree, but as I walked out of the dressing room the Bradford coach, Albert Fearnley, stopped me and asked when I had left Rovers and how long had I been at Keighley. I told him what had happened and he said, "Don't sign anything till I get back to you next week." It seemed that he wanted me at Bradford, but I told him that I had just given my word to Mr Mitchell that I would sign for Keighley, and would not go back on it. I had just finished five years of playing second fiddle to a team full of stars and internationals and wanted to try and make a name for myself with a smaller club, with no disrespect to Keighley.

My second appearance with the club was in the floodlit trophy at Castleford – these were Tuesday night games with the second half shown on BBC2, so of course I told all my mates they would see me play on telly. I was propping against Dennis Hartley, at the time the Great Britain No 8, and felt that I was having a decent game. Cas were well on top, but I was gutted when Don Metcalfe in his wisdom took me off at half time. I thought, here we go again, another coach who does not like me. I was fuming and went to him after the game to ask him what was going on. He had the audacity to tell me I was playing well.

"Then what the fuck did you take me off for?" I asked, and he told me the chairman had told him to take me off.

"What are you on about, you fucking idiot" I replied – I would never had made the diplomatic service. At this moment, Norman Mitchell came in to the dressing room and I collared him.

"What's going on? You can forget about me coming to this club, I will go back to Rovers after my month is up." He told me to calm down and confirmed that they still wanted me, and explained that they had taken me off because if Rovers had seen how well I was playing they would have put the transfer fee up. Just like they did with Terry Major, I thought, and I had to see his point. But I was more annoyed about not being on TV and how to explain it to my family and friends afterwards. I walked into the tea room and Eddie Waring, the great TV commentator, came over to me.

"Hello Keith, what's the injury?" he asked. In those days, you were supposed only to be substituted due to injury, and I told him what had happened.

"Oh, I can well believe that," he said. "You were having a great game." He pronounced the word 'great' with a broad grin and huge emphasis on the 'gr' in the way only Eddie could. What could I say? In the end, I accepted what Norman Mitchell said and joined his club.

In my first season, 1967/68, we did not do too well in the league, finishing fourth from bottom, but we did get to the third round of the Challenge Cup. Alan Kellett arrived from Bradford to take over as player/coach in February 1968. I may come across as a rebel who has a problem with authority – I am not really like that, but I do call a spade a spade and a lot of coaches do not like that. Allan Kellett was one of those, and was another I did not see eye-to-eye with. The main problem this time was that he brought a couple of his mates with him from Bradford, prop-forward Barry Potter, and a centre called Brian 'Ada' Larkin. He wanted them in the team, and I was one he decided should be left out.

I had a running battle with him all the time he was at the club. I actually asked for a transfer at one time and the directors got me in to the office to discuss the situation, as they wanted me in the team even if he did not. I was coming out of the director's room as he went in. He must have said the wrong things because they sacked him. I was sitting in the bar with Mick Clarke when he came out and told us he was going – I just smiled at him and did not say a word, but inside I was bubbling. I said to Mick, "I bet you are in for the job aren't you?" He shrugged his shoulders but winked as he got up, just as the new chairman Clifford Coates walked in to the bar, and they walked out together.

Years later I met Alan when I came home from Australia and we had a heart-to-heart talk. He was coaching Halifax and I was playing for Hull FC in the reserves at Thrum Hall. We had a couple of pints in the bar after the game, talking about things in general and my time in Australia. He gave me a sort of apology for the way he treated me at Keighley, saying that he had promised Barry first team rugby. I accepted it because I see no point in bearing grudges.

Of all the players I ever played with, Alan suffered most with nerves before the game. I was bad enough, always on and off the toilet from getting up in a morning to just before going out on to the field, but Alan used to be violently sick. He would be sat on the side of the bath giving his pre-match talk about who to watch out for, what he wanted from us, and so on, whilst all the time balking, spitting, and vomiting in to the bath. He used to make feel ill just seeing him – no wonder we did not win many under him; we all felt too ill to play! That's my excuse anyway.

There were some memorable days – and one very sad one. On February 28th 1968, we were drawn away to Widnes, later to be known as the cup kings, in the second round of the Challenge Cup, having beaten Batley 7-2 at home in round one. We had won three out of our last five games, having overcome a really bad run of eight consecutive losses, but they had won three of their last six games, including Doncaster away 10-9 away in the first round. We went to Widnes thinking we had a really good chance of winning. Our preparation was spot on and our main plan was to nullify their attack. They had some great players in the squad like Ray Dutton, Mal Aspey, Ray French and George Nichols. I was given the job of shadowing Ray French; my orders were if he looks like getting the ball flatten him. It worked, and half-way through the first half, as I tackled him for the umpteenth time, he said, "Pollard will you fuck off, you are fucking nuisance!" I thought this is the not the language you would expect from a school teacher, but I knew I was getting under his skin.

We went in to the break leading 5-0. Norman Mitchell was still our chairman then and he came in the dressing room at half time to tell us that we were on another £5 each bonus if we could hold them out. Now, a fiver may not seem a lot but we were on £14 a win and £7 a loss, so it felt like a fortune. We went out and did the business, running out winners by 15-5. We were over the moon and returned to the dressing room, laughing, joking and really enjoying the moment. Then I saw Joe Flanagan, the reserve team coach, crying his eyes out. It was not that good, I thought, but everyone celebrates in their own way. Then John Leach, the vice-chairman, asked for quiet as he wanted to say a few words.

"Fucking hell," whispered our international second row Geoff Crewdson in my ear, "more bonuses!!" But it was not more bonuses, it was bad news. Norman Mitchell had collapsed on his way back to the director's box and had died from a heart attack. I went from being on a real high to the lowest I had felt. The room went silent and no-one knew what to say. Mr Mitchell's son came in to the room, and whilst he was obviously desperately upset, he told us how his father had been just before he collapsed. It was indeed tragic that he should die without knowing of our great victory.

After that, it was Geoff who broke the silence with, "Does this mean we are not stopping on way back for a pint?" Sometimes it is that kind of black humour that is what is needed. We all went to the funeral on the 9th March. I broke my hand playing against Rovers a few days before and so I missed the third round game at home to Wigan – a game we only just lost.

The following season, 1968/69, we were fifth in the league at one point, with 14 wins and one draw out of the out of the first 23 games, and we finished just inside in the top 16 for the first time. We had several big scalps that season – including Rovers, Bradford, Featherstone, who were all strong in those days.

I had got fed up with the 'fire bending' at Abba's, the summer was coming and I asked if I could go back to working onsite. But Jack told me they had no vacancies for the site crews, so I would have to stay on the bending block. I was a bit pissed off and after some deliberation decided to go labouring at Drax Power Station, because it was more money and I fancied the change. I lasted a week.

I left there and went to work at the Humber Graving Dock in Immingham, North Lincolnshire. In those days Immingham was just starting to grow, they were building two oil refineries and had dug a deep water channel to allow large tankers to berth in the river. Jacky and I wanted to get married and, at that time, you could get a new council house if you had worked in the area for a couple of months.

I rang Keighley up and told them I had retired from the game. They were not very happy about it as I had only been there just over 12 months and they had paid a transfer fee for me. I told them that I was planning to get married and needed a house, but they were not happy bunnies. I lasted a couple of weeks at Immingham and got finished because I was in the wrong union. I had 'welder' on my PTU card, but I needed to be a member of the Boiler Makers Union to work as a welder in a ship yard. I got paid off, but once again I was out of work.

A couple of days later I was driving past Abba's works and saw the foreman, Pete Thomas, standing outside. I pulled up and shouted, "Need any good pipe benders, Pete?" He laughed and said, "Cheeky fat bastard!" But he came over and we had a few quick words. He then told me to hang on and disappeared into the works. A couple of minutes later he came to the side door and shouted, "Jack says 'you are a cheeky bastard, but you can start on Monday!'" As it turned out, I was not back for long.

RED & WHITE PHOENIX

KEITH WAS VERY MUCH A MODERN DAY TYPE PROP...

When I was asked if I would write a few words for Keith's book about his life, I jumped at the chance to pay my tribute to him.

As a childhood Keighley fan, then later a player and coach, as you can imagine I noticed many things which took place at the club from my first year supporting the club from the age of eight in 1964.

The signing of Keith Pollard and Eric Palmer in 1967 from Hull KR were headline news back then.

Eric had played at Wembley in Hull KR's loss to Widnes in 1964 and Keith was an up and coming prop who was given the chance to develop his game at Keighley with regular first team football. I watched eagerly as these two new signings boosted Keighley's squad no end.

Keith was very much a modern day type prop. Quick and played flat to the ruck as I remember, gaining valuable yards in the days of the slower play the ball.

At the time Keith became my favourite player and he embraced his move to the club by settling in the area for a number of years before moving on to Australia in 1971 to try his hand in the renowned and tough Newcastle Competition.

Being a keen Rugby League fan I followed Keith's career and I believe he learnt a lot In Australia and enhanced his coaching potential...but sadly was never given a chance to prove his worth as a coach over here on his return.

Peter Rowe
Ex Keighley, Bradford Northern, York and Hunslet
Coached at Keighley - 3 occasions, Halifax, Barrow – twice, Swinton – twice, Featherstone Rovers and Wakefield Trinity.

Keith Pollard

Our Wedding Day, October 26th 1968

RED & WHITE PHOENIX

CHAPTER 7
FAMILY MAN

The happiest part of my time at Keighley was my marriage to my wonderful wife and best mate, Jacky, who has been with me now for 45 years. Some people say that they never have a cross word in their married lives – well, that must be bloody boring, is what I think. We have, but I would not swap her for the world. My mother reminded me that I had once said, 'the only girl I will want to marry is the one I will bring home to meet you and dad' – and that is exactly what happened.

A couple of weeks after I told them I had retired, Keighley got in touch with me and said they had a club house they could offer us if we wanted it. I told them that we did not have enough money at that time to get married and they said they could get round that, and offered me an interest free loan to be paid back out of my rugby earnings. We thought hard about it and decided we would get married as soon as possible. When I told my old man, he said, "What, is she up the stick?" When I said no, he replied, "What the fuck are you getting married for then?"

We got married at St Michaels and All Angels Church on Holderness Road on October 26th 1968. It was a great day and one I will treasure always. We had a night out in the 'tin hut' that was the Rovers Supporters club, and the wedding night was spent in the Paragon Hotel in Hull.

When we arrived there, I was ready for what was going to be a memorable moment in my life, the equal of being the first man on the moon. The porter carried our bag up to the room and showed us the usual stuff before asking, "Would there be anything else you would like?"

"No thanks, mate," I said, biting my lip.

"Yes, some coffee for two please," Jacky interjected.

"Certainly ma'am," the guy smiled, winking at me as he disappeared.

"Fucking Coffee" I said, just to keep the romantic moment alive.

"We have waited a long time for this moment darling, let's enjoy every minute of it," Jacky whispered in my ear. Was this the shy girl I knew 24 hours previous to our wedding ceremony, I wondered. When the coffee arrived, Jacky had gone into the bathroom to prepare herself for our big moment. We drank if eventually but it was cold when we did completely finish it. It was well worth the wait and I do not mean the coffee!

Keith Pollard

We moved in to 41, Shann Avenue, Black Hill, Keighley on October 27th 1968. It was a modern type of house for the time, built on the side of a hill, with a panoramic view of Keighley from the front window. The only problem with it was that there was no central heating, only a coal-fire. It was freezing in the winter, as we were to find out within a few months of moving in.

The club organised job interviews for both Jacky and me. I got a job at a company called Fulworth Engineering Foundry Equipment on £16 per week (40 pence an hour in today's money), but I had been working for £14 per week in Hull. Jacky got a job in the office at a wool mill of John Haggass and Sons at the same pay that I was starting on. This was a hell of a raise for her, as she had only been on £9 per week running an office for an engineering company in Hull. I have always thought Hull wages have lagged behind the rest of the country.

There were quite a few foundry engineering companies in Keighley and, in hindsight, I left Fulworth over a quite a trivial matter. I fell out with the foreman, Bert Wynn, during the summer, when they were working on a contract to install a new furnace at a company in Doncaster. We employed an outside contractor to do the site installation, but everyone was called on site to push the job on. We were working too many hours and tempers were getting a bit frayed. I was working on installing some platforms and Bert came up and was whingeing about why it was taking so long and complaining about everything I had done. I told him to fuck off and leave me alone, and that it was a two-man job and I was working unaided. He left me alone at that, but the next morning the gaffer, Roy Staines, came through from Keighley and told me I was going back to work in the shop. I asked him if Bert had asked for me to be taken off the job, he said not, but some more work had come in and he wanted me on that. Later, however, one of the lads told me he had heard Bert on the phone whinging about me and telling someone at the other end he wanted me off the job.

I confronted Bert afterwards and, although he denied it, the atmosphere was never the same after that episode. I started to look for another job and found one literally next door. I was walking in to work one morning and a son of the guy who owned it asked how I was. I told him I was pissed off and looking for another job. He offered me one there and then – they needed someone who was used to pipe-work and I fitted the bill perfectly. I went in told Roy I was leaving and worked my weeks' notice, starting next door the week after.

I had not told Roy where I was going, and he was livid when he spotted me loading their truck with equipment to take on site. They worked for a tyre remoulding company and I was employed to install some new moulds, including all the steam lines to feed them.

RED & WHITE PHOENIX

It was more money than Fulworth, but after about three months I once again had a 'run in' with the gaffer. He had ripped me off over some bonus he had promised and I was seething about the fact that he had gone back on his word.

I used to drink in the same pub as a bloke called Mike Wilkinson, who was the manager of yet another firm, Cootes. I was telling Mike about what this bloke had done to me and he offered me a job at Cootes. I agreed and said I would give my notice in on Monday, which I duly did. I was then offered an extra £1 per week to stay, and the gaffer said he would sort the bonus problem out. I agreed, but was still unhappy deep down. I used to go home for lunch in those days and on the way back that day, I saw Mike in his car. He stopped and asked me if I was still okay to start with them. I told him I had been offered more to stop, to which he replied, "Fuck him, we will give you £1.50 more, if you say yes now."

Ever the mercenary, I promised to start the following Monday. Back at work I told the gaffer I was still leaving as I was upset about him trying to get out of bonus payment. We had bit of an argument and he lost his temper. He was a spoiled brat and he spat his dummy out and told me to fuck off there and then. I pointed out to him that he had more or less sacked me, so he paid me for the week I was working and my week-in-hand. I went round the corner to Cootes and Mike said, "Start with us tomorrow then." It was quite a result for me really. Cootes was a family-run business who looked after their employees, and I stayed there until I emigrated. You worked hard, but they were good outfit and was a pleasure to be there.

There was a foreman who was a bit of an oddball, who was always telling tales about the staff. I think they were looking for reason to get rid him but he had been there quite a while. It came to a head when the lads on the shop floor were looking for an increase in money, as other rates in the town had gone up, and Cootes always said they would pay top dollar to keep the workforce. I was asked, along with another guy, Alan Crosher, who was also originally from Hull, to be a spokesperson. We were not in the union there, so we had to do own negotiations. We asked the foreman if we could see Alec Green, the man that actually owned the company. He said he would organise a meeting, but nothing happened for about three weeks or so. The lads were getting a bit restless and a couple had already been to see other companies about a jobs and possible vacancies. I went in to the office one day and spoke to the company secretary, Anne, and told her what was going on. I said that the foreman was supposed to be organising a meeting, but nothing had happened, and that some of the lads were talking about leaving. She agreed to look in to it. Apparently, the foreman had never told Alec, who then called him into the office

Keith Pollard

Mam and Dad with Jason just before we left for Australia in 1971

and sacked him. I am sure that was the excuse they wanted, and they paid him off there and then.

Alec then asked me if I wanted the foreman's job. No way, I thought! I was 24 at the time and not ready for supervision, also we were starting to think about emigrating, and I did not want to take that job then leave them in the mire later. We got a pay increase above the going rate in the town – I think it was £23 per week. In later years, I went been back to Cootes on a few occasions to see one or two of the guys who were still there, but sadly I heard that they ceased trading in 2011.

Another great day in our lives in Keighley was on May 21st 1970, when our son Jason Wilson was born. That day and the day we got married were two of the proudest days of my life so far. His was a difficult birth - it must run in the family! - and Jacky had a hard time in labour, but she got through it like the fighter she is. We toyed with different names for him, I came up with Troy but that was rejected. We were discussing it at work one day and a mate suggested we name him after where he was conceived. We were on holiday in Scotland on the banks of Loch Ness in a tent at the time – and I didn't think that 'Nessie' or Lomand were right. I asked the guy where he got the idea from and he said all his kids were named after where they were conceived. When I asked if he did a lot of travelling he said no, but his wife had a thing about making love in cars. After that, I never quite looked at her in the same way when we met in the pub. He told me his kids were called Austin, Morris, Alfa (Alf for short), and Royce. I said 'Royce!?' and he replied, "Yes, the lad was lucky, I wanted to call him Bentley, but my wife put her foot down and said no to that one." When I pissed myself laughing at that he looked quite indignant and asked what I found so funny about it.

We settled for Jason in the end, and his middle name was suggested by Mary, the wife of our then local MP, John Binns. We used to drink with them in our local, the *Royal Inn*. We had popped in on the way home from the hospital to 'wet the baby's head' – or more accurately to show him off to Jack and Marguerite. John and Mary were there having lunch and whilst we were chatting the subject of names came up. We had not given much thought to a middle name and Mary said to Jacky, "What's your maiden name?"

"Wilson," she replied, and Mary said, "Wow! that does have a ring to it, 'Jason Wilson Pollard!'" We thought she was right, so Wilson it was.

Back on the rugby front, we started the 1969/70 season well – winning three of the first four games – but fell away badly and won only 12 games all season, finishing fifth from bottom. I then had a disastrous start to the 1970/71 season, being suspended for 10 games after being sent off against Bramley and Halifax before Christmas. The Bramley one was my own fault. I hit Robin Dewhirst with a late stiff arm as he tried to sidestep me. I was clumsy – he always stepped to your right and knowing this I should have timed it better. Referee Billy Thompson said, "That was a bit late," and I gave same old answer all us props give, "I got there as quick as I could, Billy!"

But against Halifax, no way should I have been sent off. They had a classy loose forward called Tony Halmshaw who played one game for Great Britain against New Zealand in 1971 and should have played more. I tackled him man and ball and, as I held him up in the tackle he head-butted me. I thought that it was not a very good attempt and that I would show him how it should be done, so I gave him one back, the perfect 'Liverpool kiss' right between the eyes. The referee shouted, "Okay, let him go Pollard, I saw everything," so I did as I was told.

"Right, get off," he said.

"What about him?" I replied, but he just told me to get off again. Afterwards, I thought my reputation was getting to hurt me, and perhaps it was time to get out of England. I did not think I was really a dirty player, I just played hard. When I played with him at Rovers, Frank Foster always emphasised that you had to put fear into the opposition or you would not get their respect, maybe I just

Keith Pollard

took it a bit too far now and again.

On the day I went up before the disciplinary committee, Tony Fisher was also there after being sent off for head-butting in the local derby at Lawkholme. Had he been found guilty, he would have received at least four games suspension, which could have prejudiced his chances of playing for Great Britain in the forthcoming world cup – and by a strange quirk of fate the committee met on the same day that Fisher was selected for the GB team. There is no way Fisher could not have been found 'not guilty' of head butting – he committed the offence not once but three times and received an official caution in front of a crowd of over 4,000 people. The disciplinary committee however found an error in the referee's report, which said that Fisher had the ball when he butted Mick Clark, instead of the other way round, which forced them to dismiss the case.

Far be it from me to suggest that the committee was biased in Fisher's favour – that eminent body should be above suspicion, but I believe that many people at Lawkholme felt very bitter and let down in what they saw as a miscarriage of justice. I had a poor disciplinary record and the committee handed out a corresponding sentence. But according to our media spokesperson, I was a very valuable member of the Keighley team, and would be sorely missed. That was an external factor and not relevant to my case – but was Fisher dealt with in the same way?

One of my favourite memories from my Keighley days was a night game away to Wakefield Trinity. They were the league leaders at the time, but we came very close to turning them over and had the home crowd very worried at one point. It was only a spell of eight points in ten minutes that finally crushed us. We had equalled them in skill, and were superior in courage and determination. I scored a 30-yard try after talking a short ball off our scrum half, Bob Smith, and bursting through four tackles to go over in the corner. The local paper reported that Kenny Eyre and I really shook the Trinity pack up, saying that, "The giant David Jeanes met his match in Pollard, who threw him around like a rag doll." I did not get many good write ups, so I remember those I did get!

Another game was on October 19th 1968, a week before we got married. I was not going to play in case I got injured and we had a lot of preparing to do that week, but the directors suggested I play in the Keighley reserve team as they were away at Craven Park. I agreed, much to Jacky's dismay. If it had been any other team, I would have said 'no' but as it was my old club, I said 'yes please.' At the time, Rovers had just signed the Aussie great, Artie Beetson, and he was being given a run in the A team to acclimatise. I will have a go at him and see how good he really is, I thought.

RED & WHITE PHOENIX

I spotted him coming on the burst on an inside ball so I lined him up. I had a knack of body-checking guys with my shoulder, which always worked but would probably be illegal now. I hit him full on, he went down with his eyes rolling and the trainer had to come on with the magic sponge. I was ridiculing him, calling him an Ozzie wanker and similar insults. Then he got up – bugger me, I thought, that is not supposed to happen. As we scrummed down, I could see Artie was most unhappy and, if looks could kill, I would have been on my way to the pearly gates. He was playing second row, on the same side of the scrum as me. He sent one through, but he must still have been a bit concussed as he missed me completely and hit our hooker Tony Pell. The team had to wait for Tony at Hull Royal Infirmary, where they were thinking of keeping him in overnight. Artie went off alright, but not injured, sent off by the referee – much to my relief. I reminded Arthur of this years later, but he refused to believe it. Must have been that hell of a crack I gave him!

The next time we met was up at Keighley, where Rovers were the visitors in a first team fixture. Artie was playing again and I thought he really is game; he has come for some more! I thought I'd get him before he got me, but like so many good plans this just did not work. I hit him with a cracking stiff arm – I think that is when his nose got bust – he blames me anyway. I stood over him as he played the ball and was once again giving him some verbals, when then I heard a whack, the lights went out and that is the last thing I remember about that game. Apparently, I was carried off and later came back, only to be carried off again. No-one bothered about concussion then – if you could stand up you went back on.

Jacky tells me that after I came back on, Rovers had the ball and passed it out to the best stand side of the ground, where Geoff Wrigglesworth, the former Leeds three-quarter, was running downhill towards the line, and just as he was going over the line I took him high. We both flew over the touchline but his head was still on his shoulders, so it was not too bad. I had prevented Rovers scoring the match winning try, but I got a two-game suspension for my trouble. I came round in the dressing room about half an hour after the game and I had not got a clue what had happened. I had to go to the doctors during the following week as I woke up one night and my whole body was riddled with pins and needles. I went for a scan and they told me I had burst some small blood vessels in the side of my head. They asked me if I had banged my head recently. Too right – by hammer blow from an 18 stone lump of prime Aussie beef!

Another game that sticks in the memory was Wigan away in the Floodlit Trophy. Wigan have always been a great side and it was no different then. We got hammered, I cannot even remember the

Keith Pollard

score, but what stands out was the way Wigan played. In the first half, there was not a footprint inside their 25-yard line – every time we looked like getting there, they got the ball and kicked it back over our heads back into our own 25. We were totally outplayed – even if you have the ball, when you are in your 25, you are still defending. A hard lesson learned, believe me.

One good thing that happened to the club was that at the beginning of the 1970/71 season, the team selection was handed over to Mick Clark and Arthur Render, the latter having by then returned to the fold as A team coach. For this reason, the club seemed more settled and Mick Clarke was, in my opinion, a breath of fresh air to the club. He was by far the best coach I had played under at that time. We won 21 of our 34 league games and finished sixth in the league, before going out to Dewsbury in the first round of the championship play-offs.

We certainly had our 'ups and downs' in the four years I was there, but I really enjoyed my time with Keighley. They were a great club and had some really good players. Dave Worthy was a solid a no-nonsense type of prop forward; Brian Jefferson was self-confident bordering on big-headed, but he was a great full-back and goal-kicker and you could not dislike him; Alan Dickinson, a centre from Castleford, was one of the hardest men I ever played with or against; Colin Evans, a Welsh scrum-half who finished up on the coaching staff, with such a thick accent he was almost unintelligible, but what a player! There were quite a few seasoned professionals who came and went whilst I was there, household names in rugby league like Terry Hollindrake, Bill Bryant and Kenny Eyre.

I must mention one other lad who played with us at Keighley. He was called Johnny Westhuisen; a South African by birth, whose family emigrated to the UK in the early 1960s. I found out later he was cousin of Joost Van der Westhuisen, the Springboks' scrum-half who was tragically struck down with motor neurones disease.

There were also three Australian guys at Keighley then; Jon Green, Tommy Searle and Ivan Pascoe, who were from West Tamworth in NSW Country Rugby League Group 4. They were a very strong club in Country RL at the time – as they still are. We became really friendly with them and their wives, and often went out socially. They were one of the main reasons we decided to emigrate at the end of the 1970/71 season. I got on well with all three but was particularly friendly with Jon Green, and he and his wife used to come up to our house regularly – his wife, Lyn, got on really well with Jacky. In a way we were all outsiders to Keighley – we were all living away from home, even though some were rather further away than us! But when you are away from family and loved ones you are still away, and there were none of the

114

communications we are now used to.

When the 1970 World Cup came around, we had a month off whilst the tournament was on. We went to a few of the games as well as the final, which was at Headingley. I had a minivan at the time, so Jon and I went in that. Jon had a couple of mates over from Oz on a trip run by the famous Sydney Radio commentator, Frank Hyde, who was to Australian rugby league what Eddie Waring was then to the British game. We met up with these lads, 'Grubby' and Jed, after the game, in the bar under the main stand. The game itself, won by the Aussies 12-7, was a torrid affair that became known as the 'Battle of Headingley.' It was little more than a glorified 'punch up' thanks to the 'anything goes' attitude from referee Fred Lindop, who took no real action until the 79th minute when Sid Hynes and Billy Smith were sent off for little more than had happened in the rest of the game.

Jon's mates were from a little town in New South Wales called Gunnadah, not far from Tamworth. The Australian hooker that day was Ron Turner who played for Cronulla, and whose home town was Gunnadah. The four of us were standing chatting when Mick Clarke came up and suggested we went into the players' bar. We told him that was like getting in to Fort Knox, but he was having none of that and took us with him. Of course, he knew the commissionaire on the door – he had been captain of Leeds for years and, if he could not get you in, no-one could. The two guys from Gunnadah were like kids in a sweet shop, seeing all the stars of the game in one room – which did not include Jon and I! As the players started to arrive from the changing rooms several came across and spoke, including Dougie Laughton, who was at Bisham Abbey with me the first time I went, and the aforementioned Tony Fisher, with whom I had locked horns a few times over the years. The two boys from the bush thought all their Christmases had come at once when the Kangaroos came in. Ron Coote came over and spoke – although I did not know him, he was quite a friendly, as was Bobby McCarthy. Whilst Ron Turner was talking to us, Aussie legend Bobby Fulton came over too.

Grubby suggested we go to the Queens Hotel, where they were stopping in Leeds. They all piled in the back of the van, Ron Turner included, and off we went. When we arrived, Frank Hyde, our media man, was in the lobby. When he spotted Ron, he shot over and started chatting like all good men in his profession would do. We were then invited to the party that was being given for the people on the trip, which was in the upstairs bar – we didn't need a second invitation. When I went to get a round in and got my wallet out, the barmaid said, "No money needed sir, it's a free bar until midnight." It just gets better, I thought. The bitter was in pints and the lager was in jugs with smaller glasses to drink from, and I was the only one drinking bitter. After a few beers I felt like a rest, so I went and sat down on a settee in the corner. As I sat there this tall guy came over and said, "Do you mind if I join you, mate?" We were chatting away and I thought he was a really good bloke. I asked if he had played himself and he replied that he had played a few first grade games in Sydney, mostly with St George. He asked me what I did and I gave him a potted version of my history, as you do when you have had a drink. When it was my turn to go for the drinks, Grubby said, "Fack me mate, do you know who you are talking to?"

"No bloody idea" was the truthful answer.

"Norm Provan," he replied.

"Who's he?" Grubby's jaw nearly hit the top of the bar.

"Who's Norm Provan!!!??" Grubby had then to explain that he had been captain of St George and Australia, one of the greatest Australian forwards ever. I later learned that he had played 256 games, 19 for Australia and 14 for New South Wales and had coached at four different clubs, finishing at Cronulla. He had played in the first ten of St George's run of premiership victories – as captain-coach for four – and made 30 finals appearances for the club. And I had asked him if he had ever played the game! I felt like a complete prat as I returned to that settee with the drinks. But I never let on I that I had been told about him and we continued chatting away. I had already told him I was going to emigrate the following year in 1971 and he said, "Listen son, if you want to give me a call when you get to Sydney, I may be able to help you. I'm in the book." He actually wrote his name on a beer mat for me – not that I needed it by then; I had been in the company of a rugby league God.

After that we moved on to Australians' hotel in Bradford. I know I was out of order but I drove, we all got into the van and off we went. Inside the hotel we met Roger Millward, who was out injured and in plaster, and we had a few beers. I had a yarn with Ron Coote and John O'Neill, the Ozzie prop, and Bobby Fulton joined us. Then Roger came over and told Bob that he was going to go and play in Australia. Bob said, "No way! You be king here, and I'll be king there." They did both became kings of their own countries in rugby league terms. John O'Neill said to me, "Look what your fucking mate Hartley did to me," lifting his trousers to reveal biggest gash in his shin I have ever seen. I told him he should wear shin pads – looking back it is a good job he had a sense of humour.

At the end of the night, I was well and truly knackered and drove home from Bradford to Keighley on auto pilot, arriving home at heaven knows what time. We did some stupid things in those days. Jacky was not up to greet us with a bacon sarnie or

116

bugger all – no heart some women! She and Lynn had got into one bed so Jon and I got into the other – so it transpired, but at the time I had not a clue, I could not remember anything. When I woke up the next morning, I looked at Jon and nearly jumped out of the bed – he had Lynn's hat on, and looked like a wolf in the cartoons. He had a look of the lead singer in Queen, Freddy Mercury, with his protruding teeth in any case. I woke him and asked why he had the hat on. He said that he was so cold when we got in he had to put it on to keep the warmth in – typical soft Aussies! When you went in their house it was like a sauna – heaven knows what their electric bill was.

Living in Keighley definitely changed our lives. I was very keen to go in to the licensing trade and worked in a pub owned by Jack Holmes, an ex-Keighley player, two or three nights a week, to learn the trade. A guy called Eric and I worked Wednesday nights, with a girl called Rita, whilst Jack and his wife went to Keighley variety club for a few hours. We stayed after closing time at 10-30 until they got home, and one night Eric asked me if I could use a blow torch. I thought, bugger me, is he going to do a safe or something? I was totally wrong of course.

It transpired that he worked for a scrap merchant in the town, who had a contract to strip out an old wool mill and needed someone to help in removing the drive shafts that ran through the building. They needed to burn through solid shafts and had never done it before – they were not alone, but I did not let on at that moment. I said that I could do it, and asked what was in it for me. They offered £25 for a Sunday morning, which was more than I got for 40 hours, so I said, "Count me in." I got there on the first Sunday and Eric said, "Right what do we need?" I thought, you are the expert, I am only here to use the torch, but they had not got a clue. The shafts were about 200mm in diameter and needed cutting down to make them easier to get out of the building. We could have used thermic lances, but they do make a mess and with the floors being solid timber I thought, no way.

"Okay," I said. "We will drill some holes in the wooden floors and put eye-bolts through with a plate on the top side. Then we can hang chain blocks off these to support the shaft we are going to remove." Remember the classic *Only Fools and Horses* sketch where Del Boy, Rodney and Grandad are taking the chandeliers down off bolts through the ceiling? That was the type of bolt we were using to hold up the chain blocks. I then hung up half an oil drum with chains, and filled it with water to catch the sparks and molten metal. It was only possible to wash the metal away using the biggest cutting tip available. It all worked out great. The gaffer came down to see how we were getting on and was chuffed to bits to see we had got down three sections in the first morning. Eric and his guys did the drilling of holes, working in front of me, and the team I had did the cutting and removal. We did the job in four separate visits to site and I was £100 up for four Sunday mornings.

After that, Eric asked if I would be interested in going into the scrap business with him. I declined because it was not really what I wanted to do. I haven't seen Eric since we left Keighley, but I heard a few years ago that he became a multi-millionaire – if you did make it Eric, good luck to you!

Another opportunity that arose one night was when Jack Holmes asked me if I was interested in running a fish shop for him, working alongside my wife. He was willing to pay good money, more than we were earning at the time but I did not really fancy that, because I was still intent on getting a pub.

Once we looked after a pub for ten days, to see if we liked the day-to-day work. It was the *Turkey Inn* in Gooseye, near Laycock, which we had used often. The pub was owned by a chap called Rex Simpson and his wife Gina. I was working at Cootes at the time, and they gave me unpaid leave of absence on top of my annual two-week summer holiday. We took it over one Friday and all my workmates came in. It was heaving, although in fairness that did not take much, as it was only a small place. Rex had gone through the day-to-day jobs and showed me how to tap a barrel of beer; he only used Hogsheads, which is 54 gallons of beer. He said I would not have to put any up on the racks as the draymen would do that when they delivered and took away the empty barrels. He showed us how to separate the money into float and how to keep records of sales. It seemed easy to me – but how wrong can you be!? It was really hard work and I'd advise anyone thinking about taking a pub to be very sure they know what they are getting in to.

On the first Sunday, I put nibbles and cheese on the bar and the locals thought it was great. Little did they know I had put extra salt on the crisps, used salty biscuits and the cheese was not salt free – all in the hope that it would make them drink more beer. It had the desired effect, because we sold more beer that day than Rex had ever done in one day – or so he told me when he came home off holiday and went through the takings. Only after he had worked the next Sunday lunch did he realise what we had done. He gave us a right reaming next time we went in, because all the customers complained that there were no cheese and biccis on that day. But to be fair to him he did congratulate us on the way we had looked after the business, and gave us a decent bonus for our troubles. This paid for our trip to Scotland which we certainly needed, as we were absolutely knackered.

Rex's son, George, actually played on the wing for Keighley, mostly in the reserves, but he was quite a decent winger. On a Saturday night after playing, I used to go in the *Knowle Spring*

RED & WHITE PHOENIX

Country Club – we would go around the pubs and finish up there later on. Sometimes, if there was a 'bit of bother,' we would help out the bouncers and for our efforts the owner would give us a few free pints of Timothy Taylor's fine ales. We sometimes used to go in on Sunday lunchtime when they had a comedian, exotic dancers or strippers on. We once were in there, sitting at a front table, when the stripper came on to do her first stint. She was also a fire eater, but with a difference – instead of eating the fire, it went into another orifice at the other end of her body. What a stink – I have never smelt anything like it before or since. But how she did not burn herself, I cannot understand.

For her second stint, she came down from the stage amongst the audience. She was going round trying to get people to kiss her breasts, and she went up to George just as he was taking a drink of his pint. Now George loved his beer, and you do not disturb man when he is drinking, but she pushed her breast into his face and he told her to fuck off and not to pester him. But she was getting a laugh out of the audience at George's expense, and she pushed her tit into his face again. Now George was really pissed off – not only was he being laughed at, but she was being smart with it. Next time she did it, George leaned forward as if to kiss it and put his lips around the nipple, sucked it and bit, not too hard but just enough to take a grip of it. She let out a yelp and tried to back away but George was stuck to her like a limpet, and we were pissing ourselves laughing. There she was, naked as a jay bird with a six-foot bloke stuck to her tit like a baby being breast-fed. She was shouting at him to get off, the bouncers came into the audience and told him to let go, but he shook his head and she screamed more as her breast swung from side to side with his head. Her husband arrived at the scene, not a happy bunny, and he told George if he did not let go he would crack him.

"Not with my tit in his mouth, you won't," she squealed. The six of us at our table stood up and told him that under no circumstances was he going to crack anyone, and with George being a local lad that the bouncers knew well, they lent support. All the audience were in tears of laughter and the comedian was pissed off because he had not had such a good reaction to his jokes. In the end George let go and she looked down at him, looked like she was going to slap him, thought better of it and disappeared off to the dressing room. I said to George, "What the fuck was that all about?"

"Fuck her, she stopped me drinking my pint and I'm not standing for that – and she had nice tits!" A man of principles was our George.

One night, the owner of the club, who was also the head brewer at Taylor's brewery, asked me if I was still after a pub. He told me

119

Keith Pollard

there was a pub coming up for tenancy and asked if I would be interested. The pub he was talking about was the *Burlington Arms* in the market place in the centre of Keighley. He said they were looking for someone to come in as tied tenants. Most of the tenants they had were older, and quite a few were reaching retirement age. He told me that it was a £200 ingoing, as they say in the trade, meaning that meant you had to pay a £200 deposit for fixtures and fittings. When you took on a tenancy, you were required to purchase the fixtures and fittings of the pub, pay one week's rent in advance, a rent deposit and any other ingoing costs. When you left the pub you would sell on the fixtures and fittings to the next incumbent, or back to the brewery. I told him I had never had that amount of money, but he offered to lend it to me to pay back when I could. He suggested we go and have a look at it and let him know within two weeks. I remember going home that night, waking Jacky up as excited as hell, and saying, "We've got a pub!"

Take my advice. 12.30 in the night is not the best time to tell your wife you want her to start running a boozer, especially when she is four months pregnant with her first child. Jacky does not usually blaspheme, but she then said, "No fucking chance – get to bed, you're pissed". We did go and look at the pub during the next week. It was an Irish pub – there was a large Irish community in Keighley at the time, and this was one of their locals. It even had *Paddy McGinty's Goat*, *Delaney's Donkey* and *Rafferty's Motor Car* on the jukebox. They sold more Guinness in there than any other pub in the area, so I was told it was a gold mine. But it was not to be. We decided it was not the right move for us, especially with a youngster on the way. So I let our man at Taylors know that it was thanks, but no thanks.

So there had been three opportunities to change our lives, possibly forever, but what we did do was even more radical, as we travelled the 13,000 miles to the land down under. We had met a lot of new friends in Keighley in the four years I was at the club and had fond memories that will remain with us forever.

120

CHAPTER 8
A LIFE DOWN UNDER

In April 1971, we were on our way to Australia, having been through the emigration process, including interviews in London. We got the nod around February time and were asked if we wanted to fly or sail. We went under the 'ten pound Poms' scheme, whereby it only cost only ten pounds each for the fares out there and Jason was free. We had to stay for two years, or otherwise reimburse the Australian Government the full fare. Our passports were stamped COM NOM (Commonwealth Nominee) which meant that you couldn't get out of the country within two years unless your passport was stamped with the appropriate visa to leave. We decided to sail on the basis that we got a month's cruise for a tenner each – a no brainer! So we set sail from Southampton on the Greek owned and run, Chandris Lines, *SS Ellinis*.

The *Ellinis* was built in 1932 for the Matson Line in Quincy, Massachusetts as the *Lurline*, sold to Chandris in 1963, and refitted in North Shields to accommodate 1,668 passengers in one class. Famous aviator Amelia Earhart was passenger on the *Lurline* from Los Angeles to Honolulu with her Lockheed Vega airplane secured on deck in December 1934 in preparation for her record-breaking Honolulu-to-Oakland solo flight in January 1935.

We were allocated an inside cabin on A deck, just below the Main Deck. The cabins were very small, with just enough room for two bunks, the cot and our three suitcases. Along with £150 cash, these were our only worldly goods as we left the old country.

We were allocated our table in the restaurant that we shared with six other people. We were total strangers at first, but after a month we knew them like relations. We had the same waiter for all our meals – a Greek named George, who was a smashing guy but could not speak much English. When he was serving dinner, I used to say "what's the fish, George" and he would answer, "fish shit, no fish, have more meat." He said this every day and it suited me down to the ground, as I would rather eat meat than fish. Some of the others on the table would have the fish and this really pissed George off as it was quite a trek from the kitchen to the restaurant, and it saved him going if we did not have the fish. The food was spot on and for £10 for a month's food and board you simply could not complain – even if the fish really was shit.

One of the couples we got to know were from Sheffield, and they had actually paid to sail round the world with Chandris Lines, going to Australia to visit family before returning via New York.

Keith Pollard

The first day we met them, George from Sheffield, not the waiter, was playing hell about the cabin he had been given. He said to me, "What's yours like?"

"Great for 20 quid," was my reply, not knowing he had paid full whack.

"Can I have a look?" he asked, so I told him it was no problem and off we went. He looked and said, "Hey, that's great compared to ours." He then took me to see his cabin on E Deck – you could not get any lower. When you went inside only one person could get in, they then had to shut the door and get into the bunk so that the other person could go in. The stern of the ship was shaped so that the cabin wall actually went up on a slope and the propeller went through a tube under the cabin, so every time the ship went up in the swell the cabin shuddered. No wonder he was pissed off! He went to see the purser and complained, explaining what it had cost him and that his wife could not sleep due to the noise from the propeller. The purser said he would look in to it, and would get back to him.

Our route was to Amsterdam and from there to Tenerife, then on to Cape Town and across the Indian Ocean to Fremantle, then Melbourne and finally to Sydney. Now 'Sheffield George' had not heard from the purser until we nearly reached Los Palmas so he followed him everywhere on the ship – wherever the purser went he had George behind him. The crunch came when he went up on the bridge, where no-one but crew were allowed. According to Sheffield George, the purser was talking to the skipper, who asked him who was with him. The purser had said that he was a nuisance who wanted another cabin and that he had him that nothing could be done till we reached Teneriffe. He said that George would not believe him, and followed him everywhere.

Anyway, when we got to Tenerife, Sheffield George was by the purser's side again, not letting him out of his sight, when the skipper was doing his rounds. The skipper stopped him and said he would organise a new cabin if he would leave the poor purser alone. Sheffield George agreed, albeit rather reluctantly, but later that day he came up to me with a grin as wide as the Humber.

"Keith, Keith, come with me," he said. "Come and look at our new cabin!" It was a penthouse suite with a great big double bed, settee and a balcony overlooking the promenade deck, the highest deck on the ship. The captain had done the business – it just goes to show that sometimes you get what you want if you keep on persevering and making yourself a nuisance.

It was a great voyage that lasted 28 days in all – with beer at only 10 pence a can and free food, what more could you ask!? There was a swimming pool and everything you would expect on a cruise. Jason was ten months old at the time and in his baby walker. He learned that if he lifted his feet up as the ship rolled he did not have to do any work with his legs. One day, as I was exercising him in the area on A deck in front of the purser's office, he was merrily rolling around from side to side whilst I was talking to our steward. When I looked, Jason had disappeared, and I saw him flying down the gangway that ran from the front to back of the ship away from me, then stopping as the ship reached top of wave and coming flying back towards me. At the time, the captain was doing his weekly rounds; Chandris was a really well-run line, and he inspected the ship every week. Anyway, just as he was coming out of one of the side gangways that ran to the cabins, Jason shot past the opening. The look on the captain's face as this kid in a baby-walker shot past him at a rate of knots was beyond belief. The First Officer, who he was with, clearly did not know what to say, but the captain started laughing, which broke the tension and everyone joined in. The captain just said to me, "If you take him on deck, make sure he has a lifejacket on, okay? We don't want to lose him over the side."

We sailed from Tenerife down the coast of Africa across the Equator, where we had the traditional party by the pool, with one of the crew dressed as King Neptune. Everyone who had never crossed the equator was supposed to be 'baptised' – they could not do all the 1,600 passengers but I was one who got covered in a slimy substance and dunked in the pool. It broke the long journey down to South Africa.

A sad occasion on this leg of the trip was when a French guy collapsed with a heart attack whilst playing table tennis. Tragically, he left a wife and young son. I had been talking to him only the day before. The ship had no way of keeping his body until we reached Cape Town, so they had to bury him at sea. It was not the same as you see on the old war films, the only ones who were at the service were his wife, the captain, the ship's chaplain and six crew members. It was carried out at midnight and the ship's engines were stopped as a mark of respect. There were still quite a few people about and it was rather eerie as we all stood in silence and one of the guys with us, a lay preacher, said a few words and we all prayed with him. I am not a religious person but that really got to me, and is something I will always remember. The guy's wife was asked if she wanted to go back to France when we got to Cape Town, but she declined the offer, saying that they were going to start a new life, and that her husband would have wanted her to carry on and make a better life for their son. It must have been very hard for her, alone in a strange country with a young son. She was a very brave young woman and I hope everything worked out for them both.

As we came into Cape Town we had a wonderful view of Table

Keith Pollard

Mountain. It was one of the most fantastic sights I had ever seen, whilst a fleet of small boats came out to meet us and escort us in to the harbour. We had to go ashore in these boats as the ship was too big to dock in the harbour. We were told we had to be back at 6.00pm, so we had a great day exploring the city. The Apartheid regime was still very strong in those days and as we walked through the spotless central train station, I noticed that there were not many people about. When I asked a porter where everyone was, he told me that, at this time of day, all the black people were leaving city to go home and had to use a separate station around the back, as the main station was for whites only. It was a disgrace and it was a great day when the regime ended in the 1990s and Nelson Mandela was released from prison.

From Cape Town, it was a ten-day cruise across the Indian Ocean to Fremantle, the port near Perth in Western Australia. There was not a sign of land for ten days – you certainly realise what a big place the earth is when you travel by sea. By the time we on the leg to Fremantle I had gained quite a few drinking buddies on the ship – mostly the younger guys who were going to Australia for working holidays and that sort of thing. There were a few young girls on the ship too, and like the boys, they were in cabins that each slept four people in the bowels of the ship. After a few weeks, I am sure that there were many mixed cabins in various ratios, depending on the preferences of their inhabitants. There were definitely four gay guys who moved into one cabin.

These changes took place without the passenger manifest being changed, so if there had been an incident they would have been looking for people in some cabins that were not there. Fortunately, it did not happen and everyone was happy. I well remember one day popping to see one of my drinking buddies, knocking on the cabin door, and hearing a voice call 'come in.' I walked in and there was Kevin with a girl naked in one of the bunks. He was laid on his back and she did not speak; she had clearly been taught not to talk with her mouth full. Another guy, Mike, was occupied with another girl whose face was buried in the pillow. I nearly closed my eyes but thought better of it.

"Sit down," said Kevin. "We won't be long." I declined the offer and said I would see them up in the bar later. I was only 24 then, but I thought I must have been getting old that day. When I saw the face of the girl who was biting the pillow I realised she was actually with her Mam and dad on a holiday trip to Australia – I suppose she just told them she was just taking in the scenery of the passage. There was a young American girl who was on a world trip with her mother, whom I am sure was on a mission to service every guy under 20 on the ship. Every time you saw her with a guy it was somebody different and I know she had been with Kevin. You

124

could see she was spoiled rotten and used to getting her own way – well I was told she certainly did that in every way you can imagine, and not just with the boys either.

From Fremantle to Melbourne took about a week and we sailed along what is called the great Australian Bight, I do not know how it got its name but I know the swell in the sea is called an upwelling and is quite incredible to watch. It is something to do with the winds blowing along the shoreline and not into the shore as you would usually expect. It is like riding a rollercoaster for a week, non-stop. Jason had a ball in his walker, the ship never rolled, it just went up and down front-to-end. To get to Melbourne you have to sail into Port Phillip Bay, past Mud Island, and you enter Melbourne, which is about 50 miles inland, through what is called The Rip. I had always envisaged it to be a coastal city; it is not, but is a beautiful place nevertheless. We did not stop long there – as for all stop-overs it was only 12 hours and then away again, but we nearly always got to each port in a morning so at least we had all day to explore and then sail out on the night tide.

It was then on to our final destination, Sydney, where we disembarked after our epic journey across the world. We sailed through the Bass Straight, past Tasmania and Flinders Island – you could not see them, but they were there, only 90 miles from the coast of Victoria. We sailed around the southern New South Wales coast, past Cape Howe and heading north past Wollongong. The first big bay we came to was Botany Bay where Captain Cook landed and where the airport runway provides a great view on a nice day when you are leaving or landing. Then past the famous surfing beaches like Maroubra, Coogee, Bondi, up to Burrowarree where you turn into the outer harbour. What a view greets you there!

If you do one thing in your life, and you can afford it, travel to Australia, visit Sydney and take a ferry boat trip that will take you to the Heads and back. It is the best scene you will ever, ever see, believe me. I am not sentimental, but even I was moved. For me, Sydney is the most beautiful city in the world. As you sail into the Bay you turn to port and past Watson's Bay, where Doyle's fantastic fish shop is right on the beach – it was first opened in 1885 and is still owned by the same family and is being run by the fifth generation. You can walk 250 metres from the fish shop across the headland to 'the Gap' and you will be looking out to the sea – that is how narrow South Head is. Further on you sail past Parsley Bay, Vaucluse Bay and Shark Bay, with Rose Bay on your left and Shark Island in front of it. Felix Bay is next as you sail towards Circular Quay, past Double Bay, Rushcutters Bay, Elizabeth Bay and the Woolloomooloo shipyards and Naval base.

Then, in front of you, is 'The Bridge' with the Opera House on

The SS Lurline, later the RHMS Ellinis, the ship we emigrated on

Jason, aged 15 months

the left. The latter was still being built when we landed; work started in 1958 and it was completed and opened in 1973. The berth for all cruise liners that visit Sydney is on the starboard side of Circular Quay, which is actually on the Rocks side – a great place to visit when you are in Sydney, with lots of bars, restaurants and shops.

The organisation for our arrival was brilliant. The Immigration people had come on board in Melbourne and had set up an office to process those that were being transported to Australia under the assisted passage scheme. We were allocated a hostel in Sydney and everything was organised so all you had to do was get off the ship, go through customs, show your passport and get onto buses to take you to your final destination, which, for us, was Bradfield Park.

We went through the necessary proceedings and were shuffled off, like wartime refugees, out to the awaiting transport to take us to our new home at Bradfield Park. Home is a very loose description – it was a tip. When we arrived, shocked is not the word to describe how we felt. I know we only paid £10 but what we had come to was beyond belief. Nissan huts that had about four so-called flats in them – flats is their term, not mine. The authorities did not expect, or indeed want, you to stop long and they encouraged you to get out as fast as your legs could carry you. It was built in 1940 as an RAAF station and later converted into a hostel. I believe that the site has now been cleared and reclaimed for housing. The flat had a metal bed that turned into a settee, but with no upholstery on it, just a mattress; an ex-army locker; two chairs like the ones you had at school in the fifties and sixties; and one formica-topped table top. No heating or cooling system, no fly-screen, no sink or even a tap with running water; there was a shower block about a hundred metres away with shower screens on each cubicle.

There were some people who apparently did like the conditions, because they could not get them out. When you went to the toilets or shower/bathrooms there were always unsavoury looking individuals hanging around outside. The eating facilities were communal; you even had to carry your own knife, spoon and tin mug with you to each meal and you often found trays of uneaten food left in the shower cubicles. Even if you had the facilities to cook in your flat, you were not allowed to. It did not affect us for that long as we were only there about four weeks but, for some people who were really tricked into coming to Australia for a better life for their kids, to live under such poor conditions was terrible. We were all shown films at Australia House in London, depicting happy immigrants lazing on the beach, having a choice of many jobs and good modern housing, and of kids riding horses to school! The propaganda worked, it all looked irresistible to many young couples living in drab post-war Europe, but the reality was very different. I understand that some poor souls had to endure these conditions for up to three years before having enough money to buy a home. Rented accommodation at the time was scarce and a lot of landlords did not want kids. There is a website called *migrantweb.com* which gives a lot more information on the conditions people endured, and they reflect shame on the Australian government who misled decent people.

We were waiting to go up to Tamworth in northern NSW, as Jon Green had arranged for me to be transferred to West Tamworth RLFC, to play for them in the Group 4 of the County Rugby League. The club were negotiating a transfer fee with Keighley whilst we were sailing to Australia, but a disagreement had arisen over the money. One of the three players who had been with the club had left debts in the town, which Keighley had paid and wanted their money back, which was around £400.

The West Tamworth club had a house they were going to rent me but the coach Billy Bischoff was living in it at the time, whilst he built his own home. He was expected to be out of it before we arrived in Australia, but there was a delay in the building of his house, so our stay in the Bradfield Park Hostel was extended. We only expected to be in this type of accommodation for a couple of weeks and we had envisaged that all migrant accommodation was like the Endeavour Hostel, which was modern brick built self-contained flats, not like the hole they put us in.

The guy in question refused to pay the debt he had left and West Tamworth refused to pay it as well, so it was an impasse. I remembered my meeting with Norm Provan and managed to get hold of him – which was bit of a struggle as he had taken his name out of the telephone book. I do not know if it was me he was hiding from, but there was another Provan in the book in Sydney, not that common name, and it was his brother Peter, who played for Balmain. I rang him and told him the story about meeting Norm in Leeds, and he gave me the number with the proviso I destroyed it after I had made contact and did not give it to anyone else. I rang Norm, who was pleased to hear from me and asked how things were – and I gave him a brief precis. I had to ring him back next day, which I did, and he had made an appointment for me to see Frank Facer at St George Leagues club for the next Tuesday. On the appointed day all three of us went to the Taj Mahal, the nickname of the club headquarters in Kogarah, to the south-east of Sydney.

It was quite a trek that necessitated two train journeys. As we made for the reception we saw a massive statue of St George and the Dragon, and I was looking at the photos on the walls in reception whilst waiting for Mr Facer. I noticed on the landing of a staircase leading to the auditorium a ten feet high oil painting of

RED & WHITE PHOENIX

none other than Norm Provan! Shortly after, Mr Facer arrived, and although we talked for a good half hour it was not very productive. He told me that, if I had been an international player, they would have jumped at the chance to get me on board, but the season had started and they had made all their signings pre-season. In the Australian close season, they get players from all over NSW and Queensland down for a few week's training and then play a pre-season competition. The club then sign who they want for their roster, which is all finalised before the proper season commences.

Frank asked me what other plans I had, and I told him about Tamworth. He suggested that I go up 'in the bush,' as they call it, make a name for myself there and then they have another look at me. They had taken Jacky and Jason away, shown them round and given them drinks whilst we were talking, so I thanked him for their hospitality. Later, I rang Norm to thank him for his help and told him what had happened. He did not sound surprised, but he promised he would help where he could, and he kept his promise.

A week later we went up to Tamworth, but another problem had arisen whilst we were waiting to travel. The Tamworth area is a large rural area and the economy is based on farming. There had not been rain for nearly three months, which was classed as a drought. This meant that no one was taking on labour. There were plenty of engineering companies in the area and everyone I visited offered me a job 'as soon as it bloody rains, mate.' I getting was really pissed off. We were living on our meagre savings of $300, admittedly rent free at the time, but that was not going to last. However, I did manage to get a job as a labourer at an animal feeds plant unloading fish meal. It really stank, but it was a job, and in the three weeks it lasted, it helped me get fit rather quickly. I had never actually done real hard labour in my life, working as a welder or fabricator was nowhere near as physical.

129

Passing to Mick McTernan in the 1971 Grand Final

CHAPTER 9
MAITLAND

Whilst I was in Tamworth, I was asked by a bloke called Tommy Driffield if I was interested in playing in Newcastle for a club called Maitland. I had played with Driffield's mate, Tommy Searle, at Keighley and he, with Jon Green, was one of the instigators of us going to Tamworth. Searle was the first player-coach of the Tweedhead Seagulls, who in 1988 became the Gold Coast–Tweed Giants. They were formed a syndicate of international players who failed in their bid to win a contract to bring a Brisbane team into the Sydney competition. Giants spanned both New South Wales and Queensland and they struggled for acceptance in either state before going out of business in 1998. Tommy's son Michael later became part owner of the newly-formed Gold Coast Titans.

Driffield had heard I was in town and had mentioned me to Terry Pannowitz, the coach at Maitland. The club were going through a bit of an injury crisis, particularly in the forwards, so they had asked Tommy if he would sound me out. Being the man he was, he did not beat around the bush and just asked if we would consider moving to Newcastle. I asked him to give us time to think about it and the next day told him I was interested. It was a good job, because by then he had got back to Maitland and organised us to visit that weekend. Tommy Driffield was a very successful insurance salesman, and he certainly sold Maitland to us!

We met at the club with their coach, president and secretary, and I had taken my scrap book with press cuttings and old programmes. They said that the standard of the competition was pretty high, as there were quite a few state players along with ex-internationals who could no longer get regular first team football in Sydney. Younger players also used Newcastle as a stepping stone to further their career, making a name for themselves in the competition, in the hope of being spotted by the 'big league' scouts from Sydney.

Maitland must have been impressed, because they asked me to sign for them there and then. They said they would pay the transfer fee, pay me £500, and get me a house and job, so everything was agreed. I went back to Tamworth to see the secretary/manager, Ken Shillingsworth, who had been away the week before we went to Maitland. Unknown to me, he had organised me a job on the ground-staff at their ground and had told the committee he would personally pay my transfer fee and the debts owed to Keighley. I

Keith Pollard

Me and Jason in Wangi Bronzing

Outside our first house in Maitland

With our Holden Premier V8 5Litre

RED & WHITE PHOENIX

would basically be his property and if and when I moved on from there, he would get the transfer fee, and hopefully a profit. He seemed gutted when I told him I had decided to move on due to the lack of job prospects in Tamworth at the time, and I felt I had let him down. But I had a wife and young son to think of.

I had not done any homework on the Newcastle competition, I had no idea what the standard of rugby was and to be honest, if I had known about the job on the ground and the other things that Ken Shillingsworth had done, I would not have gone to see Maitland. But I had, and I had also shaken hands on the deal with their president, Dave Moreland, whom I found to be a great guy and a gentleman. I had never heard of Maitland, never mind going to play for them, but when I looked into their history, I was very proud to be representing them.

Maitland Pickers' proud heritage began in 1927, and they are one of the best-known teams in country rugby league. The term Pumpkin Pickers started as a sarcastic reference to players bringing produce to sell at the markets when they travelled by train to Newcastle. Working class men turned the term of contempt into a badge of honour, and to be called a Picker made me as proud as being called a 'Hessle Roader.' Maitland had an era of dominance the 1950s, including seven consecutive Grand Finals and three titles between 1954 and 1960. They were then to re-emerge as a force in the 1970s, having made the decider on five more consecutive years, and taking three titles in 1969, 1971, 1973. Apart from a Grand Final appearance in 1977, it would then be ten years before Maitland were triumphant again, in 1983. Their players gained a reputation for courage and tenacity and a loyalty to Maitland, which is now all-too-rarely seen.

Maitland organised transport for all our gear, which had arrived in Tamworth in our two packing cases. Tommy had ensured that he was in Tamworth on business and he drove us to Maitland. We were put in a hotel for a week while we got a house, and I used the £500 to put deposit on a VW Golf Estate for us to run about in. I also went for two or three interviews for jobs, of which there were plenty. I took a job in the Rutherford part of Maitland with a company called Monosteel. They were general fabricators but specialised in overhead cranes, also manufacturing the units that go to make up tower cranes, and had what appeared an indefinite a contract to supply four of these a day. Industry in Australia at that time was booming. Monosteel worked shifts, 6.00-2.00pm and 2.30 to 10.30pm, but because I played rugby, they said I could work 6-2 all the time that the rugby season was on. This suited me down to the ground, and all that they asked was when the footy season, as they call it, was over, I would do my bit and work alternate shifts like the other guys.

Jacky and Jason with our Holden Premier V8 5L

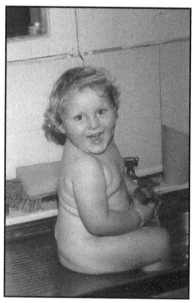

Jason takes an 'early bath'

RED & WHITE PHOENIX

I never heard of anyone moaning about 'that Pommie bastard' who did not work the 'back shift,' as they called it – they were a great bunch of blokes to work with. The guy who owned the company was a man named Jack Kerr, and what a tremendous bloke he turned out to be. We did not see that much of him, but when we did, he made sure he came to speak to everyone and asked how they were doing. After a few months, the shifts finished and I never had to work the 'back shift.' On Melbourne Cup day, the workers in Melbourne get a day off, but although we were in New South Wales, Jack Kerr used to bring a television into the workshop and set it up in the on a table with a few beers and a 'barby,' and we all sat and watched the race.

I was there four years all but about six weeks, when I went to work at the state dockyard. You may think our workers used to be militant but you have seen nothing like them. The unions ruled the roost. It was the best place to work for conditions and pay, but you never got a full week in – we were out on strike nearly every week for some reason or other.

When I was working at Monosteel, they had won a contract to fabricate some sections for two 'roll, on roll off' ships that they were building in the Newcastle dockyard. The two inspectors that the latter sent to our facility were both Poms, and they asked me if I fancied a start with them. The money was a lot more and the conditions were fantastic, with subsidised food and travel reimbursed – you could not go wrong, or so I thought. I gave in my notice and went.

But the working practices were a joke. You clocked on at 7 and you had half an hour to go to the changing rooms, change for work and get to where you were working – which really took about ten minutes. You were then taken to where you would be working for the day and had to sit waiting whilst all the equipment you were supposed to have was fetched – whether you really needed it or not. By then it would be tea break, after which you would start work – but not until you ensured everything was there. One of the problems was that they did not have enough fans to give to each welder, so if the foreman told anyone to start and they would say, "Sorry, no fan." He would give them a warning and the shop steward would call a stoppage.

It was all done in a friendly way, but it happened on numerous occasions and we never got a full week in. It occurred to me that the company was saving money by having stoppages – even if we did not go on strike there were meetings every week that always overran the break. We had a mass meeting one day about the fans. If you were working in an open area you did not need a fan or sucker anyway; the fumes from the welding just dissipated in to the atmosphere. It was only necessary if you were in a confined space.

135

Keith Pollard

Jason, ready for the Grand Final

Jason on his first set of wheels

Jason's second birthday

RED & WHITE PHOENIX

The shop steward was stood on a stairway with a megaphone so that everyone could see him, and after he finished his spiel, he asked if anyone had anything to say. Me being me, I could not resist. I pointed out that each time we stopped work, the money we were losing was paying for our bonuses. There were murmurs of agreement at what I had said, and the steward grabbed the mike off me. He stopped me later and said was I trying to make him look stupid, so I gave him the old answer, "No, you do that quite well on your own." He muttered something about Pommies and questioned my parenthood before disappearing.

I had not been there long when I was asked to work a weekend. I said that it was awkward due to my rugby commitments. I had mentioned this before I started and had been told that I would not be forced to work overtime. But the foreman said, "don't worry, I will give you a note so you can go home on Saturday lunchtime sick, and still work on the Sunday." We were playing Western Suburbs on the Saturday this particular week, and it was on TV as the Newcastle match of the day. I went off on Saturday lunch as agreed, and was doing some welding the following morning when I got a tap on the shoulder. It was the general foreman, with the sick note I had put in his hand the previous day.

"Are you Keith Pollard?" he asked. When I admitted that I was, he said, "You did not put a full shift in yesterday but you are in today - why?" I explained that I had gone home sick and my foreman had agreed to give me the note so that I could work the following day.

"You did not look too facking sick last night on the TV, when you were knocking hell out of our forwards at the Sports Ground," he said.

"Do you support the Rosellas then?" I asked. He nodded and started laughing. Up to that point he had not cracked his face and had really taken me in. But then he then sat down and started to discuss the game in more detail, finishing by telling me to let him know if I needed time off again.

You could not ask for a better place to work, but it was being ruined by a few militants most of which, I am sorry to say, were fellow Poms. They had buggered up the shipyards in the UK and where trying to do the same in Australia – it was known as Poms' disease. What a great impression we Brits made abroad in those days. I had had enough of working there.

When I left Monosteel, things were getting a bit quiet on the order front, which is one of the reasons I had gone to the dockyard. But then Doc Lawrence, the foreman, came round to our house and asked if I would go back there. I said I would let him know, but as he got up to go I said, "Okay, you're on – I've thought about it!" I gave my notice in at the dockyard on the Monday and started a

Keith Pollard

Radnidge and McTernan celebrate

The 1971 Grand Final

Captain-coach - Terry Pannowitz

Les Drew in the 1973 Grand Final

138

week later.

We had settled in our little rented house in the Maitland suburb of Telarah and made friends really easily. The early dark days were behind us, and life was starting to be good to us. Jacky had handled our difficulties really well; she has never liked uncertainty, but she was a tower of strength over that period in our lives and I owe her a hell of a lot.

Next door to us were a fantastic couple, Reg and Lorna Morrison. They had a son, Wayne, who worked at Bradmill, a local fabrics factory. Reg and Lorna became Jason's adopted grandparents, and doted on him, spoiling him rotten. One day, Wayne said they were looking for someone with office experience at the mill and Lorna suggested to Jacky that she went for it. Jacky said that she could not, as she had no-one to look after Jason, but Lorna said that she would look after him. Jacky was not too sure about it, but she was talked into it, and she went for interview and got the job. She started work the following week, and Jason was in good hands with his new grandma.

They were wonderful people and we kept in touch with them over the years, but sadly they have both now passed away to the great bowling green in the sky. They loved their time at the nearby Telarah Bowling Club where all the family were quite proficient bowlers. They won many prizes – I doubt that they ever bought meat because it was all won at the Bowling club.

I had missed the first game after arriving in Newcastle because my clearance had not come through from RL Headquarters in Leeds. This was against North Newcastle and was chosen as the game to be shown on local TV. The standard of the football was really impressed me; it was a hard game and no quarter was given by both sides. Norths had a good pack of forwards and tended to bully teams in the first 10 to 15 minutes. They won in the end, not by a big margin – but they had totally outmuscled Maitland. Norths had a prop called Karl Hutchinson, who had the reputation of being a bit of a hard case, but I thought a guy called Dennis Maddison was a lot harder and better player, and I later gained a lot of respect for him.

We went back to Maitland Leagues Club after the game and I had already had a few sherberts when Dave Moreland came up to me and asked what I thought of the game and the team's performance. I may have gone over the top a bit, as I tend to be rather frank when I have had a drink, and I told him what I had thought of our forwards and how they had let 'Hutcho' get away with murder, which he had, and I added that he would not get away with that with me on the field. A big statement that I had to back up later.

My debut game was in third grade against Macquarie and, to be

Maitland's 1971 first team squad

A skirmish in the 1971 Grand Final v Lakes United

140

honest, I was very ring rusty and did not have a very good game. The way they played did not suit me at all either. I had a word with the coach, Gus Ryan, and asked if I could do my own thing in the next game – let me run the game and bugger the plan. Well, they did not really have a plan as such – the forwards were there just to drive the ball up whilst the half-backs ran the game. I was used to letting the ball do the work, making half-breaks and putting guys through gaps.

We trained three nights a week, which was a shock to the system. But my few weeks in Tamworth, training and working in the animal feeds store, had taken a few pounds off me and given me a little fitness, but I was still well out of condition for rugby league. I played in the third grade again in the next game when we played Waratah at home and I thought I have to make a bit of a show here – they have paid money for me! There were a couple good hard running and willing young forwards in the team, Gary Oldfield and Glen 'Surfer' Marquet, so I told them to follow me around and when I told them to run and where to run, just do it. It worked out perfectly. They went straight through the gaps and had blinders. The opposition couldn't handle it – they were not used to props passing the ball. When the rest of the team saw how I played they all wanted a bit of it – they thought I was Paul Daniels! There was a young stand-off called Ross McKinnon who followed me round like a puppy, always on my shoulder. It is a simple game if you back each other up and pass the ball!

In Australia, they played three games in the same afternoon starting with third grade at 12.00, reserve grade at 1.30 and first grade at 3.00pm. I had played a full game for the thirds and was substitute for the reserve grade, but did not go on, so I was made substitute for first grade. The game had been going about 15 minutes when Max McMahon dislocated his elbow and I had to replace him in the second row. He was a tackling machine, hard as iron, and was to become a good mate of mine, as were most of the guys in the club. I went on to the sound of Rule Britannia, which was quite funny at the time. They had couple of other Poms playing for them at the time, Alwyn Hammond and Tony Finch, who were from Wakefield area. Tony and Alwyn were taking the piss when I ran on, they had formed a scrum and as I put my head down in second row, Tony said, "Hello old chap, how the devil are you?" in an upper class accent. I gave him a two-word reply.

Waratah at the time were top of the league and we were second. It was a hard game in front of a capacity crowd, but we beat them to move top. I had not trained with the firsts and did not know their plays or moves, so I just did my own thing again, much to the annoyance of the scrum half, Brian Burke. At the time, Brian was the New South Wales representative and Combined Country

Keith Pollard

Maitland's 1971 Grand Final winning team

captain and, in general, 'top dog' in the area. I went in first man a couple of times, pushing him wider and telling him to come with me and run off my passes. But Burky was king of the castle and he was not going to have some 'Pommie bastard' coming in and stealing his thunder. After the game he pulled me over and explained, 'how things work here at Maitland.' I listened to what he told me, but did not take a blind bit of notice. But I must have had quite a good game because I was selected for the next game away to Kurri Kurri. Waratah coach Frank Adams, also a Hull man, congratulated us on our victory and added, "I see you had to get a Pom on board to help you do it."

I suggested to Burke a clear-the-air meeting with Terry Pannowitz, the player-coach. We had this after training on the Monday. It was quite amiable and we had a frank and open discussion on what I thought I could bring to the team. It all boiled down to me being a totally different type of prop forward to what the Australians were used to. Burky did have an edge, as most scrum halves do, but he was a great player who should have gone to play in the big league in Sydney.

I played in the next nine games, of which we won eight, and we were second moving in to the last game of the season, the return game against Norths. The papers highlighted that 'the clash of the props will be a feature of game' and said that I would have to be at my best to contain the Norths dynamite prop, Hutchinson. I played blind-side prop and when the first scrum I collapsed, I rubbed his face as I got up. He did not like that and got up throwing punches. I caught him with a cracker right on the jaw and all twelve forwards joined in. He tried to head-butt me, but that was a game I learned off the best, and I grabbed him by the shirt and said, "No Karl, if that is the best you can do you are in for a hard time son," and showed him how it was done. All my experience gained in the UK, playing with and against some of the hardest props in the game, stood me in good stead – frankly, these players were not in the same league.

We won the Norths game and Waratah lost so we finished as 'Minor Premiers' – or league leaders – on 28 points, whilst the reserve grade also finished top and the third grade finished fourth. The club also won the Mal Woolford Club Championship, for which points in all three grades throughout the season were added together. It was a great achievement and honour and showed what strength the club had in depth. We beat Waratah in the Major semi-final replay, having drawn 11-all the first time. This took us into the Grand Final where we met Lakes United, who had beaten Waratah the week before.

Lakes were a good side full of experienced players and were coached by Ray 'Wagga' Johnson, a very good front-rower who

143

Dressing room celebrations in 1973

Maitland's 1973 Grand Final winning team

previously played for Western Suburbs. I packed down opposite Country first prop Brian Sullivan who, along with Peter Linde, who previously played for Parramatta and Penrith, and had a big influence in the way Lakes played. They played a fast, open style of rugby with a powerful three-quarter line, including Des Kimmorley, father of Australia scrum-half Brett, and centre Peter Cootes, brother of Australian World cup centre, Father John Cootes. But we were just too good on the day, and after a hard-fought encounter we came out victors by 30 points to 19. Veteran second-rower Joe Radnidge had a blinder and won the man-of-the-match award. Our winger Mick McTernan scored one of the best winger's tries I have ever seen. After a set move, I gave him a short blindside pass and after his pace took him clear of the first line of defence, he rounded the full-back and went in under the posts.

Our player-coach Terry Pannowitz was a freak. I had the honour of playing alongside and against some of the greatest players the game has ever seen. From the smallest, Roger Millward, to the biggest, Artie Beetson; from Harry Poole, Frank Foster and Bill Holliday in the English game to Johnny Raper in Australia – but I have never been involved with a guy like 'Panno.' There are no words to describe his work-rate – he was like a machine, and his tackling was magnificent. His quick thinking and running from set plays and play the ball movements was unparalleled. His only weakness in my humble opinion was that sometimes needed a ball to himself – not in a greedy way, but he just had to be in everything.

We were playing Central Charlestown one day at the International Sports Centre, the ground that the Newcastle Knights now use. 'Panno' had taken a crack to the eye and it split like a melon; the strapper came on and told him he had to go off for stitches. He went off and returned with some insulating tape wound round his head – he always wore it anyway, but this time it was a bit lower.

"Are you out of your mind? Get off!" I said to him, but he just muttered something and took no notice.

"Okay," I said, "just go full back and get out of the way. Swap Shiny over." Ken Shine was our full-back, a very good player who later went on to be the South Sydney First Grade coach, but he always fancied himself as a loose forward. They swapped for a while, but a bit later I made a break and as the full-back half tackled me I turned to look for support and there was Panno screaming for the ball. I gave him the pass and he went in under the posts. We won the game quite easily, he played right to the end, and when they took the tape off there was a huge gash right across eyebrow. St George wanted him to go there, but they had Johnny Raper at loose forward. He was the Australian captain at the time, and

Keith Pollard

The 1973 Grand Final pack

The guy on the right actually broke his arm as he hit me

146

probably the best player in the world. They asked Panno to play scrum half but he said that he was a loose forward or nothing. When St George said they had already Raper there, he told them to let him play for his spot alongside him, otherwise he would stay in Newcastle. He stayed in Newcastle – a great player and a great man.

At the end of the 1971 season, Terry suggested that I meet him twice a week during the off-season to go for a run around East Maitland, where he lived. It was not really a suggestion, so I agreed. We used to run four miles around a quarry, up and down hills that to me might as well have been Everest. I have never met a man so fit in my life. I used to set off with him and within 15 minutes he had left me. I used to finish the course every time, but by time I got back to his place, he was laid out on the lawn with an orange drink reading the paper. I improved my time every night, week in, week out, and I was getting fitter by the week. I even started going up behind where I lived in Telerah on my 'nights off' and running up the hills around there, to try and get up to his standard, but he was so competitive he would just not be beaten.

A guy called Bob Hensby joined us at Maitland from Kurri Kurri in 1973 – he had also played for Balmain and Eastern Suburbs in Sydney, and was another fitness fanatic. Pre-season training was hard enough without him, but with him it was murder. Just like Panno, he hated coming second at anything and the more Panno gave us to do, the more Bob tried to come first, but he had Terry to beat. I have never been as fit in my entire life as that time in Maitland. I had played as a semi-professional for nearly eight years but I had only played at it. We were so far behind the Australians and we neither have nor will catch up with them, in my opinion.

During the summer of 1971/72, the free transfer system came in, similar to the Bosman ruling in Europe, where players were not tied to a club for life. In 1969 a guy named Dennis Tutty had initiated legal action against the retain and transfer system of the NSWRL. His contract with his club, Balmain, had expired, but he was unable to take up employment with another club unless Balmain granted him a free transfer. A clause in the rules stated that a club was 'entitled to retain players' names on their registers indefinitely.' Dennis believed that this was wrong and decided to do something about it. Dennis did not receive any financial or moral support from any other players or clubs in his fight. He actually financed the case himself by working as an unskilled worker. It took him more than two years out of football before the courts found the transfer system to be an unreasonable restraint of trade and that all players out of contract were free agents. Whilst waiting for the results of the case, Tutty returned to play for

Keith Pollard

Balmain during 1971. He played seventeen games but did not receive any remuneration from the club. After the case, he signed for Penrith, moving on to Eastern Suburbs before, somewhat ironically, returning to Balmain in 1976 to finish his career. The court judgement resulted in all the clubs hitting the panic button, and one of the big losers were South Sydney, who lost three internationals in John O'Neill, Ray Brannigan and Ron Coote.

It worked out perfectly for me. Having just played in a Grand Final Premiership winning team, I became a wanted man. I was contacted by a couple of clubs in Newcastle asking if I would be willing to join them. I listened to their offers but I was quite happy with Maitland. They had been good to me, I had a good job and Jacky was settled there, so I decided to take Maitland's new offer. One club actually offered me more money, but for once in my life, I turned it down. I knew other players in the team got more money than me, but that was how it was and as long as I was happy with what I was getting, I thought why bother about what some other guy has managed to get.

Halfway through the 1971 season, I had a visit from the local junior club based in Telarah. Their president and secretary called round at the house out of the blue and asked if I was interested in coaching a junior team. At the time they had an under 12s team and the guy who had coached them for four years, Max Howard, would be unavailable for the following season, due to work commitments. They were looking for someone to take his place. They trained two nights a week at Telarah Oval, which was at the top of my street, and played on Saturday mornings.

I agreed to go down and take a look at the boys and the set up. The first night I went down I was impressed with the manners and attitude of the boys. They called the coach Mr Howard, they took it seriously, they were as keen as mustard and did exactly what he asked. There were about nine teams training on the oval, and there was plenty of room as it was a cricket pitch in the summer months. I went down a few more times towards the end of the season but I did not want to tread on Max's toes, as they were still his team. I took over for the start of the 1972 season when they became under 13s. We struggled a bit for numbers but always managed to turn out a side and the team actually finished as Major and Minor premiers for the first time in that first season. The experience I picked up coaching the boys for a couple of seasons stood me in good stead for later on in my career, apart from which, I enjoyed every minute of it.

I cannot remember all the boys' names, but big Grahame Brown and a young hooker called McGillivray, who just could not keep still, stick in my mind. The captain of the side, Craig Cox, was a good all-rounder, not a star, but a genuine trier and a born leader.

RED & WHITE PHOENIX

Fred Bowen was a very good full-back and Mike's son, Greg, was a very capable centre or second row. Another, prop John Hamilton, told me about his grandfather, who was one of the first motorcycle speedway stars. The first ever speedway racing was started in West Maitland.

I was very impressed the way the game was being run in Newcastle and NSW in general, so much so that I wrote a letter to the Rugby Leaguer Weekly Newspaper back home.

The letter went as follows:

Regarding several letters in your 'Post Bag' on the subject of schoolboy football, I felt I had to express my opinion on the topic.

After playing five years at Hull KR and four with Keighley, I would like to point out the difference in just these two area towards schoolboy and junior football, and also inform on the aspect of the game here in Australia.

Coming through schoolboy football in Hull (you will note I have picked up the Australian for rugby is football) which has always been a good area for the code, and then on to Under 17s with Constable Youth Club, we were coached by teachers from the school at which we learnt our academic subjects, one of whom in my case was the late Stan Adams who was deputy headmaster at the time, and also ex Senior Referee.

I am led to believe that nine out of ten teachers have played Rugby Union at either college or University, so some schools played this code. I feel that if the teachers did not know anything about league the boys did not get the chance to play it, but I am only surmising.

Nearly every school in Hull played Rugby League. This is why both Hull clubs have always had plenty of local talent to choose from. On the other hand, in Keighley, they did not play league in the schools while I was living in the town. In this case, as a couple of your contributors have pointed out, once they have been left the code it is hard to get them back.

Another point there was only three junior clubs in Keighley Albion, Worth Village and Shamrocks and they were dissolved just before I left the UK. No wonder Keighley RLFC found it hard to get support and junior talent.

Here in Australia the boys start off in under seven years, I know of one boy who is 4 years old, and play in groups up to the age of 15. After then they go on to junior league which is run by the senior league club.

Here in Maitland, which is in the Newcastle competition, where I am now playing, there are nine schoolboy teams and twelve junior clubs. These teams are nothing to do with schools' rugby, they are run by groups of men and women who have only the good of the game in their minds. It is all done on a voluntary basis, and

Keith Pollard

Pickers' hard man ba

By BEN QUINN

WHEN word gets around, former footballers from Newcastle and the Coalfields will share a collective shudder.

Keith Pollard is coming to town.

For those not fortunate enough to see him play, or those too weak of stomach to stay after arriving, Pollard was an innovative prop who played for Maitland in the 1970s.

He was very severe on anyone not wearing the famous black-and-white

Newspaper cuttings from the 'Maitland Mercury'

Pollard took pain out on Wests!

● By Wes Cornish

An injury to prop Keith Pollard was one of the best kept secrets of the rugby league grand final which Maitland won 27-18 over Wests at the Sports Ground yesterday

150

a lot of the current player at the club coach teams I coach under 14 sides.

I feel the same should be tried back home, let junior clubs take over the schoolboy league and have support from senior clubs. For example, if a boy lives in West Hull, he could play for that area against East and North Hull and other areas if each junior club had school boy teams in Leeds, Wakefield, Castleford, etc, the prospects are limitless.

Just imagine if players with the calibre of Millward, Hardisty, Sullivan and other stars were to give up a couple of hours a week to coach as they do here, how many boys would love to play under them. Let the players put something back in the game now before they are just past players and forgotten, for they get enough out of the game.

Let's look after our own boys first and maybe the money the clubs spend on union converts could be saved. After all the greats Like Ashton, Whiteley, Drakes all came through the school and don't forget the boy player of today is the star and supporter of tomorrow.

September 1971
We still have a lot of catching up to do in Britain. It took long enough for us to realise that we needed to look after the grassroots of the game, but how much have we actually done it?

We started pre-season training for the 1972 season just after Christmas. The lads had warned me it would be hard, but I had been running with Terry and by myself, so I was not too worried. How wrong was I. In the first week we did long distance stamina runs, starting with four miles on the first night and increasing by one mile each night up to 12 miles by the end of the third week. To top it off, you had to do a circuit of exercise around the 400 metre track. I was out on my legs – you would not believe the state we were in. All the portlier ones, if there were any left, were at the back and Panno used to run up and down geeing us up with comments like, "Come on you Pommie bastard, get a move on – push it!" We ran 12 miles but he must have run 15, going from the front to the back – up and down relentlessly. You just had to admire the man – he was mental, but you had to admire him.

We then got down to circuit training and speed work. We used to do a circuit of 10 exercises set out at points around the pitch. In the first session you had to go round three times, doing 10 of each exercise, then a full lap of the pitch as fast as you could run sprint – if you could manage to sprint at all by then! I had been given the nod by one of the lads who had been there in previous pre-seasons not to rush the first circuit. You were timed on it and after that session you had always to beat that time, no matter what the

151

increase in repetitions were. If we thought that was hard, as the weeks went by sprinting was increased and everything was done at pace. I have never been as fit in my entire life. No wonder the Aussies were getting better, because according to what I heard, this was only a smidgen of the work they did in the Sydney competition.

We played a pre-season competition of five rounds in the evenings at either West's home ground, the Harker Oval, the Cahill Oval, home of the Lakes, followed by two semi-finals and the final. That was a total of eight pre-season games you had a chance of playing, and you didn't get a penny for playing in any of them. I complained and was told, "If you don't want to play, don't. But you will start in third grade when the real season starts and if the man in the higher grade is playing well you will not get promoted. We don't give a fack who you are!"

Merv 'Osher' Brennan and Brian Jennings were the two selectors who picked the teams, along with the three coaches. Naturally, the first team was picked first, with the first team coach and the two selectors having votes, whilst the reserve grade coach and third grade coach could comment but had no selection vote. Next was reserve grade and the first grade and third grade coach could comment but had no vote, and so on. In my opinion it was a great system. There were no favourites – if you had one bad game you were given a second chance, two bad games and if the guy who was playing in reserves was going better than you and deserved a shot in first grade, he took your place and you had to fight for it back. This happened to me in 1972. I played in all of the first five pre-season games, but when we reached the play-off against Waratah, I missed out because I had not been on form in the previous couple of games.

When we welcomed Lakes United to Maitland Sports ground for the start of the season proper, I regained my place. Lakes had taken on board Frank Adams, who had parted company with Waratah, as their coach, and, as defending premiers we were looking forward to starting the season off well. We won, but unfortunately, I had another indifferent game. As I have said, there was a lot of competition at Maitland with a lot of good players vying for positions. So the following week, I was left out for the game against Macquarie United, and Glen Wilkes took my jersey. The first grade team won again, 47-19, whilst we lost 25-20 in the reserves, which did not help my cause at all. I just could not reach the form I had in my first season and the first team kept on winning and winning. I just could not get back in and fair play to Glen Wilkes, who fully deserved what I saw as my place. We had recruited a few new players that season, one of whom was Peter Dimond, one of Australia's best ever centres. He had bought a pub in Maitland and had been coaching South Newcastle, but had decided to play one more season and joined us. Sadly, he did not finish the season, picking up a bad injury and hanging up his boots after a fantastic career.

At the end of the season, Maitland finished joint Minor Premiers with Cessnock. Phillip 'Fishy' Mullard, who started the season in the front row with me, and Ken Shine who had both played representative football in the Country Divisional Championship, finished the season playing with me in reserve grade. Both the first team and the reserve grade got through to the Grand Final. The firsts played local rivals, Cessnock, who were coached by ex-St George hooker Norm Henderson, who was a good player-coach and had done really well with a lot of young kids. The reserve grade was up against a tough Western Suburbs side, who had played in 10 of the last 13 grand finals, winning 10 of them and beating Maitland on six occasions. They were going to be two hard games for the Pickers that day and unfortunately we both went down – the first grade lost 18-10 and we were beaten by a better 'Rosellas' side 12-6.

We had a great social life in Maitland, where we met some fantastic people – friends too many to mention with whom we have kept in touch for over 35 years, which is now so much easier now we have Facebook. It was a great time in our lives and our friends certainly made it easier for us to integrate. The language may be the same and they drive on the same side of the road, but it is totally a different way of life. There are lots of New Australians, as the locals used to call us, and there was a type of prejudice against non-Australian people. My opinion is that this was caused by newcomers who did not mix, or worse, closed ranks and created mini-Englands, Italys, or wherever they came from – trying to feel as if they were back in the 'Old Country.' They often asked the question; why do the locals not treat us like Australians? But it was a prejudice that was usually started by the minorities themselves.

The Maitland area had quite a few New Australians from all parts of the world, you only had to look at the surnames on the team sheets, for example, Pannowitz, Wolinkski, Meskauskas, Wawszkowicz, Kowalczuk, etc. Ziggy Nizcot played 114 games for South Sydney, captaining them in 1980 and playing twice for New South Wales. Pronouncing those names was a commentator's nightmare.

We were at a barbeque one night at Gus Ryan's place, when John McLane's wife, Betty, who was actually Irish, was going on about home and saying, 'we don't do that in England,' 'this is not the same as in Hull,' and suchlike, and she shouted to me, "This isn't as good as Hull, is it Keith?" I didn't even know what she was talking about, I was not even listening to her, but one of the lads who obviously had heard enough and shouted at her, "Then why don't you fack off back to Hull, Betty?" He looked at John, who just shook his head. I felt sorry for John, he was a great guy and was embarrassed by the situation. Betty had hell of a tongue on her, once giving me a hard time when John got left out of the first team and I took his spot, as if it was my fault. She was an example of why we were not fully accepted. Sadly, though, she passed away quite a few years ago, whilst still in Australia.

We used to have some wonderful days out with our friends who nearly all were involved with the Pickers. We organised barbeques at a local park in Maitland and days at the beach, especially in the pre-season. We used to train on the beach as running on sand is really hard on the legs and great for stamina. We also played rugby in water up to your knees, which is really tough work. The full club would go, with the guys training for a couple of hours, before all the wives and families arrived and we had the 'barby' on the beach. Gordon 'Coogan' Lawrence was in charge of the organisation; he was brilliant at it and we nicknamed him 'Sarge.' All the equipment and the barby would be set up and there was always a big pan of new potatoes on a fire, which they called 'chats.' Rhonda Cousins was the ladies' leader and would ensure that there were salads, coleslaw, bread, cheesecakes, etc. Transport was arranged for those who could not drive or where the husbands were using the car to get to training. It was like a very precise military operation and 'Sarge' would oversee everything. There was a serious purpose, but they were also get-togethers that everyone enjoyed.

People also used help each other out by giving their skills and labour free of charge; to help build car ports, patios and the like. A gang of guys would give up weekends to help each other out – there was a real community spirit. The barbeque area Gus Ryan had at his place was affordable for Gus because we had all gone down a couple of weekends to help him clear the block of land he owned next to the one he lived on. It had been grassed over and Gus was getting pissed off having to cut it all, so he had decided to concrete part of it over. We were the 'tidy up brigade,' going with our shovels and barrows to dig out the foundations. It took two weekends, one to dig it out and the next to lay the concrete and bricks for the barbeque. I made the plate and grill rack at work, Dick was the builder, and all the other lads just mucked in. The reward was a feed and a piss up on Gus, using the new facilities. The meat did not cost him a lot as he worked at the abattoir, so we feasted on fillet steak and a great night was had by all. Sadly, Gus passed away a few years ago, after moving up to Brisbane to live.

We moved from down Raymond Street to a flat in the centre of Maitland. I still used to drop Jason off at his 'grans' in the morning and pick him up at night, so he was happy as Larry. Jacky was doing well at her job and had been promoted. From not being too sure about going back to work, she was glad Lorna had talked her round. But we were not in the flat long when the opportunity arose to rent a house within the grounds of the plant where Jacky was working. It seemed odd going through security on the gates to get home, but the house was great. There were three of them in a T formation and we had the back one, with a decent garden. One of the managers, Doug Perry, moved into one of the others and we got really friendly with them. They also had a young daughter whom Jason got on with, another excellent result in our transition from the UK to Australia.

My third season, 1973, started with the pre-season competition again. We did okay, winning our first game against Cessnock 24-8 and I got off to good start. In another game we beat Central and I had a great game, especially in defence, Panno said he only had to make eight tackles in the game, the lowest he had done for years. All I wanted was the real competition to start, as I needed to get back in that first team. A lad I had met briefly in Hull when he was playing for Rovers, Geoff Drury, came back to Australia. He was a teacher and been touring Europe, as all Aussie kids seem to do at least once in their lives, and he joined us at the Pickers. John McLane, who used to play in Rovers under 17s with me, and went on to play for Hull FC, joined the club after being in Wollongong the previous season. We both made the first team squad to play the opening round game against Wests at home. It was a disaster for me – absolutely awful is all I can say. Why does it happen? You try and get yourself up for a big game and nothing, absolutely nothing goes right. What made it worse was that we all met at the leagues club before the game and we were shown a film called 'The Will to Win' that was presented by Vince Lombardy, the famous coach of the Green Bay Packers American football team.

This sort of thing was all the rage in Sydney since Jack Gibson had been over to the States and come back with a lot of ideas. Well it did not work for me. I went out there with all these sayings floating around my head – 'Winning's not everything, it's the only thing' was one of them. I am not blaming that, but it was not what I needed before a big game. I am a great believer in doing the same thing every week as a pre-match ritual, and watching some Yank spout a load of tripe about thinking positive and visualising how the game will go, was not for me. They call it sports science now, but it is just bullshit to me – if you can play, you play; if you cannot, you sit in the stand. I have no idea why someone needs a load of waffle to make them play.

Anyway it did not work for me, and I was that bad that they left me out for the next two games. As it happened, they lost one of the games and won one. Unfortunately, after the defeat, John, my mate

Keith Pollard

from Hull was dropped. I was picked for the home game against Macquarie United along with a young kid called Robert Finch, who was only 17 and in his first season in grade football. He had just come back from England, having been with the Australian Schoolboy side. Macquarie were coached by Peter Jacques, a seasoned professional who had played union for a time and also four years with the North Sydney Bears. We beat them 66-7 and I had a blinder, winning the 2HD radio station man-of-the-match. I had really come back with a bang, which I can now admit was a great relief.

Apart from missing one game due to injury, I kept my place in the team for the rest of the season. We won 13 of our 18 games, finished third in the competition behind West and Waratah and scored more points than any other team with 555. We played Cessnock, our Grand Final opponents the previous year, in the Minor semi-final and beat them by 19 points to 8, with Brian Burkes' goal-kicking the deciding factor, and earned the right to play Waratah in the final. Unfortunately, Brian got a bad injury and missed the Grand Final. The 'Tahs' always gave us a good game, the played some really good rugby league and could score from anywhere on the ground, so it was going to be a hard fought encounter.

Sunday September 9th was the big day. We had prearranged a bus to take us to the ground, which was a one off, as we usually made our own way to the venue. Before the game, Terry received a letter from the mother of a 12-year-old boy from Waratah, who had multiple sclerosis, requesting the players' signatures on a match programme. We decided to pick up the boy on the team bus and take him to the ground with us. His smile was more motivating than any captain's speech or motivational videos – it has always stuck in my mind as one of the most memorable moments of my life. Because of what he had gone through and what he did, we thought we could win it for him. Winning that day was a big thing for us, but for this young boy in a wheelchair it was his world.

In addition to Burke's absence, we went in to the game with five players requiring pain killing injections. I myself woke up the morning of the match with severe pains in my neck and shoulder. Terry had the physio round and I was under a heat lamp all morning. That eased it considerably and by the time kick off came it was bearable.

The plan was to blitz them in the first 10 to 15 minutes. We were to let them have possession and knock the hell out of them. If we received the ball from the kick-off we would kick right back to them – they could not hurt us while they had the ball. It was a really hot day, 26 degrees and not a cloud in the sky.

We gave away two penalties with the first two tackles. We knew that Dennis Ward would run the game and that everything would come from him, but we also knew that he was obsessed with his teeth. If he took his mouth guard out, he was not going to get the ball, he was only directing play. It was decided that it was to be my job to try and get his mouth guard off him. Not cricket? Probably not, but this was the biggest prize, and we wanted it. I managed to get the mouthguard off him and he shouted, "You're mad, you Pommie bastard!" He has gone I thought, and he had, and just hoped he did not have another in his kit bag in the dressing room. But I had put him right off his game.

I was on a mission now, and my next target was to try and nail Father John Coote, the test centre and catholic priest. He took the ball in his own twenty-five and I covered across, hit him like an exocet missile with everything I had in a man and ball tackle, and he hit the ground like a bag of the proverbial. He used to do an advert on the TV for SW Millers Electrical store, at the end of which he used to say, "If I did not believe in this product, I would not do this." I said to him as I looked down at him, "If I did not believe in this fucking tackle, I would not do it." I do not think he heard a thing though – his eyes were glazed over. He had not a clue where he was, but he stopped on, fair play to him, although he was playing on auto pilot.

We then got a penalty – their heads had gone. We got to the 15-yard line and on one of our set moves, a simple 'run around' with big Ray Wawskzowicz taking the final pass in full flight on the blind side. They could not stop him going in at the corner. We were flying now and we moved down the field with a series of well-timed passes. Wests were summoning some inner strength and their defence was strong at this point, but I spotted a gap and I told 'Panno' to follow me. I ran at one of their forwards, who knew better than to try and go high to stop me, and as he came in low I slipped the ball to Terry, who went in under the sticks. Finchy was the next to score after taking an interception off Dennis Ward, who was having a shocker.

That really helped Finch and he had a blinder against Father John, something I remind him about whenever I see him. We went in at the break 20-2 up. I was in agony when I got into the dressing room – my neck and shoulder were killing me. The club doctor told me to come off and I think you can imagine my reply. Les Drew had four stitches in his lip, caused by an elbow from John Monie. That was the only injury Wests inflicted upon us – they had no fire whatsoever. Terry told me after the game that one of their players actually picked him up after an early tackle and asked him if he was alright. We went in to a scrum at one point, remembering that then the hookers actually had to strike for the ball to win it, and Karl Hutchinson kicked out at Nabby as the ball came in. I said to him,

Keith Pollard

"Do that again and I will take your knee cap off". He said, "I didn't mean it Pom, I didn't mean it!" I couldn't believe my ears; the so-called 'firebrand of Newcastle rugby league' as the press had called him, was apologising to me. I did not have much respect for him the first time I saw him, but I had absolutely none now.

I was talking to Johnny Raper after the game, when he came in to the dressing room to congratulate us on our win, and he told me he was looking to get a bet on Wests before the game but they were such hot favourites that no-one was taking any money on them. Apparently, he then walked past our dressing room and heard us singing our theme tune, '*We Will Not be Done*' and could not believe that we were singing even before the game. He then watched us before we ran on to the field and thought, 'Wests have no chance against this mob today,' and went and put his money on us. As I was sitting taking in the euphoria I got a tap on my shoulder and looked up to see Frank Facer, the St George manager, who said, "We should have signed you, son." It was one of the best compliments I had during my career.

"Thank you," I replied, "but I am happy here," – just in case he was thinking of offering me a deal! One guy they did sign was Robert Finch, who spent the next 10 years at St George, and a hell of a player he turned out to be. His son Brett was not too bad either – playing 329 games and scoring 83 tries in his career. Robert came back to Maitland and coached them to a Grand Final victory in 1983 – ten years after winning their last premiership. He then moved on to other pastures and after holding different positions in the game, including eight years as Director of Referees, he is now as Executive Manager Football Operations at St George Illawarra Dragons. He has had a great career and it was well deserved.

Sadly, the brave little boy, who gave us such inspiration, died from his illness several months later. I can only hope he passed away without too much trauma and with fond memories of that big day when he helped us win the fight and the Grand Final.

Another summer came and we did the usual Aussie things again. We sweltered in the hot sun, drank plenty of beer down at the Rutherford Hotel, and had plenty of barbys. Great days and nights were had by all. Then we started pre-season training again – and it was not getting any easier. This time we swam the river and I took plastic bag to put my clothes and trainers in, which I tied up and used as a floating device. Smart eh?

The river was running faster than I could swim, that is for sure. When I took off I seemed to be going okay – we had set off well down the river, in order to allow us time to use the current to get across to the other bank. When I was getting close I threw my float onto the bank and stood on what I thought was rocks. Wrong! It was mud and I slipped and went under. The current was taking me

away and I panicked as I went under again. If it had not been for
Burky, I could have been a goner. He picked up a branch off the
bank and held it out as I floundered towards him. I grabbed the
branch and that stopped me for a short time, but the current was
stronger than we thought. There were some trees on the side of the
bank and as I was being pushed towards them I managed to grab
hold of something with my free hand – the other still holding the
branch onto which Burky was hanging on for dear life. That just
about stopped me and a couple of the other guys were able to grab
me and haul me ashore. I lay there floundering like the proverbial
white whale, and spitting water out. The lads were all rolling about
laughing. Pannowitz had already set off to the sports ground and
came running back to see where everyone was.

"Come on you lot we have a circuit to do," he shouted. "What
the fack are you laid there for, Pom? Get your arse up and get back
to the ground!" That was all he said to me, and I hated him at that
moment.

We played the unpaid pre-season competition again – it still
went against the grain, but I should have got used to it by now – it
was my third time. We had quite a few changes in the ranks – Brian
Burke had left to coach in Wagga and John McLane had gone up to
Muswelbrook as coach. We did not do too well this time, not
making the play-offs and finishing only in fifth place. A few new
faces had joined the club; including Rod Sneesby, a classy winger
and Newcastle representative player; Kevin Hortle, a front rower
from Cronulla; Steve Buffer, a big raw-boned second rower from
Kurri; and John Carmody returned from Bathurst.

We made a good start to the season proper, with wins against
Kurri, Norths and Central but lost in a close game at Macquarie,
who had recruited well during the summer. They were a different
outfit from previous years and beating us put them top of the pile
after five games. I played in two more games, winning at Souths in
the first, but the next against Cessnock I broke my hand. This was
the second time in my career and was the base of my thumb on my
left hand, which was classed as a Baker's fracture. According to the
doctors, it would keep me out for five or six weeks. They were
wrong. It would not heal, and only after eight weeks could I start a
come-back in the reserves.

By then, things were not looking good at the club. For the first
time in many years the first team missed out on the play-off places.
They had won or played in 13 out of the previous 20 Grand Finals
but this time finished sixth in the regular season, with the reserve
grade and thirds both finishing second in their respective leagues.

Whilst I was injured I was sounded out about a coaching job at
Kempsey, on the north coast of New South Wales. It was only a
tentative offer but they came to see me in Maitland. It was all done

with the greatest of discretion and respect to the Maitland club, as I was under contract to them at that time. I had previously discussed the possibility with Maitland of coaching the first grade when Terry retired; he had one more year on his contract and they were talking about me taking over. The problem was that they would not guarantee me the job, they said they would look at it in the middle of 1975 season, but at this moment in time I was front runner if I wanted it. So I was still thinking about that scenario.

The Kempsey President, Eric Lahey, and two committee members, Clem Rankin and Bobby Laut, travelled down the 175 miles to Maitland. They came to my place and we discussed their town. When I moved 'down under,' I looked into the history of Australia to find out more about the place – it was good to know some of the story behind the name. So when the possibility of a move to Kempsey came up, I did some research and found that Kempsey was a reasonably large country town situated on the Pacific Highway approximately halfway between Brisbane and Sydney. It was a lovely town, with terrific weather most of the time, not too humid, and great people.

At the initial meeting, we discussed housing and jobs – all the things that they thought might entice me into leaving the Pickers and living in the Macleay Valley on the mid-north coast. It all sounded great and we finally we discussed the rugby league club, and what we could commit to each other. They told me that the Kempsey Kowboys was a relatively new club, formed only two years previously when Kempsey CYM and Kempsey Central joined forces. In Kempsey, that was like Hull FC and Rovers merging, and no-one could see it working. Apparently the two clubs hated each other with a vengeance, but the town was not big enough to support the two teams financially. Perhaps something that the two clubs in Hull should consider – but it will never happen.

Rugby league clubs in country areas in those days, and I believe it is still the same today, were semi-professional. They may have had three or four 'paid players,' guys who because of their ability and experience were paid more money than the local guys, who would be contracted, including signing-on fees, match payments, and a job and accommodation in some cases. Where the local players got bonus payments, some clubs at the end of the season took out all expenses and contract payments from the seasons gate and sponsorship receipts and split the rest amongst the remainder of the players. It was the accepted way that it was – a lot of guys in country towns never left the area, lived in the same place, worked at the same company, and played for the same team from being a kid in under 8s, right through open age and then served on the club committee when they retired. All they want is their club to be successful and if it meant bringing in the paid players, then so be it. Clubs were run on sponsorship from local companies, raffles in pubs and clubs, and gate receipts. In Kempsey, each of the committee men and coaches were designated pubs from which they had to try and create revenue.

A lot of the guys that came into these towns never left – they just settled down there – and it was the same with the coaches. Most coaches that go into 'the bush,' as it is called, are captain-coaches. Clubs usually look for experienced players who have played at a higher level in either Sydney or Newcastle, which in my days in Australia were the strongest two competitions. A lot were guys who no longer could command a regular first team spot, and rather than play lower grade would rather 'go bush.' You also got guys like me that just wanted to coach, it was something I had set my heart on since I started playing, and had some experience coaching youth teams, which in my case wetted my appetite even more. I just loved the feeling you got when things went right, things you had practiced on the training field, and when you put into action they come off – it is a feeling of deep satisfaction, similar to what you get when you know guys taking on board what you tell them and it improves their game, helping not just them but the team as a whole.

Kempsey had quite a young team, made up of players from the two clubs – most of the older guys were too set in their ways and had not joined the merged club. They finished next to last in Group 2 the previous season and were not much better in the current season. There were quite a few good players amongst them, they just needed pointing in the right direction. I felt that if I could get the guys on my side and play the way I believed was the right way, it would work. The final thing on the agenda was terms, how much did I want and how much they were prepared to offer.

Having talked for quite a while, we asked for some time to think about it and they agreed a couple of weeks. They were not pushing me, but they said that they had heard glowing reports from contacts in the Newcastle area and I was their number one choice. Apparently also someone in the Maitland ranks had been asked by a mate in Kempsey if he knew of anyone who would be interested in taking up the very big challenge of the player-coach position of a new club, and had mentioned me. They left, giving me a couple of weeks to mull over the offer.

Jacky and I discussed the pros and cons in depth. Prospects were not really good for Jacky at Bradmill as there had been a lot of redundancies, or retrenchments as they called them, whilst, for me, Monosteel was booming with a full order book. Jacky had been told she was safe, but if she lost her job, we would have to look for accommodation again. So if we moved it might as well be to another town and another challenge in our lives. Jacky spoke to her employers, and again they told her she would not lose her job, but were not sure who was going to go. Having given it a lot of thought, Jacky was told if she went now, or told them now, it could save the job of someone who needed the job to survive, and they would keep her on until we left. This was a great gesture on their part.

We were also at the time contemplating going back to the UK for holiday. My mother and father planned to come out to see us, but Mam was taken ill and could not travel. My old man said that we could have the cost of their air fares for spending money, to reduce our costs. When Jacky went back to discuss the job again with her boss, he told her if she got retrenched, the government would give her a full six months' pay. Now that was too good an opportunity to miss, for if we did decide to go to Kempsey and she gave her notice in she would not get the severance package on offer. It was a no brainer really, and we decided we would take Kempsey's offer and relocate to the Mid North Coast.

At that time, I was at a game watching South Newcastle when their chairman sidled up to me and asked if I had time for a chat. He asked me if I knew Terry Clawson, which I did, as I had played against him many times over the years. He then told me they were hoping to get Clawson as first grade coach for the following season and had the audacity to ask me, "If we don't get him, would you be interested?"

"Look if you want me make me an offer, do it," I said. "You have seen me play for the past three years and if you think I am the man to take you forward, then great, but please do not insult me. If you think I am playing second fiddle to Terry Clawson, forget it". It did not bother me, as I did not want to play against Maitland in the Newcastle Competition, apart from which, I do not think I would have got on with Souths. They had a bloke in the club called Bobby Bugden who ran the Leagues club, who was also commentator on the games televised on a Saturday night but who never had a good word to say about me.

I had been asked some time before if I would be willing to go on a Saturday morning 'Footy Show' on the local channel and was interviewed live on NBN3. I was a bit nervous as I had never been on TV before. They welcomed me to the show, all that stuff and then asked me what I thought about the standard of the competition, how it compared with the league at home – the usual questions. I had got over the nerves, was enjoying it, and was in full steam by the time Bobby Bugden chipped in his two penneth. I thought he was a smart arse, and had taken a dislike to him straight away. He kept on about why we didn't use Mick McTernan, our flying winger, more, and he appeared not to have any time for Maitland. He got under my skin, and I stopped him in his tracks halfway through another question on Mick and said, "Bobby, I don't know if you have ever played the game, but we, and most importantly Terry Pannowitz, believe that our centres, who we consider to be as good as any in the competition, should not furnish our wingers with the ball unless they have a very good chance of scoring a try." One of those centres was, of course Mick Bickley, who had come to us from Souths. There was a silence in the studio; the anchor man, Noel Harrison, went white, Bugden went red and started spluttering, and another guy on the panel chipped in to diffuse the tension. Apparently, Bugden had played for St George about 150 times in the early 1960s, and for Australia a couple of times, and was quite a handy player. Obviously I did not know this at the time and learned my lesson – if you go on a television sports show try and do some homework on the pundits – it may help!

As I was getting ready to leave Bugden, confronted me and said I tried to make him look like a prat, and the other guy on the panel stepped in to calm things down. Bugden used to write a column in one of the Newcastle papers, and never had a good word for me, and whenever the game Maitland were playing was on TV, I never got a good mention from him. But he was only one man, and I did alright without his help.

Surprisingly, I got asked back on the show in 1973, when we got through to the Grand Final. I cannot remember Bugden being there, but here were two guests, Karl Hutchinson, West's front rower, and myself. I had never spoken to Karl, other than on the field of play, and that was hardly a sociable atmosphere. But he came over as quite a decent bloke – quite different to how he was on the paddock.

We went up to Kempsey in September to meet the guys who had wanted to employ me, finalise the terms of the contract, and look round at houses. We stayed at the Railway Hotel owned by Don Rampling. He and his wife Corinne became very good friends to us. They had five kids, two of whom turned out to be very good rugby league players. Dean played for South Sydney from 1979 to 1984 and Tony, who started his career in 1981, played for several of the big Sydney clubs, had three games for New South Wales, and a season with Salford in 1989/90. Don had come to Kempsey after selling his plumbing business in Sydney and buying the pub. In those days he was an avid South Sydney supporter and I can see why the two boys finished up playing with them. When we arrived on the Friday evening at around tea time, the pub was heaving. I was going in at the back door looking for the reception, when Corinne came out of the kitchen and asked if she could help. When I told her who I was, she cried out, "Oh, you're here! Hang on,

Keith Pollard

hang on!'

"Whoa," I said, "no panic!" We were tired and ready for a meal and a drink, but we had left Jason with Lorna and Reg for the weekend, so we did not have to worry about him. Corrine ran into the bar and brought out Don, who introduced himself and invited us into the bar to 'meet the guys.' I said we needed to have a shower and change first, so he gave me a key and whispered, 'room 3.' I wondered why he had whispered and he told me later he did not want anyone pestering us – if anyone knew we were there they would be pestering us to get in the bar. Jacky was dreading meeting a lot of strangers, but she knew that it was part of the job. So we freshened up, went down, and met them. There were committee members, players and supporters – it was packed with people. I could not believe the number of people that had come to the pub to see me – it was unreal. I ended up pissed, as you can imagine.

The next day, I was met by Eric Lahey, Mick Evans, the secretary, who could drink for Australia, and two committee men, Pat Clarke and Jim Challinor. Jim was a Pommie, as he reminded me on several occasions over the two years I was with them. I was taken in to the restaurant area of the pub where there were the media – radio, newspaper men and a couple of photographers, plus a few other guys I could not remember meeting before. Eric gave short speech about me and my previous history, explaining why they had picked me from the other six players on their shortlist, which was as much a surprise to me, as to anyone else in the room. I signed for one year, with the club having the option for a second season. After a few questions, the meeting broke up and Eric introduced me to other committee members and some club sponsors. He then said we were going to meet the people who had agreed to employ me. Jacky was to remain with the other ladies.

They then took me to the golf club to meet Ted Bird and Bruce Lovett, the two guys who owned a local Engineering Company called H.F. Hand Engineering. I shook hands with them, but did not think I really got a warm reception. We discussed what I had done workwise, what experience I had, and I provided references from all my previous companies, including in the UK. I had a full set because they were needed to qualify for emigration and to obtain a Tradesman's Rights Certificate from the NSW Government. If you did not have one of these, you were classed as a process worker, but I was classed as a Boiler-Maker Welder First Class, which would give me priority over anyone without that certificate. I did not feel I got very good vibes from Bruce, although Ted was okay. I was a bit unsettled after the meeting and said so to Eric, who was a bit taken aback as they were personal as well as business friends of his. But it was too late now, as I had signed, and there were not many other places to get employment in my trade as a boilermaker/welder. I did not tell Jacky about my doubts, as she would have worried herself sick over it. We spent the rest of the day meeting going to the five pubs the club used to raise funds sponsors, meeting other people involved with the club, and even the ABC radio station. It was a long day!

On the Sunday morning we went to see a couple of houses that were going to be available to rent and then had a barbeque at the pub Sunday afternoon, to end a great weekend – my only problem was the job! On Monday morning we travelled back down to Maitland. Kempsey sent a truck up to pick our belongings up to put in storage for three months as we weren't due back till beginning of January. I put my car in Kevin Cousin's fathers lock-up and we said goodbye to all our dear friends in Maitland. It was a sad day for us all. We had and still have some great bonds with people of

TIME WILL REMEMBER HIM AS ONE OF NEWCASTLE RUGBY LEAGUE'S GREAT PLAYERS...

Greatness is a label easily bestowed in these exaggerated times, but Keith Pollard earned such high praise. It is my honour to speak of Keith Pollard, a man I stood proudly next to each week on the footy field and someone who is and will always be my lifelong friend.

He joined Maitland in 1971 when we picked him up as a result of his originally destined club in Australia, Tamworth, being unable to foot the transfer bill... Enter Dave Moreland, president of Maitland Rugby League club, who had heard of Keith's talents through his 'black book' of contacts. And so it was that Keith Pollard became a Pumpkin Picker.

Whilst Maitland may not have been his original destination, it soon became the foundation for his Australian journey on both a family and personal level. They say the discovery of oneself is the most powerful of all, however as the coach of Maitland, the discovery of Keith Pollard was one of the most enriching times of my playing and coaching career.

Keith found the pre-season training regime to be most confounding. A typical session saw us belt out an 8-10 mile run followed by a series of sprints on the sandbanks of the Hunter River. I'm sure in those first few weeks I most likely earned the nickname to him... 'that f*****g Aussie bastard', as exercising and Keith weren't natural bedfellows.

On one such occasion I decided the boys needed a change... a swim across the Hunter River, then back again it was. Keith looked at me the same way Hillary Clinton looked at Donald Trump before

Keith Pollard

the election as if to say, "what the F?". He paced back and forth as the boys, one by one, entered the water and swam easily across the river... after all this is what we do in the bush.

Keith, never one to let the team down, entered the water with great gusto. I couldn't really say he was using a swimming stroke that was known to any Aussie, but it was some type of movement nevertheless. Looking more like a Wildebeest swimming for his life in the Serengeti Keith eventually started to propel his body forward. I momentarily turned thinking he was on his way when one of the boys sung out, 'The Pom is in trouble'. The look of impending death was all over his face as the reality of his predicament, not being able to swim, sank in.

As he gulped for air and steeled himself for his eventual fate I sang out, "Hey Keith, try standing up!" He soon realised the water was only three feet deep. He stumbled to his feet and looked at me, again like Trump looked at Clinton on the night he won the election, as if to say "I will survive... hey, hey."

Keith's first game for Maitland was what could only be described as a mixed bag. He started off in 3rd grade however was taken off after twenty minutes as the second grade coach liked what he saw. He then played another twenty minutes in second grade before being taken off again as I too liked what I saw. Keith then came on as replacement in first grade and it was here in first grade that he remained for his playing career at Maitland.

Time will remember him as one of Newcastle rugby league's great players. Keith was fearless in both attack and defence which earned him the nickname...'that F*****g Pommy Bastard". He played in concert with how the game was played back then, tough and tougher. He had two types of defence... knock em down or knock em out and if the truth be known he didn't care which one took precedence over the other.

My coaching position was made so much easier by having Keith in our side. His natural ability to work magic with the ball was well ahead of the times. He was often reading the play two or three tackles ahead and we all learnt to hang off him as inevitably he always put you in the gap.

History will show we played in three straight Grand Finals 1971, 1972 and 1973 with the results being two wins and one loss... thank you Keith Pollard. His infectious humour and sense of true belonging with both the club and his team-mates stood him apart. He may have travelled 10,553 miles from his place of birth, however he became part of the fabric of the club, the city and to this day the name Keith Pollard is one to be revered.

"He never set out to be extraordinary, he just did extraordinary things." Hale Keith Pollard.

Terry Pannowitz-Maitland

166

RED & WHITE PHOENIX

KEITH IS ONE OF THOSE BLOKES YOU WANT IN THE TRENCHES WITH YOU...

If Rugby League was all there was to Keith Pollard's life... his book would still be a great read. But it would hardly tell the story of this 'Mad Pommie'.

I am not really sure how or why Keith arrived to play at Maitland. I think he was to play in Tamworth, perhaps they couldn't afford him... then again perhaps it was the Country Music of Tamworth that was the reason that this talented player became one of my great memories of playing Rugby League for Maitland.

From day one he just fitted in.

What did Keith bring to our side? His expert use of the now banned shoulder charge. How to tackle with one's elbows. Sledging to a new level.

Swimming was not one of his strengths - nearly drowned in Maitland's famous Hunter River

But I should include 'The hands of a Surgeon'... no better demonstrated than by the pass that sent our flying winger Mick McTernan (now deceased) away for in my opinion, the best Grand Final try ever in Newcastle Rugby League.

I will always remember Keith's great statement "my job is to put the ball in the hole... your job is to be in the hole."

Football wise, for Maitland the timing of Keith's arrival was great... Maitland were in a period of playing in five successive Grand Finals.

Being the halfback I have to say I really don't have the words to describe what it was like playing behind our tremendous pack of forwards of which Keith Pollard was an integral part, led by our once in a lifetime Captain Coach Terry Pannowitz.

At the end of the day when the going gets tough, Keith Pollard is one of those blokes you want in the trenches with you... His book on the highs and lows of his 'life' clearly demonstrates the character of my POMMIE MATE.

Brian Burke - Maitland
First grade games for Maitland
years 1968...1973 Newcastle Rep
years 1968...1974 NSW Country v City
1972 NSW Country Player of the year
1970 Newcastle v England
1972 NSW Country Capt v NZ
1972 NSW Country Capt v Qld
1974 NSW Country Capt Undefeated tour of NZ
NSW v QLD...1970, 1971, 1972

Keith Pollard

ONE OF THE BEST FRONT-ROWERS EVER TO PUT ON THE BLACK AND WHITE COLOURS...

My very first memory of Keith 'The Pommie' Pollard was midway through my first season with the Maitland Pumpkin Pickers in 1971. I was making my first grade debut against a strong Waratah-Mayfield side that also included a couple of Pommies in hooker Alwyn Walters and a very tough second rower by the name of Tony Finch.

Keith had started the day in 3rd grade, then came on in reserve grade and was now making his way out as a replacement in first grade.

My open side prop forward that day was the very experienced Ron Clarke who was as strong as an ox and only knew one way to run and that was straight over the opposition. We slotted Keith in to the blind side of the scrum and he immediately head butted the equally tough Winston Loades. Then, all hell broke loose with Loades and Tony Finch attempting to get square with the Pom. It was a very fiery initiation for Keith who later became famous for his tackling style of 'they can't run without a head'.

Over the next four seasons Keith would go on to establish himself in the same calibre as former English Internationals Nat Silcock and Terry Clawson who both played for South Newcastle in the local competition. They were all game breakers because of their tenacity and skill.

Keith displayed all of those qualities in the 1971 and 1973 Grand Final wins where he managed to display all of his greatness.

As the season progressed, my family became close friends with the Pollards and especially young Jason who was the same age as my son Steven. We have been very fortunate to have visited the Pollards in England and then entertained them a few times when they have visited Australia.

Keith was nominated in 2015 in the best 40 players to play for the Pickers and without any doubt will go down in the annals of Maitland as one of the best front-rowers ever to put on the black and white colours.

ALAN 'NABBY' McNAB
Hooker, Waratah-Mayfield, Maitland, Newcastle
Representative Team 1972

RED & WHITE PHOENIX

WE THOUGHT HE WAS A GOD FROM ANOTHER PLANET

It was a cold, dark, rainy November afternoon in 1979 when three young Aussies from Maitland on a European vacation - Me, Tim Quinn and Neil Newman - rolled into Withernsea near Hull in the UK to catch up with an old friend.

That old friend, who had left a lasting impression on each of them, was Keith Pollard, a giant of a man who the boys both played with and supported during his time at the Maitland Pumpkin Pickers. When Keith arrived in Maitland with his huge personality, his infectious laughter and the way he approached the game of Rugby League, we thought he was a God from another planet!

Keith arrived in Maitland in 1971 and immediately set tongues wagging with his aggressive approach and deft ball skills. His approach to the game was something we hadn't seen in that part of the world. His charges into the ruck, his crash tackling defensive style, along with his pre-line and offload passing, changed the way we thought about the game.

During his time in Maitland Keith played a massive part in a highly successful team, playing in three Grand Finals and winning two in the very competitive Newcastle Rugby League Competition.

Not only was Keith a wonderful player but he was also willing to lend a hand and offer words of encouragement and guidance to the younger players in the club. I am sure these words and advice sparked and instigated my interest in coaching the game of Rugby League.

Keith brought with him to Maitland his beautiful wife Jacky and his son Jason. He also brought his wonderful sense of humour from the north of England, his sharp wit sparking my interest in UK Rugby League and my love affair with the people of northern England.

I had the pleasure of returning to Hull many years later to coach Hull FC in the Super League and many a great night was had over a few pints discussing Hull FC and its fortunes and battles against the dark side, Hull KR, where Keith played and supported KR for many years. A great man with a great story, enjoy the read.

PETER SHARP - MAITLAND - 1973 to 1981 playing.Reserve grade and 1st grade coach 1985 and 1986 - Newcastle Knights Junior rep and Reserve grade coach 1988 to 1996 - Parramatta assistant coach 1997 and 1998 - Manly Sea Eagles and Northern Eagles coach 1999 to 2003 - Melbourne Storm assistant coach 2004 - Parramatta assistant coach 2005 - Hull FC coach 2006 to 2008 - Ulster Defensive coach 2008 and 2009 - Parramatta assistant coach 2010 and 2011 - Cronulla Sharks assistant coach 2012 to 2014 - Parramatta Head of Recruitment 2014 to present

Souvenir brochure in the Maitland Mercury

KEITH SENT FEAR THROUGH THE OPPOSITION RANKS, BUT WE LOVED HIM...

It was a stinking hot afternoon, 40C plus and unrelenting, and all that the Maitland Pickers' players assembled for pre-season training wanted to do was slink in the shade and quietly expire.

Enter Keith Pollard and his great mate Alan 'Crackers' McNab and after ten minutes the young Pickers had found not one but three or four extra gears.

Pollard, McNab and their teammates from the star-studded Maitland Pickers' team of the early 1970s are still royalty in this fiercely rugby-league mad slice of the Hunter Valley.

Every youngster dreams of repeating their feats and entering the famous club's folklore.

Pollard, the English forward with a bushy moustache and barrel-chest, was a key part of Maitland's 1971 and 1973 premierships and many believe if he had played in 1972 the Pickers would have achieved a hat-trick of titles in what was then the toughest and most talent-laden competition outside of Sydney.

RED & WHITE PHOENIX

"Keith sent fear through the opposition ranks, but we loved him. You needed to duck your head when you ran near him as he was likely to take your head off," McNab said of his front-row partner in pain.

A typical ball-playing prop from the north of England, he set up three tries in the 1971 Grand Final and out-muscled opposition in 1973 decider and was part of the initial squad in the Pickers top 20 players from their glorious past.

Still very much a student of the game, Pollard was in his element on that hot summer afternoon catching up with Super League players Dane Tilse and Luke Dorn.

"Unfortunately, we never got to see the best of Dane at Hull KR because they insisted on using him as a battering ram," Pollard said of the Australian style of game adopted by Hull KR during Tilse's stay, which equally bemused him during his time in Maitland.

Pollard was revolutionary for the Maitland fans who expected their forwards to charge at the opposition's line and get up and play the ball.

His passing game and ability to offload divided fans but they all sung his praises when he set up three tries in the 1971 title win. There were no knockers when it came to his defence.

Teammate and former NSW representative Brian Burke remembered Pollard fondly as the best tackler with an elbow he had seen. A lot more fondly than Pollard's opponents no doubt.

Pollard said captain-coach Terry Pannowitz, who played lock for Australia winning selection while playing for the Pickers, and half-back Burke were the stand-outs but every player at Maitland during his era was a great player.

"We probably should have had three balls, one for Panno, one for Burkey and the other for the rest of us," he said.

"They were all great players, Alan was a tremendous dummy half and Max McMahon mowed down the opposition with his tackles. To be named in the top 40 of the Pickers was one of my greatest honours. We were great mates and stuck together which made us an even better team."

Still very much a young man at heart, Pollard's sage words of advice to the young Pickers during his visit struck a chord that spanned the decades.

"The thing I say to them is enjoy every minute of it," Pollard said.

"You can never go back, so make sure you make every game count. If you're as lucky as I have been playing with the Pickers from my era, these men will be your best mates for life."

Michael Hartshorne
Maitland Mercury Sports Correspondent

Keith Pollard

Phil Amidy, Graham Mathews, Errol Ruprecht and me training with the
North Coast Squad for the game against Newcastle in 1975

Pollard to coach Kempsey in 1975

CHAPTER 10
KEMPSEY

We departed from Sydney at the end of September for our trip back home. We had arranged to stop with Jacky's brother, Ian, while we were in the UK, and he offered to lend us his car when we needed it – which turned out to be quite a bit. We visited everyone we knew in Hull, and even went over to Keighley for a few days.

I had rung Rex Simpson, at the *Turkey* Inn, to tell him we were coming over, but he said that he had sold the pub to another guy I knew, called Brian Eastell. We stopped just across the road from the *Turkey*, with an old friend John Sayers. Rex told me he that he sold the *Turkey* as a free house and how much he had got for it. We thought if we had known, we would have come home and bought it to run ourselves. It was a great pub, and I know Brian did quite well whilst he was landlord there.

I trained with Rovers when I got back, just to keep myself in shape. The then first team coach, Arthur Bunting, asked me if I fancied playing while I was there but I declined his offer. Although my contract with Kempsey did not officially start until January 1975, I did not want to take the risk of injury. After all the hype there had been, it would not have looked great going back with an injury to start pre-season training.

I had forgotten what the weather was like in Hull after being in the sunshine for four years – it was cold, miserable and grey. One day, I was standing outside British Home Stores in town, watching the world go by whilst waiting for Jacky. Everyone looked so depressed; it was like looking at a life-size Lowry painting, with the matchstick men and matchstick cats and dogs. I could hear a girl in the shop on the tannoy system saying something about special deals and, as Jacky walked out, I had to ask, "Do we sound like her in there?" I even wondered what the hell we were doing back in Hull, and that we must be mad. But it was soon time to return, and when we got back to Kempsey early in January it was around 30 degrees with glorious sunshine and not a cloud in the skies. It was great to be back! We went to pick the keys up for the house that we were going to call home for at least the next year. The guys from the club had put all our cases in one of the bedrooms, put the furniture into the relevant rooms, filled the fridge up with food, and even put a pack of beer in the fridge! It was a great gesture and the place already looked like a home.

For the first night at training, we had over 40 players down for the two grades, which according to the committee men was a fantastic turnout. I emphasised to the troups that it was a clean sheet, and that everyone started afresh. I did not know anything about of them – I had not even asked for opinions from the reserve grade coach. All I knew was what positions they played in. I told them about the goals I intended to set, and what I expected of them for the coming season.

There was a deathly silence when I said we would be training three nights a week – Monday, Wednesday and Friday. In most Australian minds Friday is about going to the pub straight from work. All games are played on Sunday in country football, so I told them that I wanted everyone down on Mondays for a light session and to see the physio if they had any injuries. Wednesday would be the physical night when the hard work would be done, and on Friday we would have a light session, run through our moves and discuss the opposition's strengths and weaknesses.

To be fair to them, they bought in to it. I believe that we were the only team in the competition that trained three times a week and to me it paid dividends. The schedule I gave them for pre-season was something they had never done before and they had never trained as hard in their lives – come to think of it neither had I! We were super fit by the time the first trial game was played; we were bouncing in every way but match fitness. I had been trying to drum into the players my ideas on how I wanted them to play and I had a blank canvass to work with, as most of them were young and willing to learn. The veterans of the team were hooker Mick Flanagan, a local guy who had been with arch-rivals Smithtown Tigers for the three previous seasons - a good player, although a bit temperamental, who had something special, he was as hard as iron in defence, could read a game well, was a good dummy half, but lacked a bit of pace; Johnny Mayhew, the scrum half, was just what I wanted in that position, with great vision and defence, and although he had been out the full previous season with a bad injury he came back stronger than ever; and Terry Anderson at stand-off, so quiet that I thought he was deaf and dumb for the first six weeks, but what a good player, with good hands and speed to burn. The rest were in their early to mid-twenties. I kept wondering how they had only finished next to last the previous two seasons. Was I underestimating the opposition?

When I joined the club, I was designated a pub that I had to, for want of a better word, 'work' in. I had to go there every Saturday morning and do the raffles, sell doubles tickets, and generally promote the team. I also used to go on a Friday night after training into another pub to show my face and speak to supporters – in fact anyone, as long as I was promoting the Kowboys. I also used to visit the other two pubs in the town centre, so with training three nights a week and going to see the under 18 squad on the other two nights, I had plenty on my plate.

We played Wauchope away in our first trial game. We had a lad called Eric Carney, a second rower, who had come from that town to trial with us, and he told us they had recruited well during the summer, bringing in New Zealand international Eddie Heatley, who had played for North Sydney in the 1974 season, as captain-coach, along with a number of top class country imports from around the state.

Eric thought he would come and have a go with us because he would not get a look in down at Wauchope. It was a good move for both parties and he earned his place in our first team squad. He was not a big fella but he could certainly tackle. I often used to move him wide when we had the ball, swapping him with our winger Dick Bailey, who was built like second rower and was very quick.

The game was played in four quarters of 25-minutes duration each. Both teams used a mixture of players in the first two stanzas, after which we were leading 26-8, not only to our amazement but also that of the opposition. It was quite evident that my message had got through to lads about letting the ball do the work. I wanted them to play 'Pommie football' and had practiced for a few weeks running at gaps and moving the defence to where we wanted them to be and not where they wanted to go. It worked a dream, and my vision was working. I realise it was only the first game, but Wauchope had not a clue how to defend against it. I was as happy as the proverbial. We won the second two stanzas by 13 points to 11 and, whilst they brought out their big guns, I kept mixing and matching to assess our best combinations.

I will always remember this day, not only for the success of my vision of how the game should be played, but also because, after the game, whilst in the local RSL club, I met Ron Coote again. I was standing at the bar when a voice behind me said, "G'day mate, how are you? Been a while!" I turned round and saw that it was Ron.

"1970 World cup final – Bradford," I replied.

"No, it was at Leeds – Headingley," he replied.

"Yes, but we met at that hotel in Bradford after the game and were with John O'Neill." What a memory the guy had. We talked about that night, what I had done since, why had not I played in Sydney, and my time at Maitland. I was pleased and honoured that he had remembered me and had taken the trouble to come over and talk. One of the Kempsey committee men told me later that he was standing near some of the Eastern Suburbs players they had been very impressed the way we were performing. One of them had said, "They play the gaps like Poms." Apparently Ron Coote had said "I know that front rower from somewhere!"

Keith Pollard

A farewell party in 1976

A cartoon drawn by Kowboys' second-rower Eric Carney

Jacky and Libby Evans with President, Eric Lahey

Saying my goodbyes to physio, Max Cameron and Eric Lahey

RED & WHITE PHOENIX

Also in the RSL was Artie Beetson. Artie was working his way through the buffet and when he was opposite to me I said, "G'day mate!" He looked up and said, "Jesus, Keighley! How are ya mate, I'll be with you for a yarn later okay?" He then continued his way down the buffet like a locust across a field, devouring everything in sight. His reputation of being a big eater was well deserved. He came over later and joined in the conversation when I was with Ron. We talked about our meetings in England and, as ever, he mentioned that I had broken his nose.

At Kempsey, we had another trial game before our first game. In between these, I was picked to play for the Group 2 team at Tamworth and then was chosen to play for the North Coast Division. I played in the Group 2 game at Tamworth, but was left out of the team for the next game, along with Ian Martin, who the season before had played regularly for Manly alongside the likes of Phil Lowe, Mal Reilly and Bobby Fulton. Ian was also picked as captain of the North Coast team. I was later told that one of the group of five Group 2 selectors, Lloyd Hudson from Kempsey, was not at the selection meeting for the next game and that the four other selectors picked 13 of the 15-man squad from their four clubs. They were beaten at Tweed Heads in the knock out series and I was told that if Ian and myself had been playing the result would have been different, but that is history now.

The divisional game was to be against Newcastle on April 12th 1975. I had played in Newcastle for three and a half seasons and for three of them I thought I deserved a shout at the representative team, but when Maitland officials put my name forward for selection they were always told, "He is a Pom and can't go any further." I would apparently be depriving an Australian-born player of the chance to represent his country. Then in 1974, when the Great Britain team was across, I was told I was going to be selected for that game to counteract the English forwards, most of whom I knew from playing against them previously, but I missed out when I broke my wrist the week before. Whether I would have played we will never know – but I was invited to the after-match reception, and that had never happened before!

It was ironic that the Newcastle team we played that day included an ex-New Zealand prop, Brian Anderson, who had played for North Sydney; together with Gary Leo and Brian Moore, who were both ex-internationals. Our coach was a guy called Ronnie Boden, another ex-international, who hailed from Toowoomba, and had played for Queensland and Australia alongside the great Reg Gasnier. He had played for Parramatta, was captain-coach of them in 1961 and was credited with playing a leading role in making the Parramatta club into one of the strongest in Sydney. He had an ear bitten off in a match in France on a

177

Kangaroo tour, and was distinguishable on the paddock with white head gear. Ronnie later coached in the Taree, area before sadly passing away in August 2015.

We met at the hotel on the Friday afternoon before the game, after making our way there in our own cars. Few of us had actually met and were introduced when we met with Ronnie. We had been invited to tea at Western Suburbs Leagues club, so Ron suggested we have only a couple of beers and told us we would have run out the following morning to go through a few plays try and get to know each other. His final comment was the best bit of reverse psychology I have ever witnessed. He said, "We will turn up and try to give them a game. There's not much chance, but we can get pissed after the game, okay?" Ian Martin turned to me and said, "Who is this arsehole?" and another voice said, "Cheeky little bastard!"

As we sat chatting in the hotel, waiting for the transport to take us to the Sports Ground, Ronnie was not there but he was still working our hearts and minds. We were all asking how this prat had got the coaching job – he had really wound us up. By the time we got to the ground we were really up for it. It is now a matter of record that the North Coast team, which had only won one game since 1963 and only two of their sixteen games in the Caltex knock-out cup competition championship, and a team that Ronnie had said had no chance, hammered a Newcastle team full of ex-international and state players, 34-5. It was a pity that there was only a small crowd to witness the annihilation and how sweet it was to go there and rub their noses in it. After the game, Ronnie came into the dressing room and said, "Well boys, I thought you would play well but not that fucking well! Congratulations, it worked!" After the game we went to the reception and had a great night – the highlight to me being when the players of Newcastle were asked by their chairman 'Mo' Wilson to stand and applaud the North Coast Team!

Later that evening I was in the bar at the hotel, where I had been on the amber nectar for quite a while, and was taking to Ronnie Bowden, who was also under the influence. He picked up a full unopened can and said to me, "Hey Pom, do you know how to tell a good front rower?" When I said that I did not, he hit me on the forehead as hard as he could with the full can, sideways on, bursting it as he did so.

"Good on ya, mate," he said, when I just stood there. "That's how you do it. You'll do for me!" My head was ringing like Big Ben.

The next day I drove back to Kempsey to play in our first game of the 1975 season away to Macksville, which we won 37-0. It was a great start for us, as the previous season Macksville had reached the final, going out to eventual competition winners, Coffs Harbour.

The following Wednesday we had to travel up to Lang Park, Brisbane to play against the star-studded Sydney outfit, Manly Warringah, in the 1st Round of the Amco knock-out cup competition. In all my chequered career I have never gone into a game thinking that we would lose. This was no different, but deep down I knew that a team that included top players like Malcolm Reilly, Phil Lowe, Bobby Fulton, Graham Eadie, Ray Brannigan and Kevin Junee were going to be unbelievably hard to beat.

Three of us, Arthur 'Fatty' Woods from Smithtown, Coffs captain-coach Peter Swanson and I drove up to the airport at Coffs Harbour, from where we were to fly up to Brisbane in a four-seater plane. Fatty had been telling me on the way up how he hated flying, which was too good an opportunity to miss. I just happened to mention this to the pilot when he came over to tell us about the flight.

"No worries, mate," he said, as only an Australian can. He told us to follow him out to where the plane was parked up. I had to laugh when I saw the name on the side - *Bananaland Airways*. It was painted white with a great Yellow banana on the body and tail – it was a flying taxi. As we were walking out to the plane, Fatty was wittering away to the pilot, telling him he had never been in such a small aeroplane and how he was worried about flying.

As we got in, the pilot told Fatty to get into the front, with me and Peter in the back seats because we were bigger and there would be more room for us. He then started to do his pre-flight checks and was acting as if he was brand new to the job. He was talking out loud, as if he was not sure he was doing it right, and it was an effort for me not to burst out laughing. Fatty kept turning round and looking at me with the most worried face I have ever seen. The pilot put his finger on first one switch and then another, saying, "this one, I think ..... err no, this one!" He then looked quizzically at Fatty before his face lit up and he said, "yes, this one!!" At which, the engine started up and the pilot gave a little jump of surprise and said, "Yes!!!" He was just classic, I loved him!

We took off and he flew the plane up the coast, more or less following the coastline all the way to Brisbane. I do not think we went above 100 feet, and it was the bumpiest flight I have ever been on. When we landed at the airport and got off, Fatty kissed the ground – I thought only the Pope only did that, but Fatty did it that day.

We were taken to a brand new hotel in the centre of the city and were given our itinerary. We then had a team meeting, at which we discussed the opposition – not that we needed telling who they were, because we knew that all too well. We were duly picked up and taken to the ground, where we got changed in the same way as for any other game. The well-known Aussie commentator, Ray 'Rabbits' Warren, was commentating even back in those days, and came over and asked me few questions, as he did with a few of the players.

We went out on to the pitch to do a few stretches and all was well for ten minutes or so. Then Manly came out onto the pitch. We kicked off to them, which was the last time we had the ball for about a quarter of an hour. I had never seen anything like their speed before. I have no idea what the score was when we got the ball for the first time. We have all had that 'what the hell am I doing here?' feeling, and I had it quite a few times during that game.

We kicked through once and followed ball up-field where full-back Graham Eadie, whose nickname was Wombat, took the ball on the full. I lined him up, thinking, 'I have got you here son, come to daddy,' but as he ran at me he changed gear and exploded into me, hitting me in the chest with his head. It was like being hit by a meteorite – I had never been hit as hard in my career. I was travelling backwards as he ran over the top of me.

The only joy I had in the game was when I hit Phil Lowe with a perfect man and ball tackle. Phil and his wife, Avril, had visited us in Kempsey one weekend before the season started and we had been talking football over a few beers on the deck at our house. Phil told me about the few moves Manly did during a game, not thinking we would ever play against each other again, and described one where if they got a penalty, he would go down as if his bootlace had come undone. They would take the tap and Malcolm Reilly would put on a run-around move attempting to send the defence to the open side of the ruck, before sending a long pass to the blind side where Phil had set off in the hope that the opposition had forgotten all about him.

During the game, Manly got a penalty, and I noticed Phil kneeling down, attending to his boot lace. I totally ignored everything else that was happening on the pitch and concentrated on Mr Lowe. As they took the tap, I set off and as the ball landed in Phil's arms I hit him like an exocet missile. He went up in the air backwards and I felt as if my spine had expanded and contracted like a concertina. Ray Warren said on the TV, "Jeez, the two Pommies have just crashed." Phil ended up on his back on the floor with me on top of him.

"You fucking bastard," he said. "How the hell did you know I was getting the ball?" I then reminded him about what he had told me. We have laughed about that many a time over a few beers – but it was the only laugh I had that day. We were hammered 44-2, and we were lucky to score two.

The following week, I had to travel to Taree to play in the quarter-final of the divisional knock out against Illawarra, the

RED & WHITE PHOENIX

Wollongong area representative team. They were a very strong experienced team that included the then Rovers international forward Paul Rose, who was playing for Dapto in the Wollongong competition. Their captain was another one-time Rovers forward, Allan Fitzgibbon, father of Craig, who was a very good footballer. They completely outplayed us and personally I had one of the worst games of rugby I have ever played. Looking back, I think four games in under two weeks was just too much for me. Players have off-days and this was a mega off-day for me. I was ashamed of my performance, and I was rightly dropped for the next North Coast game which was against New Zealand.

Our next opponents at Kempsey were the previous year's Minor Premiers and grand finalists, Bellengen, who were coached by former Newtown Sydney forward Graham Mathews. We drew with them 10-all and then beat Woolgoolga away 21-0. Next up were last year's Premiers, Coffs Harbour, who came with a big reputation and were coached by the giant South African Peter Swanson, who the previous year was at the Penrith Panthers in Sydney. Swanson had been on the controversial 1971 South Africa rugby union tour of Australia, which was marked by anti-apartheid protests all around the country. Coffs had endured a bad start to the season. They had lost the legendry Phil Hawthorne, former Wallaby and Kangaroo scrum half, who had joined them after a great career in Sydney. Sadly, Phil was later diagnosed with leukaemia and died in September 1994. Coffs had signed Peter as a big name player, but he was on a hiding to nothing. They had lost a lot of their experienced players and he was in a similar position to me with a lot of young kids. Fortunately for me, our kids were better than their kids and we hammered them 48-13. After the game they dispensed with Peter's services. In those days, sackings of coaches and managers were rare, particularly in 'bush football,' where the pressure was not as great. I do not remember a coach being sacked in Sydney then either. I felt sorry for him. If the boot had been on the other foot, it might have been me.

We ended the first round of matches with six wins and a draw, and with 13 competition points on the board we were sitting at the top of the league table. I was more than pleased with that, and so were the committee. They told me they were taking up their option of another season, with a pay increase for me too. Happy days!

We started the second half well, and after completing the double over local rivals Smithtown Tigers we secured the Minor Premiership. We then went in to the play-offs as favourites. We played our last regular league game on 20 July, not playing again until 10 August when we played Nambucca Heads, who had beaten us in the last regular game, in the Major Semi-final. We duly beat them to go straight through to the Grand Final which was to be held

Keith Pollard

at our home ground, the Verge Street Oval, on 31 August. A Grand Final on your own pitch is all you can ask, but we were underdone, and by far the best team on the day won. Nambucca turned us over 19-4 in a really hard fought game in front of a record 5,000 supporters paying a then record $3,027.00. We could just not lift ourselves, and as coach it was partly my fault. I had convinced the team they were unbeatable, and they actually thought they were. From being second bottom the previous season to Grand Finalists was all too much, and I could just not bring them back to earth. Winning the Major semi-final did not help either because from 20 July to 31 August 31 we played only one game, whilst Nambucca had played three. Paradoxically there was no benefit from having a successful run – we were the best team all season but we did not benefit from having three weeks off.

Personally, I have never liked play-off systems and never will. Manchester United would not finish top of the Premier League after a hard season and then have to play off to win it. For me, if you are top of the league at the season's conclusion, you are top dog, it is as simple as that. But those were the rules, and congratulations to Rod Urquhart and his boys, who deserved their win on the day.

The summer came, our first in Kempsey, and we loved the climate on the Macleay, which was not as humid as Newcastle. We did the things you usually do in Australia – going to the beach, having barbys, and relaxing with friends. But whilst we really enjoyed the lifestyle, at the back of our minds were always thoughts about family and friends back home.

Another great thing in my life happened in January 1976, when my daughter Tracy was born. We now had a boy and girl, and decided to leave it at that. The only guy who was not happy for us was Ruben Saull, with whom Jacky had got a job at his Mazda garage in town. He had been looking for someone to run the office, and whilst Jason was at infant school the agreement was Jacky could work hours to suit school times. Jacky had got the job on the understanding she was not going to get pregnant and leave. When she did, he really gave me some stick over it as well. He started another girl to take Jacky's place but this did not work out. Fortunately for Ruben, when it happened I had broken my thumb, so Jacky used to go in to the garage leaving Tracy with me at home. When she needed feeding, and she knew how to let me know, believe me, I used to take her down to garage to fill her up, with milk, that is. We did this for a few weeks until Ruben could make other arrangements.

Nearly every Saturday morning, I used to go fishing with Toddy Watts, Johnny Mayhew, and the latter's brother Greg, or 'Skippy' as we called him. We would be up at around 3am to load the gear and head down to a place called Christmas Cutting, near the little town of Bellbrook, 30 miles up-river from Kempsey. We used to fish for Pearly Perch, also known as Bull-eye, Epaulette-fish and Nannygaiit, or to give it its proper name *Glaucosoma scapulare,* which was a fresh water fish mainly only found in Eastern Australia. This was great to eat and always gave you a great fight when you got one on the hook.

I had bought myself a little eleven-foot aluminium 'car topper' boat with 3hp Mercury outboard motor and John had a Canadian canoe. We would go up river in both cars, unload the canoe and leave Toddy and Johns' car there. Skippy and I would the drive back four or five miles down-river, unload the boat and go upstream against the current with the motor, whilst they came down stream using the current to propel them. We would pass somewhere along the river, stop for a beer or two and discuss the 'ones that got away.'

One morning we came round a bend in the river and found Toddy sitting alone in the canoe, tied to a tree in mid-stream. Skippy was worried about where his brother was, and as we stopped, John appeared out of the water with his bowie knife in his mouth, saying, "That bastard fish has got my Mr Floppy." A Mr Floppy was a special lure that we used to use to catch the fish that lived on the bottom of the river, but that come up to the top to catch flies or frogs. We used lures in different shapes, like flies or fishes, of which the daddy was the Mr Floppy. This was cast under the branch of the tree and then reeled in. As it moved across the top of the water it made a flip-flop sound like a frog swimming, hence the name Mr Floppy. The idea was that the fish would hear the sound or feel the vibrations and come up and catch it.

A big fish had seized John's Mr Floppy, had dived down and in its' frenzy wrapped itself round a tree branch on the river bed. John being John wanted his lure back as well as the fish. We waited around wasting precious petrol whilst he went up and down, before there was a burst of water like a big white shark coming out of the sea and he appeared with his knife speared in the fish, which still had the Mr Floppy stuck in its mouth. John was naked at the time, having left his clothes in the canoe, and it was quite amusing seeing him go under, as his brown body suddenly became a white backside, then the brown legs again. Eventually, his perseverance, and greed, paid off. It was all fantastic fun and a great way to spend warm summer mornings, before returning to the Kempsey hotel for a few beers and to do the raffle for the club funds.

I was still not impressed with Bruce my boss at HF Hands, but the guys were a great bunch to work with. Geoff 'Gully' Trees was a charge hand who had been there for years – although admittedly there were not many other places to work in Kempsey. He was also

Keith Pollard

under 18s coach at Smithtown and had, I understood, been a very good player in his day. Bobby Nelson, Cec Peters and a young apprentice, Wayne, were the workforce, and there was an old guy we called 'Smiddy,' who used to come in part time to do a bit of shot-blasting and painting. Overall, I was happy at Hands, and stopped there the full two years I was in Kempsey.

My main bone of contention was that Bruce used to 'penny pinch' incessantly. Once we were fabricating some high specification bridge beams out of plate steel. The joint on the beams had to be thoroughly inspected to ensure there was no foreign matter in the weld. Being used to this type of work, I asked Bruce if he could get some large cutting discs that would fit the hand grinders, that we could use to clean out the welds. He disappeared into the workshop and came back with just one. I could not believe it as he handed it to me and, to add insult to injury, said, "Don't use all of it, save some for Bobby."

"You are taking the piss, Bruce, where are the others?" I could not hold back from saying. He looked at me as only he could and muttered, "What others, you won't need more than one." He was as tight as the proverbial duck's backside!

At the start of my second season at Kempsey in 1976, we had quite a few changes to the previous season's squad. Mick Flanagan had spat his dummy out of the pram because I told him my thoughts about the play-off system. When I said that finishing top of the league was more important to me than winning a Grand Final, he refused to play with me or in any team I was that I was involved with. He was free to go anywhere and I expected him to go back to Smithtown so that he could prove a point to me, but he had other ideas.

We brought in a young lad called John Secombe, perhaps not as good as Mick, but he had something Mick did not – he wanted to play for me and, more importantly, for the Kowboys. We had also lost Kevin Bannerman, our loose forward, who had gone to University in Sydney, whilst Johnny Mayhew was injured at the start of the season. To have three of our spine, as they call the more influential players, not available for one reason or the other was a blow, but one we had to get over. I drafted in a loose-forward, Geoff Studman, and Alfie Drew, a young indigenous scrum half from the reserve grade.

After some settling in, we were soon firing again and at the end of the first round we were on eight points, four behind the league leaders, Bellengen. During part of this period, I had been side-lined with a broken thumb, which occurred against Smithtown in the fourth game of the season. I came off at half-time and asked our strapper, Max Cameron, to strap it up, without saying anything to the other players in the dressing room. He replied that I would have

184

to come off and go to hospital.

"Fuck off, you don't come off in local derbies!" I replied. We won the game, so all the pain was worthwhile.

We won the first four games in the second round, one of these being Bellengen. By this time, I had called up one of the veterans of the club, Billy Kennedy, from the reserves to take my place and to bring a bit of experience to the team. He had already come out of retirement to help us out with the injury problems – he was a great man and a tower of strength. I can never thank him enough for what he did.

One of our wins was at home to Smithtown Tigers. The previous season when we played them at their place I had been a bit overzealous in a few of my tackles. A Mr F.S. Hughes of Smithtown had written to the local newspaper, under the heading of 'Footy Thugs,' castigating me. What he failed to mention was that during the week previous to that game, I had received a lot of abuse and threats from Tigers supporters and even players, detailing what they were going to do to 'the Pom.' I have had critics on both sides of the world about my tackling techniques and use of elbows on attack, but this was different, and I was well primed up for the game. In my opinion, it was case of, 'first in, best dressed.' I made sure the so-called players who were going to do this or that to me were the first to go. I was given four cautions, three in the first half and one in the second – all this with a broken hand. To be fair, Mr Hughes did admit it was one of the best and hardest fought-games seen for many years. Maybe if the boot had been on the other foot and the Tigers forwards had been good enough and tough enough to dish out what they said was supposed to happen, he might not have complained so much.

I mention this because a certain prop forward for Smithtown, who had retired the season before, came up to me after that game and said, "Have you got a minute, Pom?" and went on to tell me what he thought of me and added that if he had been on the field I would not have dared to treat the Tigers in the way I did. I told him that if he thought he was good enough, the only way was to prove it was on the field of play, or outside if he so wished, but he declined my offer.

This 'gentleman' did make a comeback a bit later in the season and played against us in the second round game. He did none of the things he said he was going to do, and after a few scrums he did not even want to put his head in. On one occasion, he came high with a swinging arm and stepped right on to the end of my elbow. He never got up and they carried him off. Later, I went through a gap and out of the corner of my eye saw a Tigers shirt coming in high. As he went down, I passed the ball to one of my support players, Frank Evill, and we scored a try. I then looked back to see the player who had come in high on me, thinking it might be my mate, who had come back on again, but it was their young loose forward, Kyle, who, I am sorry to say, then had a broken jaw. He had been promoted for this game, and Geoff Trees had emphasised to him not, under any circumstances, to 'go high on the Pom, or you will suffer.' But he did and he did. I have always been a great believer of give and take – if you give it you have to be prepared to take it back.

In those days, rugby league was a hard game, in my opinion a lot harder than it is now, and it was a case of if you do not get them, they sure as hell will get you. In those days, there was a lot more underhand stuff went on – scrums were competitive, stiff arm and head high tackles were common, as was the use of the elbow, and shoulder charges were the norm. The occasional punch up was not such a great offence, and often a word from the referee after a melee was all that players received. I would add that a lot of the players in 'my day' would never get a game in today's modern rugby league.

We then went to Woolgoolga for what was, on paper, a certain win, were on the end of a shock 33-21 defeat. We had to come back fighting the following week when travelled to Coffs Harbour, but we had to make even more changes to the team due to injuries, losing prop Billy Kennedy, second-row Eric Carney and full-back Paul Thompson. We brought in three players from the reserves – Garry Kemp, Father Kevin King and our indigenous under 18s full-back, Fred Kelly. We also had a couple of newcomers in Tommy Sines and veteran winger John Niland. We were leading at the break 8-4, but not playing well, so I got stuck into them and gave them a real bollocking. I still had the previous week's shambles at the back of my mind.

Every time he touched the ball, Father King was being knocked about by their second row, who had obviously marked the priest as an easy target. I ripped in to Kevin, saying that I did not give a stuff what his job was off the field. Afterwards, I did think I was out of order but at that moment I had to lift the boys.

"You may be a priest," I said, "but if that bastard out there cracks you again and you turn the other cheek I will crack you myself! Stand up to the bastard! Now get out there and do it!" I noticed a couple of the faces of the Catholics in the room went ashen, they had never heard that sort of language to a priest before, nor do I suppose have they since. We started the second half not much better than the first, but one thing did please me. When Kevin ran onto a short ball from me and ran through a gap, the guy who had been giving him a hard time hit him with a head high shot, but Kevin hit him back with the best left hook you have ever seen and dropped him like a stone. After looking to the heavens for some divine inspiration, Joe Gauci the referee, 'Maltese Joe' as we called him, just shouted, "Play on!" We never saw that second-rower again.

Then Coffs scored again, we were 17-8 down with 15 minutes to go, and looking for inspiration – divine or otherwise. Then our centre, Geoff Vale, scored and Niland kicked the goal to bring us back to 13-17. Joe then gave us a penalty and I called up Toddy Watts to go for goal. There were some moans from our supporters but it was a great kick, straight between the sticks, making it 15-17. Tommy Sines, who had come on for Kemp, was having a blinder. He made a break into their 25, and after another couple of drives, was there again, taking the full-back with him to score. It was 20-17 to us after the conversion, with just five minutes to go. Then Tommy put me over to make it 23-17 and seal a great win for us.

Sines was an indigenous lad, who had come up from Sydney, where he had been playing for South Sydney Juniors, for 'personal reasons.' I will say no more than that, but he was great for us whilst he was in town, before going walkabout again. One day, he said to me, "Hey Pom, why you no drink in our pub mate?" I thought I would be the only white face in there, but one of the other guys in the team, who had a liking for aboriginal women, had overheard the conversation and butted in, "Yeah Pom, we will go in on Friday after training!"

Friday came and we duly arrived at the Great Western Hotel, where the 'locals' drank in the beer garden round the back. At the time, the Aboriginals still lived in tribes and had tribal laws, which they lived to. One of the main laws, I was led to believe, is that they have to share everything. If one person has money, he is expected to share it with his relations – and I think the same rule must have applied to their women. I was chatting to a few of the lads over a beer when one of the younger guys, who played in the under 18 team came up to me and said, "G'day Pom! Okay? You wanna root?" Root was Australian slang for sexual intercourse, and he asked if I wanted to 'root' his younger sister. According to the guy who was partial to these girls, and who was by then deep in pre-sex with a girl in the back of the pub, if an aboriginal man told a relation that she was to sleep with a guy, she was expected to carry out the deed. I told the kid I was not interested and thanked him very much for the offer. He went away and, thinking that was the end of the matter, I went into the front bar to have a yarn with the landlord and a couple of other guys.

Pubs closed at 10pm in those days and I went to my car to drive home, leaving my team-mate in the safe assumption that he had gone off with the girl with whom he appeared attached at the lips. At that point, out of nowhere, a young 'local' girl came up and said, "G'day Pom, I's with you."

Keith Pollard

"Like hell you are, love," was my reply.

"My bro' told me you wanted to root me," she said. It was unreal. I was standing in the street with a young aboriginal girl who was adamant that I was going to 'root' her. I told her to go home but she whinged on about not being able to get back to the 'Mission,' which is what they called the area where the majority of aboriginal people in Kempsey lived. She started crying because I did not like her and saying that she was stranded, so I said, "Get in the car. I'll take you home, but keep your head down. I do not want anyone to see you in my car."

As I drove her up to the Mission, she kept asking why I did not want to 'root' her, then she started trying to put her hand inside the leg of my shorts. I nearly crashed the car trying to fight her off.

"Come on, Pom – I want white cock," she kept saying. It was like being raped in my own car. I managed to get her to the Mission and dropped her off. Even then she asked me if I was going to see her again. I could not get away quickly enough. At the game on the Sunday, the team-mate who had talked me into going to the pub actually asked me how I got on and I told him the story about the journey.

"Oh, I saw you coming off at the Mission," he said. "I was in a layby near the turn-off. I thought you had been for a root!" I told him I was never going in that pub again – I was not going to be compromised like that again. It only needed someone to see you with a 'local' girl and it got around that you were 'playing up,' as the Ozzies call it.

Kempsey lost the next game at Nambucca, but finished the regular season on a winning note by beating Sawtel 18-8. This gave us third place in the 'ladder' as the Ozzies call the league table, so we had a preliminary-semi against Bellengen at Coffs Harbour. They were far too good for us and the inconsistency that had hampered us all season struck again as we lost 30-15. That meant that we had the game all the locals wanted – a minor semi-final against our old foes, Smithtown Tigers, on their own pitch. In our last encounter we had turned them over by 20-12 and in the first round they had beaten us 16-5, so this was our own Grand Final. It was a torrid affair in which we had too much speed and organisation for them, and came out worthy winners by 32-15.

The win took us into the final against Bellengen, but after being fantastic the week before against the Tigers, we were equally mediocre against the Magpies. We did not resemble the team that had put in such a fine performance seven days earlier. I had completed my two years with the Kowboys and it was the end for me another chapter in my life over and done with. I thought that I had taken them as far as I could. We struggled at times, especially in the second year, but you can only play with the cards you are

RED & WHITE PHOENIX

given, and sometimes they are not quite good enough to reach the very top of the pile. I like to think we left some good memories for the people we met, and we made friendships that have lasted for over 32 years. I may not have pleased everyone all the time, but I hope that I pleased most of the people some of the time.

I believe we left both clubs in a better place than when we joined them. I was once thanked on one of our return trips a few years ago by a guy I played with at Maitland, Kevin Cousins. We were at a reunion at a pub owned by an ex-player, when he put his arm around me and said, "Thanks, you Pommie bastard, for all you did for this club."

"What are you talking about?" I asked.

"You taught us how to play footy properly and made the team what it was," he replied. "But Jacky too – she really joined in with us Aussies and became one of the family." That's what the 'Pumpkin Pickers' were – a family. We took the same attitude to Kempsey and took a next to bottom team in one season to Minor Premiers and beaten Grand Finalists the next, then to third in the league and finalists in the second season, with just a set of young willing kids. As far as I know I only made one enemy – Mick Flanagan in Kempsey – and that was because I believed that finishing top of the league was more important than winning a Grand Final, which, as a 'Pommie bastard,' I stand by!

Before leaving Australia in September 1976, we called in at Maitland to see some of the friends that we would be leaving behind. There, I was approached by the chairman of a local club and asked if I would be interested in a coaching position in the Newcastle competition with Cessnock, one of Maitland's arch rivals. I declined the offer, telling them that I was going home – all our possessions had already been sent by ship and all we had left were three suitcases. We had come out with a ten-month old baby and were going back with another one, but there were four of us now. For good or for ill, we had set our minds on returning to the UK.

We arrived back home on a nice sunny autumn day, a lot wiser and a lot richer than the family that sailed away from Southampton nearly six years earlier. The four of us were now financially sound. We went with just £150 in our pockets and came home with £12,000 – most of it saved from my earnings from rugby. Those earnings set us up to buy things we could not have afforded if we had stayed in the UK. We could now afford to buy our own home, furnish it with all new furniture, buy a new car, and have a few quid left in the bank.

I always try to use the word we. It was a joint venture, and none of it could have happened without the help of Jacky. She was my 'offsider' as the Aussies call your no 1. Without her going along

Keith Pollard

with the move in the first place, then making new friends 12,000 miles from home, before upping sticks after settling in Maitland, it could not have happened. She was my tower of strength.

Scully Park, the home of West Tamworth, the club I was supposedto join in 1970

KEITH WAS YEARS AHEAD OF HIS TIME

Keith had a profound influence on my life in sport as a player and a coach. We have re-connected in recent years and share similar views on many issues relating to Rugby League in Australia and GB.

In the mid 70s a Englishman came to my home town of Kempsey in NSW to Captain & Coach our newly formed Kempsey Kowboys RLFC. I was in my mid-teens and all I wanted to do was to one day play for our Kowboys.

My dad was a student of the game and from the very first time Keith played and coached our town team my dad & I both agreed that Keith was the real deal and an exceptional, tough and smart

190

RED & WHITE PHOENIX

ball-playing forward. We had heard that he had played with outstanding sides in the rugged and extremely good quality Newcastle comp. We also heard he was a stand out player. The talk and rugby league gossip was 100% correct.

A few years later I have been lucky to sign to play grade in Sydney for North Sydney Bears & to have a fulltime career in rugby league coaching and working for the ARL and Super-league, NRL High performance at the Canberra Raiders, West Magpies and then Pro Rugby Union in Japan and NZ, so I hope I have learned a little about the rugby codes over the past 50 years.

Keith took a new club that wasn't any sort of contender before he arrived to a grand final in one year. He generated massive local community support and worked with a predominantly home-grown squad. Keith was years ahead of his time, he created never before seen plays that regularly left opposition sides dumbfounded and forced players to rise in their personal standards and performance. He was a big, tough, skilful forward with a magically subtle passing game. My dad often said the players were not game smart enough to fully exploit Keith's talent with the ball and his ability to carry and create space.

Later in my playing and coaching career I used many of the running lines and shape and plays I had seen Keith introduce 20 years earlier, that's how advanced Keith's game knowledge was and still is. Keith always had time to talk to, coach and encourage all of his players and my mates and myself. In Keith's second year I was fortunate enough to make rep teams for the Group and the North Coast and this opened doors for me later in my career. I only played Under 18s in Keith's last season, but he had a profound effect on my future. I dreamed of playing overseas because of Keith and later John Gray, the great English forward who I later played with at North Sydney.

Keith inspired me to not limit my goals and he showed me that thinking about the game we both played and loved meant that rugby league when correctly thought about is definitely a science. I have had the good fortune to work and coach with Mal Meninga, Bob Lindner, Michael Hagan, Craig Bellamy, Anthony Seibold and the late great Steve Rogers amongst others.

I value Keith's opinion and influence on my rugby league life in the same category that I rate my good fortune to have worked with the previously mentioned rugby league identities. I will forever be grateful for the influence Keith had on me during his time in my little home town and I am thankful for the fire he ignited in me to become a student of the game.

Paul Hamson - Coaching (Lev3 NRL HPC) Wynnum Manly RLFC U/20s & Academy S&C. PNG NRL Coach Consultant (ASCA Lev2 Pro)

CHAPTER 11
BACK IN THE OLD COUNTRY

We stayed with Jacky's brother and sister-in-law, Ian and Angela, again for a few weeks when we got back. I went looking for a job as soon as we settled in, but had not realised how bad things were in the UK, with over 1.5 million out of work. In Australia in those days, you could change jobs like you changed your underwear. We had heard about the 1973 oil crisis, the economic downturn in the United Kingdom, the three-day week imposed in 1974 as a result of fears about power shortages, but had read that economic growth had restarted in 1975 and the recession had ended. But we did not appreciate how bad things were. Inflation remained high, strikes continued to cripple manufacturing and public services, and the economy had only been bolstered by a multi-million IMF bail-out.

I still managed to find a job though. I went back to Abba's, the last company I had worked for in Hull, where the old manager, Jack Hutchcroft, had told me when I got married and left for Keighley to go back and see him if I ever wanted a job. Jack had left though, and I was told that they did not need anyone then. But, as I was walking out of the works, a lad I knew called Mike Smith was walking into the out-sales department. He asked what I had been doing and I gave him the story and told him that I was now looking for a job. Mike told me of a couple of outfits he thought might be looking for men, one of those being a firm called Croft Pipework. It transpired that Jack had left Abba's with Graham Evans and started Crofts, carrying out similar work. I found their workshop in Hessle, where I was greeted by Johnny Chapman, an old foreman from Abba's, who had also left to join them. Whilst I was talking to Johnny, Graham appeared. He was a great kid when I had last seen him – now he was in his thirties and a qualified engineer.

"Now then stranger, how are you? What you after?" he asked.

"A job!" I replied, "Anything doing?" He said that Jack had popped out but invited me into the office for a cuppa. Whilst we were catching up, Jack returned.

"Hello there! How are you? Nice to see you again," he said – a very polite old English gentleman to the last.

"Are you still living in the West Riding? Was it not Keighley you went to?" he asked. I gave him a quick version of the story – by this time I was getting fed up of it myself – it would have been easier to say I'd been in jail! Anyway, I was in luck, they had just been given a contract at Croda Chemicals, on Oak Road in Hull, to build new Hexane plant using equipment they had purchased from a factory that had closed down in Selby. They were reassembling it at their works. Crofts gave me a start the following Monday.

I reported to the works manager – Crofts had no foreman on site, so Croda were looking after the labour. I was taken to the cabins that we were using – two old railway goods wagons that had electricity wired to them – you would never get away with that now, but in those says it was the norm. I was introduced to the three guys on site – Keith Woods, Pat Ginelly, and Dave Woods. They showed me the job and generally filled me in. Pat was a fitter welder like me, and Dave was a pipe-fitters mate, but Woody was a was a semi-skilled fitter. Dave and Pat were already working together, so I teamed up with Woody.

It was an easy enough job. They had installed the two old vessels into a new steel structure in the hope that the original pipe-work would fit like for like. Their mistake was that the steel structure had been designed from old photographs and it being a mirror image everything was back to front. This meant that all new pipe work had to be manufactured and fitted on site. Another problem was that the workface was inside a 'no hot work' zone on the plant, so we had to take measurements, go to the temporary fabrication area, make it up, take it back and try to fit it. Without going into detail, the flanges on the vessel did not align either – it was a right cock-up. Instead of taking weeks it took months. We were working 54 hours a week and it was a gold mine for Crofts and us. With no supervision, we just plodded on – the Croda guys never came near the job, they had a plant to run. It was open season and, to be blunt, some of the guys were taking the piss. I would have sacked them, but it was not my place to say anything. The unwritten law of the construction game was that you did not 'dob' your workmates in, even if you thought what they were doing was wrong.

They thought I was odd because I was actually 'playing the game' – but, after six years working in Oz, I believed in a fair day's work for a fair day's pay. Back home, it was 'get as much as you can for doing as little as you can.' No wonder the country was going downhill. I could not believe it; I had been brought up to work hard. My old man was a hard worker and had taught me that to get on in life you had to work – no-one gave you anything for nothing. I had quite a few arguments with the guys I was on site with, and in the end I did my own thing. I told them I would not cover for them or tell lies for them.

I had been on that site for about six months when Graham came to see me and asked if I fancied a foreman's job. I thought, 'yes – on here, bloody hell yes!' I was disappointed when he told me it was on another Croda site – the edible oils plant on the river bank

Keith Pollard

on Stoneferry. The foreman they had was leaving to go to a job in Venezuela, and they wanted me to take his place. I was to be on more money and even if I was on a site without men to supervise, I still got the higher rate. I agreed and started the next week. Frank Charnley was the foreman who was leaving, and he showed me all the paperwork, order procedures and day-to-day site management. It was quite straightforward really, but I got £1 an hour more for doing it. I was introduced to the lads I would be working with – Harry Chatterton, a pipefitter/welder, Barry Middlebrook, a semi-skilled pipefitter, Ray Wealsby, a pipefitters mate, and Mick Rex, a welder. It was a good little crew and they turned out to be a decent squad of guys. I was a working foreman, which meant I still had to produce, whilst running the job at the same time. I was also the contact for the Croda engineers and site supervisors, so if anything wanted doing, they came and told me. It was all straightforward and simple; Frank left after a couple of days and I took over.

I noticed that, like Oak Road, the site was somewhat lacking in discipline – the guys seemed to come and go as they pleased. You may wonder, why spoil a good thing? But my mind did not work that way. It was not that they did not work hard when they were there, they did, it was a case of not getting there on time. They were nearly always late, especially one guy, with whom I had words after a few days on site. I did not want to start ruling with an iron fist, but if it was brought to Crofts attention – and you never know, when you are working alongside a plant workforce that have to clock on and off, who might complain about contractors – I would be the one to get it in the neck.

The official hours where 8am to 12-30pm and 1pm to 5-30pm; a nine-hour day with a quarter-hour tea break in the morning and afternoon and half an hour for lunch. I sat them down after a few days and told them what my ideas were as foreman and what I expected from them. I got a couple of looks that said, 'who the hell are you coming here and telling us what to do?' Frank had never laid the law down obviously. We were working every Saturday morning and every Sunday. In fact, I worked every weekend for the 18 months I was there. Most of the jobs that we had to do on a weekend were maintenance jobs – stripping out pipework or plant, replacing it and so on. Working every weekend was too much for most of the lads, so I told them that as long as we got the required jobs completed and running, ready for the process guys to come in on Monday and start work, we would be away Sunday afternoon before 2pm. I did this unbeknown to either Crofts or Croda management, but what they did not know did not hurt them and all went well for a while.

Then, in February, we were given the nod to tie some new pumps and tanks into the main oil feed lines to the bottling plant.

RED & WHITE PHOENIX

John Sutton from Croda came to me at the beginning of the week and said we could do it the following weekend. We did all the preparation work, I got the lads to prefabricate all the tie in pipe-work spools, which we then put them aside out of sight, as we often did to make it look as if we had done more on the weekend than we had. Then, on the Saturday morning, it was all hands to the pumps – forgive the pun! We stripped out all the old stuff and by lunch time we were running on gas. We then stopped for lunch and during the break the heavens opened and the snow came down – and I mean real snow. In those bygone days, the lads would not work in the rain or snow – three spots on a *Daily Mirror* and they were all in the cabins. I was up the creek. I told the lads if we worked through it, I would pay them 12 hrs for Saturday and Sunday. They agreed to the deal, but by mid-afternoon it was three inches thick and laying fast. We were okay with the job, the prefabrication work had been measured and fabricated accurately and went in with no problems. I told them to go home but needed them to turn up the next day or the deal was off.

I was living in Withernsea at the time, but managed to get home with no problem. The next morning it was a 'white over,' but I had to go in, and I struggled through the blizzards, arriving a bit late. The lads were out and working when I arrived on site. We worked right through with no tea breaks or lunch break and just had a cuppa on the run. The job was complete by 2 o'clock – we were drenched and cold but we had succeeded were others would have failed and I told the lads to get home.

The next day I got in and John Sutton was in rather early, for him anyway. He was chuffed as a dog with three tails. "How on earth did you get it finished?" he beamed. "How did you get in? I live in Hedon and couldn't get out of the drive."

"I had to drive through Hedon to get to Hull but I managed it" was my reply. He said "I am really grateful, I thought the bottling plant would be down and my balls would be cut off by production management"

"How grateful?" I asked. "I have told the lads they would get 12 hours for Saturday and Sunday." I did not know what his reaction would be, but he just told me it was no problem and to put it on the timesheet. Bingo! I thanked him and he went on his way. Then Graham came for the time sheets as usual on Monday morning and when he read them he said, "What's this? They won't pay those hours!"

"Don't argue, just do it," I told him. "John has agreed to the hours, and the more we get, the more you get." He was about argue but I interrupted him and said, "you pay me to run the job, and that is what I do – so off you go".

A few weeks later, he came in one Monday morning and said,

195

Keith Pollard

"I came on site on Friday afternoon and there was no one here."

"What time?" I asked.

"About 4ish," he said.

"Well, I am not surprised! Have you tried driving through Hull on a Friday afternoon?"

"But you are on pay until 5-30," he replied.

"What the fuck has that got to do with it?" I asked. "Listen Graham, we had this conversation the other week, leave the site to me. You get paid don't you? The work gets done doesn't it? Everyone is happy. Do you ever get a complaint from John? No! So don't rock the boat." Looking back, I was a bit out of order but never again did he come again on site at an odd time – or if he did he never let on.

After that, Crofts won a contract to install some refrigeration plant at the Birds Eye factory on Hessle High Road and Graham asked four of us to do a welding test for the job. I told him I was not prepared to do a higher class of work for the same money as I was already getting. Coded welders earned a far higher rate of pay than guys who worked in the industry we were working in. He asked me to do the test anyway and said we would sort it out later. We went up to Stockton to carry out the test. None of us had ever done this class of work before, but Harry Chatterton, Dennis Ferguson and myself passed; only Frank Charnley, who by this time had come back from his South American folly and was back at Croda, failed. Frank was then working under my supervision, something that did not go down well with him.

At Croda the following week, Graham came on site and said that he wanted me to go back to the shop to do some fabricating work, as they could not afford two foremen on one job. I told him to take Frank off the job and relocate him, as this was my site. He then said my money was going to drop by 50p an hour, so I reminded him about the deal that had been struck when I took the foreman's job originally. We argued, but at the end of the day he was the boss and there was not a lot I could do about it. I went into the workshop the following Monday not a happy bunny. When I got in, I was greeted by Johnny Chapman, who was plodding along towards retirement as workshop foreman.

"I have cut and prepped this lot for you.," he said. "So you can start on these drawings". When he gave me the drawings I saw the words *Birds Eye, Hull*.

"Fuck off!" I told him. "I am not working on this for the same money". He shot off to see Graham and Jack in the office. Graham came out and asked what the problem was I told him and reminded him of what I had said about coded work. I told him to get Harry or Dennis off their jobs to do it. Little did I know that I was the only one left. Dennis had fallen off a scaffold and hurt his back, and

RED & WHITE PHOENIX

Harry was on sick for some other reason. But he never told me that.
We argued and he asked me what I wanted extra to do the work. I
said I wanted 20p an inch per butt. He said, "No chance!"

"Okay, no problem. Sack me," I said. I was calling his bluff, but
deep down shitting myself he would. He disappeared into the office
and I stood my ground. He came back out and he said, "Jack thinks
you're holding a gun to our heads."

"Get the others to do it then," I said. "In fact, I will drop down
to tradesman's rate and fuck you and your foreman's job. Put me
on another site or swap me for Harry or Dennis." I was really
pissed off by this time. He went back in to see Jack, and then asked
me to go into the office. We had a bit of a heated discussion before
Jack said, "What if the butt is a repair or a cut out – who pays for
the repair?"

"I will do it in my own time," I said. "You will only pay me
extra for 100% x-ray passed welds". I pointed out that I would be
doing the other work as well, including fitting and preparation,
which coded welders would not do. In those days as well as now,
coded class welders did nothing but weld; whilst coded
fitter/welders were an animal that did not exist. In the end they had
no option to agree to my demands, as they were getting a good deal
and they knew it.

The job started and all the fabrication was completed in the
shop in about a month. We went on site and started the installation.
I heard through the grapevine that Harry and Dennis were really
pissed off when they heard what I was getting out of the job. They
tried their best to get a transfer onto it, but I made sure I worked
bloody hard to keep it all to myself. I completed it in about four
weeks without one repair or cut out. Every butt was 100% 'A
okay'. I was then transferred back to Croda Oils with Frank, but the
atmosphere was never the same and they did reduce my money by
50p.

I had been looking for another job for quite a while – I was sick
of working every weekend and thought I might as well be abroad
or offshore. I had tried several companies but you had to be
experienced or know someone in the game. There were quite a few
guys from Hull that were in the offshore industry and had done
quite well for themselves, but being away from Hull for nearly 10
years, I did not know most of them well enough to ask – apart
which it was not my style to grovel to some of those arseholes,
which is what some had become, with their inflated opinions of
themselves.

I know a few of them, like Tony McGowan, Howard
Laybourne, Dave 'Ginna' Robson and Pete Abba, but they told me
to ask others who were in more powerful positions. I did not want
to give them the satisfaction of knocking me back, I would rather

197

try and get on myself, which I did later on.

It was well known in the construction industry that Hull guys had a poor reputation. They would rather see you out of work than working in their industry. I was later on a job that was full of Geordies, who, unlike the Hull mob, do look after each other. At a tea break a guy asked me where I was from and when I said Hull the place went silent, so I followed up by saying not to worry because I was not like the rest of them.' Outsiders, or people other than the 'Hully Gullys,' as they are known, do not trust Hull people, and I am led to believe most of those to blame for this reputation are those who were the first to join the offshore industry in the early 70's.

I left the company in 1978 after nearly three years, when I got a job with Pullman Kellogg's in Algeria. I gave my notice in to Graham and he said he did not want me to leave. I did not fall out with him but just told him that I wanted to work abroad, that the opportunity had arisen, and I wanted to try it. Jack came to see me and said, "I would not go abroad to work."

"Jack, if I had my own company, lived in a big house up Heads Lane in Hessle and drove a fucking Range Rover I would not either," I said. He just nodded, wished me well and left. Crofts told me that if ever I wanted a job, to go and see them because I was always welcome back.

During my time with Crofts, we had bought a house in Withernsea, about 16 miles east of Hull. We had looked around Hull for a house but could not really find what we were looking for, and two of my cousins and Jacky's brother lived out at 'With' as we call it. We went out to look at houses there and found the one we wanted. It was a detached chalet-type bungalow joined to the next door by garages. It was perfect for us and we fell in love with it soon as we saw it. They wanted £12,000 for it, we agreed to buy, and arranged a solicitor.

That is when the trouble started. The bastard who was selling the house was bankrupt and to cut a long story short we had hell of a job with it. They could not give clear title to the land until her debts were paid, and she could not pay because she had no money. Even the flowers in the garden where not paid for. It was a mess. We had paid the £1,200 deposit and the problem only arose when they did the search on her. In the end, it took about nine months to sort out. All the creditors had to remove their writs on her to allow the sale to go through, then they served them again to get paid once the money was in the bank. We had been living in my Aunt Mary's holiday chalet through the winter, and had just started renting a flat when the sale went through.

So we eventually moved in to 9, Chellsway, Carrs Meadow, Withernsea. We were really happy there – not far from the town centre and the shops and pubs. With was then a busy little holiday, resort with quite a few static caravan sites, a large number of them holiday homes for people in the West Riding. It had a decent beach of mostly sand – not stones like a few on the east coast. We used to holiday in With' when I was younger and it was to Hull what Brighton was to London. I remember walking down the main street one day with Tracy, who was about six at the time, and she asked me what all the people were doing there.

I said they were on holiday, to which she replied, "On holiday in Withernsea? Why?"

She had been spoiled – we had been to Spain and Portugal quite a few times since we had returned from Australia, but had never holidayed in the UK.

Keith Pollard

CHAPTER 12
HANGING UP MY BOOTS

Hull FC had approached me when I got back home and asked if I fancied going down to the Boulevard. As I had always been a black and white when I was a kid, I thought it would be nice to finish playing by wearing the famous irregular hoops. By then I was 30, so I was getting towards the end of my career. I went to see the directors and discussed money. They told me they wanted to see me play before they would agree to any terms. I did not want a lot of money, but I did want a yearly contract, as I had been used to in Australia. At the time, this practice was not the norm in the UK, and they were not keen on the idea. I only signed forms allowing me to play as a trialist in the reserves and I played six reserve team games, the last one being at Bramley on a Friday night.

At the time, I was working for Crofts on a job at the Capper Pass smelting plant to the west of Hull, and arranged for the club coach to pick me up on its way to Bramley at the top of the Melton Lane. When it arrived, Mick Trotter, Ray Edmonds, Steve Mallinson and Peter 'Flash' Flanagan were about the only faces I recognised – the rest were mainly trialists. When we got to the ground, another couple of new faces turned up. I scored a try but we got beaten, which was not surprising given the team we had put out. After the game I overheard the assistant coach, Kenny Foulkes, a former Hull FC scrum half, discussing the game with one of the directors, Mike Page, in the bar. They were basically slagging the players off. I took umbrage to this and told them what I thought. Page tried to interrupt me when I was in full flow, so I told him that what he knew about rugby league you could write on the back of a postage stamp. I did not agree with the ideas of David Doyle Davidson, the head coach at the time, and was not enjoying being there, so I decided to end my association with the club.

Then, three weeks later, whilst in town on a Friday, I picked up a *Hull Daily Mail* and saw on the back page that I had been selected for the first team for the that Sunday. I was to make my first team debut at Keighley of all places. We called at Jacky's parent's house on the way back to Withernsea and her old man told me that the Hull FC secretary had been trying to get in touch with me to sign the forms to enable me to play in the first team. He had left the paperwork at a Hull director's house in East Hull, but it had to be done before 5pm that night. I went round to the house, and we discussed the signing-on fee. What I had asked for was agreed, so I signed. As it happened the game was off due to bad weather. I never got my signing on fee and they never contacted me again. It was a total shambles.

I went to watch a game at the Boulevard a few weeks later, where I met Brian Lockwood, the ex-Castleford and Great Britain player who was head coach of Wakefield at the time. I had known Brian whilst I was out in Australia and he was, and still is, a very good friend of mine. He was playing at Canterbury Bankstown when we left Oz to come home, and he and his wife Anne came to the airport in Sydney to see us off. He asked me if I fancied going to Wakefield to play in the reserves and bring the young lads on. I told him the story about signing for Hull FC but he called Alan Pearman, the Wakefield secretary, across. They agreed to pay me £8 a trip expenses and what they called squad money – £11, which was the first team losing money. It was as simple as that – no involvement of directors to verify the deal! Alan took me in to the Hull secretary's office to get my clearance from them.

"We haven't got his clearance from Australia yet," the secretary said.

"But you were going to play me in the first team at Keighley a couple of weeks ago, how could you do that without a clearance?" I asked. The clearance was duly provided.

I trained with Wakefield on the following Monday night, and played on the Thursday in the reserves against Castleford. We won and I fitted in with them as if I had been there all season. I had been told by Locky to organise them as a player-coach would, and they responded well to my prompting. I was in my element again. They were a great set of kids – the two Rayne twins, Keith and Kevin, who later moved to Leeds; Mike Lampkowski the ex-England rugby union scrum-half; stand-off John Crossley; and Paul McDermott, the younger brother of the current Leeds Rhinos coach. I played about eight games and everything was going well.

I did not want first team football as I was working every Saturday morning in Hull, and all the reserve team games were in Yorkshire in those days. Wakefield were happy the way things were going, and after a game at Batley the chairman congratulated me in the tearoom on the way the players were developing. Freddie Williamson was the reserve team coach, he was great to work with and I loved it. Then I got a call to play in the first team at Wigan because George Ballantyne was injured and they wanted me on the substitute's bench. I travelled over to Wakefield to pick up the team bus. Now Wigan at Central Park is no place to make your debut. I had never trained with any of the first team, I did not know any of the moves or plays, and Brian Lockwood had gone back to Oz to play for Balmain.

After about 20 minutes or so, one of the props came off with a foot injury. Freddie, who had taken over the first team duties, said.

Keith Pollard

"Get on and go number 8." As I went on, Ray Handscombe, the hooker said to me, "Get a grip of their prop – he is giving me a hard time". The prop in question was Brian Hogan, the ex-Warrington and Great Britain front-rower, who was bit of a handful to say the least. At the next scrum, I gave him a head butt and told him to leave Ray alone. He came up throwing his fists at me, so I grabbed him by the front of his shirt to make sure I did not get any more. I noticed that Bob Blackwood, their second-row, who was also no mug and did not mind a scrap, was trying to line me up to give me one, so wherever he went, I put Hogan in between us until the referee intervened. Hogan was moaning about me head-butting him and that I had started it. I think he was a bit taken a back that I had the audacity to hit him first. I said if he left our hooker alone, I would leave him alone, easy as that. We had no more problems with them for the rest of the game. We lost, as most teams do at Wigan, by about 15-8, but they had a very good side. Vince Karalius was coach, so they were taught never to take prisoners, so to speak. Internationals George Fairburn, at full-back, and Bobby Irving, in the second row, helped make them a formidable outfit.

That was my only first team game and my last game of any sort for Wakefield. The following week they were at Dewsbury in the Challenge Cup. Freddie told me I was in the squad – either playing if George Ballantyne was not fit, or 18th man if he declared himself fit. He declared himself fit and they got beaten. I went to training on the Monday, and as I walked in to the dressing room at 6pm, Freddie told me I was selected at No 8 for the first team for the next match at Rochdale. By 9pm I was on my way to Doncaster.

I was asked to go in to see the secretary, Alan Pearman, who asked me to take a cut in expenses, as I was costing them too much money when they were trying to cut costs. It seemed rather a coincidence that as I was picking up my wages that week, David Topliss, who was standing behind me, saw on the wage packet how much I was getting, and in his broad Yorkshire accent he said, "By! You're on't a good thing, Keith!" I said it was my travel expenses and he said no more. But when he asked me to take a reduction, Pearman told me that something had been said by one of the senior players about expenses payments to out of town players. All the locals got were bus fares. Pearman was adamant that I had to take a cut in expenses if I was to stay.

But a deal is a deal in my language, and if they wanted to break their word then that was it for me. I told him I would not take a cut, and if they did not like it then they could let me go. They did, and in the end they got rid of anyone who was costing them money. Mick Morgan, Ian Ellis, Howard Firth and Graham Idle all left for one reason or another. Topliss was the only one who had seen my pay packet that night, but I never met him again and did not the chance to confront him about it. There is no doubt that he was a great player and played in over 600 first class matches, but my experience of him left a bad taste with me. He passed away suddenly in 2008, so I will never find out the truth now.

Pearman also told me that Doncaster wanted me. At the time, Doncaster were the whipping boys of rugby league, and I was not keen. Those with longer memories may remember the film, '*Another Bloody Sunday*', which was based on their struggles. But the chairman of Doncaster rang me, and we talked. He told me they had been to watch another player in the Wakefield reserve team and were very impressed with my style of play. He said they wanted to build a team around me. He told me that money was no object and invited me to go to a game and discuss it with him. The old saying that when something sounds too good to be true, it usually is, was certainly right in this case. But greed got the better of me again, and I agreed to join them.

"Where are you playing this week?" I asked. It was Keighley again. I could not get away from that town. When we came home from Oz, we went back once with our kids when Jason was about 12 and Tracy six. We had been to Blackpool for a weekend and came home that way to show them where we used to live and the town Jason was born in. After driving around a bit we went to the *Turkey* for lunch. How it had changed since the last time we were in. It had been extended to about three times the size. Brian was behind the bar and told me he knew my face but did not know why. When I told him who I was, he greeted me like a long lost brother. We had a really good yarn and he told me how he had just sold the pub for ten times what he paid for it. I said that was not bad for a thirty thousand pounds outlay and he gave me a 'how the hell do you know that' look. He explained that he had sold it to furnish his conversion of the old mill into a hotel complex, which it was costing him a lot to do, as planning permission for buildings in that area was all conservation-related. He told me that he had started a brewery, *Turkey Ales*, and that one of his latest was '*Pommies' Revenge,*' which was his response to all the Australian beers that were coming onto the market then. I understand that he eventually sold everything up, but started up the brewery again, as the *Goose Eye* brewery, with Jack Atkinson in 1991. Sadly, Brian passed away in 2012, but *Goose Eye* is still brewing excellent local beers and has won a number of awards at CAMRA festivals.

I went to Keighley the following Sunday. They were midway up the second division, whilst Doncaster were bottom. I went into the dressing room to meet the coach, a former Hull FC man, Don Robson. I saw the most depressing dressing room I have ever been into. Each player was given a little black bag with shirt, shorts and a pair of socks. They were not laid out in the changing room, just

Keith Pollard

My swansong at Hull Dockers

thrown at the players by the baggage man. Hardly anyone was talking, and I was already thinking that I had made a mistake.

Don gave his pre-match talk and we went out on to the field. I tried to play my normal game, which was hard when I knew hardly any of the players' names. Tony Banham, another former Hull FC player, was one of the few I knew. I tried to read the game for the first few minutes. Then I spotted a gap and called to one of the second-rowers, a young lad from Wakefield called Norman Cooper, to come with me. I drew in the defence, put him through a gap, and we reached their 25-yard line. I then said to Tony Banham, "Come with me, you will score here." He was nigh on impossible to stop close to the line. I ran towards three of Keighley's players who were bunched together, and as I reached them I turned, expecting Tony to be with me. There was not a soul there and I was flattened by three of my old team-mates.

"Where the hell were you?" I said to Tony.

"I'm fucked" was the reply. I reminded him we had only been playing for about fifteen minutes and asked how could he be fucked when he had done bugger all. I have never professed to be a superstar, but I was too good for this mob. Luckily, just before half time I took a crack to the jaw, and honestly thought I had broken it. I could not open my mouth properly and my speech was like the ventriloquist's 'gottle of geer.' I came off and they sent me to hospital for x-ray. It was not broken but was misaligned, and I was told that that it would go back of its own accord in a few days.

When I got back to the ground to pick up Jackie and my car, Jacky was sitting in the tea room. I knew what she was thinking. I bumped in to Colin Evans, an old Keighley team mate, whose opening words were, "What the fuck are you doing playing there?"

"Good question," I mumbled. Colin went on to ask if I fancied going back to Keighley, but it was too far to travel and I was not going down that road again. No, this was the end of my professional career. 14 years as a pro and finishing on the scrap heap at Doncaster. I left the ground that night and never saw anyone from the Doncaster club again. No one asked how I was, or said see you next week – nothing. What a shower. It was no wonder they finished bottom of the league that year with just one win from 26 games. I waited a few days before I could talk properly and rang the chairman up. I told him I was not going to join them and gave him a few home truths. He put the phone down on me.

A few months later, I was training with Hull NDLB and whilst sitting in the dressing room picked up an old *Rugby Leaguer* weekly. My attention was drawn to an article that entitled 'Shortest Trial Ever.' It was about me. It not only said that I was not wanted by Doncaster, but that they knew by half-time that I was not the player they wanted. I got the name of the reporter, rang the editor of the *Rugby Leaguer* and managed to get his telephone number. When I rang him, he told me that what he had put in his article was what the club had told him. I told him my side of the story, and advised him to get back in touch with them. I said if I did not get a written apology in the *Rugby League*r, he would be hearing from a solicitor. As far as I was concerned it was a pack of lies and a defamation of my character. I rang him the following week and he apologised to me, saying that they had lied to save face. I told him that I had never been paid for playing that game, or given any expenses, in addition to which they had even kept my boots!

Two weeks later, he wrote an article that appeared on the front page of the paper, giving a more accurate version of events and saying that I had decided I did not want to join the Doncaster club. Sadly, that was the end of my involvement in the professional game. To be honest, my experiences at the three clubs since I had returned to the UK had left me totally disillusioned with the professional game.

The next season, 1977/78, I started playing with NDLB, which became Hull Dockers, in the Hull and District league. An old Hull KR pal of mine, Colin Cooper, was coaching them. I played a few games, including one in the John Player Trophy against Hunslet when we did very well, only losing by a narrow margin. But, once again, I broke my left hand a couple of games later and I realised that my career was finally over. I could not afford to be off work on sick with a young family and no insurance.

I went to work at Croda the next morning, the Sunday, and got the lads working before telling them I was going to the Infirmary to have an x-ray. I knew it was broken, just by the way it ached. I had enough experience of broken bones by then. They put it in a plaster cast and put it up against my chest in a sling. I said, "This is no good, I have to go back to work!" I had some welding I had to complete to finish a job off for Monday morning.

I rang Graham on the Monday and asked him if it was okay if I stopped at work. I could still weld, but not do the fitting side of it, and he agreed. The lads carried me for about six weeks whilst I acted as foreman and welded, whilst they did all the man-handling, erecting and whatever else was needed.

Whilst I was living in Withernsea and playing for Dockers I met an old mate of mine from Rovers, Danny Raper. Danny did a bit of bouncing, or door work, as they call it nowadays, and was working at *Withernsea Pavilion* on Friday nights – the dance night. He asked me if I fancied doing it, as they were short on numbers. Another lad I knew from Rovers, Charlie Mennell, was the organiser and he started me on. It was a doddle. They paid you cash in hand and you could have as much free beer as you wanted – so long as you were not drunk and unable to 'manhandle the clientele.'

The duties varied between being on the front door; patrolling the bar, where most of the trouble started; walking around the dance floor; keeping people from getting onto the stage when acts were on; and guarding the stage door to stop people going down to the dressing rooms. Another part of the job was to get the artist out and into their transport after the show. Sometimes, idiots full of drink thought they would be the big man and try to start a fight with the artist, and often young, and sometimes not so young, girls would try to get down to the dressing rooms for autographs, and anything else they could brag about after meeting the so-called pop stars of the day.

They did have some decent artists from time-to-time – Bonnie Tyler, Gino Washington and Alvin Stardust were all on when I was there. I was on the dressing room duty when Alvin Stardust finished his second spot and it was my job to get him into his motor and away after the gig. I knocked on his dressing room door, he called me in, and I had a yarn with him. He was a great guy with no airs and graces, and I told him I remembered him as Shane Fenton with his group the *Fentones*. He said, "Fuck off, you are not that old!"

Another night *Smokie*, the group from Bradford who had top ten hits with *If You Think You Know How to Love Me*, followed by *Don't Play Your Rock 'n' Roll to Me, Living Next Door to Alice* and *Oh Carol.* They were a really good set of lads too. A few extra bodies were brought in to help out as a large crowd were expected, and sure enough it was packed. I was with a few of the lads on seats in front of the stage with a scaffold-type barrier between the stage front and the audience. We had been over the barrier a couple of times to sort out some minor fights that had started, as the crowd were getting a bit rowdy waiting for *Smokie* to come on, and one or two scuffles had broken out. The music started but the curtains were still closed and there was a smoke machine working. Smoke was rolling out and over the edge of the stage when the curtains opened and the band ran forward to what they thought was the front of the stage. The lead singer game right over the top and landed in my lap guitar and all. With that a huge guy picked me and the singer up and threw us both onto the stage. Fortunately, the lead singer was okay, got himself together, and the band played on.

Afterwards, I asked the monster who picked us up why he had picked up me as well as the lead. He told me it was easier to pick up both of us than try and untangle us in front of a load of screaming girls. He said he did not have time to think, he just acted as best he could as I happened to be in the way, I had to go as well! He apologised and asked if I was okay. Apparently, he was one of the roadies, who acted as a body guard for the group. I was talking with the group later and they said they thought the edge of the stage was where the crowd were, they did not know about the gap in between.

I was standing at the door to the dressing rooms that night when a young lady asked if she could go down to the dressing rooms for some autographs. I politely told her no, but she started to tell me how she was a great fan of the group. She was obviously very well brought up, because when I refused her again she said, "I will give you a blow job if you let me go down." I thanked her for the offer, and told her that I was happily married. I am sure you can imagine the response when I told the lads about it later. I believe *Smokie* are still performing – not the same group of guys, as one of the originals died after their tour bus was involved in accident in Germany later.

Bonnie Tyler was a real decent sort and a very talented and good-looking girl. I went down to the dressing room to see if she was ready to leave, and when I knocked on the door a Welsh voice called out, "Come in!" She was standing with her back to me zipping up her dress – quite a sight to behold. She said, "Hello love, help me with this would you?" in her Welsh singsong voice. I walked forward and, ever the perfect gentleman, zipped up her dress for her. She turned and smiled, "Thank you love – what's your name?" she asked.

"Keith" I replied.

Keith Pollard

"Thank you, Keith, it's a good job you arrived. I was struggling there a bit – I was just about to take it off again. Bloody zippers!" I was quite surprised how small she was – she always looked bigger on TV. She offered me a drink and we chatted for a quarter of an hour or so then she said, "Okay, let's go love – I'm ready for bed." There was no answer to that.

Not long afterwards, I got the nod to leave on my first overseas job – apparently employment agencies do not class emigrating 12,000 miles to Australia as working overseas!

KEITH WAS ONE OF THE MOST UNDERRATED PROP FORWARDS IN ENGLAND

It is a pleasure to be asked to contribute to Keith's book as we go back a long way.

I first met Keith when playing for Castleford under 17s in the Yorkshire Cup in 1962, when we were drawn away to Constable Youth Club on Reckitts ground over in Hull. At the time it was thought that we were reputedly the best Youth team in Yorkshire, but found that not to be the truth when they blew us away and Keith was one of the forwards who kicked us off the field.

We played against each other on numerous occasions over the years both at Hull KR and Keighley. Also often having nights out in Castleford, as Keith and his wife Jacky used to stop over with Keighley hooker Tony Pell.

We met up in Australia socially when he was up in Newcastle and I was at Canterbury Bankstown, but never actually met up again until I was coach at Wakefield Trinity. We were looking for someone to assist the Coaching Staff to help bring on the crop of good young players in the reserves, an 'Old Head' so to speak.

I met Keith one night at the Boulevard and asked him why he wasn't playing as I had heard he had gone there on his return from Australia. He told me he was not playing for one reason or another. I had always thought Keith was one of the most underrated prop forwards in England and was sure he could do the job we wanted at Trinity as he had been a player-coach in his last couple of years in Australia.

We signed him straight away, and he played his first game in the reserve team against Castleford at Belle Vue the following Thursday. I went back to Balmain later that season, happy that Keith was doing just as I thought he would, but things changed whilst I was away and when I returned Keith had left the club.

Brian Lockwood - Great Britain, Yorkshire, Castleford, Hull KR, Oldham, Widnes, Balmain and Canterbury Bankstown

RED & WHITE PHOENIX

CHAPTER 13
THE GREATEST GAME

I would like to continue my story with some personal thoughts on what I believe to be the greatest game of all – rugby league.

Rules: In my humble opinion, the powers that be have tried to make a science out of a simple game. Australian Jack Gibson, who I believe was the daddy of all coaches, was the first to go to the USA and bring sports science back to our game. For example, eating the right foods, living the right lifestyle, the mental side, and so on. I do not knock that, but we must never lose sight of the fact that there are only five basic aspects of rugby league – running, tackling, backing-up, passing the ball and kicking.

For a prop-forward like me, the game was a lot harder during the days of the unlimited tackle rule. It was a lot tougher to make the hard yards then. Now there is more room to run, and the game is a lot faster and better organised. Around 1967, when the four-tackle rule was introduced, it was said this would be the end of the big forward. People thought that the big men would not cope with the speed required in a game requiring more mobility in forward play. I had been playing under the old rule for five seasons against some very big packs like Huddersfield and St Helens – and even the lower sides had big men, like Trevor Walker at Batley and David Horne at Bramley. But when the four-tackle rule came in, other big men, like Mike Harrison at Hull FC and Jim Mills at Widnes, thrived on the new rules. Also, younger more mobile forwards like Phil Lowe at Rovers and Mal Reilly at Castleford were coming through and were thriving on the open play in the 'new game.'

In Australia, the star forwards under the unlimited tackle had been men like Artie Beetson at Easts, Elton Rasmussen at St George and Jim Morgan from South Sydney, but they were all massive men who could run like backs and revelled in the new rules.

When I was in Newcastle, there were some members of the board of directors of the NSWRFL who wanted to revert back to the unlimited rule for the 1974 season. There had been a sharp decline in spectator interest, gates had dropped quite a bit, and the board was very worried. The thinking was that if they brought back the unlimited rule, crowds would come back. Who knows what the outcome would have been if Mr Ken Charlton's motion had been passed.

I would have liked to see a 10-tackle limit introduced. There is

209

far too much panic football when teams get to the fifth tackle, and to me it has become stereotyped. Most teams do much the same thing – three or four drives, maybe a set move and then a kick on the last. Having ten tackles would give teams the opportunity to try different things and express themselves more.

Over the years, there has been much nonsense written about rugby league being a dirty and violent game, fit only for thugs, and efforts have been made to 'clean up' the game. In the past each team had one or two 'star' players, who were often heavily marked or subject to rough treatment to take them out of the game – but now the players are of very much the same standard and are often of a similar size, so opponents cannot single out anyone for 'special treatment'.

Most of the foul play was reported to occur in and around the scrum. I have played against some of the wildest, hardest, and most powerful men ever to put on a jersey and I believe all the hype about foul play is grossly exaggerated. Occasionally games did erupt, and there were odd 'head bangers' at some clubs, but mostly the game was played hard but fair. Nowadays all games are scrutinised by the judiciary panel and there is very little foul play at all.

If rugby league had been such a dirty game, so many players could not have played for ten or more years. Most injuries are invariably to knees or legs, and occasionally arms and shoulders – but not heads. Players learn that the most important thing is always to try and position yourself to take the ball on the move, so that you are much less likely to get hurt. If you take it standing still, you are asking for trouble. The best players will always be those who can 'read the game,' and can maintain their concentration.

Training: One lesson I learned 'down under' was that the player who is prepared to train hard, has faith in his own ability, does what his coach tells him, and, most importantly, plays for his team, will do better in the game than even he thinks he can. Many forwards discovered that since the new rules came in, they opened up new opportunities.

Being quite honest, until I went to Australia and joined Maitland, I had never really properly trained. That is no disrespect to any coaches I had trained under, but the training in Oz was just more intense and harder. I remember two Great Britain internationals who played down there telling me that, 'the game is the easy part of the week.'

There are a lot of people who do not know much about the game, who can only see the 'stars' in the team; the real supporters will appreciate the workers, the lads who put in 80 minutes every game. Any player who enters the arena less than one hundred per cent fit, is not only kidding himself, but letting down his coach and team mates. He will not be able to produce the performances that the coach, team-mates and supporters expect of him. The effort a player must be willing to put in during a game will quickly expose his weakness if he is not in top condition and will show him up to be the fool he is. One word sums up what is required alongside being fit for the job – enthusiasm. This is a crucial quality a sportsman requires when putting his body through the pain barrier both in training and on the field of play. Lack of both effort and enthusiasm in a player often leaves great talents undiscovered, and if players do not have this in their youth, they never will have.

In rugby league, as in any other sport, a player's success is largely determined by his keenness rather than his natural ability. It is often the case that players have 'not made the grade,' not because they did not have the ability to play the game, but because they did not put everything they had into a match when it mattered. A player must be willing to train until it hurts. That is the only way it will get him into the kind of physical condition required to get him fully fit. For being in top condition makes you brave, whilst being unfit brings the coward out in you. When a player can go the full eighty minutes in a game and come off battered and bruised but looking forward to next week's game, that is a sure sign that he is fit.

A player who has no stomach for training will only go through the motions as far as he has to, and when it starts to get hard he will pack it in. He will never reach the level of fitness required – he is a wasting his own time, the coach's time and is letting everyone down. He might as well stay at home with his feet up.

Coaching: The Australians used to use the term 'patterned football' which meant that the game was being played strictly to a set pattern, a trend that follows American Gridiron, which is probably the most completely pre-planned of all football codes. The game has become a challenge between coaches, each trying to out-plan his opposition coach. Every week, clubs plan and rehearse every likely scenario, both in attack and defence, that can occur during the 80 minutes of the game. In this, the game has become a bit robotic, with players having to be in certain places at certain times. The old way, of playing what is in front of you, has largely dropped out of the game. I believe that whilst they have cleaned up the game to protect the skilful player, they have taken the skill out of the game.

In today's game every player has a greater responsibility in defence than ever before. This is because each player has a specific defensive job to do. If he fails, someone must try and cover for his mistake, or this could totally wreck the whole defensive pattern. One of the worst situations is when a man 'shoots the line,' where he runs up to make the tackle much quicker than the players alongside him, but most times misses the tackle and leaves a gap or

Keith Pollard

an overlap for the opposition to exploit.

Let us look at a few of the components that make up a successful rugby league team, starting with the 'Head Man,' the coach. What is a Rugby League coach? He is a tactician, slave driver, father figure, diplomat, peacemaker and, in some people's eyes, he has to be a super hero. But when taking on the job, he is first of all an idiot – for when a team plays well it is the players who get the plaudits, but as soon as they start to lose games he will get the blame.

Coaches need various different qualities to create a successful Club – not just a team but a club, because if you do not have the right atmosphere at all levels within the club you will not get success. I played under numerous coaches during my chequered career, all of them different, most had different qualities and odd ones no quality at all. They all left an impression on me in one way or another, and here is a list of them starting from my first rugby league team that I played for at age 11.

Jim Watts, Boulevard High School 'C' team - Only had time for his star players (which did not include me)

Stan Adams, Boulevard HS 'B' and 'A' teams - School deputy head, ex-professional referee; very good - a disciplinarian and good man-manager (also gave us a three penny piece each if we won)

Ronnie Everett, Constable Youth Club - One of the best 'father figure' coaches I played under, not very technically minded but could manage and get kids to play for him; left to join Hull KR as their first academy coach

Jim Tong, Constable Youth Club - Ex-Hull KR captain; took over from Ronnie, to whom he was assistant when we won the Yorkshire cup; a great bloke with similar qualities to Ronnie

Wilf McWatt, Hull KR 'A' team - Ex-Hull KR captain; my first professional coach, a quiet man who never said much and did not demonstrate coaching qualities

Bob Coverdale, Hull KR 'A' team - Ex-Great Britain World Cup winner, player-coach; hard as iron but a true gentleman, led by example and really looked after the younger members of the team (something I feel is lacking now there is no reserve team football)

Ronnie Mills, Hull KR 'A' team - Ex-Hull KR half back; nice guy but never said much at training or offered any criticism or guidance

Tommy Harris, York RLFC - Ex-Hull FC and International hooker; I learned more from him in a six-match loan spell than anyone I had previously played for (he asked me to join York permanently but Rovers would not let me go)

Colin Hutton, Hull KR First team - Ex-Widnes & Hull FC full-back; often credited with instigating the rise in Rovers fortunes, but undoubtedly was given a much stronger playing squad to work with (big players like Alvin Ackerley, Harry Poole and Frank Foster did not need coaching and did all the organising on the field of play); only once in my five years at Rovers did he offer me any help with my game

Don Metcalfe, Keighley RLFC - Don and I did not hit it off at all – we just did not see eye to eye, he was not there long after I joined the club in 1967

Alan Kellett, Keighley RLFC - Ex-Bradford Northern; another who was on the same wavelength as me, I was playing in the same positions as Barry Potter, whom he had brought from Bradford with him on the promise of first team football, no matter how well I played, he always brought me off to put his mate on

Mick Clarke, Keighley RLFC - Ex-Leeds & International forward, player-coach; without doubt the best coach I had played for until then, a master craftsman at his job, knew the game inside out, took the time to help everyone in the club; a great bloke of whom I cannot speak too highly

Gus Ryan, Maitland Pickers RLFC 3rd Grade - Gus was a very good coach with the hardest job in the world; every week he was given the guys who had been left out of the two grades above his, in a very strong club; I was lucky enough to be picked to play in his squad when I first joined the club and he was a great help to both me and my family in settling in with the club

Gordon 'Coogan' Lawrence, Maitland Pickers RLFC 2nd Grade - Another great assistant coach; he was a hard task-master who ruled with an iron fist, an excellent communicator, I played a lot of games for him in my second year and learnt a lot off him in many ways

Terry Pannowitz, Maitland Pickers RLFC - Ex-NSW and Australia, player-coach; there are not enough adjectives to describe this man, I had never trained properly in my life until I joined the Pickers, he was a fitness fanatic and without any doubt the best leader I had ever played with, he actually coached the team so they knew exactly what was expected of them

Lloyd Hudson, Kempsey Kowboys RLFC - 'Lloydy' was my assistant at the Kowboys when I joined as captain-coach in 1975, he was very helpful and a very good coach in his own right, we bounced ideas off each other, he was a very good listener but always ready to offer his opinion; all first-team coaches need someone who they can trust and who they know will not stab them in the back to get their job – Lloydy was such a man

Ronnie Boden, North Coast Representative XIII - Ex-Australia and NRL player; I played for Ronnie twice and without doubt we won one of those games due to his input (the other we had no chance of winning), a great man manager, especially for

213

one-off representative games.

David Doyle Davidson, Hull FC First team - One of the worst coaches I have ever played under, I did not see eye-to-eye with him on this ideas, he was always criticising his players publicly (one of the most important lessons for a coach is to praise in public and criticise in private); he was the main reason I lost interest in the professional game

Ken Foulkes, Hull FC 'A' team - Very much in the mould of Doyle-Davidson, a laughing assassin who stabbed his players in the back

Brian Lockwood, Wakefield Trinity RLFC - Ex-International forward; I was not long with him at Wakefield but I always respected him

Freddie Williamson, Wakefield Trinity RLFC - Worked with him when he was A team coach at Wakefield – he was great to work with and seemed to know his game

Don Robson, Doncaster RLFC - Held possibly the least wanted of all coaching jobs in the game in the UK – a poisoned chalice if ever there was one – the club needed more inspiration than he could offer

The coach's first priority is his players and he must learn to be a bit of a psychologist, working out which guys need a good bollocking when they deserve it and which need an arm around their shoulder away from the group. He must also be someone to confide in if things are not going right. This applies from junior level to seasoned professionals – a coach must take responsibility for his charges throughout. A coach must have a bit of an edge, not being big-headed or cocky, but with an air of confidence in himself, that he can convey to his players. They must believe in him, and want to work both on the training pitch and on the playing field for him. People like Jack Gibson and Wayne Bennett seem to be able to get the best out of sometimes average players and turn them in to stars.

A coach also has to be thick-skinned. There are always supporters and ex-players who know better than he does and could do the job better. He must not let these outside influences get to him, which, believe me, is harder than it might seem.

The coach needs a good assistant; someone who he can trust, who will give another opinion, or whom he can bounce ideas off. Trust is the most important facet. He needs to know that he always has an ally, a person who will be honest with him, and who is not after his job. The assistant does not have to have been the best player in the world, but he obviously must know the game and what the coach is trying to achieve. The best scenario is that the coach has actually brought the assistant into the club with him, or if he was already there, at least had the opportunity to find out if he

214

RED & WHITE PHOENIX

can trust him and work with him. If he cannot, then unfortunately for the assistant he must go.

Coaching is a hard game and if things do not work out, that will be the end of it – so you must be sure you have guys around you that buy in to your ideas and plans. If you do get the right guy alongside you it gives you the opportunity to try and tutor each player individually as well as in the team scenario. By working on a one-to-one basis you can learn about a player's temperament and personality, how you can use his strengths, and work on his weaknesses, so that when you pick him for your squad he fits into the jigsaw. The main objective is to produce a squad of 17 players, working as a team, using each other's skills and strengths, and covering each other's weaknesses.

I have always thought that only group coaching brings the best out of players, but others will have different views. The ultimate ambition is to send on to the field 13 players all thinking alike, knowing what each other is going to do, both in defence and attack. This does not come from just playing together, it comes from playing for each other, for the team and for the club. Once a coach has engendered that team and club mentality and loyalty, it is that spirit that wins games.

A coach must ensure that no-one else is in the dressing room at half-time and at the end of the game, when he is talking to his team – there is nothing more belittling or embarrassing than for players to be bollocked publicly as a team or individuals. I cannot over-emphasise, 'praise in public, criticise in private.' Sometimes, especially in junior rugby, I have seen coaches standing in the middle of the field calling hell out of individual kids in front of their mates for some mistake or other. Sometimes, you even see parents trying to talk to their kids whilst the coach is talking.

Having said all that, there is no better feeling than when you see an improvement in an individual player's performances after you have worked with him, or when you see a move that you have practiced on the training field week after week come off to perfection. You can feel real pride.

Unfortunately, however, I have found that often an interfering relative can be the worst influence on a player. When you are coaching at youth or amateur level, you may only have them two nights a week at the most, plus a couple of hours on match-day – whilst relatives are with them much more and can have a greater influence on a player. Some relatives are frustrated coaches and cannot resist telling the kid how he should play – and most times they would not know a scrum from a tea party. The poor player is torn between what his coach is telling him and relative. It can be disastrous for the player, who ends up getting left out of the team, and for team-mates when the player does not do what they expect him to. Sometimes a quiet respectful word may work, but a heavy-handed approach will mean that you have an enemy on the touchline telling everyone how useless you are.

Often the coach is required to come up with some inspirational quote in the dressing room and I have sometimes used little things I have picked up during my career. One of the most famous was back in 1914 before Great Britain's decisive third test match in Australia. The team had several injuries and the players were in need of a rest. Mr John Clifford, the team manager, addressed the players.

"Sit thi'sens down and shoot oop," he said in his broad Huddersfield accent. He stood there for a few seconds to let the players absorb the dressing room atmosphere before restarting, "You are playing in a football game this afternoon, but more than just that you are playing for your country and even more than that, you are playing for right against wrong. You will win because you have to win. Do not forget that message from home – Great Britain expects every one of you to do his duty"

The captain, Harold Wagstaff, wrote later, 'We were tremendously moved and thrilled as never before or since. You could see our fellows clenching their fists as he spoke those words. When he left the room no one spoke not even myself. At one stage the team were down to nine men, but Great Britain won by 14 points to six to keep the Ashes.'

It is the coach's job then to mould a match winning formation even although some of the players are journeymen and not superstars. As long as they can carry out the basics of the game and are willing, the so-called stars can use them to give the coach everything he needs to mould the squad into a winning combination. There is no room for pig-headed individualists, selfish players who play only for themselves. They not only undermine the team spirit, but disrupt any co-ordination that the coach is trying to instil into the squad.

Captaincy: The next most important member of any team is the captain. That means he not only leads the team on the field and directs operations, ensuring that the coach's instructions are carried out were possible, but also he must be allowed to put his stamp on the team. I believe that he must be allowed to play what is in front of him, whilst having a structure to fall back on when things are not going to plan. The captain must know when to settle the team down, which can be very difficult in the modern game when there are times when teams are try to score tries from every set of tackles. But, in those circumstances, the game needs to be slowed down so you can regroup.

If you are on top in defence, it is ok to just make some hard yards and let the forwards drive in for a full set of tackles – on which subject, I will never understand why wingers are now used to drive the ball out from their own quarter when they simply do not have the strength and weight to do so.

The captain must have a thorough knowledge of the game, good playing ability and gift of leadership. But the best captain in the world will struggle to be a success leading a team of brilliant players who will not play for each other – 13 individual players who just happen to wear the same coloured shirt. No matter whom the captain is if he does not have the support of his players and their desire to play as a unit, he may as well not be there. Captaining a team of average players who are willing to but their bodies on the line for 80 minutes and play as a unit will be a hell of a lot easier at any standard. The very best captains will be able to mould disparate individuals into a team.

A captain should also form part of the 'social committee' to ensure that there are functions, throughout the year including off season, to get players and their families together. Wives and partners need to be involved – if the partner is happy, it is a hell of a lot easier on the player, especially in the modern game where players are living away from home. If a partner is at home, bored and with nothing to think about, and the family other side of the world, it puts extra strain on the player.

Creating a family atmosphere engenders a bonding that money cannot buy. Our time at Maitland contained some of the happiest days of our lives and we made friendships there that have lasted nearly 40 years. Few of us were star players but we played in three grand finals in four seasons and we were a star team.

In my years in the game, with no disrespect to any of the captains I played under, Harry Poole, Terry Pannowitz and Mick Clark where the best ones that I had the honour of playing with, but the daddy of them all must be John Sattler, the former South Sydney Rabbitohs prop. Sattler played a full grand final with a broken jaw and led his side to victory. To play through the pain barrier is the ultimate sacrifice any man can give to his team. Sam Burgess did the same later on, but Sattler's performance, when the game was a lot more physical and the scrums were a real battle, makes him the 'king.'

Ironically, if Sattler had been playing now he could well have been overlooked. He did not start playing rugby league until he was fifteen when he was a Maitland boy who joined Kurri Kurri in the Newcastle area competition. By the time he was nineteen he had made the Newcastle Representative team and was chosen to play against the British touring team in 1962. One of his main attributes was his strength. His cousin, Max McMahon, who played with me at Maitland, once told me he used to train horses to trot by putting on reigns and running behind them, without the buggy. He held them back with his arms and reckoned it was better than gym work as you used every muscle in your body at same time – arms, legs, the works. I take his word for it.

Junior Rugby League: The whole of schoolboy and junior rugby has changed dramatically since I was a boy. We only played at school and then we started at the age of 11. There was no 'mini rugby' in those bygone days. The Australians were ahead of us when this started to change in the 1960s. Instead of starting in their early teens, kids were starting to play at five or six years old. When I first went to Maitland I could not believe how young they were playing competitive rugby. Some were playing three games a week for school and their junior clubs and some trained every day. Boys who did not pick up the game until say, ten, were disadvantaged, as they then had to catch up the other lads. Some of the lads had reached a hundred games before they were ten years old.

In addition, there was such an intense competition between football codes in Australia that was almost obligatory to supply schoolboy teams with free passes to professional games, whilst a lot of clubs supplied kits and equipment for training. It is often said now that kids are given too much and are spoilt, but that clubs have to try and get players to play the game. Often parents would rather go away for weekends or have their young protégé play the piano or violin rather than get himself knocked about chasing a leather egg. I read once that in Australia, the game was founded by men who sometimes walked ten miles to play a game and then ten miles home, because they could not afford train and ferry fares. In those early days, first grade got $1-50 a season and actually thought they were well done by. It is a sharp contrast to clubs bribing kids to play for them by giving them stuff. In my opinion, a boy who needs this kind of wooing is better off out of a team as he is unlikely to give a full effort to the team. He will think he does not have to try that hard as he was begged to join them.

When I was first in Oz, I could not believe the standard and numbers of kids that played the game. At the annual NSW schoolboy carnival, over 200 teams took part, on 18 grounds with over 3,000 kids in one place, and with ages ranging from five to 18. I read some years ago that there were over 100,000 boys playing rugby league in Sydney alone and this has grown over the years. A couple of years back, 34,500 kids played in a carnival in the western suburbs of Sydney, shared between Penrith and Parramatta. No wonder they are that far in front of us. This is without the Country RL and all the other 25 divisions split in two groups – just imagine the pool of players they have to pick from.

Learning positional play and where to run is vital at an early stage. Naturally, everyone wants to handle the ball, it is a ball handling game after all, but every player cannot get his hands on the ball all of the time. At under-six to under-nines they run about like bees around a honey pot, all wanting the ball. It is not until they are about 10 that they start learning positional play. I believe that a coach at this age should be talking to them individually and explaining clearly what their duties are within the team, and teaching them to remain in position. There is nothing worse or more frustrating to a coach than seeing a kid wandering out of position and putting pressure on other team members. I believe that there is nothing more beneficial to a team of young boys than knowing where to be at the right time in the right position – this improves them faster than anything else.

There has often been a difference of opinion on the benefits of touch rugby games. Boys must be allowed to play it or they tend to lose interest quickly. Coaches must mix the training and touch rugby together – it is called game conditioning. I have often stopped a game mid-stream and told the boys to stay where they are. You can then see if each boy is in the right place, and ask them why they are in a particular place. This teaches them positional play on the fly. It is best to try and train away from the parents, who may be waiting or watching the session. Boys do not like to be watched by parents, as they get self-conscious about it. If it happens, and a boy does not appear to be listening, because he keeps looking at his mother or father, the coach should have a quiet word later – the boy thinks he is special because he is being picked him out, and he is not being reprimanded publicly.

Coaches must never discriminate between the better players and the ones not so naturally gifted. Sometimes those not so gifted at the beginning become the better players, because they have often worked harder at their game to apply themselves more. I have seen 'star' first-team players who were the no-hoper at school. I was never a star, but I was always the last one picked when we used to play in the street and the two 'best' players picked the team from the rest.

Defence: The Australians have always based their game on defence. Tackling is the main priority. If they win a game 1-0 they are happy because the opposition have not scored. They do not think the tackling is as good here, and when I first went to Australia they used to have a go at me saying, "They can't run without their legs, Pom!" After playing there for six years, I now realise that there is no better feeling than when you hit a guy with a full 'ball and all' tackle – the surge of elation that goes through your body after stopping him is immense.

But the Aussie game was totally different in everything. For example, at half-back, it always used to be said that English half backs were not supposed to tackle, whereas the Aussies have always made their half backs tackle, going back to the times of the great Barry Muir. Muir came up against Alex Murphy many times and I am led to believe that the honours were 50-50, not that I think Alex would agree.

Some of the Australian forwards were quite brilliant in defence, and probably the best of them all was Johnny Raper, whose timing and execution of the tackle were superb. To be fair though, the British had some great tacklers, and Vince Karalius, one of our best, was to me on a par with Raper.

I think that in retrospect, the reason why we could match the Australians in the period up to 1970 was that our forwards were better all round. The majority of our 'greats' could do everything, especially the props, whereas the Aussie props were not allowed to pass the ball, and in some cases could not pass the ball.

My best players: During my career in the professional game I played with some great players, both at home in the UK and also in Australia. Below is my selection of the best three players in each position that I played alongside during my career. They are not all big name players but were all excellent in their positions and would always be there when you needed them.

1. Full back

Cyril Kellett (Hull KR) – a great defender; not very quick but could shepherd the opposition player towards the touchline in defence; excellent goal-kicker

Brian Jefferson (Keighley) – to me the inventor of the 'up n'under;' a wonderful player could do anything; read a game from the back; never stopped talking; represented England; great goal-kicker

Ken Shine (Maitland) – fantastic goal-kicker; very strong in defence; clever footballer (finished up as Head Coach of South Sydney Rabbitohs)

2. Right wing

Graham Paul (Hull KR) – 'the Cornish Express;' not big in stature but nevertheless a great finisher; one of the all-time greats at Craven Park

Mick McTiernan (Maitland) – the fastest winger I ever played with; actually raced a horse on a handicap system and the horse beat him by a nose; with better eyesight he would have been a world beater

Dick 'Hooker' Bailey (Kempsey Kowboys) – Dick was a winger in a second-rower's body, on the wing; coming inside to run off the edge of the ruck he was devastating; speed to burn; should have been played at a higher level

3. Right centre

Terry Major (Hull KR) – the hardest centre I ever played with; GB under 24 team captain and would have been a full international had not been for the number of great centres around in his day

RED & WHITE PHOENIX

Robert Finch (Maitland) – a class centre even as a boy; great side-step and turn of pace; played ten years at St George and had great career in management

Alan Dickinson (Keighley) – similar type to Terry Major, hard as iron and had no fear; he took no prisoners; moved into the pack as hooker before returning to his home town club of Castleford; real character on and off the field

4.   Left centre

John Moore (Hull KR) – a classy centre; strong in defence and wonderful turn of pace for big guy; good vision and a brilliant pair of hands; became a great assistant coach to Roger Millward

Mick Bickley (Maitland) – wonderful in defence and rarely missed a tackle; quick and had a great pair of hands; great presence in the dressing room with a wonderful sense of humour, one of those who weld the team together

Ziggy Niztcott (Maitland) – played with him when he as younger and you could see his class then, but he finished up as club captain of South Sydney Rabbitohs; as a late developer he would have been lost to the top level today

5.   Left wing

Merv Wright (Maitland) - indigenous Aussie winger or centre; strong as an ox; lightning speed; could tackle like a front row forward; not only one of the best I have ever seen, but a great bloke

Chris Young (Hull KR) – I played against Chris when he played for Craven Park juniors and he was always a star player; we signed for HKR around same time; a very good winger who represented his country

Geoff Drury (Maitland) – I first met Geoff when he came over as a young guy and played for HKR in the early 70s then we played together at Maitland; he was a solid performer and a good finisher

6.   Stand-off

Roger Millward (Hull KR) – pound for pound the best player ever in either hemisphere; a great player who could do everything; we played against each other as under 17s when he played for Castleford; a great bloke too

Ian Martin (North Coast NSW) – I played with him in 1975 when we represented the North Coast; a fantastic player who he had everything; played for Manly and Australia

Alan Burwell (Hull KR) – a great player anywhere in the backs; had a spell with Canterbury Bulldogs; had as much skill as Roger Millward, but was very laid back; if he had taken the game more seriously he would have been a 'great'.

7. Scrum-half

Brian Burke (Maitland) – a great scrum-half; very quick; an organiser and play maker; great goal-kicker; played representative football for Country NSW and was the Country Player of the Year

Keith Pollard

Alan 'Doddy' Dickinson and the late, great Terry Hollindrake

Albert Eyre, Geoff Crewdson and me at the Keighley Reunion

in 1972

John Mayhew (Kempsey Kowboys) – one of the best defensive scrum halves I ever played with; what he lacked in pace he made up for in guile, and could really play the game

Colin Evans (Keighley) – Colin was a Welsh international in both codes of rugby; started with Leeds and finished at Keighley; hard as nails and played like a forward, although quite slim; really broad Welsh accent

8. Prop forward

Mick Clarke (Keighley) – had a great career with Huddersfield, Leeds and GB, before becoming player-coach at Keighley; good old-fashioned prop-forward; the best coach I ever played for and was always honest with his players

Dave Worthy (Keighley) – a great number 8 who was solid as a rock and never took a backward step; always there to do the hard yards; a great scrummager; never let you down and could hold his own with anyone

Bob Coverdale (Hull KR) – one of only six players to make more than 100 appearances for both Hull clubs; GB international; player-coach with Rovers reserves who looked after his young players and passed on his experience

9. Hooker

Peter 'Flash' Flanagan (Hull KR) – a great player and a great character; played 415 games for Rovers before finishing his career with Hull FC; toured Australasia three times with GB; was very quick and had a great side-step

Peter Walker (Hull KR) – a very good all round hooker who was kept out of Rovers team by Flanagan and ended up having a great career at York, Bradford & Salford; one of three brothers who all played professional rugby league

Alan McNab (Maitland) – greatest strength was dummy half play, with a good eye for an opening and could pass the ball straight off the floor; very good in the scrum; a great engine; very rarely injured; represented Newcastle

10. Prop forward

Phillip 'Fishy' Mullard (Maitland) – a very good front rower who could play either side of the scrum; made up the front row with McNab and myself in 1971 Grand Final, represented Newcastle; career ended by a bad car accident

Jim Drake (Hull KR) – a rugged Cumbrian; a legend in Hull who played 243 games for Hull FC and twice for GB; **a** fantastic man to play alongside, and I learnt a hell of a lot from him, not just about rugby but about life

11. Second-row

Frank Foster (Hull KR) – one of the hardest men ever to play the game; he had everything - good ball skills, fair pace and was a fearsome tackler; played with real aggression and led by example; stories about him are legion

Eric Palmer (Hull KR & Keighley) - a journeyman player, never a star, but was pretty quick for a second row forward with a good pair of hands, solid defence and a good engine; just needed a bit of Foster's aggression

Geoff Crewdson (Keighley) – a stocky forward with surprising pace; part of a great Hunslet pack; GB international; later career hampered by a bad knee; sadly, overlooked for the Keighley coaching job after Metcalfe sacking

12. Second-row

Max McMahon (Maitland) – 'the lawnmower' I called him – he tackled non-stop; a great engine; could run like a stag and although he did not pass a lot but he was always on my shoulder; one of the nicest blokes you will meet

Phil Lowe (Hull KR) – one of the best running forwards the game has seen, a majestic sight in full flow; not the best tackler at first but his spell at Manly improved his defensive work and he became a fine cover-tackler

Bill Holliday (Hull KR) – a strong running Cumbrian with a very good all round game and a decent goal-kicker; a member of what I believe was the best ever 'back three' that Rovers have ever had – Holliday, Foster and Poole

13. Loose-forward

Harry Poole (Hull KR) – probably the best I played with; hard as iron; a great thinker and ball player who could do anything on the field; great leader; GB captain; starting to show his worth as Rovers' coach when he passed away

Terry Pannowitz (Maitland) – captain/coach; another of the best; a fitness fanatic who never stopped running and tackling; always wanted the ball; St George wanted to sign him to play scrum-half but he only wanted to play 'lock'

Cliff Wallis (Hull KR) – a very good all round ball-playing forward; showed his true worth when moved to loose-forward; played for Yorkshire and was near to GB selection in the early 70s

I could have named more players, and I apologise to anyone who I have forgotten who should have been in that list. There are even more that I have played against who have really impressed me and I could probably have written a separate book about them!

What I must add is that any boy, youth or man who puts on a rugby shirt and crosses the whitewash to put his body on the line is a star in my eyes, for unless you have played the game, you do not have any idea what you are letting yourself in for.

CHAPTER 14
ALGERIA

Once again I did some homework on Algeria before I left for North Africa. I found out that The People's Democratic Republic of Algeria, commonly referred to as Algeria, is the second largest country on the African continent. It is bordered by Tunisia in the north-east, Libya in the east, Niger in the south-east, Mali and Mauritania in the south-west, and Morocco, as well as a few kilometres of its annexed territory, Western Sahara, in the west.

Algerian society has been subjected to a number of external influences and migrations. Fundamentally Berber in cultural and racial terms, its' society was organised around extended families, clans and tribes – predominantly in a rural rather than an urban setting, before the arrival of the Arabs and, later, the French. Skikda, where I went to work, is a modern city, founded in 1838 by the French on the ruins of an ancient Phoenician city that flourished in Roman times as Rusicade. It lies on the coast of the Gulf of Stora in the Mediterranean Sea. The landscape is hilly and forested, with high ridges on both the western and eastern sides of the city. The weather is really hot in a summer with temperatures sometimes reaching over 116° Fahrenheit in July and August, whilst it can fall as low as 30F° in winter. The rainy season is from November to February, and at times there are monsoon-like downpours. Our site was built on a sand base and in a winter when it rained it was like a paddy field.

Before I left Crofts, I had been for a trade test and medicals at Pullman Kellogg's offices in London, which allowed me to work in Algeria. The money was a lot more than I had been earning, and I wanted the experience on my CV. The rota was 16 weeks away and two weeks at home, which was harsh on Jacky, who was left looking after eight-year old Jason and Tracy, who was then nearly three, but she went along with it. I left amidst a lot of tears from all of us, including me. After a night in London, I flew to Algiers via Geneva with *Air Algerie* – definitely not one to recommend! In Algiers, we changed planes to fly the 550km to Annaba, where we were bundled into a little minibus for the 100km journey to Skikda and the Sonatrach camp.

It was late at night when we got there, and we had nothing to eat except what we were given on the plane – which was not worth eating. Fortunately, there was some decent food left out for us in one of the canteens, before we were given keys to our rooms in the camp huts. The rooms where about eight feet by six feet with a bed,

225

a table, a chair and a tin locker – quite similar to those in the Bradfield Park Immigration camp in Sydney! I was in H Block at the back of the camp, a bit away from the rest of the huts, and there was also had a communal area in the middle of the block with a couple of settees, a table and a great big fridge with a bike chain wrapped around it and massive padlock.

There was no one around by the time we got into the rooms, so it was off to bed for a six o'clock start in the morning. I did not sleep much, and was missing home and the kids already. I was starting to have doubts that I had made the right decision, but it was a case of making the best of it. We went down for breakfast, which came on a single stainless steel tray with compartments in it, like you see on war films. The eight of us that had travelled together picked a table that was empty, sat down and were eating our breakfast when everything went quiet. I thought the Harlem Globetrotters had come into the room. There were four big black guys, and I mean big, looking down at us.

"Morning," I said without looking up, "how are you?"

"We usually sit at this table" was the reply from the giant of the four.

"Please take a seat – there's plenty of room to join us, if you want," I replied. I admit that I was feeling rather twitchy in the nether regions by this point. He shrugged his shoulders and he nodded to the other three to sit down. The big guy asked if we were new and I nodded and smiled. Apart from that there was no conversation between us and I breathed a sigh of relief when they disappeared to catch the bus. We had been told to wait to get our site passes, induction and all the other paraphernalia required to work on site. We were then loaded onto a bus and taken to the site, where we were introduced to a couple of foremen, who picked those they wanted for their crews. I was warned to try to avoid the fabrication shop because it was run by a little American, who was reputedly a really mean bastard. My supervisor introduced himself, but I never really caught his name, which did not matter because I never saw him again. He resigned, or 'jacked,' in construction slang, later that morning. He said to me that he had 'just the job for you' as we set off for the stores to pick up our tools and equipment. After that, we went to the site office, where he gave me some drawings and introduced me to my Algerian mate. I called him Charlie, because he was Charlie Chaplains double, with even the little moustache above his lip.

We then went to look at the 'job.' I knew it was going to be large pipe, it always was – must have been my build! To be blunt, it was a bastard of a job. They wanted two trunnions to be manufactured in position on a valve station. A trunnion is a support made out of a piece of pipe smaller than the pipe it is supporting, which had to be cut to shape similar to a saddle on a horse, and then welded to the parent pipe in position. It would not have been so bad if it had been a straight length of pipe but these were on bends – the worst scenario you could imagine for a fabricator. It was hard enough to do in a workshop, never mind on site and in position. My supervisor then took me to the compound to show me the materials and then disappeared, never to return. We struggled along with no supervision whilst the piping engineer, Don Stillwell, looked after us until they could come up with a replacement. They could not keep men, it was world-renowned as a bad job – people in the trade used to say that they had more men in the air flying to and from Algeria than they had on the ground.

Sam Warmington, an Irish guy who was sound as a pound, was our general foreman. He was on leave when I started and returned about three weeks later. As it took me about three weeks to manufacture and fit these two supports, I had just finished them and got to know Sam, when the site superintendent, Wes Wheldon, came up to me and asked if I had ever been a foreman. Wes was a real American, a Cherokee Indian, and by the look of him he was at the battle of the Little Big Horn with Custer. He looked a day older than Father Christmas, had a real slow drawl, and was always whittling a bit of wood.

"You wanna be foreman for me son?" he asked. He called everyone 'son.' Ever the mercenary, I asked him what extra I would get and the benefits were. He gave me his spiel, which ended with him telling me that I would not 'have to work, son.' Now my ears picked up at this. I agreed to the promotion, went over to the HR department and had all the paperwork for my contract revised, before returning to Sam, who would now be my immediate supervisor.

The following morning, he introduced me to my squad. I had six ex-pats, four Philippines and 18 Arab mates or labourers. Poor old Charlie was heartbroken that he was no longer working with me – I had treated him well and taught him out to use a burning torch and an electric grinder. The Arabs had their own foreman – a real mean-looking snake-eyed individual called Bettith. The word was that Bettith had been thrown out of the Algerian Police force for being too brutal, which said it all. He spoke decent enough English to get by, but the others only spoke a little English, Arabic and French. This is where I learnt to speak some French, and I was surprised how quickly I picked it up. Anything else was just a case of hand signals and gestures.

The job was okay, but the camp was dreadful and the Algerians did everything possible to make life hard for us. The food was abysmal. I was talking to the chef one night, a big black guy from Liverpool, who was telling me when he arrived on the camp he was

Keith Pollard

interviewed by the camp boss, who at the time was a local. He went through his diplomas and when he mentioned hygiene, the boss said, "You won't need that here." The health and safety diploma got the same comment. The chef said we were lucky that they had changed camp bosses a couple of weeks later. The new one, an Australian, had really cleaned it up.

There were two canteens or restaurants; one for supervisors and above, the other for all other workers on the camp. There was not a lot of difference in the food, but it kept the workers away from supervisors and avoided conflicts – and it was the American way of doing things. Not long after the Aussie took over, the lower one closed for a few days whilst they fumigated it. I was told that they took cockroaches out of there by the barrow load.

The local labourers were useless and you could not give them anything to do on their own. All they could do was to help carry materials, but we were supposed to be teaching them how to be tradesmen. If they made a mistake and you chastised them, you could find yourself up in front of the 'syndicate.' This was an organisation that protected the Algerian work force, rather like a union, but was, I understand, run by the government. If a local had a father who had been in the Algerian forces when the uprising started, or was a terrorist, he was guaranteed a job for life, When Kellogg's took the job over they were told they had to use as much local labour as possible. The project manager wanted to keep them in a compound for eight hours a day, rather than let them loose on site, as they were a danger not only to themselves but to others working alongside them. But he was refused permission to do this – they had to be used on site.

One foreman was hauled up in front of the syndicate and charged with swearing at one of his crew. He was more than upset because the Arab had actually spit in his face. When the company interpreter asked the foreman what had happened, he said that he had been spat at, full in the face, and was lucky he was not up on a more severe charge. The interpreter asked what he had said to the man and he replied, "Fish finger." The foreman explained that he was totally pissed off with having to bow down to the Arabs but, as he knew the consequences, he said 'fish finger' in a nasty snarling way. He knew full well that he would be charged but would make a mockery of the whole process. The outcome was that the foreman was found guilty, but with extenuating circumstances, and the Arab was made up to foreman because he 'had shown guile in standing up to the ex-pat foreman." That was Arab justice.

One Arab law we were told about was that if a guy who was under your supervision had an accident and died, it was your responsibility to look after his family forever. If he was ill or immobilised, you had to help to pay to keep his family. Fortunately,

RED & WHITE PHOENIX

I never heard of this happening. We never had any formal training as supervisors, you were just made up and you got on with it. I only heard of these so-called laws by word of mouth, and in conversations with management. I am sure this was at least part of the reason why the company did not want to give the local labour any work to do. They were not allowed to work at heights, such as on steel erecting, rigging or on scaffolding. Even if you arranged a taxi, which had an accident, it was your fault. We never took taxis anyway, because it was well known that people who did often had to pay for repairs after being involved in 'set up' accidents.

You could not get beer on the camp but you could buy it from another camp down the road. The only problem was that you could only buy a crate, and only if you had an empty crate to exchange – and how did you get an empty crate if you had not bought a full one in the first place? You had to wait until some guy 'jacked,' and hope that he had an empty crate to sell. It was a lager-type beer, which was not too bad, but the breweries never washed the bottles out, and you had to make sure there were no slugs or insects in the bottle before you drank it. After my first 16-week trip, I took homebrew kits back with me, as a lot of us did. I had moved blocks, as I had become pals with some of the guys that used to brew their own beer and then mix it with the local brew. Half of the block was called the Caribbean club, for obvious reasons, and our half was called F Troop. The lads in our half were a mixture from all over the UK.

Our big night was Thursday, as Friday is a Muslim festival and we did not work. We worked a six-day week. We also used to bring a bottle of spirits back with us after being on leave, so we always had a bottle to share on a Friday. That is how I got into drinking whisky – *Glenfiddich* was the favourite tipple of the majority of the group, although I now prefer single malts.

We got a rugby union team together and played a few games against a couple of university teams and a team from the steelworks at Annaba, which was made up of ex-pats who worked there. Our team was organised by a Welshman, one of the electrical engineers, who was called Clive Jones. We had a couple of ex-rugby league players; Don Stillwell, who was from St Helens but had immigrated to the USA and had arrived in Algeria via the London office; Kevin Watson, the foreman welder was from real rugby league country, Egremont in Cumbria; Alan 'Pit-Prop' Lord, was from Tylerstown in the South Wales valleys and became one of my closest friends. It broke up the boredom and there was good banter between us. We trained a couple of nights a week, which kept us a bit fitter and gave us something to do. We asked an American engineer, Randall O'Brown III, who used to play grid iron, to play but he watched one game and said we were crazy. He would only play if he could wear the padding and helmet that they used in their 'football,' as he called it.

After our game at Annaba to play, we went to a local institution for ladies of the night – a brothel to be blunt. I must make clear that I did not avail myself of the services on offer, but I went along for the craic. Most of the women had been disowned by their families for having sex out of wedlock, which is frowned upon in Arab countries, where girls are supposed to be virgins when they get married. There was a little bar area, where you could sit and view the wares, but as soon as you went in the women grabbed you and showed you porn magazines and pointed pictures depicting positions that they would copy. There were some sights there, with the women dressed in what they obviously thought were sexy outfits. Even if I had been single I do not think I would have been tempted. We had a drink in there and left, although I do believe some did partake in the delights on offer.

The ironical thing was that if you were in the Algerian Forces, and there was an army camp near Annaba, a soldier could avail himself of one of the womens' services for one dinar a time. The official exchange rate was four dinars to the pound, whilst on the black market you could get twenty dinars – which worked out sat 5p a time, or 20p at the higher rate – still not worth it in my mind. Apparently sexually transmitted diseases were rife and it was no surprise that a few months later some of the lads that had visited the establishment were infected. It was not a pleasant experience for them – the medical facilities on the camp and site were good, but it did mean they could not go home for a few months, until it had cleared up, and a couple had to postpone their leave. Try explaining that one to the wife!

It was difficult for healthy young men to remain abstinent for four months at a time, but their right hand was their best friend in the circumstances. It is natural as you mature through adolescence to masturbate, but to be sitting in a room with several construction workers and hear someone say, "Bugger this, I'm off for a wank," is somewhat surreal. When I hear football and rugby crowds calling the referee a wanker, it brings back memories of that camp somewhere in the desert. It was what kept many of us sane.

Pornography is a very rare commodity in Algeria. If it was found in baggage at the airport it would be confiscated, so some of the men put boxes of sanitary towels on top of their clothes. When the bag was opened and they were spotted, the Arab officials would not touch anything in the case, it was taboo for them to touch anything like that. Pork scratchings were an alternative – anything to do with pigs drove them crazy. I took some back once after a trip home, and was giving them to the lads who worked for me. I had put them in a plain bag and they were enjoying them until I told them what they were. Their extreme reactions seemed funny at the time, but I was very lucky not to end up in front of the syndicate.

The mixture of guys you meet when you are working abroad is very diverse, and each one had a story to tell. In our block, we had six welders who were all black guys who were great blokes once you got to know them. Danny McNaughton was in the room opposite to me and I got to know him quite well. He was a bit of a show pony and a smart arse, but deep down he was ok. He was telling me one day when we were talking about unions that he was in Equity. When I said that's an actor's union, he said, "I know I am an actor, I've been in films."

"Fuck off," I said, "you're winding me up."

"No, I was in Zulu with Michael Caine," he replied. I did not believe him until he pulled out a load of photographs of him and there was one of him with Michael Caine. There was another of him in his Zulu costume with his lionskin shield and spear – he was a big guy but it made him look even bigger! He also showed me photo of his wife, who was an interpreter who apparently spoke about seven languages. There are times in your life when you feel you have wasted your time at school, and that was one of them – all I could speak was one sentence of German! She was standing with Danny, who was wearing a white suit, and in between them was the King of Jordan. She was at a function as the interpreter, and Danny was invited along as her escort.

My first leave from the camp was at Christmas. We were having our Christmas dinner when the phone rang. Tracy shot to the phone and said, "There's a funny man on the phone, daddy." I went and picked up the phone and it was Danny.

"Merry Christmaaass," he said in his Jamaican accent, "howsyadoinman?" I was quite surprised to hear from him to say the least, but it was really good of him to call. He was very sound and I really liked him.

Drake was another character. I never ever got to know his real name, and I never knew why they called him Drake, until one morning in the showers he came in and took the cubicle opposite me – there were no doors or curtains, they were all open type of communal shower blocks.

"'Morning," I said. He had his back to me and when he dropped his towel, which was around his waist and turned round I knew then why they called him Drake. To say he was well endowed was an understatement. I am no connoisseur in these matters, but I have played in rugby teams and seen a lot of naked men – but nothing like him. I was told when he went to Annaba some of the girls would not take him, and the one that did would not take any money off him. I am surprised she could walk afterwards. He told me one day he had been in porn films when he was younger and that did not surprise me. He had to leave the job after a few months because his father had died and he had to go home to run the hotel the family owned back in Trinidad.

Pretty Boy was a real character who was permanently on 'wacky backy.' In his room, he had used a candle to put patterns all over the ceiling and he was always playing Bob Marley tapes. He used to drink a white rum similar to Bacardi. Danny was partial to this tipple as well, and I tried it once – it was like aircraft fuel. Viv, to use his real name, used to mix it with pure orange juice and keep it in the communal fridge. I can see him now walking along with his shorts and flip flops on in the way that only Caribbean men can, a sort of dancing walk, whilst humming Bob Marley with a smile as wide as the Humber.

"Howsyaalldoin?" he would say. "Don't worry, be happy!" and off he would go back to his room and his smoke. He worked on the same unit as me but under a different supervisor, although we used to swap welders about as and when needed. During the rainy season, he was working under a tent, or 'elephant' as we called them in the trade, when he had had a bit of a 'run in' with his other supervisor, a little Irish guy – another Charlie Drake lookalike. He went to his room that night and made a little doll of this guy complete with red hair. He had got some hemp that was used to make screwed pipe joints with, dyed it with raspberry juice, stuck pins in it, took it up to the top of the camp where the married quarters were, left it on the doorstep, knocked on the door and ran.

The following morning, 'Charlie' came up to Viv, fuming about this doll, which he assumed that Viv was responsible for. Viv looked and pointed at him, at which there was a flash of lightening and an instantaneous clap of thunder. I nearly shit myself, let alone Charlie. Steven Spielberg could not have directed it any better. As he pointed Viv shouted, "Don't you talk to me like that, fuck off you little fat bastard!" He never worked for Charlie again and my opinion about voodoo changed.

There were quite a few older guys on the job, mainly because they had such difficulty getting men and were quite happy to take anyone. There was Snowy, from the London area, whom I reckon was nearer 70 than 60. He was a great old guy, his hair and beard as white as snow – who would have made a great father Christmas. Unfortunately, he just had no family at all – his wife had died very young, he had no children and no home to speak of. He just travelled from contract to contract around the world living on construction camps. Sometimes you realise how well off you are.

Vince, was a Welsh guy who was well in to his 60s. He was a 'very down in the dumps' type, who used to play a mouth organ. When he was drunk, he used to play the old Irish folk song, *Danny Boy*. One evening I was in another block talking to a guy called

RED & WHITE PHOENIX

Mike about an upcoming rugby game when we heard Vince start up *Danny Boy*. With that, all you could hear was doors closing and locks turning and I asked Mike what was going on. He told me that Vince used to go from room to room telling the same old story about how he had no family, how his wife had left him, on and on. All the guys in the block locked him out because they had all heard the story so many times and felt like slashing their wrists after a quarter of an hour with Vince. It was bad enough being away from home in the back of beyond, without having someone moaning about missing their family.

We used to go in to the town of Skikda now and again, often walking along the sea front to a little village called Storra. At the time we were there, it had been ravaged following the revolution – it was only about 15 years since the uprising had ended, so there were still a lot of ruins and bad feelings towards the French. The little bay at Storra was great for swimming, and I used to enjoy our trips there. It was a break from the camp where there was a beach nearby, but it had bad rip currents and was not safe to swim in. We were there on one of our days off and took our swimming trunks and towels for a day on the beach. There was no one around so Pit Prop suggested we swam naked.

"What the hell for" I said.

"Apparently it's great to let the water run around your dangly bits when you are swimming," he said. Now this was something I had never done since I used to go in 'penny buff' at the swimming baths when I was a kid, and in those days one did not have that much to dangle. So that is what we did that day, and he was right, it was quite a nice feeling. If you have never done it, I suggest it is one to put on your list to do before you die! Only do not do it in Algeria where it is illegal! When we were in the water a police car pulled up on the road top of the beach. We had to stay in the water until they went, but as they had got out of the car for a smoke, it seemed like an eternity until they got back in car and disappeared.

I had just got back off my first leave and walked onto the site when I was met by my then supervisor, Sam Warmington.

"Great to see you back," he said, "I'm away tomorrow"

"Why? You've not long ago had leave"

"I know," he said. "My mother's died."

"Oh, I'm so sorry Sam," I said, "when"? he looked at his watch and said,

"About 10 minutes ago," he said, looking at his watch and bursting out laughing. I called him a twat and started laughing myself.

"Shut up, the gaffers here," he said. With that, Leroy Walker, who was the Project Manager, walked up.

"Morning guys, how 'ya all doin'?" He said – he was another

of our cousins from over the Pond. "Wes is looking for you, Sam. He's in the office – go and see him now," As we were walking to the site office, Wes walked round the corner and spotted us. Sam whispered to me to say nothing.

"Hi guys, Hi Sam, got some bad news, son" he said, looking at Sam. "Your Ma's died." He said it just like that, no warning or anything.

"Get yourself over to HR they are organising your flight," he added, before looking at me and saying, "You take over while Sam's away son, ok? Goddam world out here in this shit hole and your Ma passes away. I don't know what I will do when mine goes." 'When she goes?' I thought – he was in his 70s, so she must have been be a hundred years old. It was taking me all my time to stop laughing. He was just playing along with Sam. When he got back Sam told me they had flown him first class back to the UK via France straight to Dublin where he came from, all in between travel by taxi, all paid for by the company. He told me that his mother had died three times on various different jobs he had been on, and he had never been caught out once. He was a real con man – all nerve and no conscience.

But he was taking a big risk because Leroy Walker was ruthless with his workforce. I had been told that he was not allowed to work in the UK because he sacked a full site of workers on one occasion and the unions would not work with him. He ruled by the iron fist, sacking one of the rigging superintendents because a rigging crew had dropped a control unit off the back of a lorry. The poor bloke he sacked was not even on site, he was down the docks organising a shipment of materials to be sent to site. But he was sent a message to get back on site and as he walked into Walker's office he was told to pack his bags. It did not matter to Walker that he had his family and everything out there. I just do not understand how some people cannot realise when making a decision that they could ruin a guy's life. But the effect on a family never came into Walker's reasoning.

Sam nearly did get caught once though. He worked the same scam on every job he went on abroad, and on one occasion he had forgotten that the boss on this particular job had been the boss on a previous assignment. After the phone call came through from his wife asking that Sam be informed of his loss, this particular gaffer said, "Sam, I seem to recall she died when we were in wherever together, or am I mistaken?" Sam quickly replied in his Irish brogue, "No, that was my stepmother, this one is my real mother – they were divorced, my da and ma".

I had done two four-month trips and my time was running down on the second when Mel Larkin, a Darlington lad who had taken over from Wes as Superintendent, asked me if I wanted to get my

RED & WHITE PHOENIX

12 months in – which meant I would get the additional completion bonus of 25% of what I had earned. We were paid tax free, any tax was left to us to sort out and you could claim tax relief on the bonus. He said that if I wanted to come back I could, and as the mechanical side was coming to an end, I could supervise the painting squads that were starting to work through the units. I told him I would think about it. On the one hand, it looked like a doddle and I would only need to stop a couple of months to get my full year in. But, on the other, had there was the local workforce to take into account. Letting this lot loose climbing around with tins of paint was an accident waiting to happen. I told Mel that I had decided to finish when I went home.

When I came home, I got a feeling that must be akin to guys getting out of prison as the plane left the tarmac. As far as I was concerned I had completed my contract, but when I had been back home two weeks, which would have been my leave if I was going back, I got a phone call from Kelloggs asking me when I was going back. I told the girl I was not going back and that I had finished because the mechanical work had come to an end. She told me they had asked for me back. I told her, 'no chance,' and that I was entitled to the completion bonus. They rang me a couple of times more and I was beginning to panic – no way did I want to go back to that hell hole. They rang me a fourth time and told me that a mistake had been made – there was more work outstanding than they first thought. They promised I would only have to do a few months – one full trip at the most – and then I would be paid off in full. I discussed it with Jacky and decided that as I only needed a few weeks to complete my year and get my tax free bonus, I would go back.

After I had been back on site a few weeks, I was really homesick, the worst I had ever felt. I was missing Jacky and the kids really badly. I got on well with the guy in admin and he organised a phone call home for me. I managed to get through after the usual hassle and we had been talking for a while when Jacky had mentioned Tracy having to go into hospital. At that point the phone went dead and an Arab voice came on the line telling me the call had ended. I asked her to reconnect me but she just said that the call had ended. I went berserk. When I had calmed down a bit, I went into HR and told them I had finished, and to get me home. It took 12 days before the authorities would give me my exit visa to get out of the country and, to top it all, Kelloggs took the flight costs off my pay, saying I had not completed my contract. I did not get the 25% bonus, or my full year in, and had to pay around a £1,000 tax. I understand now why guys used to wait until they were home on leave and the money was in the bank at the end of the month before they told them to 'shove it'. Another lesson learned.

Keith Pollard

The hassle we experienced out there was unbelievable. When you were due to come home on leave, you had to personally go to the police station in Skikda and get a visa to get out of the country. They made you sit outside an office for hours before being interviewed by some petty pen pusher who treated you like something he found on his shoe. Many of the lads sat there all day, only to be told go back the next day. When you entered Algeria you had to declare how much sterling you had with you. Occasionally you were searched and if any undeclared sterling was found on you, you were not allowed in the country and were put back on the plane. When you departed, you had to be have exactly the same amount with you. This was to try and stifle the black market in money that I mentioned earlier. The dinar was practically worthless – even the national airline, *Air Algerie*, would not take them on their flights. We used to take a few extra quid hidden in our suitcases and then put a porn magazine, some pork scratchings or ladies' sanitary towels on top, so that the officials would immediately close the suitcase.

Arabs do not know how to queue. You had to get to the airport hours before your flight, the two or three hours here is nothing in comparison. At the check-in desk, we made sure that the lads off the job stuck together and formed a semi-circle round the desk to stop the Arabs from pushing in. When the flight number came up, the passengers went outside and had to stand and wait until the stewardesses called, then walk towards the plane. The nearer you got to the plane, the faster you walked and by the end as you got to the steps you were sprinting. This was to ensure you got seat. There were no seat numbers allocated and they always overbooked the plane. You had to get yourself into a seat, buckle up and look out of the window. You did not make eye contact with any of the stewardesses, because they threw Europeans off first if they had stuffed up. It never happened to me but I do know of guys who had got this far on their way home, only to fall at the last hurdle.

If we were lucky we flew back via Geneva on *Swiss Air*, which provides a fantastic view over Lake Geneva on daytime flights as you reduce height for landing. That was one of the best things about working in Algeria!

One lad brought his car back after being home on leave. He drove it through France down to Marseille, then on the ferry to Algiers. He had been back about a month when he crashed the car into a tree. He was ok and left the car overnight, but when he went back it had been stripped bare – even the seats had been taken out. But worst of all, his paperwork, including his passport, had gone. He was arrested for damaging Algerian property – the tree – and given a month in jail. An Arab jail is certainly not the best place to be, especially if you are a European. He had his head shaved, was put in a cell with about 20 Arabs, and put on bread and water. We used to visit him and take him food, part of which he gave to a couple of 'heavies' in his cell – every night someone got raped in the cell and, if it had not been for these two guys he was feeding, his turn would have undoubtedly have come. He also was giving them money, which we had smuggled to him in our shoes.

After his release, all he wanted to do was get home as quick as he could. It took him a while to get a new passport and when it arrived he had more hassle getting the visa, because did not have a stamp in his passport to show he had come in to the country. Then when he did get to the airport he was turned back as he had no slip showing the amount of sterling he took into the country. When he tried to explain he hit the language problem and he had a lot more hassle before he finally 'escaped.'

When I asked myself why I put myself through it, there was only one answer – it simply came down to the money. At least I think it made me a stronger person – if you can work there, you can work anywhere. I have been for interviews since, and people have said with amazement, "You did nearly a year in Algeria?" It was as if I had been to the moon and back.

After a few weeks back home I got a job with Pipe Fabrications of Burstwick, a village about half way between Hull and Withernsea, where I was living. Like Crofts, they carried out site installation work in the oil and gas industries. I started with them at Marfleet refinery in Hull, which became Seven Seas Oil, where they were installing a new tank farm and associated pipe-work. I was only there two weeks before they asked me if I would go to BOCM at Selby to run a small team on that site, so I agreed and started there a week later. The then manager at Pipe Fabrications was a guy called John Kilvington, who met me onsite and introduced me to the engineers and the BOCM contractor supervisors, and generally showed me round. We covered the jobs that had been allocated to us and it all seemed in order. It was another six and a half days a week job.

Selby is about 46 miles from Burstwick – just over an hour's drive, which we did every day in the works' Transit van. I then had about another nine miles to and from Withernsea, but that was my problem. I was on pay ten hours a day Monday to Friday, six hours on Saturday and ten Sunday, plus weekend overtime rates. It was not a bad earner and I was effectively my own boss – no-one bothered me as long as the job was getting done. We finished up with just two of us on the site most of the time, and if we needed extra bodies at the weekend, I used to contact the works to organise men from other sites to make up the numbers.

When I first started, we had a cabin by the side of the railway track inside the main works. I soon got that moved to outside, across the road on the riverside – away from the site security, who used to log us in and out. I used the same system as I did at Croda – work extra hard during the week to get stuff done ready for weekends, then ensure the job could be completed in good time ready for Monday morning. I certainly did not want a record of our movements! It worked a treat. We never worked past 1pm on a Sunday as we always had the jobs finished. I never had any hassle off the engineers or supervisors – they did not care as long as everything was running smoothly.

We had a bit of a slack period when I was sent on a job in Leeds at an *Esso* storage facility. There were six large storage tanks that needed a skirt installing on the inside as they were going rotten near the floor plates. After having a look, John Kilvington asked if would I do the welding on a price. I calculated how long it would take and said £220 per tank, for the welding, and the fitting at my hourly rate. John went to talk to Harry, the boss, and they agreed the price. I told him which rods I wanted, knowing if I got the right rods I was laughing. I had another fitter welder with me as well as a mate. *Esso* would only release two tanks at a time, so whilst I was working on one and finishing the welding, the other two would be preparing the other. We finished the lot in six weeks.

I rang the office and asked what they had for us next. Harry came to the phone and asked what I meant, saying I had six tanks to finish. I told him they were all done and that he owed me £1,320 for the welding. The next day John arrived on site – the first time we had seen him in six weeks – to see how I had managed to do the tanks so quickly. Harry had told him he thought I had conned him with the price. I reminded him that they had agreed and in the end they had to pay me, but it took some getting out of them and I never did it again. They never asked or offered a price for a job again – but they must still have made money out of the deal if they thought it was going to take longer.

Shortly after, I went away for my summer holidays and when I got back I had a message from John Kilvington to contact him as soon as possible. He told me that he had left Pipe Fabrications and started his own business JVK Engineering Services. He had taken the BOCM Contract with him, as he had obtained it at the beginning and he considered it his job.

When I went back to work at the fabrication shop in Burstwick, old Harry, who owned the company, said to me that as there was no work at Selby I was to go back to Marfleet and work on there. It looked like I might be getting paid off as things were slack, so I said I would leave at the end of the week and gave in my notice.

I went to see John at his home in Kirk Ella, one of the nicest parts of Hull. I thought he must have had some other income to afford such a house – the word was that he was a wallpaper salesman before he joined Pipe Fabrications. We discussed terms, and I got the impression that he only got the work at BOCM because I was going with him, if I had said no he was snookered. He gave me an increase and said there would be the odd bonus now and again if things went well, so I started with JVK the following Monday at BOCM.

I went in to see Dennis, the lead engineer there, to discuss what work was needed, he showed me the schedule they had planned and it there was work for quite a few months ahead. He said to me, "John must be paying you some money to get you; he would not have got the contract if you weren't included." My impression was right but I was happy with the terms and had no pressure other than to turn up and do my bit. My mate, 'Big Harry,' had been paid off from Pipe Fabrications at the same time and had come with me.

I did ask Dennis whether, if I had gone self-employed, I would have had a chance of getting the work. He said, "Yes, why didn't you go for it when you knew Pipefabs were being relieved of the contract?" I told him that I did not know, but he did not elaborate about what had happened, and I did not ask. I was quite happy with my lot. John was a bit tight when it came to money. He said there would be a van to transport us from Hull to Selby, but it was a clapped out Ford Escort Estate car. However, I did get to use it to and from Withernsea at no cost to me. All I did was put the petrol bills in each week with my time sheet and they were paid the next week.

I stayed with JVK for about 12 months before things started to get a bit slack. He had all his eggs in one basket and, although he did try to get other work, he was not very successful at it. After a complete disaster on a small job at a local animal feeds factory near Beverley where we did not have the right equipment because John was trying to do everything on the cheap, I thought it was time to look elsewhere. A mate rang to ask me if I was interested in going to South Africa with Fluor, who were recruiting pipefitters. I rang the agency, had an interview in London, was offered a job and agreed terms.

Keith Pollard

CHAPTER 15
SOUTH AFRICA

As you might expect, I did my homework before taking the job in South Africa. Secunda is a small town in what was then the Eastern Transvaal (now Mpumalanga) to the eastern side of the country. It is 1,620 meters above sea level and around a hundred miles from Johannesburg. The weather was supposed to be quite good, with an average summer temperature of around 25°C, and although the winter nights are cold with regular frost, it is usually quite dry, sunny and warm in the daytime with an average temperature around 16°C. That was certainly good enough for me!

The town of Secunda was built in the Transvaal coalfields in the mid-1970s following the 1973 oil crisis. It had then been decided to establish an oil-from-coal industry that would make South Africa less dependent on the importation of crude oil. The town itself therefore is quite modern and well-designed, albeit with very much an industrial backdrop of mines and refineries. I was to work as a pipefitter on the construction of Sasol 3, which was opened 1982, and is still the largest coal liquefaction plant in the world.

We flew out from Heathrow with all the lads for Sasol 3 in one section of the plane. When the stewardess came along to ask if we would like anything to drink, I asked for a beer, and when I asked how much it was, she said it was complementary. Sipping my beer, I turned to make conversation with the Liverpudlian to my right.

"We haven't got time to talk, it's free ale," was his classic response. We never spoke again for the rest of the flight and he was probably incapable of speech when he got off the plane at Johannesburg. On my other side was a very decent guy called Graham Spittle, with whom I got on right from the start.

The site was a good bus ride away from the airport, and we were all well knackered after the long flight. We were allocated our rooms in the blocks that are standard on construction sites the world over. There was a decent bed for a change, although, unlike Skikda, there were no social amenities in the block. But there was a large bar and gymnasium building, which also provided a free laundry service. We soon learned that if we gave the guy who ran it a few rand, your gear would came back ironed and pressed – a lot better than the standard service. We were provided with all our meals in the canteen, where the food was not bad at all. I was paid £50 per week which was then around 200 rand. A six-pack of the local beer, Lion, was three rand and although they were only small tins, one pack a night was sufficient and some nights I did not bother at all.

The working schedule was based on nine or ten-hour days, Monday to Thursday, finishing at lunchtime on the Thursday, and then Friday to Sunday off, which suited me fine. Sometimes, I went to Johannesburg for long weekends, and occasionally further afield, A few guys went to Mbabane, which was the capital of Swaziland, and was about a three and a half-hours drive away. The furthest I went was Durban, which was about an eight-hour drive.

I started on the job on the Monday morning and was picked up at 6.15am for a seven o'clock start. We were transported on the backs of trucks across the massive site. It was so big that the job was split into separate projects, each with its own management team. I had heard rumours over the weekend about what the job was like, where not to go, and which unit to try to get onto. Apparently, the Afrikaners supervisors were the ones to avoid, they hated the Brits more than they did the blacks and treated them like the proverbial on the bottom of your shoe.

Luckily, I was sent to section three, which was run mainly by British management and supervision. I was given green overalls, which denoted the section you were supposed to be on – if you were in a different area you stood out as you would have the wrong coloured overalls. There were armed guards on the manmade hills around each section – they did not tell you that at the interview for the job in London!

I was on the offsite area of Tank farm, working mainly on pipe tracks rather than process units. Our Foreman was a great bloke, an Irish guy named Liam Flynn, and our supervisor was from Gloucester – so I had struck lucky! The welding supervisor was a big Afrikaner called Fricky Botha, but he was a decent enough bloke and was the only local I had to deal with. The section superintendent was an American called Ken 'Spitting' Smith, so called due to his rather disgusting habit of chewing tobacco and spitting a foul black concoction out of his mouth. He used to drive about in a bright green Ford Escort that had black slimy lines down the driver's door where he had spat out of the window. A lot of the access roads on the site were above the pipe tracks, and if you were working down an embankment and you spotted him coming as he was driving around the site overseeing his domain, you always made sure you stood clear to ensure his spit did not land on the back of your head. He did not do it on purpose though, and probably did not even realise he was doing it.

I was working one night when my foreman asked me if I would do him a favour and weld a flange on a length of pipe for a level float instrument. I asked him if he wanted it doing properly or just slapped on. He told me to do it right as it might be inspected and that he intended to put a welder's number on it, just for reference.

Keith Pollard

As I was doing it, Fricky Botha rode up on his bike. I did not even know he was there until I lifted my welding screen up. He had been watching me welding.

"Hey, vot you velding?" he asked, "you not a velder." I thought I am in it here and so is the foreman. Fricky then started to laugh as only he could, from deep in his belly.

"Hey Keit, you are very good – you come vork for Fricky!" he bellowed.

"No fucking chance," I replied. "No way I am having my head stuck in a welding screen all day." They were very short of welders at the time. They had a welding school, which they used to put local blacks and coloured guys through, and they could turn out a welder out in four to six weeks – from being a bricklayer to a welder in less than two months maximum! Their policy was to teach the younger guys additional trades, according to their needs. But they only taught them a particular process because if they were fully qualified they would just leave and get work nearer their homes or on other projects.

There were men there from all over South Africa. One guys who worked with me told me that he had friend in the camp, a black, who had walked for a full month and the spent three days sleeping in the back of the truck, just to get to the camp. But when he got there he was treated like an animal – I really felt for those guys. When we worked the middle weekend, our supervisor used to let them use the truck to go back to their camp, and this was the only day of the week when they got meat. Their lunch pack-up was a half loaf of brown bread and a carton of mealie-meal, which is a coarse flour that is made from maize and is a staple food in many parts of the southern African continent. It is usually eaten as a thick porridge or as a mashed potato substitute. It is similar to Italian polenta or American grits, except that it is usually made of a white rather than a yellow maize.

To me it stank, but they liked it. I thought the doggy bags we used to get were pretty poor. I was once given a tin of sardines in my bag, which said on it, 'not fit for human consumption.' Most of the Brits bought plastic lunch boxes and filled them the night before with salad or took stuff at breakfast. We used to give the doggy bags to the blacks. They thought we were great – white men had never done anything for most of them before either. I once had an argument with Fricky Botha, who said I would make them ill giving them the doggy bags, as they were not used to good food.

I made only the one visit to the Kingdom of Swaziland, but it was educational to say the least. Swaziland is a small land-locked country in bordered to the north, south and west by South Africa, and to the east by Mozambique. The climate is very varied depending on the height above sea level – the terrain is quite mountainous, particularly in the west – and it is home to several major game reserves. The population consists mainly of ethnic Swazis and their main language is siSwati. The Anglo-Boer War saw the United Kingdom make Swaziland a protectorate under its direct control, but it gained independence in 1968. The King is the head of state and appoints the prime minister and a small number of representatives for both chambers of parliament. It was one of the poorest counties in the world at the time, and life expectancy was comparatively low at the time.

Swaziland was then the place where South African white men took their 'coloured' girlfriends, as such fraternisation was illegal in South Africa. Unfortunately, it was rife with sexually transmitted diseases and Aids, not that this put off some of the guys on the job, who were smitten with the young black girls who offered whatever you fancied. It was strange to see very mature men with these young girls, young enough to be their granddaughters never mind daughters. It was as if they were trying to live a second adolescence, going back to when they were teenagers, with no thought to their families back home or their health. One guy actually left his wife and family to go and live with a young girl in Mbabane, and was proud of it. He told us that he had once taken her shopping to feed the family, and when they were in the bed at night he heard a rustling under the bed. Thinking it was a snake, he was alarmed to say the least, until his girlfriend told him that it was the chicken for the following day's dinner, that she had left there in a bin-liner. At the time, there was no electricity, no sanitation or running water – it was like going back a hundred years.

When I went, a few of us got together and went with a young Afrikaner who used to take his black girlfriend to Swazi. We booked into the Highland View hotel in Mbabane and I shared with a guy called Ray from Newcastle. It was a really spotless and comfortable place. When we went into the bar, there were one or two guys off the site and a few locals. One of the girls came over to Ray and I – quite a bonny girl she was. Ray wasted no time, and when she went to the ladies, asked if it was ok to use the room. I thought, bloody hell we have only just come into the bar, but I told him to go for it anyway – just to make sure he had protection. He then went to the toilets to see if they had a machine, and the girl came back and started talking to me. When she asked if I fancied some fun, reminded her about Ray.

"Oh, after him if you want," she said, "or both together if you fancy going twos up." I thanked her and told he to give Ray a good time. After that, whilst standing on my own, I was propositioned by three girls within 20 minutes, so I took my beer out into the garden. It was a fantastic view out over the hills and valley below. There was no-one out there and I thought I was safe at last. When it

Keith Pollard

started to fill up, I headed for the restaurant and joined a few of the other guys. I had a Monkey Gland steak, so named because of the sauce it was served in – sweet and hot, made with Worcester Sauce, tomatoes, onions, Tabasco, and brown sugar. Apparently it is a traditional South African dish and was very nice indeed.

I met an Ozzie guy there called Skippy and we got talking. He was a Parramatta supporter from Sydney. He asked me if I wanted a root and I said no again, making the excuse that I did not like black women – which was the first thing that came into my head. He called over a Zulu girl, who called Mildred – she must have been at least six feet tall and was a go-go dancer. Skippy told me that she said she wanted me to be her 'cherry' – the Swazi term for a boyfriend or girlfriend, or to put it another way, 'meal ticket.'

I was around 17 stone at the time and found out that day that if you were a well built guy like me, you were highly esteemed amongst the Swazi people. Apparently, it was a sign of authority and power. Mildred came and sat next to me and she kept eyeing me up – to be fair she was very nice. After a while she disappeared downstairs to do her dance, and told she would see me after her performance. I asked Skippy how I could get rid of her. Once again he asked me why, and I simply asked how many 'cherries' she'd had that month. By then, the drink was starting to get to me, I'd had a fair few beers and I could never take a lot, so I went to hit the sack before my un-adopted cherry returned.

Ray was not in the room when I got in, so I took the made-up bed. His was bedclothes were everywhere and a pair of skimpy knickers were hung on the mirror. I never heard a thing all night and woke up with my head pounding and my tongue like a budgie cage bottom. The sun was shining through the venetian blinds onto a sight I will never forget. As I opened my eyes slowly, they alighted on the most perfect girl's bottom – a boilermaker could not have sculpted a better rounded bow to an oil tanker. The sheets had come off them both and the sunshine through the blinds formed stripes like a zebra on her. They were both asleep and I did not move for a minute or so, just laid there looking at this perfectly smooth skin, black as coal, and without a blemish on it. I was getting aroused, so I stirred, at which Ray opened his eyes. He never moved and smiled with a grin as wide as the Tyne. I soundlessly mouthed, 'who the fuck is that?' to him and he shrugged a 'I don't know her name' look. I started to get up and the girl turned just as I stood up, so I grabbed the sheet to cover myself – ever the gentleman! She smiled and said 'hello,' so I returned the greeting and said I was going for a shower. I then got dressed, went for some breakfast and left them to it.

After a feed, I went out into the garden, where a few guys who were around were under the influence of the demon drink. Then more people started to arrive. It appeared the Highland View was the meeting point for guys going back to the camp and the place was bouncing by mid-afternoon. I got talking to a guy who I had apparently been talking to the night before – I had to apologise as I could not remember talking to him. He was a Scottish guy called Graham who lived in Swazi and was a pilot for the Royal Swazi National Airline. He asked me about Ray, who had apparently told him he used to be in the SAS. I thought it was bullshit myself, but I did not know, so I could not comment, and the conversation turned to other matters.

One of the guys, who had told me about the 'big fella syndrome,' told me I would be a prize possession, one they would love to show off to their family and friends – he made me sound like a Great Dane. As we were talking a waitress walked up to us and started talking to Graham in the native tongue, and I noticed that both of them smiled at me as they were talking. After she left us, Graham said she wants to get to know you – it is your size, she wants to be your cherry! I said he had to be joking, but he assured me he was not. I must admit that I was flattered because she was drop dead gorgeous – she reminded me the girl who used to be in the Tia Marias advert years ago. Time to get out of here before I do something I would regret, I thought. I did just that, and never went back.

It had been a great weekend – the food and drink were cheap and the hotels spot on. But to be honest the whole town was like one giant brothel. Girls would fill the bars and hotels with one thing on their minds – to earn some money in any way possible. I had been warned about the place, but also told it was worth going, if only once, to have a look – 'keep your dick in your trousers and see how the other half live,' was how it was put. I had seen how the non-whites were treated in South Africa and it was good to see the freedom the Swazis had. Although poor they always had smiles on their faces and it seemed a really friendly nation. It was a tragedy that they were so poverty-stricken they had to subject themselves to prostitution.

One of the guys picked up a local girl one night and she went back to his room with him. The next morning as he was getting dressed, he noticed that his wallet was missing. He asked the girl if she had seen it, but she denied any knowledge. There were only the two of them in the room and he was certain he had it in his pocket when they went in. He asked her to empty her handbag and he searched her clothes, but there was no sign of the wallet. He was convinced she had it, and as she stood in front of him wearing nothing but a smile he realised that she had a wig on. He reached across, lifted the wig, there on top of her head sat the wallet. The guy did not involve the hotel management or the police, but she was no longer his 'cherry.'

Back on the site I was enjoying the work, and my supervisor asked me one day if I fancied taking a welding test.

"No, thank you," I told him, "I don't want to just weld, it is so boring with your head stuck in a bucket all day. But I don't mind doing both fitting and welding like I have done on other jobs."

"But you are doing two jobs then" he said.

"That is the only way I will do it," I replied and left it at that. A few days later I was told to report to the tank farm office and ask for the Superintendent, a guy called Mendez. He introduced me to a guy called John Beek – 'Captain Beeky,' as he was known. They asked me if I would take a weld test and subject to me passing it I would be working for John, off-site and on the tank farm, completing all the small bore pipe stations that needed installing and making good any outstanding work. I took the test, passed with flying colours, and was teamed up with a Geordie, Brian Robson. We got on really well and could not believe our luck in getting this job. We spent a few days turning a dump truck into a mobile workshop, removing the tipper unit and fitting a flat base with a tool box, a bench, a mobile welding machine and generator.

John used to give us a list of outstanding jobs in a morning and off we went – no-one bothered us all day. We were picked up at night by John, who had a rough idea where we would be and would turn up with his pickup truck to get us back to our pick-up point to get back to our quarters. It was a brilliant job for us.

Whilst I was working on some pipe-support steelwork, one of the young local welders came to watch me working. He asked me would I show him how to weld with a stick on steelwork, as he could not do it – as I said earlier, they would only teach them one process at a time. He was a welder on the stainless steel pipe-work and a very good one, I was told. But I could not believe he had no idea how to weld steel. I was working in the same area for about a week so he came across at dinner time and I showed him what to do. I did not mind doing the kid a favour.

We used to sit and have tea breaks with a few local guys, a couple of whom were Spanish. They were full of questions about what it was like in England and why we were in South Africa, and the subject of pay arose. It transpired that the black guy, Joseph, was the lowest paid; the coloured guy from Cape Town, Abie, was the next; then the Spanish guys; and I was the highest paid. I could not believe how poorly paid the black guy was. Abie was on about three rand more an hour just because of the colour of his skin. It was hard to try and explain why the Spanish guys and I were on more money than them. The Spanish guys were on a lot less than me and I never told them my exact rate – it was really unfair as we were all doing very similar work. The only thing I said was it was

246

very expensive to live in the UK, which has not changed. I said I
needed more money to live and keep my family back home, which
they accepted and never asked me again. As it turned out though,
Abie, who was away from home for nearly a full year before he
went on leave, would have enough to buy himself a new home
when the job finished and he returned to Cape Town. We certainly
could not say that – and nor could the Black Guy!

We went to Johannesburg for a few long weekends and had one
extra-long weekend in Durban. It was the Republican Weekend,
which is usually as near as possible May 31st, the anniversary of
South Africa becoming a republic in 1961.

Graham Spittle, another guy, Dave Marshall and I got a lift with
a young South African kid from Durban who was going home. He
was grateful for the extra money for his petrol costs – and I think
it also paid for the wacky backy he smoked on the journey. The
further we went the higher he got, and by the time we got there he
was as high as a kite.

He dropped us off outside our hotel, which Davy was supposed
to have booked. He ended up blagging our accommodation by
asking to see the general manager and dropping in the name of our
camp boss, who was apparently a friend of the manager, and had
recommended the hotel in the first place. Later, in the bar, Davy
admitted he had never booked the hotel, but he had remembered
the camp boss telling him about his mate. By the time the manager
had spoken to his mate, we would have long gone.

As I mentioned earlier, during the first few days on the job I had
been introduced to a few Hull lads, or 'Hully Gullys' as Hull people
are called in the construction game. Three of them, Norman Carr,
Johnny Haite and Bill Scholey, who had all been on the site quite a
while, had travelled to Durban for the long weekend and were
staying in a hotel just round the corner from the one we were in.
They were with a lad from the Black Country who was only ever
known as 'Yowser.' The four of them could drink for England.
After sorting out our hotel we went to meet them, only to find them
embroiled in a booking fiasco – not helped by the drink already
consumed. I had not had a drink at that stage and I tried to make
some sense of the situation. I went in to the bar where Norman was
sat talking to a guy I had not met. Apparently, when they had
arrived at the hotel about three hours earlier, they had gone straight
to the bar without checking into the hotel. I talked to the
receptionist, apologised on their behalf, and laid it on the line to
them that they booked in then and there or lost their rooms. I ended
up marching them to the desk.

After that, John, Davy and I went out for a meal at a seafood
restaurant not far away. Davy wanted fresh oysters but I am not
keen on them. I much prefer Oysters Kilpatrick, a classic English

recipe involving oysters, cheese, Worcestershire sauce and bacon. I was about to pick something else when the owner came out and asked if everything was ok. I explained about the oysters and he asked me how was the Kilpatrick dish was prepared. He had never heard of it, but was more than willing and get the chef to do them. When they were brought out the owner came to sample one. The look on his face was enough, "Fantastic, I have never tasted anything like them," he said. For the main course we had a wonderful seafood platter – clams, crab, langoustines, fried fillets of fish, all washed down with South African white wine. It was a great meal. When the owner brought the bill, he knocked off the cost of the wine, thanked us for visiting his restaurant and said he would put Oysters Kilpatrick on the menu. It worked out at only about 20 rand each – about £4 then.

When we went back to the hotel, Davy started talking to two girls, who told us they were in a beauty pageant in the hotel the next day. Davy could not resist saying, "Oh yes, we know about that, Keith and I are two of the judges." When the girls' partners came over, they introduced us as two of the judges – incredibly they all believed us. A few free drinks later, we bid them goodnight and said we would see them tomorrow, before moving on to a London-themed pub nearby. Davy soon found a local blonde beauty to turn his attention to. She was way out of his league, but you would never convince him of that. Graham and I were starting to flag a bit, so we made our way back to the hotel via a couple of other bars and were back in for midnight.

On the next morning we could not raise Davy, so Graham and I went out to explore Durban, which is a very nice place. It was their winter, so it was a bit cold and there were not many people on the beaches, apart from the surfers coming in on the big rollers. After a 'livener' at a beachside bar at around noon, we went to a shopping mall before heading back towards the hotel. On the way back, we spotted the London pub we had been before, and went in to see if Davy was there. Sure enough, there he was, this time with four girls in tow. As we left, the giant of a bouncer on the door suggested we take Davy with us before he got in to trouble. Apparently, Davy had left the night before only just before he was about to be thrown out. I tried unsuccessfully to get him to come with us, and as we left 'Giant Haystacks' was beginning to glower threateningly in Davy's direction.

When we got back to hotel, we decided on a couple of hours' kip before our evening adventures. We were not asleep long when there was a banging on the door. It was one of the Hully Gullys, Bill Scholey, and he was well under the influence even then. He wanted us to join him at a party they were having downstairs in the bar. We gave him short shrift and he stumbled off out – or tried to.

RED & WHITE PHOENIX

In fact, he went into a 'walk in' wardrobe and as the door closed behind him the automatic light went out. He was then in pitch blackness, panicked, and started banging and yelling, so I had to let him out

We went down later and joined everyone, including Davy, who had returned. We sat with what you might call some 'more mature' ladies and a guy I had seen the night before but did not know. Last night he had said he was a helicopter pilot with the marines but now he was a submarine commander in the Royal Navy – Norman said that he came from Manchester and was a pipefitter back at the plant. But the ladies were entertained by his James Bond-type tales.

On the way out, we passed through a lounge area where they were having the beauty contest. I had forgotten all about it, but the two husbands from the night before spotted us and came over. They did not look too happy and one of them barked, "Hey you two, what was this judges thing?" in his Afrikaans accent. Davy came out with some waffle about them changing the format and not needing as many judges. They bought it and finished up buying us another beer, which we supped and left, before we were asked any more questions. The rest of the weekend passed with no more dramas and we set off back on the Monday lunch time to the job – and reality – again.

I went to Johannesburg a few times during the time I was out there, stopping at the Casamia Gardens Hotel in Hillbrow, a suburb of the City. It was near to everything and was cheap. Sasol workers got a special deal of 30 rand for two nights bed and breakfast – about £8 for two nights was hard to beat even then! We drank on Saturdays in the *Victoria* Hotel, which had rock bands on during the afternoon and was a meeting place for the lads off the site. We went there on the weekend of my birthday and had a good session – I had been on *Lion* beer and brandy and coke most of the day. We were having a bit of a singsong, with Marshall leading the choir, when the bouncer came up and told us to stop singing and shut up. Now Davy does not like to be disturbed in mid song. He pointed at the bouncer and beckoned him over with his finger. When he came over, Davy whispered in his ear, "Pick a window."

"What you talking about? What window?" this rather large South African gentleman replied.

"Any window! You are going through the bugger if you don't fuck off and leave us alone," was Dave's statement of intent. There were about ten of us in the room at the time maybe more – it would have been another Rorke's Drift if it had kicked off. I had picked up a bottle, and when the bouncer came back with another giant, I gripped it a bit harder. He looked at us and said, "The Boss said you can sing, ok?" turned on his heels and left the room. The atmosphere cleared as the band came back to do the next session and they kicked off with Thin Lizzy's *The Boys Are Back in Town* to rapturous applause.

On our next visit to Jo'burg, Graham and I went into a bar called the Carousel, just for a change. We have all been into somewhere and thought we have made a mistake – and this was one such occasion. I thought we were in the land of giants. The shortest person there must have been six feet – and she was a girl. As we walked in, the place went silent, like a Wild West film, and as we walked up to the bar, Graham whispered to me, "Come on, let's go."

"Bugger that," I said, "We are here now, I'm having a beer!" although I admit to a certain twitching in the nether regions. A guy came over to us and asked if we were new there.

"Nosey bastard, aren't you?" I said – full of bravado, gripping my Lion bottle just in case.

"Ah Brits!" he said, "Okay, no problem. We thought you were police – you have to be careful, my friend!" He put his arm which felt as if it weighed about three stones on its own, around my shoulder. He asked if we were at Sasol and when I said we were, he nodded and walked away, saying something to the rest of the crowd in Afrikaans. That seemed to resolve the problem, and one or two looked over and gave us a smile and a nod. Even Graham relaxed – after saying that we should leave, he had not uttered another word at that point. A rock group came on and we ended up having a great night – so much so that it was dark when we came out.

Then the fun started. The guy who had first approached us was ranting and raving about his mates having gone and left him on his own and that someone had cut the leads to the spark plugs on his motorbike. He told us that bike thieves go round the parking lots and cutting the leads so that people left their bikes, and then return with a lorry to pinch the bikes. I then had a rare flash of inspiration – where it came from I have no idea – I do not have a clue about cars and motorbikes. I pulled some wire off a fence behind us and took the end of the lead, pulled the covering back, wrapped the wire round the bare cable, and then wrapped the other end round the spark plug. I asked him if he had any insulating tape in his pannier, just to hold it together, and luckily he had. I wrapped it in the tape and the engine fired up first go. When he thanked me and took off, I felt very pleased with myself.

Another weekend when we went to Jo'burg, we stopped at the *Carlton* Hotel, which was linked to the Carlton Shopping Mall. It was a lot more expensive than the Gardens, but they had starting giving discounts to Sasol workers so we thought we would give it a try. We shared rooms to save money, but they were much more luxurious and well worth the extra.

RED & WHITE PHOENIX

One night, we were having a few beers in the bar and one of the lads, Gerry, was trying to get into the knickers of a rather elegant-looking woman whom had met at the bar. He was lavishing her with drinks – Irish Coffee was her tipple – and he was matching her with beer, drink for drink. Now she was a seasoned drinker, and was knocking the coffees back like there was no tomorrow. We were sitting in the bar chatting and watching what was going on. He was putting on a bit of a posh accent, acting like an upper-class Englishman in the company of a colonial lady. We were pissing ourselves laughing, and she just kept knocking the coffees back. I went to the bar for some beers and heard her whisper, "What room are you in?"

I turned to the boys and put my thumbs up. A cheer broke out and as she turned around to see what was going on, I could see by Gerry's eyes that he was well gone. As I was going back to the table he ordered a bottle of wine and two glasses, at which she finished her latest coffee and he his beer. She stepped down from the high, swivel-type bar stool whereupon Gerry attempted to slip coolly down from his, and fell flat on his face, spark out. His companion looked down at him with disdain, picked up the bottle of wine, stepped over his prone body and went out of the bar without another word, smiling across at us and giving us a wink as she went. Classic.

Whilst in the Carlton one night, one of the younger guys, Russell, who was from the Southampton area, was sitting talking to me at the bar. He was only in his early twenties, was really missing home and was really down in the dumps. He was very close to his family, especially his father, who owned a pub somewhere in the New Forest. He told me about a job he had been working on back home when the site foreman had taken him under his wing and introduced him to the engineering side of the work. They were staying in a small B&B whilst working away, and one night they had gone out for something to eat. After their meal, whilst they were having a few beers, the foreman put his hand on Russell's groin area under the table and said to him, looking straight into his eyes, "I like you Russell; do you like me?" He then asked him if he had ever made love to a guy. Russell said he was somewhat taken aback by the situation and did not know what to do. He told the foreman that he had not, and quickly left. The next morning the foreman, obviously worried that Russell would blow the whistle on him, asked if he wanted to transfer to another site. Apparently Russell said not, but never to try anything like that again, or he would tell everyone that he was bent.

Russell then looked at me and said in his naïve way, "Do I look queer, Keith?"

"No," I answered, but at the same time I touched the top of his thigh and stroked it slowly as I looked into his eyes and said, "But you never can tell Russell, you never can tell". I never cracked my face although I was bursting inside. He was dumbstruck and I wished I had a camera to capture his priceless expression. He started stammering, "B-b-but, I'm n-n-not", and I could not stop myself from laughing.

"You bastard! You fucking no good bastard! I was beginning to think there was something wrong with me", he burst out. I was pissing myself when I told the guys about what happened. They really gave poor old Russell a hard time, but that was just the craic, the harmless fun and camaraderie we had on the sites. I suppose some would say that it was some kind of abuse now, but that was how it was then. Banter amongst men who were away from home, in their 'temporary families.' I often think about the TV programme, *Auf Wiedersehen Pet*. It was one of the best things I have ever seen on telly, and I can watch it time and time again. I can relate all the characters to someone I have worked with or come across, and to the situation they are portraying.

We went to Jo'burg several times whilst we were there, although towards the end we stopped at the camp for a while, as we were saving our rand for presents to take home. Our last visit to Jo'burg was to be a big shopping trip and I took 1,500 rand that I had saved. I did my shopping and the usual weekend things like having a few beers with the boys and then, on the Sunday lunchtime, the one 'must do' thing, we went to the *Castle* bar. This was the only bar on a Sunday that had live bands on – and was also the meeting place to get the transport back to site. Once again, the place was rocking. It was heaving, as usual.

I had been to the gents and on the way back I had to pass a group of girls. In my best English, I said, "Excuse me, please," to a tall blonde girl in front of me. She turned around and said in a South African accent, "Hello, where are you from?" When I said I was from the UK, she said she knew that, but where in the UK. When I said I was from Hull, she said that her parents were from Castleford. We talked for a while and I told her that I used to spend quite a lot of time in Cas playing rugby league, and that a lot of the lads I played with were from that town. She told me that she was called Caroline and asked me my name. I told her that she would be too young to remember it, but when I told her anyway, she said she had heard of me – probably being nice, but it was still good for the ego! She told me she had followed Cas as a kid and used to go "down't Road" (the Wheldon Road ground where Castleford play).

Caroline said that she had come out to SA to work, enjoyed the lifestyle and had settled there, and that whilst she missed Yorkshire a bit, she was living with it. One thing she said she did not like about South African were then men, whom she thought were arrogant – she had not met many that she had warmed to. It was not easy for single women in South Africa – it could be very dangerous to go out alone at night, particularly in Jo'burg, and the social life is very different to the UK, with very few pubs as we know them. Caroline told me she was going back to Castleford in a few months and would be touring around. I said my number is in the book – give us a call if you can remember my name and call in and see us if you have time. I told her I was married and that I was not looking to chat her up and she giggled and said, "That's ok; it's nice to talk to someone who is honest."

I had spent quite a few minutes chatting to her before I went back to the lads, where I got the third degree – all the usual male questions when you chat with a woman. I was sitting down with the lads when one of her mates brought a note over and whispered in my ear that she was too shy to bring it herself. She had given me her phone number and the note said, 'call me next time you are in town for a coffee and a chat.' I turned and smiled back at Caroline and nodded, she gave a little wave and the boys gave a cheer. I never went back to Jo'burg again and I lost the note – the last time I had it was in my jeans pocket. It had been eight months since I had last had any intimacy with a woman and I was aching to get back to Jacky for the companionship that marriage brings. That chance meeting with Caroline gave me more understanding of why men away from home can be tempted into indiscretion.

The job came to an end and it was time to return to the UK. I think South Africa is a great country but I do not believe that there will ever be true peace there. There are too many tribes that have centuries of conflict between them. The Zulu nation will always be 'top dog' amongst the blacks in my opinion, there will always be corruption, no matter who is in charge, and the minority will always be at the bottom as in most African countries. Nelson Mandela was a great man to say the least, and at least he got rid of apartheid, but at what cost, only time will tell.

We were flown home on KLM via Nairobi and Amsterdam. We are in one section of the plane and attacked the bar with enthusiasm and when we got to Nairobi we were well gone. We went into the terminal whilst they refuelled and a black guy started giving us some grief about 'taking African gold out of the country' as he put it, saying that the money should be spent in Africa. I had heard enough, so I had a go back at him – the beer was starting to take over. Luckily, the airport security had heard what had happened and took him away. Thinking about it afterwards, I was fortunate they did not take me away too. It is not a good idea to start on the locals in a foreign country when you have been drinking.

I must have been more drunk than I realised because when I got back on the plane, I found a steward's cap and started walking up and down the aisle thanking everyone for flying with KLM – what an idiot! I then got into my seat and woke up in Schiphol airport. We were transferring to a flight for Leeds Bradford airport. We had been warned not to overdo the duty free allowance as Leeds was very strict on its customs, so I only brought in what was allowed. As we came through customs there was no green line like nowadays. Everyone had to go the same way and there were loads of customs officers. They asked each individual what they had, and if they were happy they let you through. I had no problem and never even opened my case but one or two unfortunate guys were really given the third degree. I was told later by one of the Geordie lads that one poor guy was stripped and given an internal search.

When I came out of arrivals, Jacky was there to greet me. She looked fantastic and had lost weight – she was back to eleven stones, which is what she was when we got married. I could hardly wait to get her home, feel her in my arms and make love to her. Working away from home either makes or breaks a marriage, and it made ours stronger. I would never have believed that before I met Jacky that I could have stayed celibate for up to eight months at a time in countries where you could meet nice women and have sex every other weekend if you wanted to. I have always felt that we were the right people for each other, had saved our love for each other, and we have been loyal to each other. I have never strayed – I have too much to lose.

Top: Constable Youth Club Under 17 - 1960-61
Below: East Hull ARLFC - 2002 - Joint coach with Lee Radford

Top: 1975 Kempsey Kowboys' Minor Premiers losing Grand Final Team
Below: Hull Kingston Rovers' ex-players

Top: Meeting up with former Rovers' front-rower Dane Tilse
Below: Daniel and I meeting Parramatta Eels' Joel Reddy and Nathan Hindmarsh

Top: At the casino in Sydney with former Hull FC coach, Peter Sharp
Below: Our great friends in Maitland, the McNabs

CHAPTER 16
THE OFFSHORE INDUSTRY

By this time, it was 1982 and after a couple of weeks off I needed to find work again. Brian Robson, with whom I had worked at Sasol rang and told me that Grootcon were recruiting for their module yards in Holland. Grootcon were a big name in the offshore industry in those days. I rang them and got an interview the following week in Stockton. After passing the interview and trade test I was given a job. I had to be at Teesside Airport the following Sunday for a flight to Rotterdam. Once again, I packed my bags and off I went. The rota was three weeks away and one week at home, which was fantastic after what I had just done. The company put employees up in a cheap hotel and paid a 'living away allowance' that covered daily expenses, whilst the salary was paid into the bank tax free. There was no pay for the week off, but when you added everything up the pay was better than you could get working at home.

I travelled up to Teesside Airport by train via Darlington and met up with the Grootcon representative and the guys who were going out to Holland. From Rotterdam, they took us to our hotel, which was the Klarenbeek in Johan De Witt Strata, Dordrecht. It was a nice little place, clean and tidy, with shared rooms, but I was used to that. I was teamed up with a guy I had never met before, Dick Longhurst from the Yarmouth area. We sat together on the way and he seemed a decent steady sort of chap, a bit older than me and also married. He looked a bit like Topol from *Fiddler on the Roof*, with a big beard. The rep was telling us what the form was on the way to the hotel and Dick asked if I wanted to share with him. It was okay by me so we booked in and then went for a walk round Dordrecht.

There were a few guys on the plane and in the hotel who had been home for a week off, so they knew the ropes and we went along with them to one of the bars that the contractors used, the *Stadt*. Another of the regular haunts was the *Frik De Witt*, which was our local and although it was run by a couple of gay men, it was not a gay bar. They did not serve breakfast on a Sunday in the hotel and there was not a lot open, so it was along to the *Stadt*, which was bouncing, not many Dutch people, or Cloggies as we called them, but full of Brits, mostly lads working at Zweindrecht, the Module yard owned by Degroot. There were quite a few Teessiders but no Hully Gullys! We had a few beers before going to the *Frik de Witt* and ended up in a Thai restaurant for our tea.

Keith Pollard

One of the lads from Middlesborough was a friend of the comedian, Roy 'Chubby' Brown. He used to bring his tapes and play them in the bars around Dordrecht. God knows what the locals thought, if any were in the bar, if they could understand him. I had never heard of him before, but I later bought some of his cassettes and have seen him live. I would recommend him, he's not everyone's cup of tea but I find him very funny.

We had to be up at 6am for a 6.30 pick-up in the centre of Dordrecht to be transported by bus to the yard in Zweindrecht on our first morning. When we arrived, we were met by our foremen and shown to our jobs. Mine was a Teessider called Brian, who seemed a decent enough guy. They were building modules for a new oil platform, the *North West Hutton* for Amoco. It was the first time I'd had anything to do with the offshore industry, so it was all new to me.

I was introduced to my welder and rigger and we worked in a small gang, which I thought was a good idea. The welder was another Teessider, a young lad called Billy Wright, and the rigger was an Irish guy from Derby. The gaffers on the job were Paul 'Pongo' Palin from Derby and Eddie 'Rapper' Robson from Newcastle, and the scaffolding foreman, Frankie Salmon, was from Cumberland. The labour was usually supplied from the areas these guys came from, so nepotism and favouritism were rife. There were quite a few guys working in the yards, especially the so-called riggers, that I would not have let loose in a playpen. They had not got a clue, yet here they were, working sometimes in very confined spaces with men below them, installing prefabricated pipe spools and steelwork. These were the days before method statements and risk assessments had been heard of in the UK.

I was given a set of drawings and shown where the spools were to go and more or less left to it. I got stuck in and was doing okay. Part of the job was checking that the pipework would actually fit in where it was supposed to. This meant checking the co-ordinates and the elevation and reporting any discrepancies back to the foreman. The first job they gave me was a load of concrete lined pipe spools that were for the sprinkler system but they would not fit. Brian came up and checked that I was correct, before he brought in the piping engineer to sort the problem. I was right in what I had said and they now had to come up with a solution to rectify the fault, which would take time. Another set of isometric drawings was issued to me and off I went again to check out the situation for installing some other pipes, and it was another 'no go' scenario. I started to think I was a Jonah. Apparently though, the whole job was one big cock-up. This was a goldmine to Grootcon, they were being paid to install the materials and all these revisions were extras, so they were coining it in.

RED & WHITE PHOENIX

I was enjoying my time in Holland. You learn after a while as a contractor working away from your home and family that there are three elements to a job. First, the work, which I enjoyed, it was a bit frustrating at times but it was an area I had not been involved in before and I loved the challenge. Second, the money, which was okay, but I took the job to get into the offshore game, so in a way that was secondary. Third, the social side or to use the Irish term, the craic, which was brilliant. These three were good indicators of how a job would pan out, and my rule was 'one out of three' – leave; 'two out of three' – live with it; 'three out of three' – stick with it! I stayed with Grootcon for over a year, working my three weeks on and one week off.

I had some great times over there. We worked a 50 hours week over five and a half days, met some real characters, and had some funny times. There was a group of five girls that hung about in the bars we frequented, and if I say that we nicknamed them the Whale, Jaws, Bigfoot, the Skull and Plastic Monkey, you'll get the picture. I could not for the life of me understand why guys hung about with these women who were only after a good time and free beer. Some guys must have spent a fortune pouring beer down their throats and taking them out for meals in exchange for sex – and they were only away from home for three weeks for heaven's sake. If they needed sex that badly, the sex capital of Europe, Amsterdam, was only an hour's train ride away. It would have cost a lot less than what they were laying out on the Dordrecht dogs, as they were called. A couple of guys whom I met in Holland later 'lost' their families through playing around with these local girls.

It was getting towards the depths of winter and it gets really cold in Holland, being so flat and low. We were out one freezing night for a few beers and were walking down a bit of a slope in Indian file, when Davy Millom passed me doing a tipple tail. He must have rolled over half a dozen times. We went to the bottom of the slope, where he lay in a heap, to help him up and he said, or I think he said, in his broad Geordie accent, "I only bent down to pick up my tab!"

At Easter we did not come home, but we did not work either as the yard was closed for the holidays. We decided to get the train to Antwerp for a day trip on Easter Saturday. We got the train from Dordrecht to Amsterdam, where we changed onto the Antwerp train, which was about three hours in all. The Dutch rail service is a fantastic system. You can practically set your watch by it, the trains always seem to run on time. Antwerp Central Station is an unbelievable building – it reminded me of a church – and I had never seen anything like it. It was constructed between 1895 and 1905 as a replacement for the original terminus of the Brussels-Antwerp railway and is, I understand, regarded as the finest

The North West Hutton Platform

example of railway architecture in Belgium. The viaduct into the station is an equally remarkable structure.

We had a wander round and headed for the square, or Grote Markt, which is probably best known for the beautiful Guilds houses that surround it. If you ever visit, look at the beautiful statues on top of these buildings.

At the centre of the square there is a large fountain depicting Antwerp's most famous legend, the mythical hero Brabo. According to legend, a giant, Antigoon, demanded a high toll for each ship to enter the city and if the ship's crew did not pay the toll, their hands were cut off. The hero Brabo fought the giant, cut off his head and a hand, and threw the hand into the river. The statue depicts Brabo throwing the hand in the river Scheldt and symbolises free passage through the river. It is a political swipe at the Dutch, who used to block free traffic on the Scheldt.

We found a fantastic restaurant just round the back of the Guild Hall. It had a U-shaped bar, in the middle of which was a massive barbeque grill, where the owner of the bar was working. He was a stereotypical Belgian, with a big handlebar moustache and was wearing a chef's hat and full regalia. The house speciality was steak in a white peppercorn sauce with Belgian fries, so we ordered steaks all round and it was gorgeous. After we had finished our

258

meal we wandered around the area and down to the river. We were lucky to be there when the Tall Ships race was being held and it was a great sight to see all these wonderful ships.

The first Tall Ships' race, from Torquay to Lisbon was held in 1956, featuring 20 of the world's remaining large sailing ships. It was meant to be a last farewell to the era of the great sailing ships, but public interest was so great that it has been held every year since in different parts of the world. The 50th Anniversary Tall Ships' race took place during July and August 2006, and was started by the patron, Prince Philip, Duke of Edinburgh, who also started the first race. Today, the race attracts more than a hundred ships.

We set off back to Dordrecht after a great day, and we decided to have a day around the town on the following day and go to Amsterdam on the Monday. Dordrecht was a good place to be based and is a very pleasant town. It is known as the ancient capital and oldest city in Holland with an interesting history going back to the end of the tenth century. It was granted city status in 1220, before becoming an important market city during the 12th and 13th centuries due to its strategic location close to the North Sea.

We took the train to Amsterdam on Easter Monday, arriving around lunchtime. We went for lunch in an Italian restaurant, which did great food, after which we went for a wander round and did some 'window shopping'. You name it, you can get it there, whatever takes your fancy. As we walked past one shop, a gorgeous-looking girl, the double of Britt Ekland stopped me and said something in Dutch. When I answered in English, she said, "Is there anything I can do for you?"

"Yes, please," I replied, but before I could continue, Dick butted in with, "Be gentle with him won't you!" I then asked her if she could change a 20-guilder note as I wanted to phone the wife.

"Fuck off!" she said as we toddled away laughing our heads off. When I rang the wife, she said, "Where are you today?" I told her we were in Amsterdam, looking in the windows, and that I had just got some change off one of the girls.

"Oh yes, I can believe that!" was her reply. We had a great day and headed back home.

I was at Zweindrecht for nearly a year, and all in all, it was a good place to work. The Dutch site manager, however, Brugeneck, was a bastard who seemed not to like the Brits. In the middle of winter it was really cold and one guy said to him, "It's warmer outside than it is in this building,"

"Ok, no problem," replied Brugeneck, "I will open the doors and let some warm air in."

It was a massive building, wide and tall enough to get a drilling rig in, and it was like a wind tunnel when you opened the doors. I

The Phillips Maureen Platform

was up a scaffold in the roof of the mud module one day and he was walking below the scaffold on the other side. I saw a guy drop a blank flange off the scaffold immediately above him. If it had hit him it could have killed him, and I could have sworn it was deliberate. Luckily it hit a lot of obstructions on the way down. Brugeneck looked up but could not see the culprit. I spoke later to the guy who had dropped the flange and he denied it. I said, "Don't deny it. I saw you do it. You tried to kill him."

RED & WHITE PHOENIX

"Pity it didn't," he replied, walking away laughing. Some gaffers are lucky they are still alive, for every friend they make, they make three enemies. Industrial sites are dangerous places and I have met some very bad men in my career. They were in a minority, but it only takes one.

One guy I worked with in Holland, who lived in the North-East told me that he was interviewed in connection with the Yorkshire Ripper case. He had returned from working away when the police came to his house and took him back to Leeds to interview him. His car had been spotted in Leeds on a few occasions and some of the dates had been around about the same time as the murder dates. Apparently, the bloke had been seeing a girl in Leeds and had been going there instead of going home. The detective who interviewed him was sure that he had got the right man, mainly due to the gap in his teeth that matched some marks on the victims. It was only the fact that he could prove from his time sheets that he was not in Leeds and was working away on several of the murder dates that cleared him.

I was transferred from the fabrication yard onto offshore hook-up and commissioning work, first on a small platform in Dutch waters off Dan Helder, doing around four trips, then onto similar work on the *North West Hutton* platform in the North Sea, 130 km north east of the Shetland Islands. That was about a four-hour flight in a helicopter from Aberdeen and sometimes longer if we had to refuel in Shetland on the way back. *North West Hutton* was the only integrated oil and gas drilling, production processing and accommodation facility on this oilfield. It was an impressive structure that rests on a 'jacket,' that weighs about 17,500 tons and is positioned on a 290-ton steel template installed under the seabed using steel piles. It comprises 21 modules including the wellhead, production, utilities, drilling derricks, an accommodation block and a heli-deck. It was cold, hard work and I did ten trips, mostly on night-shifts, some of which towards the end were in mid-winter. In those days I had a moustache and after working a shift outside it would be frozen solid.

It was whilst I was on this platform that I had an accident. I was on a day-shift working on piping in the well-head area. The pipes were not very big in diameter but were very heavy and in awkward shapes due to the complexity of the design. I was dragging a spool across the gratings and one of the flooring panels had not been installed correctly. In fact, I found out later that none of them had. As I pulled the spool it caught on something and stopped but my momentum took me forward and my feet pushed the grating away from the steelwork supporting it. I dropped through the opening upright and feet first. All I remember was the pain in my back as my feet hit the floor about nine feet below. I fell backwards onto

261

some pipes and lay there for a few minutes, not daring to move. Having played rugby, I knew how to fall and maybe that saved me from a worse injury. Within a few minutes, I started to get some feeling back in my legs. I tried to get up but by this time there were people around me telling me to lay still and saying that help was on its way. My safety helmet had been dislodged and I remember someone putting it back on my head. Next, the medics were there, asking me how I was as I laid on the floor, wet through with mud and freezing cold water.

"Let me get up and I will be okay – I will die of pneumonia sat in this water," I said.

"Take it easy," was the reply. "We are going to get a stretcher to get you to the hospital bay."

"Like hell you are!" I answered. The only way they could get a stretcher to the hospital with me on it was using the crane, as the hospital was situated under the heli-deck. No way was I going on a stretcher at the end of a crane hook that high! I do not know how high it was, but whatever it was, it was too high! I managed to walk up the stairs, very slowly I admit, but I got there in the end. When I got into the medical bay I was examined by Phillip, one of our medics, who was as camp as Christmas. I held my breath and thought of mother England as he moved his hands up and down my spine. What he was feeling for I do not know but I put my trust in him. He 'oo'd' and 'ah'd' for a while and asked how I was feeling.

They kept me in the hospital overnight and a day later I was back at work, a bit sore but none the worse for my ordeal. When I got back to the well head area under the mezzanine level where I had been working, I had a good look around. If I had fallen a couple of yards either way, I would not be writing this. On one side there was a six by four metre sheet of plate standing up on its edge, which would have cut me in half like a cheese slice. And on the other sides were holes for extra drill pipes, about four feet in diameter each and covered with bits of thin sheet plate. I would have gone straight through any one of them, right down to the spider deck about a 100 feet below. If I'd been a cat, only eight lives would be left.

One good thing about *North West Hutton* was the accommodation barge. This was the *Treasure Hunter*, a Norwegian semi-submersible barge. It was an old vessel but the beds were fantastic, each were about three feet wide and for me they were heaven. The food was also great. For the first time in my life I had venison, or reindeer as the Norwegians called it. I thought it was really good and had it two or three times a week. At one point I was transferred to live in the accommodation on the platform, where the beds were so narrow that I could not sleep for the fear of falling out. They were four-man cabins, with the top two bunks on either side about two feet wide and five feet from the floor. I only slept up there one night and then put the mattress between the two bottom bunks on the floor. When the others in the cabin complained they had some weirdo in the room that slept on the floor, they soon moved me back to the *Treasure Hunter*.

Whilst on this job there was also a near miss whilst I was in the helicopter. Due to bad weather, the barge had pulled away from the platform on its anchor chains. Men were being transferred to and from the platform by helicopter at either end of their 12-hour shifts. We were going over to start the night shift and it was really blowing a gale. We could see that the pilots were a bit apprehensive about flying in such bad weather but the pressure was on to get the men to work. When we got on board, the pilot had the rotor going fast to try and keep the helicopter from blowing over. After we had got on board and buckled up, he hit the throttle and the helicopter went up in the air like a bullet. I never had a take-off like it. We went really high and then arced away from the barge and the platform before curving round back to the platform at speed to land. They abandoned flying for the night after that.

Apparently, what had happened was the wind changed direction just as the pilot started to lift off. Witnesses told me the following day that the rotor was shaped like an onion as we went up in the air – if it had not been for the pilot's quick reactions, there would have been a disaster.

One trip coincided with Christmas and New Year. They asked for volunteers to work one of those periods so that everyone got either Christmas or New Year at home. If you were married with young kids they tried to arrange it for you to be home at Christmas. I returned to work after Christmas and had been back a couple of days when I started to feel rough, so I went to the medic to get some paracetamol. But after the shift I was feeling even worse. The medic took my temperature, which was soaring and I was put into the hospital. I thought my time had come. My chest was really tight and I was coughing up blood and phlegm. I was flown off first thing in the morning and taken straight to a doctor in Aberdeen, who prescribed antibiotics. I was then taken to the airport, where I had to sit until six at night, as the usual flight was not running that day. When we arrived at Teesside, a taxi was waiting for me. The driver was most unhappy when I said I wanted to go to Hull. I got in the back of the car, which luckily was a big Merc, and the driver was wittering away all the way down the A19 to York, but I was so dosed up that most of it passed me by. When we got to the Humber Bridge and he asked how much further it was, I said, "Withernsea, just the other side of Hull!" That really pissed him off.

I was in bed for a full week and lost over a stone in weight. The doctor said I had been as close as I could be to getting pneumonia.

Keith Pollard

He was most unhappy about the way I had been treated and suggested I should take it further. But if I did that, they would have looked on me as a trouble-causer and got rid of me. You just did not do things like that if you wanted to work offshore. Most companies treated you like the proverbial, but to be fair Grootcon were quite good to work for, so I did not rock the boat. When I went back, I got some right stick off the lads. They thought I had worked it to get New Year off and no one really believed that I had been ill.

It was then back to nightshift again, but that was okay with me, I quite liked it. One night, we were going around the pipework finishing off things that had been missed or needed correcting when the foreman, Charlie Simpson, one of the better ones, asked me to do a little job. He then said that, when I had done it, he would not be looking for me for the rest of the shift. This was unheard of, so I immediately thought there must be some catch.

"Ok, no problem," I said. "What do you want me to do?"

"Go out there and fit these two penetration sleeve covers," he replied. These were similar to a bandage, conical in shape, which were wrapped around the pipe penetration and the pipe itself, with the ends glued together and fastened on with jubilee clips. I went out and it was blowing a hurricane and freezing. I got up the scaffold and the wind was cutting through my coat, overalls, thermal underwear, the lot. I have never been as cold in my entire life. My hands were so numb that I could hardly hold the screwdriver to tighten up the clips. I did one then went back inside for a warm. Charlie was standing there and said, "Done 'em both, have you?"

"Fuck off! Not yet – I'm frozen!" I replied.

"What's up? Are you getting soft?" he smirked. It took half an hour to get any feeling back in to my hands. I went back and did the smaller of the two and got back inside. Low and behold, there was Charlie again.

"Have you done 'em?" he asked.

"Yes – what a fucking job that was!" I replied.

"Fine," he said. "Just come and have a look at this now, will you?" I was just about to erupt when he started laughing.

"Go on, get a drink and get out of the way!" he said. "A deal is a deal. I won't be looking for you".

It was a good job to be on. When I came to the end of my time there, they paid me off and I got another job straight away on the Gas Terminal at Easington, down near the mouth of the Humber estuary. They had combined the Amoco and BP terminals into one and I was working in the onsite fabrication shop for Laing Industrial Engineering. It was a steady enough job but I was not there long when I got a call from Grootcon to go offshore again, this time on a long term hook-up on the Phillips *Maureen* Platform.

264

RED & WHITE PHOENIX

The *Maureen* was built to a unique design and was the only large tripod steel gravity base and oil storage structure of her kind. The base was the world's first steel platform to combine flotation, ballasting and oil storage. The gravity base structure comprised three large cylindrical tanks, each measuring over 25 metres in diameter and standing 74 metres high. After completion, the base was floated and towed to Loch Kishorn on the west coast of Scotland, where the deck was being built at the Howard Doris yard. The deck and base were mated by submerging the substructure and floating the deck over on a barge. The platform was then towed out to the Maureen field in the North Sea and, by using controlled ballasting procedures placed over the drilling template through which some wells had already been drilled using a mobile drilling rig. Some eighteen years later, with the field exhausted, in an operation no one was certain would succeed, the tanks were de-ballasted and the 112,000-ton platform was floated away to be scrapped in Norway.

We flew out to the platform, where we were to live on a nearby drilling barge, Selco 6, as the platform accommodation was full. We shuttled to and from the platform in a small, five-man Bolco helicopter. A couple of days later, we had just arrived on the barge in this fashion, when the Heli-deck Landing Officer told us to go below and stay there. Apparently, there was a problem with the Bolco. One of its engines had blown and it was returning after aborting the flight. A mate of mine, Terry Foster from Maltby, had been on board at the time, and he appeared in the accommodation as white as a sheet. He told me he thought he was a goner. There had been a big bang and the helicopter fell about 15 feet with flames and smoke coming out of the engine cowl. They were very lucky that day that's for sure.

The Bolco was stranded on the heli-deck and it was going to be a few days before they could get a replacement engine out to the rig. Great, a few days' rest, we thought – but we were wrong. It was decided that they would shuttle us over to the *Maureen* by boat. We were asked if we were willing to use what is called a 'Billy Pugh,' which is a basket suspended on the end of a crane, which is banned in the North Sea unless under exceptional circumstances. The Billy Pugh was cone-shaped with a floatable ring about eight feet in diameter and the net was about eight feet high, in four quadrants around the ring with gaps between each segment. I asked if we sat inside the basket and was told that we did not – we stood outside on the ring, holding on to the net.

"Is this for real?" I asked. I have no real head for heights at the best of times, but to be lifted heaven knows how high was not for me. We were told we did not have to go, but we knew the consequences if we did not – 'not required back'. The first lot of guys went out on to the heli-deck and were lowered down using the

Keith Pollard

drilling crane onto the supply boat. We were then told that we could watch and if we did not fancy it we did not have to do it. I went out and watched and said, "I am not happy about it, but I will do it if I have to." The landing officer came back to me and said, "Don't worry Keith, they are not coming back for the last two." That was a rigger called Bill and myself. We then sat and had a coffee, until the landing officer came in and said, "Okay guys, there's been a change of plan, they are coming back for you." My nether quarters started to twitch as we put on our survival suits and got ready to go. Bill said to me, "Just stand in the gap between the segments, put your arms through the net, clamp your hands together and close your eyes. Do not look down whatever you do and I will tell you when to open them."

We were lowered down into the supply boat and sailed across to the platform. It was dead flat and there was no problem. We sat in the galley chatting to the crew until one of them told us we were there. I was sweating by this point and the next bit really turned my bowels to water. We went outside and were told to stand back whilst the basket was lowered down. I looked up and up – I needed a hinge in my neck to see that far up – it was a hell of a height. I got on the net and did as Bill had told me. I felt us lift off but the crane driver took it easy and it was not too bad. As we got over the heli-deck Bill said, "Okay, you can open your eyes now." The bastard! We were still hovering over the deck! But I did okay, even if my hands were white when I unclamped them.

"Thanks for coming lads, where the hell have you been!?" Eddie 'Rapper' Robson, the Superintendent, greeted us. I told him a few home truths and he just laughed.

"Bugger off and get a drink, I'll catch you in a minute." After our twelve-hour shift, the fog cleared and we did not have to go back by boat as the Bolco was now repaired and took us back. A couple of days later we moved over to the platform to live and I was there for eighteen months. It was the best job I had ever had. I was one of the first six pipe-fitters on the job, which meant something in the days when it was 'first in, last out.' The gaffers were good, the owner's staff were spot on, as were the food and accommodation, even the work was interesting and the platform was spacious and not congested like so many are. It was supposed to be the first one of its kind and all platforms were to be built like that but of course that never happened, as they started to introduce sub-sea engineering and using sub-sea wells and then floating production, storage and offloading facilities arrived.

In keeping with tradition, the bulk of the crew were from the North-East. One of the Geordies asked why a Yorky, Terry Foster, and a Hully Gully, me, got on before him – and was told, 'Because they're both better than you, that's why.' Even a 'Mackem', Vince

266

RED & WHITE PHOENIX

Robson, got on before him, which was an insult! I had worked with lots of lads from Newcastle before, they certainly look after each other and these were no different, they were a good set of lads to work with. My foreman was Dave 'Sleeper' Neilings, a young Geordie who seemed destined for bigger and better things.

When working offshore, pipe-fitters were usually paired up, one of the main reasons being that you needed one to do the work and the other to ensure that nothing caught fire – as you can imagine, fire is the biggest threat to an oil platform. Even if the platform was not 'live', you still had to work as if it was – using the work permit system as laid down by the operator or owner.

One lad I was partnered up with on the *Maureen*, Smithy, had a terrible tragedy when he was home for Christmas. His young son had gone out on his new bike on Christmas day and was knocked down and he died of his injuries. It was terrible for him and his family, the sort of thing that should just never happen. I never thought he would return to work offshore. But he came back to work a couple of trips later and was sent to partner me. I was on a job installing a spray curtain over the side of the platform on a scaffold. It was hard for Smithy. I could see he was suffering. He kept going off the job to be on his own and when he returned would pour his heart out telling me all about the accident. It was heartbreaking and I was also getting worried about him. I went to the foreman and suggested they give him a job somewhere that was not so precarious. I was concerned that because he was feeling so low, he could have done anything. Working on a scaffold overhanging the North Sea is not the best place to be if your head is not right, and his was not. It was too hard for him being away from his wife and family at such a time and finally he packed the job in and went home.

Our foreman, Ronnie, had the nickname of 'the Wounded Buffalo.' We had safety meetings in the platform cinema, which were scheduled to last for an hour. We used to keep asking questions to try and make it last longer and every time someone asked another question Ron would look at his watch and his left eye would twitch along with his leg, just like a buffalo that was shot and wounded in the old Westerns films. The more we asked the longer the twitch. We all thought it was hilarious and used to organise questions beforehand.

When I eat ice cream, I always remember Joe Nelson, the Offshore Installation Manager. Whenever he returned from leave, his first question was, "What flavour ice cream have we got this trip?" I had never seen anyone who loved ice cream like Joe and it amused me that the flavour of the ice cream was his main worry!

During the period I was on the *Maureen* we moved house from Withernsea to Hedon, about six miles east of Hull. Jason had

Keith Pollard

moved on to senior school and was not doing too well at Withernsea High School. However, South Holderness School in Hedon had a good reputation and we thought that if he went there it might help him. It proved to be a good move and he improved out of sight.

I volunteered for redundancy in late 1984 as there were going to be pay-offs and I'd been offered a possible long-term job as a piping supervisor at Torness nuclear power station on the Scottish Borders. The guy who took my place, Ted 'Six-pack' Collins, told me years later that he was made redundant three times, which meant he was paid 80 hours in lieu of notice each time. He thanked me very much for what he called 'a great favour'. It cost me money, but you win some and you lose some. It was the end of me working offshore for a while.

I accepted the job at Torness for Aitons of Derby. A mate of mine, Harry Hodgins, who was already working there, was asked by the management to contact me and ask if I would be interested in a supervisor's job. I had never worked in the nuclear power industry and thought it would be a change. My new shift manager was a guy called Tommy Carter and the Project Manager was Harry Poynton, both of them were real characters in their own right, to say the least. They had worked for Laing at Easington where Tommy was my foreman.

I started on the day shift for a couple of weeks before we started working on a two-shift system – 6am to 2-30pm and 3-30pm to 11pm. There were five of us from Hull who travelled home every weekend together – Barry Middlebrook, Norman Carr, Neil Hagger, Harry and myself. At first, we used each other's cars every fifth week, but it was putting too many miles on the new car I had just bought, so I proposed that I buy a car and they pay me to run it. They agreed and I bought an old Ford Granada off a mate of mine for a grand. We shared the fuel costs between us, with a bit extra for the extra insurance and road tax. It worked out fine and I sold the car to Barry when I left the job for the same price as I'd paid for it.

The supervisor on the other shift was a guy called Gerry Houston, a great lad from Glasgow – as were most of them until a few Hully Gullys came onto the job. The shop steward was the secretary of the CEU and he told me that after this job he would not get on another site for about four years. He was not militant but one or two of the riggers were a bit red-necked and often tried to create friction on the job. We had to try and keep a tight rein on them as we had lost a few days through them 'going out the gate,' as it was called. They could be quite intimidating to some of the other lads on the job, but we could not prove any wrongdoing. I did not have any hassle on my shift but the manager on the opposite shift did not

268

appear to give Gerry a lot of help. Tommy just let me get on with the job, whilst the other guy was always interfering. We used to have daily meetings between the shift changes and I had my handover meeting with Gerry whilst Harry was having his. He would often blow up when he saw us talking quietly together.

"How the fuck do you get all that done in eight hours?" Gerry asked me. "I can't get half the production you are achieving."

"Job and knock – especially the back shift," I replied, meaning that I used to get the lads to get really stuck in for at least six hours flat out, cutting the odd corner here and there to get the work done. Then I let them go and clocked them off at the end of the shift. They took it in turns to go early, two or three a shift depending on who travelled with whom.

I had a 'run in' with the Irish planner one meeting. We had a programme of work laid out for each shift. The reactor was round, so they split the work areas in half.

We did one half on all floors and Gerry did the other half. My erectors installed support and steelwork along with pipe spools for Gerry, and he did the same in my half for my squad. The planner had told me that if we got held up in any areas, I could fall back to doing the boiler start-up pipework that was not yet in the programme, as it was not a priority.

We had been having problems with access due to civil work being undertaken, so I started on Plan B. At our weekly meeting we worked down our list and I suggested that we had problems with most of the work planned. When we got to the end Harry said, "Well, what the hell have you been doing this week? Every day you have been having problems!" Then the planner said, "Why did you start on the Plan B work? I never told you to do it."

"Yes, you did," I said.

"No, I never!' he replied. I then called him a liar and asked Harry if he had a toilet roll, 'to wipe up the shit coming from that Irish bastard's mouth.' The meeting erupted. Harry was shouting at me to apologise but there was no chance of that. The Irishman was also having a go too, whilst Gerry and I sat there chuckling. Tommy gave me the thumbs up sign, he did not like the planner either. In the end the Irishman said, "Well, I may have mentioned it to Keith, come to think of it." He was a liar, he'd told me alright.

We often had rather lively meetings but all in all it was a very good job. Tommy Carter told me that they needed more good pipe-fitters and asked if I could recommend any. I gave him four names and they were all started on. Davy Marshall was one of them. I was quite open and told Tommy that he might be a sausage roll short of a picnic, he was not the best pipe-fitter, he did not particularly like work because it got in the way of his social life, and sometimes the drink affected his output. But he would sort out the cabin and the harassment that was going on. It had started to creep in on my shift, but no one complained, and I could not prove anything, I had my ideas and had words with the guys I thought were responsible, but they flatly denied it.

On his first day onsite, Davy was put to work with one of the other fitters for familiarisation. He was up on a scaffold as Harry Poynton was doing his weekly walkabout with Tommy. Without warning, Davy jumped off the scaffold, right in front of the two of them, introduced himself to Harry and thanked him for giving him a start on the job. Then off he went, as quickly as he'd appeared. Harry turned to Tommy and asked, "What the hell was that all about?" Tommy just laughed and shrugged his shoulders.

A couple of days later there were rumblings about there being a stoppage and I was expecting the steward to request a meeting in the canteen after lunch. Sure enough he came to see me with the request, which I granted. At the meeting it came to a vote about striking, and the steward asked if anyone had anything to say.

"Yes, I do," Davy said. "No one is going to tell me what to do and, even if you vote to strike, I am carrying on working." This was all the majority needed – a leader to speak up for them in front of the bullies. They had a show of hands and the vote was to stay at work. I don't even know what the problem was, it never got back to us. I heard that a couple of the so-called heavies tried to intimidate Davy, but that fell on stony ground. Apparently, he told them that if they wanted to sort it out on the car park, he was quite willing to oblige. They did not take up the offer and things were quiet for quite a while.

The craic was good both on and off the job. As I've said, I usually got home every weekend – it was a bit of a rush when we changed shifts from 'backshift' to the earlier six till two, but that was just part of the job. We did the main steam pipe-work, which involved preheating and stress-relieving the butt welds. I did not want weekend work but one weekend we needed supervision on the site and Tommy asked me if I would do him a favour and work. I told him that I had brought the lads up with me and needed to take them back home, so he lent me the site pick-up truck, and I let them take the car. All I had to do was to supervise the cooper heat stress guys. It was a doddle but when I went in, I could feel there was a bit of a tense atmosphere amongst the four guys who were on shift. The charge hand was a good guy, so I pulled him to one side and asked him what the problem was. He was quite open and said the rest of the crew where a bit worried about getting 'flyers.' He explained what was expected from them and the scope of work that needed to be completed. I was not sure if he was taking the mickey as I was on my own and I did not want to rock the boat. I was a bit apprehensive about his breakdown of the work schedule, but then Tommy came on site.

"Come on, we're going for a drink," he said.

"What about the stressors?" I asked.

"Oh, just leave them to it, we'll sort them out after," he replied.

We went into Dunbar and visited most of the pubs that Saturday afternoon. We met a few of Tommy's mates and had quite a session. When we went back about 3.30pm the guys had left the site and we clocked them off. The same thing happened on the Sunday. As a supervisor, I did not have to clock on and off, so I did not go in until about 10.30 and then went in to Dunbar again for a pint and pub lunch for an hour or so and then clocked the guys off.

If Harry Poynton knew that this was going on, he would have had a coronary. But the work was done and everything was running smoothly, so everyone was getting something out of it. If the guys had not gone in and checked the stressing process was running correctly it would have been a lot more expensive to correct a fault later. This had been going on every weekend, so I had missed out on a few easy weekends, but I still would rather have gone home every weekend.

For our first Christmas on the job, Davy organised a get-together at the Holmes Arms in Eyemouth. We all put money in each week for a month or so leading up to the event. As usual it was a great night out. One or two outsiders tried to gatecrash the party but they had obviously not heard about Davy. They soon did, and they soon left – our one-man wrecking ball made sure of that.

By September 1986, we had been back from Australia about ten years and had discussed going back on holiday. We decided that if Aitons would let me have two weeks unpaid leave we would go back to Oz for a four-week holiday. We had saved about £7,000 and we said that if we would have £2,000 left after the holiday it would be worth going. I asked Harry and he agreed but said I could be away no more than four working weeks.

So off the four of us went. We flew with *Garuda*, the Indonesian airline, which was the cheapest – we had a couple more stops than the bigger airlines, but we got a good deal. We had three days in Bali on the way there, stopping at the Sanur Beach Hotel, which, though not the most expensive, was still good. The food was spot on and the kids loved it.

There was a great restaurant just along the beach, which was recommended by an Australian couple, Jack and Karen Hicky, whom we had kept in touch with for years. We'd had a chance meeting and had stayed friends – we even went to see them on another visit later. You could walk to the restaurant along the beach when the tide was out, but otherwise you could only get to it the long way round via the village – which was rather run down and a bit dangerous, especially at night. The locals were very poor and

Keith Pollard

Kowboys' reunion in 1986

272

RED & WHITE PHOENIX

mugging and robbing was quite common. We had a great night with Jack and his wife, but we had to walk the long way back as the water was high. The back streets of Sanur were certainly not pleasant at night, but we got back safe and sound.

The beach outside the hotel had its own security guards, to keep away the beggars and junk sellers, who could be a nuisance. I do not know how they made an existence – even in the shops and arcades you could barter them down in price to next to nothing. Bali was one of the Australian most visited holiday destinations in the 1970s and we did not have long enough to see more of it. We would love to go back for a bit longer one day.

We flew in to Sydney where Alan Fris, a Kiwi friend, came to the airport to pick us up. I always think that if you have a friend in the southern hemisphere, you have a friend for life. They will do anything for you and, whenever we go back, they all want us to stay with them. It can be embarrassing because you cannot cut yourselves into bits to keep everyone happy – but that is just the way they are. They are great people and will do anything for you. We have never been asked for a penny, but we always chip in, take them out for meals, buy a weekly shop, or whatever we can do to ensure they are not out of pocket. I do know some guys in Hull who would not go to Australia or New Zealand unless they had people to stay with, to save on hotels and expenses, which is just greed in my opinion.

We stayed with Alan's family in Maitland for a week or so. Jason really loved being back although he did not really remember much about Oz, as he was only six when we returned home.

"What the hell did you take me back to Hull for – why didn't we stay in Australia?" he said to me one day, and he wanted to come back when he was older. Alan's daughter Caroline took Tracy to school, where they thought her Pommie accent was fantastic.

We had a great reunion at the Pickers. It was fantastic seeing all our friends and talking about old times – and plenty of amber nectar was thrown back! I was even offered a coaching job with the Macquarie Scorpions in the Newcastle competition. Strangely, having been away ten years and out of the game for a long time, someone wanted to offer me a coaching job straightaway – whilst clubs in the UK would not give me a chance. Along with the coaching job came a job in the mines, which was like winning the lottery – it was a real closed shop. A few of the committee members at Macquarie were union men at the Toronto pit and they said they could get me a job there with no problem. A house would also be included as part of the contract. They were an 'up and coming' club and had quite a few decent players pass through the club over the years, including Willie Mason and Craig Bellamy, the Melbourne Storm Coach. Obviously, I had to decline the offer, but it was nice

Keith Pollard

to be asked.

From Maitland we travelled up to Kempsey to see our friends there. We went to a couple of Kempsey Mustangs games – they had changed the name of the club by then. They were in the play-off semi-finals and we went to Bellengen to watch them play the old enemy, Smithtown. I was standing outside the dressing rooms when Skippy Mayhew, who was on the Kempsey Committee, asked me if I would go in and have a word with the team. I agreed providing that it was ok with the coach – but he had apparently actually asked Skippy to ask me if I would do it. I went in and gave them a bit of a Churchillian-type speech, saying that I had not travelled 13 thousand miles to see that bunch of wankers in the other dressing room beat them. Also, I said, even if you never ever win another game, if you turn them over you will still be talked about in years to come as the kings of the river in 1986. I cannot remember everything I said, but it seemed to work. The coach told me they had played the best they had all season, when he came to thank me for my contribution. I felt really proud that, even after 10 years, I was still regarded as a decent coach and motivator.

The win put them into the Grand Final for the first time since I took them there in 1975. He asked me if I would be there on finals day but that was the day we flew back to the UK. History repeated itself again – they lost to Nambucca Heads, the same team that beat us eleven years earlier. Kempsey have never been in a Grand Final since and they do not even have a team in group two now.

We had another reunion with a few old mates in Kempsey. We had a great time and once again they were good people – apart from one bloke. My old team-mate Mick Flanagan apparently still held a grudge all those years later. He was in the Kempsey Heights bowling club on the same night as us and had told some of the lads that he would not speak to me or even shake hands with me. I went over to him and said, "G'day mate! How's you? Okay?" and put out my hand to him. When he somewhat reluctantly took it, there was a huge cheer from the other side of the bar. He then brought up his feelings once again, but he did admit that, having watched a lot of football on the television over the years and understanding the mentality of the English towards winning championships, he understood now how I felt. He never apologised, but I would not expect Mick Flanagan to say he was sorry to anyone, about anything. He was always right, he was just that sort of guy.

We travelled back home after a month away, not knowing if we would ever see our friends again. A month is not long enough to travel to Australia for a holiday – it is too big a place to travel around in that time. But we have been back a few times since.

I went back to work at Torness and was not a happy bunny. Harry Hodgins told me on the way back that they had altered the job and that it was not as good as it was when I left on my holidays. He told me they had abolished the 'extra hour' that supervisors were paid for doing the paperwork at the end of the shift, saying that it had to be done during the eight hours we worked. I was told that Tommy had accused Poynton of waiting until I was away before he reduced the hours because he knew I would not stand for it. He replied that he would worry about that when I got back. I was back and I was fuming. I went straight in to see him when I got back on site and he gave me a load of bollocks about not being able to pay the hour. I told him to stuff his job and gave my notice in. I was unsettled by being offered a job back in Oz, and my mind was still there. Tommy talked me round after Poynton had reinstated the hours to the original format, but I was still unhappy.

I went home that weekend, and whilst I was still annoyed with him, I was even more annoyed that my colleagues had just accepted what had been done. I went into town on the Saturday and bumped in to Graham Evans from Croft Pipework. He had won a contract to build a prefabricated module for Croda Chemicals, was looking for someone to run the job for him and offered me the job. It was less money, but I could make it up with overtime and I would be at home for a while, as he expected to get more work out of it. I accepted and told him I would start a week on Monday.

I went back to Torness and gave my notice in to Tommy. Poynton was away on holiday, so I did not have the satisfaction of finally telling him to shove it. Once again, Tommy tried to talk me round, but he understood how I felt. I had been at Aitons for about eighteen months.

Back at Crofts, I was working at first mostly in the fabrication shop in Anlaby. It was a pain travelling across Hull City centre every day, but it was not for long, as we then went on site at Croda to install the 'module.' They had quite a lot of work on at the time, and a few of the old hands that had been there when I worked for them in the '70s were still there. Harry Chatterton was the manager and Dennis Ferguson was the site foreman at Croda, but as the latter was tied up with another project, they asked me to be foreman on the module and associated work. One of the jobs that I had to work on was a drain line from the new reactor. I asked Graham if I could do it on a price, but he would not have it after the Birds Eye job. The line ran for about 150 metres across the plant, but it had to have a gradual fall in it as there would be no pump, as they wanted it done as cheaply as possible. It took some working out, but I managed to do it with dirt pockets and drain points in at several positions. To cut the story short, when the plant closed for the Christmas break, they did not drain the line and it froze solid. When I got back, every flange joint had split and the cheap plate flanges they had insisted on using were all bellowed and split. We had to go along the line, cut out every flange joint and install a short piece of pipe, and replace all the small-bore drain valves – all this before they could restart the plant. It cost them a fortune and someone paid for not draining the line.

In all the supervisory jobs I have had, I always tried to do the right thing by anyone who worked for me – but I expected some sort of respect in return. Whilst I was at Crofts this time, I had one guy who for the want of a better expression, was 'taking the piss'. At this point, we were in a shutdown situation, needed all hands and were working the weekend. On the Saturday, one of the guys asked if he could have the Sunday off. I had previously told everyone that they would be expected to work all hours required to complete the job – they all agreed and said they would ensure they were available. This guy now said he wanted the Sunday off because he was playing football and could not work. I told him that there was no chance as we needed him at work. The workload was planned, and he was needed in. He was not a happy bunny and went away mumbling about me, casting doubts on my parentage.

He came in on the Sunday and went off to start work, but just after tea break, he came up to me to say he had slipped and twisted his knee. One of the other guys said that he had heard him cry out in pain and had found him behind a container holding his left leg. He said he could walk but could not put much pressure on his leg. No one had actually seen him slip, so although I had my doubts, I had to let him go to hospital. I asked him how he would get there, and he said he would get a bus – he was not on his bike that day, as one of the other lads had given him a lift. I offered to get him an ambulance or let one of the lads take him, but he said he would be fine on the bus. I felt there was something not right about it, and, not having heard from him by late afternoon, I rang Hull Royal Infirmary A&E to find out how he was. They informed me that they had no record of him on their register. I asked them to check, but they were positive he had not been to the hospital that day. I was fuming.

The following morning, he came into work as usual, I did not ask him how he was, as he was walking fine, with no sign of any limp. During the tea break, I asked him how he got on at hospital – he went a bit red and held his right knee, saying that it was ok.

"It should be, it was your left yesterday," I said. "Now get your gear together and go back to the shop. I do not want you on site." I cannot stand liars. I told him I knew that he had not been to A&E and that he was not only taking the piss out of me, but also the rest of the lads, who had to cover for him. He said he was sorry, but to top it all he asked if he would get paid for the full shift. I usually booked guys in for a full day, even if they needed time off to do something important during working hours. I blew my top and told him to leave and not come back. He asked, "How do I get to Anlaby?" I told him to go the same way as he got to the site – on his bike.

"But it's a long way to Anlaby," he whined. I told him he should have thought about that before he deceived me.

I then rang the office and told Graham I had sent him off site and why. But I did not know that he was was one of Graham's mates. I was told that he had to come back.

"Not a chance," I said. "If he comes back, I go! It would make me look stupid and the workforce would have no respect whatsoever for me. They would think they could do as they like."

We argued, and Graham said he would come to site to have a chat about it. About an hour or so later Graham arrived with the guy in his Land Rover and his bike in the back. He came into the office and we talked about the situation. I was adamant I would not have the guy back on site and told Graham that if he wanted him to work there, he had better make him foreman and sack me – but that I would see him in court for wrongful dismissal. That went down really well. Instead of sacking the guy, he swapped him for another guy on another site.

This was the beginning of the end for me, after that, as the work load at Croda reduced, I was sent to another site in Hull to work with a mate and another welder, and my foreman's pay was cut again. Not long after, I and one of the other pipefitters, Martin Oldfield, were offered jobs with Press Offshore if we could be in Yarmouth two days later. When Martin rang me and asked if I was going, I said, 'Yes,' straightaway. We would leave the next day. As far as I was concerned, I owed Crofty nothing after the way I had been treated. Martin, who was on another site, said he would do the same. When I rang the office and told Graham he blew his top and came on site quicker than an Exocet missile. He said that Martin had rang him just after me, and that we were going against our contract.

"What fucking contract?" I asked him, "I have never had one. I am on PAYE." Okay, he was due a week's notice, so I gave him a week's notice, but I still left that night, and so did Martin. Unsurprisingly, I have never been back to work for Croft Pipework.

I picked Martin up the following morning at around three o'clock to be in Yarmouth to complete an induction course, which allowed us to go offshore two days later on the Shell indefatigable platform. We arrived at Yarmouth Heliport at about seven o'clock to travel to the platform. On arrival, we were allocated cabins on the accommodation barge, after which we were taken to the stores and issued with our gear. We were told we would be picked up by our respective foremen after lunch. It was all very civilised, which was the exception rather than the rule offshore, I must say.

Keith Pollard

After lunch, we met in the cinema and the foremen were there as expected. One of the piping supervisors, Mal, called out my name along with another couple of guys who had travelled out that morning. I was teamed up with a Geordie lad and we were taken to the cellar deck area and shown the job we were going to work on, which was to install what is called a sphere tee. Rubber 'pigs' are used to clean out the main pipeline that carries the gas or oil that is being drilled for. They are sent along the pipeline under pressure, and at each end of the line are pig catchers which are accessed to install and remove the spheres. Just before each catcher are the sphere tees that slow the 'pig' down.

Normally, an oxyacetylene cutter is used to cut the pipe and install the tees, but the drain valve attached to the underside of the pipe restricted access, and a fair amount of cutting had to be done by hand. Then, an angle grinder had to be used to put the weld prep on by hand. It was really hard work, as we had to lay on our backs under the pipe and hold up the heavy grinder with our arms. I did most of it – the Geordie I was with was a lazy bastard to put it mildly. He kept disappearing for a smoke – and whatever else he was on. As I have said, there is an unwritten law amongst the rank and file that you do not tell tales about your work mates, no matter what the situation – you just grin and bear it. If they will not toe the line when you ask them yourself, then you have to accept it. I put up with this prat for a full two weeks, asking him time and time again to do more, but the only reply I got was that I was mad for working as hard as I did and no way was he doing that – whether I liked it or not. He had been with Press for a while and he had mates in high places.

I was asked to do an extra couple of days on my first trip, so I missed him when I came back off leave. When I asked who I would be working with, the foreman winked and said, "I will get you someone better than last trip." He obviously knew what was going on but had simply let him get away with it. I was paired with another Hull guy, Alan Brattan, who was as sound as a pound, and we ended up becoming good pals. The job finished up working out well and I worked for Press again on quite a few occasions after that.

An old friend of mine, Howard Laybourne, was working for Heerema Hook Up Services, a Dutch company who had opened an office in Hull on Albert Dock. They serviced supply boats and assisted in small-scale work. Howard decided to try and get more work, which he did when he managed to be awarded the hook-up of the Arco Thames project. ARCO stands for the Atlantic Richfield Company, which is one of the richest private oil companies in the world, with operations in the United States, Indonesia, the North Sea, and the South China Sea. It is known for its low-priced gasoline compared to other national brands.

Heerema took me on board to work in the THC fabrication yard at Hartlepool, punching out the modules prior to load out and preparing the hook-up work packs. I was in Hartlepool for about six weeks with another Hull guy, Vince Finnerty, who was to carry out the same sort of work on the electrical and instrumentation side. When I was punching out the hook up positions for the pipe work, I found a big problem. The dimension shown on the drawing was wrong and the spool would not be big enough to tie in at both ends – it was about a foot too short. I got quite a few brownie points for finding this mistake. If it had happened offshore the cost would have been monumental, to say the least.

Hartlepool is like going back in time on Hessle Road. The *Globe* where we stayed was near the docks and was a real old-fashioned type of pub. There were four of us in one room, but it was okay, it was clean and the food was decent. The job would take six weeks before the jacket, the legs and the topside, were in a single piece ready to go to the North Sea. The social life was good – there were quite a few parties put on by THC's different sub-contractors, which were a 'thank you' to the gaffers, as this was near the end of the job. We were invited along as we were part of the hook-up team and part of the management.

At one of these parties I was approached by a young 'lady' who asked if I would like a good time. I was not tempted, and, rather surprised, one of the lads told me that she would do things I had not even dreamed of. I left the party quite late with one of the other lads and as we were walking back, full of free ale, she was standing outside a house and asked me if I fancied a coffee or night cap. I declined once again but the lad who was with me immediately said, "Can I come in?" She agreed and went in, with him following, grinning from ear to ear and giving me a 'thumbs up'. I went back to the *Globe* and about half an hour later, he came in. I said to him, "That was a bit quick – no good?"

"You missed out on something there, Keith," he said. "She lived alone. She offered me a beer and then we sat down and chatted. She asked if I fancied her and I said, 'Yes' She was quite a looker. She put some music on and started to do an erotic dance in front of me. Off came her top, then she turned her back to me and slipped off her skirt. She was wearing a thong, stockings and suspenders. Even though I'd had a drink I was getting aroused. She took off her bra and exposed a pair of magnificent breasts, then turned around and slipped off her thong. She then turned around again, and you've never seen anything like it!"

"What do you mean – was she shaved?" I asked.

"No – but she had the thickest cock you've ever seen!"

"She was a bloke?"

Keith Pollard

"Yep," he replied. "I thought, 'how the hell do I get out of this? Do I succumb to her abundant charms or piss off quick?'" Needless to say, he took the latter option.

In work the next day, they all knew what had been going on. She was a regular at these parties they held and always someone fell into her trap.

We completed the work and I was asked if I would go offshore as general foreman/field engineer. It was expected to be a short hook-up and I was told I would get three, three-week trips out of it. I accepted the job and did quite well out of it. It was the first time I had worked on a self-employed basis. I was to be paid 18 hours a day to cover both day and night shifts, on £12 per hour – £4,536 per trip. I did the three trips as promised and I finished up with £13,608 in my hand. It was the most money I had ever earned for nine weeks' work. The job was a great success – it was the fastest ever hook-up resulting in 'first gas' in the quickest time ever. The whole job was a pleasure to be involved in. It also put me in the frame for future work offshore, which later turned out rather well for me. On completion of the contract, I was paid off as Heerema decided to close the Hull branch and make everyone redundant. I never did find out why, but I have my own ideas, and the least said the better.

I then got a call from Press Offshore again. They had won a three-year contract to refurbish the West Sole gas-field off Humberside and I was asked if I fancied a supervisor position. I accepted, although the money was not that good, but it was three years' work on a 'two-weeks on, two-weeks off' basis, which meant working 18 months in three years. John Hopwood, who had been with them years was the project manager, he was the guy who gave me a start with them on the Shell Indies project.

I was asked if I could make up the crews from local labour and was given a pile of CVs to go through and pick out some people that I could rely on. I duly picked the squad from guys who I knew I could trust, although a couple let me down after one trip, complaining about the pay, and had to be replaced at short notice. I got a bit of grief when I put another couple of names forward – 'I hope they are better than the last two!' I gave the pair of them some stick when I next saw them and they never worked on any job for me again. I had told them what the rate was, and that if they did not think the job was going to be right, then not to start because the rate would not go up. But they did and dropped me in the mire.

Whilst I was on this project, on the *Bravo* platform, there was a tragic accident on the *Charlie* platform. We had just finished our shift and had our evening meal when I got a call from the Offshore Installation Manager. He asked me if I could get the lads out, as the crane had fallen off the *Charlie* and into the sea, taking the driver with it. He wanted floodlights pointing down into the sea, in case the tide pushed the guy towards our platform. We had been having bad weather for a few weeks and supply boats had been unable to get out to the field. They had started to run out of fresh water on the *Charlie* and a supply boat had been able to get there, but they needed the crane to unload the water. There was still a bit of a swell on and it was decided they would try to unload the boat, so the driver, Vince, was air-lifted over from the *Bravo* to carry out the task. Whilst he was lowering his hook, it caught the back of the boat. It was an old crane and due to be replaced, and as the hook caught, the wire did not break but the crane did, at the weakest point, which was the mounting of the crane on its pedestal.

A helicopter was scrambled to help in the search but sadly, when they found Vince, he had died. It was a very sad time indeed and one I will never forget.

Towards the end of my three years, there was quite a bit of union trouble up north, off Aberdeen. There were a number of long-term Press men, quite a few of them militants and mostly welders, who thought they could not be sacked as they had been with Press for years and had some of the Press management in their back pockets. Some were transferred down to us and one of them, a welder, was a real pain in the arse. He caused quite a bit of upheaval on the job because he thought he could work it so that he could get transferred again. He asked me if I would transfer him to a job off Aberdeen, so I told him he would have to put it in writing. He did so, asking me to keep it quiet, as he did not want the lads to know he had asked for a transfer after all the rubbish he had given them about solidarity. I said I would but, unbeknown to me, someone in the office copied the letter and put it in a set of drawings which he gave to one of the foremen, whom he knew would tell everyone. The foreman showed me the letter and I told him that it must have been put there by mistake, and not to tell anyone as it could cause some problems for the welder. But that welder had caused this foreman a lot of problems, so he was not going to do him any favours. We got the guy off on the first chopper the next morning and his name was mud. It must have spread like wildfire up in Aberdeen, because I got a call from the project manager later that day to say that the guy had left due to the number of threatening phone calls he had received.

I was going off on leave one morning soon afterwards and went into the canteen early for my breakfast. There was a deathly silence about the place. I had never heard the canteen so quiet. Some of the lads were in the TV lounge watching the news, so I asked what was going on and was told about the tragedy that had occurred. As I came out, another of the lads was going in and asked me what was wrong. I told him that a rig had gone up off Aberdeen and his words were, "I bet it was the *Piper*, that platform was always an accident waiting to happen." Apparently, he had worked on it, and told me the conditions there were terrible.

I was back home later that morning when the onshore rep phoned me. He told me that all the crew had finished and he was in the process of getting them off the platform before they could organise a 'sit in' – something that oil companies are very frightened of.

At about six o'clock that night, one of the lads rang me and told me they had all finished, so I asked what was he going to do? When he said they had organised a meeting, I asked what about? - saying that they did not have jobs any more as they had all finished. I told him that I had received a phone call from Mike Marshall in the office to say they were organising a new crew to send out on the Monday and had been inundated with calls from men looking for jobs – so much for solidarity!

I have been involved in several strikes. You can never win. Workers seem to forget that to withdraw your labour is your last weapon, because you can never get back what you have lost. It is amazing how many men put their hands up to go with the flow, but if you ask them afterwards why they wanted to go on strike, they say that most of the guys wanted to and that they did not want to go against them. When they get home, they always say that it was not their idea, that they wanted to stop at work, but it was the others. I have heard it so many times and it does not cut any ice. The workforce had their meeting and were taken back by Press, but the issue was not taken lightly by BP, and Press lost the contract for the southern North Sea. In fact, they seemed to take the blame for all the industrial unrest taking place at the time in the offshore industry and lost quite a few contracts.

It was a pity really. I always thought they were a good company to work for. But I never worked offshore again after I got paid off. The job was changing. Companies started making the labour force pay for their own survival courses and stopped flying men up to Aberdeen, sending them on trains and even making them drive there. I had a good run, but by 1991, I'd had enough and decided that it was time to try something else.

CHAPTER 17
LE TUNNEL

After finishing offshore, I briefly took a piping supervisor job offered by Harry Poynton, my old boss from Aitons. It was the worst job I had ever been on – everything was being done on the cheap, there was nowhere near enough equipment – it was unbelievable. Harry and I had words early on. Harry said to me, "Well you have been here a week now – what do you think of it so far?" There was only one possible answer. Using the old *Morecambe and Wise* line, I said, "Rubbish!" I told him a few home truths and you could cut the air with a knife. No-one ever talked to Mr Poynton like that. I lasted there only a couple of weeks more, before I told him to shove the job up his arse.

I had only been out of work about a week when I got a call from Laing Industrial Engineering, asking if I was interested in a job on the Channel Tunnel as a construction manager, on a two-shift rota – two weeks on and two weeks off, similar to offshore. Was I interested? Too right I was! I went to Folkestone for an interview with the project manager, Ian Jameson. He was a mad Scotsman who ruled with an iron fist. But I thought the interview went well and he told me he had another two guys to interview, and would let me know before the end of the week. I had travelled down by train, and the HR Manager had phoned me at home and to offer me the position before I had even got back that night. I rang the next day to accept the position, and started the following Monday. I travelled down again by train as I was being given a company car when I got to the site office. Company car, I hear you thinking – from pipefitter to construction manager!! Little did I know what I was letting myself in for.

I arrived at the site offices in Folkestone, where I was introduced to my fellow shift managers – Jim, a Glaswegian, and Peter, from Sunderland. The 4 construction managers, John Alt and myself, would be covering the cooling water plant and pipework installation in the running tunnels. John and I were always on a two-week rota together. Over the days and nights, we worked approximately 14 hours a day to cover 12-hour shifts, with an hour at each end for a handover. The cooling water section was covered by a day shift manager called Reg de Boltz, who was from Southampton – a decent guy who was easy to work for. We had a two-week induction course, which covered everything you could think of, from Health and safety to bomb searches.

I was given my brand new car on the first day and found some

Keith Pollard

A plaque made from an actual
piece of rail used in the tunnel

A bronze statue of the
breakthrough of the service
tunnel on December 1st 1990

great digs in a pub called the *Tiger Inn* in Stowting, about 10 miles from Folkestone. The landlord had just bought a house in the village and wanted some people to stay in the pub. It worked out great for John and I, and a couple of other lads from the job also moved in. I was there for the entire three years that I worked on the Tunnel Project, paying £60 per week, which included the pick of the menu for our evening meal. We were given four weeks' lodging expenses a month – even for our two weeks off.

The *Tiger Inn* had live music a couple nights a week and Sunday lunches were very popular. When I worked the night shift, I used to go down for my lunch every day, then go back to bed for a few hours. There was an Italian family who came in every Sunday and always made a grand entrance, as if they owned the place. They were always immaculately dressed and the father looked like a mafia don. The *Tiger* had a piano player who used to play background music and every time the mafia family came in, he started to play the theme from *The Godfather* movie. Everyone used to watch the looks the old man of the family gave the piano player when he walked in. I said to him, "One day you will wake up with a horse's head in bed with you!" I understand that the *Tiger Inn* is now a very posh eating place.

RED & WHITE PHOENIX

The Laing Offices were at Sandgate, about three miles from Folkestone, and the works entrance was about two miles from the docks at Dover. The latter is now called Samphire Hoe and is man-made, using all the spoil taken out of the tunnel.

I will not go into detail of the tunnel construction, but it was a privilege to work on the project. It was hard and at times very frustrating, largely because the offices and worksite were so far apart, and my time was sometimes spent either on the radio or on the telephone twelve hours a day. The work was done using locomotives and flat-bed wagons especially designed for the individual tasks and fitted out with specialised equipment.

The cooling water section had ten crews at any time, working in the four 'running tunnels.' There were actually only two, but during construction each was split and identified as North and South Land, and North and South Marine. This reflected the way the boring machines travelled from Shakespeare Cliff – 'land' was from there towards Folkestone, and from there towards France under the channel was 'marine'.

The tunnels are now used by the Eurostar and the shuttle trains. There is also a service tunnel that runs the full length from the UK to France, which is joined to the running tunnels by cross passages every 1,500 metres or so. The cross passages are isolated from the running tunnels using air tight doors, and contain all the electrical equipment and instrumentation, along with fire-fighting manifolds to cover each particular section. There are also three crossovers, where the trains can cross from one tunnel to the other, in case of accidents or maintenance requirements.

In 1993, during my time on the tunnel, Jacky and I went on holiday to Carlsbad, between Los Angeles and San Diego, to celebrate our 25th wedding anniversary. We flew with *Delta* – not an airline I would recommend – and had to change planes at their hub airport at Newark, just outside New York. The first problem we had, was they had overbooked the flight. We were supposed to have been booked in right through to LA, but when we got to the desk at the airport to go through as 'in transit' passengers, we found out that we had not been, so we had to go and check in at the desk. After quite a heated exchange of words and arguments with different people we managed to get two seats – although not actually together.

Delta were asking people if they would be prepared to volunteer to stay over in a hotel with all expenses paid and fly on a later flight. We considered it, but we'd had enough by then – all we wanted to do was to get to LA. Jacky was not very keen on sitting by herself, but it was that or wait over. The flight was then delayed by five hours whilst we sat waiting at the gate. I asked at the desk a couple of times and got the standard, 'it is a technical

Keith Pollard

fault; it won't be long sir – you have a nice day now.' Some chance!

Then the flight was called, not where we were waiting, but at another gate on the other side of the airport. So we ended up running through the airport with our hand luggage and coats. Both of us were by then built for comfort rather than speed, but we managed to get to the other gate as our names were being called out. It was all a bit much and we were both well knackered and pissed off. I complained to the stewardess who told me, "Don't worry about it sir, it happens all the time at Newark!" Be warned!

Jacky was up at the front of the plane and I was at the back, where I got talking to a pleasant young black guy in the seat next to me. He asked me where I was from and I was telling him about the UK. I asked him why was he going to LA and he said, quite openly, 'drug rehabilitation.' Apparently, he had been in all sorts of trouble just to feed his habit, and it was either that or a jail sentence. He was put on the plane at one end and was being met at the other by someone from the rehab organisation. I wondered who Jacky had got stuck next to!

My new friend told me he was using about $100 worth of drugs a day and had no job. He asked what I did for a living and could not believe that a mere pipefitter could afford expensive holidays abroad. Without really thinking, I said, "One reason we can afford to come here on holiday is that we aren't shoving $700 worth of drugs up our fucking noses a week for a start! You're a fucking idiot, you're ruining your life!" A bit late, it flashed into my mind that he might go off his head at me, but he just looked shocked and said that no-one had ever spoken to him like that – he ended up actually thanking me! When we got off the plane he had to remain in his seat to be escorted and I wished him best of luck.

Whilst we were standing at the carousel waiting for our luggage, about ten young black guys all about six and a half feet tall came up and one of them said, "Great meeting you, Jacky – have a great vacation!" It transpired that they were a University basketball team travelling to play in some big game in LA, and her seat was right in the middle of the them. She must have made as big an impression with them, as I had done with my companion!

As we were going to the car rental desk, I noticed him talking to some guy and pointing at me. The guy waved, gestured me over and introduced himself. He told me what the young guy had said to him about our conversation, how it made him think about what he was doing to himself, and that he wanted to get off drugs. If it helped to save his life, it was well worth calling him a fucking idiot!

As usual, the car rental people tried to get us to upgrade to a more expensive car. I had been through this before, so I said that they had tried to rip me off like that last time. We ended up with a top of the range car for just a few dollars a day extra – they do not want any agro at the desk in front of other customers, and they could not get rid of us quick enough. It was Friday teatime by the time we hit the expressway, and there were seven lanes of traffic. It was bedlam – the London rush hour does not compare. It took us an hour to do about twenty miles until we got outside LA. When you are not used to it, the overtaking on both sides is certainly quite frightening.

In the end it was not too bad a journey though. Our destination was a 'time share' resort right on the beach at Carlsbad. It was a nice spot, perhaps a bit dated, but with great pool bars and a small shopping Mall was across the road, which had plenty of restaurants and bars. There was also as a bandstand right in the centre of the square, where local bands played in the evenings. I was into *Eagles* music and, as they are a Southern California group, it was good to hear different renditions of their songs – and for free too, always a bonus for a Yorkshireman!

There was a music show going on nearby with Jimmy Buffett, an American singer–songwriter, author and actor. He is best known for his music, which often portrays an 'island escapism' lifestyle, as well as some humorous experiences from his life. Together with his Coral Reefer Band, Buffett has recorded hit songs that include *Margaritaville*, *Come Monday* and *It's five o'clock somewhere*. You could hear the music from where we were staying– it was brilliant. Buffett is still performing to this day, despite having made his fortune, with over five resorts and 30 restaurants around the world, all inspired by his visions of a laid-back life in paradise.

The area was inundated with many small independent antique shops, which I love browsing round. It was interesting to see the American idea of antiques, which is vastly different to ours, with our much longer history, and I spent several happy hours browsing around.

I am interested in animals, so we naturally went to San Diego zoo. The 100-acre site is home to more than 3,500 rare and endangered animals representing more than 650 species and subspecies, and there is also a prominent botanical collection with more than 700,000 exotic plants. There is also a Safari Park, which is a huge wildlife sanctuary that houses more than 3,000 animals. Over half of the Park's 1,800 acres have been set aside as protected native species habitat. It is 30 miles north of downtown San Diego, and is well worth a visit. I suppose that some of my rugby and work colleagues will be surprised to hear of my interest in animals and antiques, but, as they say, you cannot judge a book by its cover!

We had agreed to spend £500 on each other for our anniversary, and so we went into a big shopping mall in San Diego. The Labour Day sales were on, so we thought we might get a good bargain. I

Keith Pollard

had fancied one of those chunky gold bracelets, and found a jeweller's shop where there was a sign saying, 'no reasonable offer refused.' We went inside and there, in a display cabinet, was my dream bracelet, with $4,000 on the ticket. At the time it was two dollars to the pound so it looked well out of my reach. A sales executive, as they call them, came across and asked if I was interested in anything.

With nothing to lose, I said, "Yes, that bracelet."

Jacky shook her head and muttered, 'No chance,' as I did so.

"Make me an offer," the young lady replied, so I offered $1000. She smiled and said she would speak to the manager, whereupon a guy came over and asked if that was my final offer. I told him the story about us being on holiday for our 25th wedding anniversary, how we had saved for years so that we could come to California, that we had dreamed of doing so all our working lives, just being ordinary working class people. The sales girl looked as if she was filling up, and I even started to feel emotional myself. The bloke smiled and said you pay the tax, which at the time was 6%, but I said I only had £500 and took my credit card out of my wallet. I laid it on the counter and said, "If you will take the thousand, we have a deal," With that he put out his hand and congratulated us on our twenty-five years together. I do not know which of us was the most shocked that I had pulled it off.

We went to another jeweller's, where Jacky spotted a watch she that fancied and we went inside. Whilst Jacky was looking at the watch and trying it on, the manager came up and asked me how I was. I asked him if he could do me a favour and told him about the bracelet – he had a few similar ones on display. I asked him to take a look at mine and tell me what it was worth. He put in his eye glass, examined it, and asked if he could do a test on it. I agreed and he took it away, before returning to ask me how much I had paid for it. When I said I paid a thousand dollars, he asked where I had got it from and I told him. He then shook his head, "Yes, I know him," he said. "Every Labour Day sale he does one crazy deal – you are one lucky guy!" So we bought the watch and left the shop feeling very pleased with ourselves. When I got home, I took it into our local jewellers for a price for insurance purposes. They said £1,500, but they could only value it as nine carat, which is a British standard, rather than 14 carat, which it is.

Just to top it all off, we then went into Macy's department store with about $800 left to play with and got a $3,500 ring and some earrings for Jacky, within our budget. If you ever go to the States, check whether your visit coincides with Labour Day – you might drop lucky with some great bargains! All in all, we had a brilliant holiday in California and were determined that we would go back again.

RED & WHITE PHOENIX

Back at work, senior management decided that we should hold a bomb alert practice. I had to contact all the supervisors on my units by radio and ask them to contact me on their nearest telephone, which were located in the cross passages. When they rang, I told them that we had a tip-off that a bomb had been planted somewhere in the tunnels and they were to use their crews to search the section of the tunnel they were working in. They were to let me know the result of their search by radio. Under no circumstances were they to use words such as bomb or explosive device to the men. Obviously, they thought it was for real, and some of the comments I received were in industrial language. A couple said that they were bringing their crews out straight away – 'fuck the tunnel!' I had to calm them down and explain that it was crucial for everyone's safety that they carry out orders. I told them that they could not use words like bomb because local radio stations monitored our frequencies for any information that could be used us. The majority of local Dover people did not want the tunnel – they thought it would cost jobs and take money out of the local economy.

It took a few hours for the search to be completed and, one by one, the supervisors called me on the radio to give me the 'all clear.' There was just one guy I was waiting for and was concerned about. He was a straight-talking Barnsley man. Eventually called me. "Hey up, Keith! All reet old cock, I couldn't find now't, no bomb down here tha'knows." The phone lines went berserk. I had every one trying to call me from the project manager to the main control room. We both nearly got sacked and it took a lot of sweet talking to get us out of that.

One evening I was sitting in the *Tiger* and got chatting to a bloke that I had not met before. He asked me if I had watched some football match and I told him that it was not my game, I was a rugby man. He then asked where I was from and when I said Hull, he immediately said, "Do you know George Kennedy?" I told him that I had played with George. Apparently this guy lived near to George, so I asked him if he had his telephone number and he said he would get it for me.

Lo and behold, George walked in the very next night. We had a great time swapping stories and regaling each other of our experiences over the last thirty years or so. At the end of the evening, George said, "You must come up to the house, meet the wife and have a meal,"

"That would be great, thanks," I replied.

"Ok," he said, "I will send the chauffeur for you."

"Fucking chauffeur! Are you taking the piss George? Do you mean your lass?"

"No, I have a driver who takes me everywhere on business trips and the like." Apparently, by this time, he was on the board of a very big city firm. He came across as down-to-earth as he always had, and I had never dreamed that he was that high up the ladder. I declined the offer of the lift and said I would drive to see Christine and himself. We had a great night and I met his boys who were home from boarding school. When we said our good byes and we said we would keep in touch – but it was not for over twenty years that we met again.

It was 1994 when I finished on the tunnel, and I was offered a job by Howard Laybourne again. This time at SLP, a large offshore engineering company based in Great Yarmouth. They had bought Crown Fabrication, the company owned by Howard, as they were confident they were going to be offered the maintenance contract for all the southern North Sea offshore installations, and they wanted use Hull as a base. Crown had won a contract at Easington, on the coast about twenty miles east of Hull, for the expansion of part of the Dimlington Terminal.

I was taken on as a piping supervisor, but was given the task of co-ordinating the supply to site of fabricated pipe spools. There was not a lot of storage area on site, so the fabrication, painting and delivery to site had to be finely-meshed into the programme. I worked with the planner and the workshop manager to devise a system, and it was my responsibility to ensure that it was carried out successfully. I then had to supervise the installation of a new gas compressor module and the relevant pipework. The site manager, Paul Bosanquet, said that the last company that installed one of them went bust in the process. The compressor is a very fragile piece of equipment and needs careful installation and fine tuning – but that one had taken too long to install.

"Thanks for that info," I said. "No pressure then!" After sizing up the job and discussing it with BP engineering staff, I made some recommendations on how the job should be done. They were accepted, and thankfully it was a great success. So much so, that they made me up to Projects Manager on a new venture they were planning. They were trying to get in to the water treatment Industry, which they thought was going to be the next big thing, and had been trying to win some work from a company in Switzerland called Ozonia, who specialised in the supply and installation of Ozone Plants. Both Ozone and UV are well recognized methods of water and wastewater disinfection in industrial and municipal markets. They are used to eliminate a whole range of viruses and bacteria. In addition to disinfection, ozone is also used for taste, odour and colour removal, as well as iron and manganese reduction.

We won a contract to install an Ozone plant at the Wing water treatment plant in Rutland. I visited the site once a week for a couple of days to ensure that the clients were happy with the work done and that all was going to plan. I had to ensure that any changes or extra work were correctly done and charged. After that, we were given two more projects, one for Anglia Water and the other for Thames Water. We completed them both, but unbeknownst to me, the site foreman had taken on himself to cut corners on the job. We were working with thin wall stainless steel pipes, which, when welded together, had to be purged with argon gas to stop the welds corroding. This means that preparing the weld joints is a longer job and something of a pain, but it is a requirement that, if not done correctly, can cause weld failure. But there was no requirement for weld inspection on the job, and I was told by my superiors not to push the subject at it had not been requested or priced for.

After we had completed the Thames Water job we were completing the paperwork and negotiating the final payment when the bombshell struck. When some of the pipework had been stripped out by the maintenance team onsite, someone with a bit of knowledge looked inside the pipe to find coking. When the shit hit the fan, I had to go to see the manager at the time, a David Walker. I told him that whenever I was at the site as far as I could see everything was being carried out according to the specification – albeit that this was very open to question, as we should have done a minimum five per cent radiography check on the welding. Surprise, surprise, the foreman concerned had already left the company, and I took the brunt.

To be fair, they did not sack me but I was made redundant. SLP was in the process of closing the Hull works down as they had not been awarded some work they had expected and the only other job they had was an ad hoc contract with BP, which ran out not long after I had gone. SLP had to go back and rework both the Anglia and Thames Water jobs. It must have cost a fortune to put right and I do not think they won anymore work from Ozonia. It was a great pity, as it was good work and there were quite a lot of the plants being installed in the UK. It was all lost due the short-sighted approach taken on the checking and the laziness of one foreman.

After being in supervision and management for a while I thought it was time for a change and went back 'onto the tools,' working for an old mate of mine, Johnny Draper. Johnny had a company that specialised in the installation of refrigeration plants in cold store warehouses and food process factories. During the time I was working offshore, I went up to Scotland once to help him out at a chicken process plant near Dundee. That was a strange experience because the chickens seemed very subdued, as if they knew what was going to happen to them. They were unloaded off trucks into a dimly-lit area and onto a conveyor belt, on which they

Keith Pollard

were hung upside down and their heads cut off. They were then passed through a trough onto a machine that removed their feathers, onto machines that sucked out their innards, and then either bagged them as whole chickens or sliced them up into portions. The whole process took less than five minutes.

This time, however, I was working at the Tesco warehouse in Doncaster, where a massive extension was being built on the side of the building. To get to the new area, we had to walk through the existing loading bay. Health and safety had not reached there at that point, and it was a most dangerous place. There were forklift trucks coming out of the freezers from all angles and into the loading bays, with horns blasting out all the time. It was hard to believe that no-one got hurt.

I did not realise how unfit I was until I went back to manual work! I was knackered for about six weeks until I got back in to the rhythm of things. We were installing 100mm piping in the void between the roof and the top of the insulation that created the ceiling of the freezer. We had to manually carry the six-metre pipe lengths from the only access point in the wall to the final installation area, and there were literally miles of it. It was really hard work, especially when I had not done it for quite a few years.

I had just finished working for John when I got a call from a mate of mine who was working for the ABB Group, who were managing a new power station at Killingholme, along with PCN, a new company that had been started by directors of a couple of Derby companies, of whom I think Shaw's was one. I was put onto the gang of a Scottish guy who had not a clue how to run a gang. He gave me a set of drawings, showed me where the job was, and that was it. I had to organise the delivery of the pipe spools, the scaffolding and just about everything else. I ended up having to stand around waiting for deliveries and could not get anything done. My so-called supervisor asked me if I would be his charge-hand, but I told him, "I am not doing your job for you running about like an idiot for 10p an hour extra – no way."

I just plodded along doing as much as I could, and a couple of times the project manager passed by and gave me a funny look. But the third time he stopped, asked what I was doing and I told him I was waiting for my supervisor to organise whatever it was that I was waiting for at the time. Within half an hour, my supervisor arrived demanding to know what I had said, and when I told him, he started giving me some verbals. I told him exactly what he could do – I was not taking that from anyone. After that, a guy from management called Terry, who I knew from previous jobs, came to see me. I told him what had gone on and he arranged for me to be transferred to another supervisor – a guy from Sheffield who was as sound as a pound and we got on well from the off. He paired me

292

RED & WHITE PHOENIX

up with another Hull guy, Rob Murray, on installing the main gas line from the British Gas compound into the station. Once again, I had got the big pipes to install!

The two welders that were put with us were two that had been with one of the companies for a long time and were on a very good deal. They told us that if they got a specific amount of butts welded during the week they would not have to come in weekends, but would still get paid for them. I informed them that if we were not on the same deal, I would make sure they did not get the amount of butts they needed. Not an hour had passed when our new supervisor told us we were summoned to the office to speak to the site manager and project manager. We duly toddled off to the site office and these two jokers were sat at the end of a conference table. They never said good morning or sit down, so I sat down anyway, and got a withering look for my effrontery. I was asked to explain our comments to the welders, which demonstrated how 'well in' they were. At this point I must clarify that a lot of power station boiler work is done on deals – to compensate for the filthy and unpleasant nature of the work. To be fair to these two, they did give us a good hearing and promised that we would be on the same deal as the welders as long as the work got done. After that, everything went really well and I was one of the last six pipefitters kept on at the end of the job, being made up to foreman to look after the squad working for ABB right until the end.

Life had been good to me over the years since I retired from being out of rugby league, but I missed it more than I cared to admit. I missed the camaraderie, the smell of the liniment – perhaps like actors miss the smell of greasepaint – and I still wanted to get back in to it in some capacity. It was still in my blood.

In 1995, I had a message from an old mate of mine in Australia, Mick Quinn, whose son Daniel was on with the Australian schoolboys' tour of England and France, and he suggested we meet up. They were going to be based in Leeds at the *Oulton Hall* De Vere Hotel between Leeds and Wakefield, and he said he could get me a good rate there. He rang when he got to the UK and we organised a weekend away. Gary Selkirk and his partner at the time asked if they could come with us, and off we went. They were playing a Test Match against an English team at Batley on the Friday night, so we went to the game and stayed at hotel on the Friday and Saturday nights.

I have never been so cold in all my life as that night in Batley. How the young Australian lads managed to play in those conditions I will never know, but they did, and they won again, as they had regularly since they first toured back in 1972. On that first tour when they played 11 games and scored 108 tries, and it was not until 2002 that they ever lost a test series.

Keith Pollard

Over the weekend, Mick told me that they had never seen a professional game whilst they had been over here so I suggested that they come over to Hull and watch Rovers, who were in Division Two in those days, playing Swinton at home. I said we would put on lunch at our house before the game, and Mick asked if he could bring a couple of the others with him – the fathers of Danny Buderus and Owen Craigie, the latter of whom is the only player to make three schoolboy tours. In addition to them, incidentally, the undefeated 1995 tour party featured future Australian internationals Trent Barrett and Matthew Gidley, and World Cup-winning New Zealand captain Nathan Cayless.

After lunch and a few beers, we went to Craven Park, where I had arranged with then Rovers' director Phil Lowe some complimentary tickets for the game. Whilst we were in the bar before the game, a coach arrived carrying the whole of the Australian schoolboys' team. It was a bit of a coup for Rovers for them to select this game and they made a real fuss of the boys and presented them with mementos.

Mick was part of the Newcastle Knights coaching set-up and had asked me before why was not I involved in coaching and was not involved in the professional game over here. I had told him on numerous occasions that it was something of a closed shop and hard get into. After the game, Mick was talking to Phil Lowe and I overheard part of the conversation.

"Why have you not got the Pom there coaching? He asked. "He is one of the best that I have ever been involved with."

"Oh, he is – he helps with our youth development" Phil replied. I could not believe my ears and it was all I could do not to butt in and call him a lying twat. Mick came over to me and said, "You did not tell me you were part of Rovers coaching staff!" I put him right of course, and I think he realised what I had been talking about.

It was nearly ten years later that I came closest to getting involved with my old club. At the time, another Ozzie, Steve Linnane, was Rovers head coach. I was talking to him one night after a game and the conversation got round to me playing in Newcastle. He looked at me and said, "Are you the Pom who played for Maitland in the early 70's –Keith Pollard?" I was very gratified that he remembered me – he would have been only quite a young lad at the time. He also asked why had I not been involved with Rovers, or in fact any club, and asked if I was interested in coaching the reserve grade. I said I would do it for nothing. He told me to leave it with him and that would get back to me. Unfortunately, he left Rovers and returned down under for personal reasons not long after, and needless to say, I heard no more.

Howard Laybourne called me once again to ask if I would work for him once more, as he was starting up another company –

RED & WHITE PHOENIX

Construction Data Services Ltd. He asked me if I would fund myself for a month until he got some work in and I foolishly agreed – a decision I came to regret. Howard wanted me to take over the estimating and cost control of the company, once it was up and running. He had rented an old garage in the centre of Hull, that was turned into be quite a good workshop with an overhead crane included. I built some offices with the help of an old friend, Col Stevenson.

Our first contract was for some beams for a structural company in Lancashire. They supplied all the materials and we had to fabricate the finished article. I had been touting CDS around various companies looking for work and we also won some work for a company in Manchester – Birse Process Engineering – for the supply and installation of stainless steel pipework on water treatment plants again. The initial order was for a quarter of a million pounds with extras, so it was quite a good contract to win. We won another two or three contracts from them, along with other work from oil and gas contractors, so everything was going along nicely.

Howard then had one of his 'great ideas.' He decided that we would not employ people directly but would use sub-contractors. His brother-in-law, Paul Birch, was one of them, becoming foreman and looking after the fabrication in the shop and the installation on site. I could not believe what was going on – I would certainly not have worked for what they were being paid.

In 1997, we went away on holiday to timeshare resorts in Arizona, for a week, and Nevada, for a few days. We have had timeshares for over 20 years in Portugal, Spain and, the one we have had the longest, in the Lake District at Pine Lake, north of Morecombe. We have used them to exchange for other resorts around the world on numerous occasions, as well as staying at our own places over the years. We flew into Phoenix, with the usual flight delays. As usual, we travelled on a Wednesday, staying a couple of nights en route in motels, before arriving at Pine Tops for check-in on the Saturday. After picking up our car rental we set off, planning to drive for a couple of hours then stop at the first motel we came to. The road we travelled on was not the best – with no cats' eyes or lighting – and after 16 hours travelling we were really tired. So when we saw a Best Western motel, we pulled in and booked a room for the night. I had gone past being tired and all I wanted was a beer. As we were taking our bags out of the car, we could hear music coming from the hotel bar, so whilst Jacky had a shower and went to bed, I wandered downstairs. It was like a scene from the wild west. There was a three-piece band in the corner playing country music, couples dancing and plenty of people sitting at the tables and the bar – most of the men wearing Stetson hats! The barmaid was wearing hot pants – and this in 1997! I ordered a Bud, which was the only beer I recognised – I am not a fan of the draft beer in America anyway.

The guy next to me said, "Hi, you are not from round these parts." I told him I was from England in as broad a Hull accent as possible. He asked what I was doing there, we got chatting, and after a while he shouted to the guy on stage with the Willie Nelson Stetson, feathers sticking out of it, the full works, "Hey buddy, we have a Limy in the bar!" With that there was a load of yahoos and cheering, as only the Yanks can do. I stood up, gave them all a wave, sat back down on the bar stool and one or two came over to say 'hello.'

The guy asked me about the UK, where I lived, and what job I did – all the usual questions people ask each other in foreign countries. It is why I love travelling – meeting different people, seeing different places, and tasting different food. Apparently the guy I had befriended was the local high school principal, or headmaster as we call them. He told me that the following day it was their parade and open day at the school and a big football game was taking place. Their team were called the Globe Tigers and I told him that our local 'soccer' team were also called the Tigers, which he loved. He invited Jacky and I to be his guests the following day, and said he would show us round. Sadly, I had to decline the offer as we had a long journey to complete, and he wished us all the best for our holiday.

The next morning, we packed the car up and left motel to travel the hundred miles or so to the resort along Highway 60 through Apache country. I have never seen so many Pine Trees in my life as we saw on that journey. We stopped off at a place called Show Low before heading up to the resort. It was made up of wooden buildings, each with four apartments in them, and a hotel block with a restaurant, bar, pool and gym. It was a bit dated, but had an olde worlde character. We visited Fort Apache whilst we were in the neighbourhood, but that was something of a disappointment. Some of the old buildings survived, that dated from when it was a proper fort with the cavalry posted there, but they had now been fitted with uPVC double-glazed windows and doors. It was sacrilege – they had ruined it. We should be thankful for our regulations about listed buildings.

We also went to the *Apache Gold Casino and Resort*, run by the local Indian tribe, where all proceeds went back into the community. It was a hell of a place and was owned by the San Carlos Apache tribe, whose land covers over 1.8 million acres in eastern Arizona, from the Sonoran Desert to the Ponderosa pine forests. The San Carlos Apache were hunters and have deep cultural and spiritual ties to the land. They have made the decision

RED & WHITE PHOENIX

to keep most of the land in a natural state, which protects the habitat for big and small game, and allows the Apache to preserve their special and personal relationship with the natural world.

Later, on our way to Nevada, we had to pass by the Grand Canyon. Of all the places I have been to, this really does have the 'wow' factor. The Yanks certainly know how to create something out of nothing. The Canyon is far more than just a hole in the ground, but it is hidden from view when you arrive at the car parks, which are surrounded by bushes trees. You have to walk along designated paths through the trees and when you get through it really does hit you in the eye – it is absolutely fantastic. I was talking to a couple from Leeds, who had been down to the bottom of the canyon on mules. They said the path was only about a metre wide in places, with a sheer drop of hundreds of feet on one side, and was really frightening. As I am not keen on heights, there is no way that I would do that – not to mention that they said their backsides were aching from sitting in the saddle.

After the Canyon, we travelled north through Bitter Springs and Marble Canyon, on to Page, then into Utah, driving past the Coral Pink Sand Dunes and heading for the southern end of the Zion national park where you can follow trails that ancient natives roamed. Things had not changed in centuries and we passed by massive sandstone cliffs that towered above us. We then arrived at St George, a small town on the Utah Arizona border, on our journey to Mesquite, on the other side of the Nevada-Arizona border, where we had booked into another time share place.

As it was not far from Las Vegas, and we were flying out of there anyway, so we took a drive along Highway 15 to the gambling capital. We had a look round and decided we would stay there a for few days before we came home. So we stopped in Mesquite for four days instead of the seven we had planned, returned to Las Vegas and booked into the *Sands* Hotel. The *Sands* had just gone through a major renovation and was offering silly prices to get people back through the doors. We paid something like the equivalent of £12 a night for a room for two people. Most of the hotels had great deals on and I would never book with a travel agent – the best deals can be obtained when you are there.

Vegas to me is like Blackpool with the sun. It was quite cheap to eat in the casino buffets, and the sheer size of the hotels and casinos is a real eye opener. It is not really my cup of tea, but we did return eight years later. We had four nights at the *Sands*, which is not on the Strip but was good value as there were not a lot of crowds and the free tram passed the front of the hotel. After that, we flew out of Vegas and back to Manchester direct. I will never again fly via hubs – I will only use direct flights if going to USA!

CHAPTER 18
A FIRST GOODBYE

By this time, my father was living in an old people's home in Hessle. He had been suffering from Alzheimer's and dementia, and had been in the home for around three years. He had stopped knowing who I was eight or nine years earlier – it was heartbreaking. He used to ask Jacky if she knew anyone called Keith, and she had to tell him that Keith was his son. It had come to a head when my mother had a fall and was taken into hospital. Whilst we went to the hospital, my cousin Elaine went to sit with dad in the house in Anlaby where they lived. Dad did not have a clue what was going on. The first words my mum said when we got there were, "Get rid of him, I can't take any more." When we went back to the house, he kept asking where she was, but when we told him, he asked again ten minutes later. Mum had lived with this for at least eight years and it must have worn her down – I know how bad it sounds, but I'd had enough after being in his company for an hour or so. It was so frustrating.

Social services sent someone to evaluate him. He was asked questions like, who was on the throne, and who the prime minister was. My dad turned to me and said, "He thinks I'm daft, but he doesn't know who is on the fucking throne! Just tell him, Keith". It was both funny and sad at the time. They decided to find a home for him because my mother could not look after him in her state after the fall. One day, we took dad to the hospital to see my mother. He was ill on the way there, as he still hated travelling.

"Look who is here," I said at the bedside.

"The face rings a bell, but I'm not sure who it is," he replied.

"It's Louie, your wife," I told him.

"Get out of that fucking bed – I need it more than you," he said. Whilst we were there, we got a call to say that there was a place for dad at a home in Hessle and asked when could we take him. I told them we would take him from the hospital, and to tell the people at the home to act as if he had been there a while, as he would not know. It was a such a hard time and we were struggling to come to terms with it. It seemed that we were helpless and had no control over what was happening.

When we arrived at the home, Dad asked where we were. When I told him we were home, he asked, "How long have I lived here?" But the staff were brilliant.

"Hiya Eddie! had a good day?" someone said. "Come on, let's have a cuppa tea." Off he went with one of the carers whilst we went in the office to complete the documentation. About half an hour later, we were just about to leave and saw dad came walking out of the main room. He looked straight at me and said, "Hey mister, where are the toilets in here? Do you know?" I pointed him in the right direction and he said "Cheers pal," pottering off oblivious to who we were.

The next day we collected all his things in a little suitcase and a carrier bag, together with his recliner chair, which he loved, and took them to the home. He was downstairs in the main room again and when he saw us he came rushing out and shouted at me, "You, you bastard! You're the one who put me in here! They are all fucking crackers in here. Call yourself a brother – if I had a gun I would shoot you!"

"What you talking about" I said, but he just carried on ranting about me being a no good bastard of a brother, before saying that his mother had abandoned him in the home. It was just so upsetting, and one of the carers had to help me calm him down. She then took him into another room, so I gave him a few minutes to calm down then went back in to see him.

"Hi dad, how's it going? Are you okay?" I asked.

"Great! Nice to see you," he replied. He was totally changed within minutes, but that is dementia. It is a terrible disease, not only for those that have it, but for all the friends and the relations. It feels like you are treading on eggshells all the time. As sad as it was, there were humorous asides in the home. One guy he frequently sat with had either the most vivid imagination or had lived one hell of a life. His stories varied from being helicopter pilot to a chef at the Hilton in London – every time he had a different story. A little old Scottish lady used to come up to me and say, "Hello! Have you got any cigarettes?" When I said no, she would whisper, "You fucking greedy bastard," and walk away to ask someone else.

It all ended after just after Jacky and I had returned from Arizona and Nevada. Tracy did not let us know while we were away that dad had gone downhill quite quickly and, when we got home, she told us we had better go and see him. We went to the home and found that he was very ill and on liquids only. When I asked what they thought, I was told he could be like that for a while. But we got a phone call at about three o'clock the following morning. The lady from the home said, "I'm afraid we have some sad news, Keith. I'm sorry to tell you that your father passed away a few minutes ago. He went in his sleep, he was not in pain, he just slipped away."

There was nothing any of us could do. Jacky said, "It's Dad, isn't it?" and I told her. It was strange, I never really felt anything. To me, my dad had died a few years before, and it was really a bit of a relief that he had gone without suffering. When you have to go, just slipping away in your sleep is the way to do it. But that was not the way he wanted to go! He once told me he wanted to be in bed with a girl and be shot by an 18-year old jealous husband – he was ever the comedian!

We went round to my mother's house early before she could hear the news any other way. Her door was locked from the inside so I had to shout through the letter box to get her up. When she came to the door, she just said, "It's Dad – he's gone hasn't he?" She took it well, she had a little cry, but there were no hysterics – I had not expected any, but you never know how people will react to news like that. We did all the organising that has to be done. A Humanist lady led the service – we are not a religious family. It all went without incident, there were not a lot of people there, just a few cousins, aunts, uncles, friends and ourselves. To be honest there were not many of them left – most of them had gone years before.

I have always had an unusual view on death. I believe that when you die the body should be quickly and quietly disposed of – the agony should not be prolonged. Sometimes it is all so drawn out, with weeks before the actual funeral. Then there should be a party for friends and family to toast the person's life and share good memories. I do not believe in moping about and mourning.

A final story about the old man. He had scarlet fever as a child, which in those days could be fatal. He told us he was in bed, the doctor was there and everyone was standing around the bed, when he had what is now known as an 'out of body experience.' He said he was looking down from the ceiling in the corner of the room and the doctor said, "I'm sorry Mrs Pollard, he has gone." He said he was shouting down at them saying, "I'm not gone – I'm up here!" But of course they could not hear him and he felt himself float down onto the bed. The doctor felt for his pulse, which was still there, and he turned to my grandmother and said, "No, he is still alive." After that he pulled round.

Back at CDS, a new face appeared on the block – a guy called Frank Rowlands joined the company. I am sorry to say that I am one of those people who, if I do not like someone at first sight, then that is it – and he was one of these people. I asked Howard what his remit was, and was told he was going to bring some work into the company, if he did not bring anything in during a three-month period he was gone. He was still there when I left in 2000 – I never got on with him and thought he was a complete idiot.

Frank got it into his head that we should try and get work in the London area and had big ideas about starting a fabrication shop down south – but of course that never materialised. Frank and I went to look at a job for Siemens in London. The job was for a piping system in a building in Mayfair that was being refurbished. We went for a meeting but the guy we were due to meet was not there, so we went across the road for a coffee. It was £2.50 for a coffee in 1999 – but I suppose this was in Mayfair! Whilst we were talking I asked Frank, who was now running this side of the business, what selling rates were we going to base the estimate on.

"A labour rate of £8 per hour, all hours," he replied.

"We won't get guys to work in London for £8," I said, "It has just cost me a fiver for two coffees" Me, you notice, no way would he stick his hand in his pocket.

"Don't worry about it – that's what we will use."

"Okay – on your head be it, my son" I told him. "The cheapest digs in London are in the Kings Cross area, which is nearly an hour across London." When we got back to the office, I talked to Howard and he agreed with me to uplift the rate to £12, plus mark ups. I worked on the estimate and came up with a cost to cover all the scope of work. We submitted our quotation and a couple of days later Siemens asked us to split the scope into sections. I told Frank and Howard that this would take some time, as all the materials and other items were in a lump sum.

"Just split it into hours," said Frank. "Divide everything by hours for each section." I told him to stop talking stupid. One section was just the risers and these were all large bore pipes, but I was shot down in flames and had to do as I was told. You can probably guess that they split the job, we got the risers and ran out of money with only one of the four installed. I told Howard if he did not get rid of this buffoon he would end up busting him, but he ignored not only me but his secretary Angie, who had told him the same. A while later he did go bust, but I had already left and, with two other guys, had started my own business – KRC Engineering Services.

Over the previous few years, I had not watched a lot of rugby league as I had been working away from home. I had seen the odd game, but the game itself was changing drastically and I had lost quite a lot of interest. But, in 1998, I saw an article in the *Hull Daily Mail* about one of the local clubs in the Hull league, East Mount, looking for a coach, and decided that I would like to get back into rugby. I had a chat with the secretary, then met with him and a couple of the committee men for a discussion on my coaching philosophies. We reached agreement and, as it was the pre-season, I had chance to get them fit and to put what into practice my previous experience. I intentionally made training a bit harder than I thought they could handle, just to see what they had in them, and some of the guys dropped out. We trained in same place as the Embassy club, one of the oldest teams in Hull, and apparently some of their guys asked the East Mount boys if I was

Keith Pollard

Jacky's mam, Vera

My mam, supporting England

The grand kids and great grand kids

trying to kill them off, saying that no way would they train that hard. As it turned out, neither would the East Mount boys. They did not want to train properly, so I packed it in before the season started.

It was not long after that when John Boland, the chairman of Hull Dockers, asked me if I was interested in helping out with their Under 18 squad to lend their coach Russ Bowering a hand. Russ was then doing the job on his own. I went along and found that they were a good set of lads. They were all as keen as mustard and there were some quite good players there. I was with them for about a season, during which time we got four players in the Yorkshire squad; Chris Stevenson, Paul Smith, John Ledger and Alex Brown – with John Ledger even making the Great Britain under 18s squad. I used to take the four lads to Hunslet and Wakefield for training and games. I brought in a few different tactics, things we used in Australia, which were far ahead of anything being done in the English game, and the young guys loved it. It worked really well and we had several good wins in the Yorkshire League Division 1. Dockers also had a squad in the under 18s National League, coached by Ivor Davies, who finished up on the Hull and District open age management committee in later life. The national league team actually folded, because the players did not like the grind of travelling all over the country, and a couple came back to our team where they were happily accepted.

Later in 1998, we went back to Australia for a month just before Christmas – a trip we had planned just after getting back from the USA. Earlier in the year, Tracy had moved out and the following day found out that she was pregnant. We decided to go on the trip anyway, and Libby was born whilst on Boxing Day whilst we were up at Surfers Paradise at friends' house at Mermaid Waters. They have some great names like Gold Coast, Surfers Paradise, and Mermaid Waters – Thorngumbald, Patrington and Skipsea do not seem to have the same ring to them!

We flew into Brisbane, planning to work our way down the Pacific Highway to Sydney, stopping off at Kempsey and Maitland on the way down. Mick and Libby Evans had been to the UK and stopped with us a couple of years earlier and had invited us to stay with them over Christmas. It was an even hotter summer than usual that year, and they did not have any air conditioning in the house – only in Mick's office, which was a garden room adjacent to the swimming pool. We lived in the office most of the time – apart from night-time when we had three fans in the room and could not sleep for the noise. When we were out, all the pubs and restaurants were air conditioned, so it did not matter.

We were sitting outside one night having a late barby, when the phone rang. Jacky said, "That's Tracy, I bet!" Libby went to answer

Keith Pollard

it and sure enough it was. When Libby came back she was in tears.

"She had a girl and they are calling it after me!" she said. Jacky shot to the phone, coming back crying and blaming me for not being there when our Libby was born. Of course, Mick and I opened another couple of cans and just smiled. What a great life! 80 degrees at midnight outside, bellies full of barby and beer, and our first grandchild had come in to the world when we were 12,000 miles away. Good planning, I reckon.

A couple of days later, we said our goodbyes to Mick and Ozzie Libby, as we had started to call her, and set off for Kempsey, which was a good 260 miles away on a single track road. We were stopping with John and Lyn Green for a couple of nights before heading down to Maitland. Obviously we met up with a few of the old Kowboys and had another bit of a reunion. Mick Flanagan was the same grumpy bastard he always was, still cranky about the grand final loss and my comments about finishing top. Mick will never change and is still pissed off that an outsider came in as player-coach without him getting the chance. If you met him, you might understand why. As ever, not much had changed in Kempsey – it was just the same large country town it always was. Kids tend to grow up and leave home to go to the city or university, as there is not that much work in the bush. Those who do stay get an apprenticeship or a job and tend to stay with the same company all their lives. I only got job in Kempsey back in the 1970s because not many tradesmen went to the town and they were very busy at time – as they were for the full two years I was there.

After that we set off on our travels again – another 150 miles down to Maitland, where we stayed with Alan McNab and his wife Gaye – two of our closest friends in the world. They had moved into their new house in East Maitland, on the way to Morpeth, which is a great little old-fashioned town where they have tried to keep the main street as it has been for a hundred years or more. It was great to wander around and visit some great pubs, cafés and shops there, it was like going back in time. We had a fabulous time meeting all our old friends again – with lots of beer and barbys!

I really enjoy meeting old friends, and I wonder how the old war veterans feel when they meet up every Remembrance Day. When they get together and discuss battles they were in and the comrades they lost, they must have really mixed emotions. I know how I feel when I meet up with former players of the clubs that I played for, and even against. Many a game is replayed, battles are re-won and re-lost – but it is great to get together with guys with whom you have put your bodies on the line, sweated with in training, and helped when one or the other was injured or low on form. People who have never played in team games, or been in a team environment where you rely on each other, cannot understand

RED & WHITE PHOENIX

how close you become to each other. 'Band of Brothers' is a good description. Wives and girlfriends often cannot get to grips with why you need to go to reunions – having said which, Jacky loves meeting the players' wives when we go to those in Oz, although not so much so in Hull and Keighley because we were never as close there as we were with the couples down under.

At the end of the 1998/99 season, John Boland asked me if I was interested in coaching Dockers' team in the National League Division 2 the following season. I said that I would only be interested if the existing coach did not want to carry on with the job, as I did not want to take it from him. John told me he was 'getting rid' of him anyway (in hindsight I should have taken note of his choice of words) and offered him the director of football role to keep him happy. I said that if he was happy to work with me on that basis, then I would do the job.

There were a couple of things I was not happy with about the way the club was run. I have always believed that everyone at a club should be treated the same, and that players should play in any team they were chosen to play in. Some of the first-teamers thought it was below them to play reserve team football and refused to play when not in the first team squad. They were amateur players and some of them thought they were better than they were. A fact I pointed out to them, and which they did not take very well.

I introduced a Player's Charter, which spelt out what was expected of them, at a pre-season meeting. They were asked to sign it before training started to show their agreement to it. I have always believed that in life, if a person knows what is expected of them before they commence any type of activity, they perform better. If they cannot use the excuse, 'well no one told me,' when they are questioned about not performing to their best, they cannot question criticism. Whenever I have been in the position, for the want of a better word, of authority, I have always told people why they are on the job, or included in a team, from the start. I point out that there are no locks on the doors and if they do not like it, they can go, with no hard feelings. At least they knew where they stood.

The captain from the previous season had left and gone to pastures new with Ideal Isberg in the National Conference Premier League, so I asked Glen Brewer, one of the more senior players in the club, to be the club captain. He accepted and after a good pre-season and start to the competition, we were second in the league and just three points behind the leaders. Des Harrison, the ex-Hull KR player, was my assistant, but he was a fireman and was not always available. Keith Farr coached the reserves along with Neil Lowthorpe. Everything was going along fine until two of our best forwards, Don Frankish and Andy Hutchinson, left to join their former captain at Isberg. It was their decision, they wanted to play

305

in a higher level of rugby, but what did annoy me was they did not even have the decency to come to me and tell me they were leaving. I was very disappointed, but you can only play with the cards you are dealt. This meant that we were a bit low on numbers and had to play one or two of the under 18 squad, but the guys stuck in and were still holding onto second place.

Then, when we went to Crossfield in Warrington, I had been struggling for prop forwards during the week at training, one had flu and the other was not fully clear of injury. On the day, one of our second rowers was totally off his game so I took him off in the second half, along with the prop who had flu. I had asked the latter to do has much as he could and when he was totally gone, to put his hand up and he would be replaced. Fair play to him, he did as I asked, but in the end, he just could not do any more. This depleted the team quite a bit and we got beaten, albeit not by a lot. I found out later that the second rower had been out on the razzle the night before and did not get in until three o'clock in the morning. No wonder the so called super-star was so crap.

In the bar after the game, I could feel there was something wrong. No one spoke to me, and none of the committee came anywhere near me. To be honest that did not bother me a bit, they were in my opinion were a set of 'yes' men – whatever Johnny Boland said, they went along with. At training on the Tuesday night, John called me into the dressing room, told me he was not happy with the way things were going, and questioned my decision to take off the two players at the same time at Crossfields. I did not bother to explain as I guessed what was coming. I asked him if he was going to sack me, and when he admitted he was, I said, "Too late son, you can shove it up your arse – I am away."

"We don't want to lose you from the club," he said, "But we are not happy the way the first team are performing". I pointed to our high league position, and said that I believed we were doing quite well considering the players we had. But he had already decided. Outside, the guy who had been sidelined to director of football was getting the gear out for the session and asked me what I had planned.

"Do as you like, I am off – Boland has just sacked me," I said. Des then came up, asked the same question and got the same answer. He could not believe it. I went home seething and Jacky greeted me with, "You're early!"

"Yes, Boland just gave me the elbow – or was going to when I told him to shove it." Later I went back and had a word with Russ Bowering, who said, "Come back and help with the under 18 squad." I did, until the end of the season, then left Dockers for good. I heard that Boland was boasting at work during the day that he was, "going to get rid of that Pollard tonight." Apparently he

RED & WHITE PHOENIX

thought that the fact that I took the two forwards off together at Crossfields cost us a win – the fact that the blue-eyed second-rower was pissed the night before was never mentioned.

There had been other things that I would not agree to though. John wanted to bring an ex-Rovers player down and pay him £1,000 and I said, "Not while I am coach." Then there was an ex Rovers half-back who was playing for York, who John wanted to play for us during the professional close season and then let him go back when York's season started up for the summer. It was not an arrangement that I wanted, and this did not go down very well either.

Deep down, I like John and I had known him a lot of years. He was the club's main sponsor and he thought that it had to be run his way, that everyone had to do as he wanted – basically that it was his team. He was a sort of early amateur version of Dr Koukash – but he appointed the wrong guy when he took me as coach. I was really disappointed in what had gone on at East Mount and Dockers, with players not wanting to commit themselves and blokes who thought that putting a few quid in to an amateur club entitled them to be a dictator, and I stayed away from rugby for a while. Dockers have always had a reputation for treating coaches badly. I remember being told by Mike Collinson who was and still is still coaching at East Hull, what they did to his father when he was down at Tower Grange. He was out putting the gear out ready for a training session when they called him in to the dressing rooms and told him he was sacked. There was no warning, he was just told to 'bugger off' – it is beyond belief.

But after a short break away from the game, I was determined to get back into coaching. I was talking to Mike Smith, the former Rovers legend, who had coached Skirlaugh in the National Conference Premier League, with quite a bit of success, before he too had been shit on by them. I always found it amusing how some of the chairmen and committee men of amateur teams get to be control freaks, and the so-called power goes to their heads. How can you sack a volunteer, a guy who puts 200% in to the job, without a thank you, kiss my arse, or anything. Mike had been approached by East Hull to go down as coach and he asked if I fancied doing it with him. He had a meeting arranged with their chairman, Dave Chester, asked me to go along with him. I went and we said we would do it together. Mike would be head coach with me as his assistant – which I was quite happy with. At that time, they were playing in the Yorkshire Premier League, which was quite a tough competition, not as higher standard as the National Leagues, but not far off it. We started pre-season training using a mixture both our ideas, and it was going well even if we did lack numbers a bit.

307

Keith Pollard

Mike struggled from the off. I think some of the guys just were not up to the standard Mike was expecting – he thought because he could do something, everyone should be able to do it. I tried to get through to him that if they were as good as he was, they would not be playing for East Hull in the first place. But in the end, it got to him and he left. I carried on and we struggled on to the end of the season. After one particular match away to Pudsey in Leeds, we were at an all-time low and had a meeting in the back room of the pub that Pudsey played from. Dave Chester poured his heart out to the guys and it was very emotional to say the least. This kind of hit a nerve with a few of the guys and things improved a bit, but overall it was not really happening.

At the end-of-season presentation get-together, I had word with the chairman and told him that if he could get anyone else involved, I would carry on, but to try do it on my own just took up too much time. Dave told me if I was willing to stay on next season, Lee Radford would be prepared to come down and do it with me. Lee was already coaching a team in the youth system and wanted to try his hand with older guys. I arranged to have a meeting with him and we exchanged ideas. Lee said he was agreeable to come down and coach the first team with me, so I told him he could take over as head coach and I would assist him. After all, the players that he said he could get to come and play for East Hull, would be coming for him rather than me. But he said he wanted us to be joint coaches – he did not want to just take over.

We discussed our thoughts on taking the club forward, and although I realised that I was a bit of a dinosaur and did not have a grasp of the 'so called' modern game, I thought we could get a mix of how I believed the game should be played and Lee's more recent experience. Lee asked if we could do some of the stuff they did at Bradford Bulls, and I said if it was good enough for them it was good enough for East Hull.

For the start of pre-season training, we had quite a few new and experienced players on board, the likes of Lee Brown and Michael Docherty from Hull FC, both of whom were young but had Super League experience; John McCracken from Rovers; and Paul and Lee Roberts from West Hull. These supplemented some of the guys from previous seasons like Gary Weymes, the Clark brothers, and Gary and Paul Blanchard. It was looking good. The way we trained was something new to me and, to be honest, far better than anything I had been involved with. 'Games Conditioning' was what Lee called it – everything was worked on the way the game is played. The fitness side, including weight training, we expected the players to do in addition to our two training nights together, and most of the players bought in to this. It all paid dividends as we had a great season, finishing up as champions and being duly promoted

RED & WHITE PHOENIX

to the National League Division 2.

Meanwhile, I had left CDS in 2000 and started my own engineering business, KRC Engineering Services, in partnership with another two guys who had worked with me. We were working in the water treatment industry and were doing ok. I was running the office, including estimating and cost control along with 'on the road' sales and promotion, which meant being away a few days a week. However, one of the guys wanted to expand the business, which meant taking out a big loan, and I felt I was too old to be getting into debt. I had paid off my house and did not owe a penny to anyone and I was not willing to mortgage my home. So I decided to give the business to my partner, Richard, and opt out. This meant that, unfortunately, I had to work away from home once again. I contacted a few agencies and obtained a position with Ondeo Degremont in St Albans, which was for about nine months, after which I obtained a job back nearer to home, in Immingham North East Lincolnshire, with Fabricom.

This enabled me to get back into coaching again down at East's. By this time, Lee was doing well with the team but I was invited back as his assistant. However, I never felt that I had any real say in what was going on. We had one or two differences of opinion, but he had his way, although I felt he was wrong with one or two of the decisions he made. I was also on the committee at the time, and writing the weekly programme that national clubs have to produce. Lee was supposed to write a few words every week but there was no chance of that, so I used to do it, show it to him, and he gave it the royal seal of approval. All joking aside, Lee is a great bloke and did a hell of a lot to make Easts a much better club.

Whilst I was on the committee, the under-17s squad under Chris Pickard were going in to the Yorkshire under 18 division the following year as under-18s. At this stage they came under the open age section of the club, rather than the youth section. We told Chris and the guys that they had to be self-sufficient and find their own funding, as being in the national completion was a lot costlier, requiring coaches to transport the team to venues in Cumbria and Lancashire, which we simply could not afford. This they understood and agreed to find their own sponsors.

During 2001, our close friends, Gary Selkirk and his fiancé, Jules, decided to get married. Following his name, Gary decided to go up to Selkirk and get married there, and we were duly invited along with a multitude of other guests. I was just glad his name was not Sydney, as that would have cost us a fortune. They were to supply all the food if we would pay for our rooms at the hotel, which seemed a fair idea. Gary rented a castle to host the reception, and laid on a bus to take us from Dryburgh Abbey Hotel near Melrose to Selkirk for the church proceedings. There was also a

309

piper to meet us when we returned.

We had travelled up on the Thursday, staying overnight in a B&B close to the hotel, and on the Friday afternoon we had a barbeque. We later had a meal outside in the grounds of the hotel – it was a really nice place, a bit posh for us, but there was a hell of a mixed bunch, from multi-millionaires driving Red Ferraris, solicitors and business men from all walks of life, to us mere mortals – riggers, pipefitters and out-of-work printers. The full spectrum was covered.

The wedding went really well, and we all went back for photos to be taken in the grounds of the hotel. Gary had organised for all the men to wear traditional Scottish dress and I had refused to wear one. But when he insisted, I had said, "The only way you will get me in one of those is for you to pay for it." So, when I arrived at the hotel, hung up in the wardrobe in our room were the jacket, kilt, socks, sporran and dirk. The latter is the knife you put down your sock – just ready to stab Gary, for making me wear that outfit.

The reception was spot on and the whole day went off really well – even the weather was great. We retired to get changed for the evening do before returning to the ballroom, which by then had been opened up and a stage set up for the artist. Gary had really gone to town. First, there was a Scottish band playing traditional music, with bagpipes and all. Then a rock band came on playing oldies, whilst Tammy Cline and Martin Jackson, two of Hull's best singers, were there. They were very good indeed – Tammie's rendition of *Over the Rainbow* was the best I had ever heard.

We were well into the night when one of Gary's mates, a guy from Liverpool, well loaded as well as well pissed, was telling me at the bar about the Ferrari he was driving, and I talked him into going outside and showing me it. We went to the car park and he let me sit in. Then he started the engine and the sound was unreal - what a motor! I sat there revving it up and suggested we go for a spin round the grounds of the hotel, but he said, "I'm not that pissed!" I suppose that will be the one and only time I ever get to sit behind the wheel of a super sports car. All in all, it was a great weekend – the best wedding I have ever been to. We really had a great time, but when we came away we were not to realise that one day we would be closer to the Selkirks than just wedding guests.

Later that year we went to Myrtle Beach in South Carolina. We flew in to Atlanta, Georgia, picking up a car at the airport again and driving down to Savannah for a couple of days. It is a really nice place, quite 'olde worlde' and right on the Savannah River, with paddle steamers tied up next to the dockside. We loved the century old buildings, which were once cotton warehouses, a lot of them converted to antique shops, modern boutiques, impressive galleries, some really good brew pubs, great restaurants, unique nightspots, elegant inns and hotels. The place was full of life with really friendly people. You can also see Savannah from the river by taking a cruise and watching ships from all around the world sail into one of the busiest ports in America.

We drove through the Historic District of Savannah, that is at the heart of one of the most beautiful cities in the world, with its cobbled streets, manicured gardens, and oak-shaded parks, where you see trees with silvery Spanish moss. I had never really imagined going to Georgia on holiday but it seemed a great place to visit for all ages. It has got everything – art, culture, festivals, concerts, live theatre, outdoor cafes, gourmet restaurants, and true Southern hospitality. There are squares filled with museums, churches, mansions, monuments and famous forts from the revolutionary and civil war eras. It was really impressive, and we would have loved to spend more time there.

After that, we travelled on to Charleston to spend a few days. We visited Patriots Point, which is a kind of floating museum, that houses the *USS Yorktown,* an aircraft carrier that was first commissioned in 1941, and served in the second World War, when she was based at the now infamous Pearl Harbour and used on missions to places like Formosa, Okinawa, Tokyo and Guam. She was later involved in the Vietnam War, and last used in active warfare in 1967 before being finally decommissioned in 1970 and given to Patriots Point in 1973. Alongside the *Yorktown* were a submarine and a coast guard cutter. It was a really interesting place to visit.

At Myrtle Beach, we stayed at a resort at a place called Barefoot Landing where we had a fantastic time. The resort was across the road from the Barefoot Landing shopping complex, which consists of sections of stores and attractions located on filled land over top of Louis Lake, next to the Intracoastal Waterway. Myrtle Beach had everything from shopping to great restaurants and cafés – even its own Theatre, The *Alabama*, founded by country music stars Alabama to accommodate their act. We went to the show, which retains its original format to this day, and included guest artists and other live concerts. There was also the Tiger Preservation Society, where you could see and even touch the big cats. A short distance away was the old town of Myrtle Beach – a visit there is like going back in time. There is so much more to the States for holidays than Orlando – we have tried somewhere different on several occasions and never regretted it.

Back home, as the 2002/3 season progressed, I was getting more and more disillusioned with my first team role at Easts. Lee had asked me if I minded if Paul Cooke, now a coaching assistant at Leigh Centurions, but then at Hull FC, could come down and help with coaching the backs. I had no problem with that, I thought

Keith Pollard

we had enough coaches with Lee and myself, Mick Collinson and Nicky Dean coaching the reserve team. But I thought that another would not make any difference – Lee was the only one who had any real say, and it was his ideas and instructions everyone was working to. But I'd had enough of playing second fiddle. I am not cut out to be a 'yes man' – I have my own opinions and like to voice them, even if I am wrong! So I decided to opt out of coaching the first team squad, and concentrate on my committee role. There were only about five games left in the season, and I told Lee of my decision. He asked me to reconsider, as he was enjoying sharing the coaching with me, but I had made up my mind – the team was his and he was doing a good job. The club had not been in such a good state for many a long year, and whilst I like to think I had some input it to the success, it was mostly down to Lee.

'Radders,' as we called him, had been brought up in the modern game and much that he brought into the club was fantastic, but I still had my ideas on how we should be playing. The Australians, mainly through Jack Gibson, brought in 'game plans,' which we never had up to when I finished playing in 1977 – you just went out and played to the best of your ability and usually the best team won. My idea of a game plan was to play to the strengths of the players you have available on the day – why try and get players to do something they are may not be good enough to do? Sometimes, teams try and play in the same structured way, with or without the key play maker. But a 'stand in' is obviously not as good as the player they are replacing, so you cannot expect them to play in the same way or as well. You need to adapt and 'play what is in front of you,' using your players' strengths. Few teams now play a bit 'off the cuff,' which in my opinion is what is sometimes needed. My only real regret in life is that I have never been given the opportunity to put my 'game plan' into practice, but that is life and it is no good dwelling on it.

A few days after I had finished with the first team, Chris Pickard asked me if I wanted to take over the under 18 squad the following season. He thought he had taken them as far as he could, and a change of coach would be good for them. They were playing at Lock Lane in Castleford the following weekend and suggested I come along and take a look at them in action. He told me they had been beaten by the same team by 36 points a few weeks previously and according to Chris they had been bullied out of it. I had seen a few of the lads around at training and, although I did not know most of them, I could not believe how they could have been bullied – most of them would rather have a fight than a McDonalds. One of the lads was Scott Wheeldon, who went on to play in the professional game with Hull FC, Rovers, London Broncos and Castleford, and is still full time with Sheffield Eagles.

312

RED & WHITE PHOENIX

I went to the game and asked Chris if I could have a few words before the game after he had said his bit. He agreed and told the lads that I was taking over the following season – even before I had made my mind up! But I gave them a Churchillian speech about it being the last chance to win some silverware – it was the play-off semi-final and if they did not give it their all, that was it until next year. I had been watching a documentary on TV a few weeks before about the British Lions in New Zealand and Australia in an interview, in which one of the All Blacks was asked if he ever wore a rugby jersey off the field. His answer, was no, he only put a rugby shirt on when he was going out to play because he felt when he went out onto the pitch that he, 'was going to war and the shirt was his battle dress.' We had just got into the Kuwait war at the time, and had lads of 18 years old out there, putting their lives on the line. I spoke of what these lads were prepared to do to keep us safe, and said, "All we are asking of you is to go out there and play 80 minutes and put your bodies on the line to win a game of rugby."

Chris said to me he could see them grow another foot taller as I was talking. I held up one of East Hull's spare shirts and said, "This is your battledress – now go out there, don't leave anything in this dressing room, and do not come back in here with any regrets, wishing you had done this or done that. Ensure that when you come back in, you can look in the mirror and know the guy looking back at you has given his all".

We won the game quite easily and Chris reckoned they had not played that well all season. Afterwards Chris was talking to Lock Lane's coach, told him about my pre-match talk, and said that I was taking over next season. When Chris introduced me and he said, "Do us a favour - don't take over! I've never seen such a change in a team in my life!" That certainly gave me a good feeling.

So, in 2003/4, I was coaching the under 18's with Dean Cox, someone who had been with them through the bad times as well as the good, and one of the most genuine and honest people you could ever meet. The lads responded well to our coaching and we had quite a good season in the Yorkshire League Division 1, reaching the final but losing out to Oulton Raiders by a couple of points at Featherstone Rovers' ground.

I was still working with Fabricom in Immingham, and had a good job as Project Estimator, where I had the opportunity to get quite a few sponsors for the under 18 team. I found that people and companies were willing to fork out money for youth teams, much more so than for open age. I contacted a few firms in North East Lincolnshire that I dealt with for Fabricom and managed to obtain around £5,000 for the club – quite a substantial amount to us. Fabricom would not get involved though. The Managing Director there was not my type – a church goer who did not like swearing –

an odd-bod in my opinion!

As the editor of the club programme for the national league team and, as part of the sponsorship agreements, I included an advertisement in the first team programme for each company. There were more adverts in for the under 18s than the open age team, and I was questioned by the committee about why this was so. I went through each advert individually and the chairman noted down the value of each donation. At the end he said, "That's about four grand." I told him that it was more like five – but that it was all the under 18's money, and that he wasn't getting any towards the open age teams coffers. He was unimpressed, so I had to remind him about the meeting when it was decided that the under-18s had to self-sufficient – and they were. He was not particularly happy, but to be honest I do not think it was so much him as the other committee members, who were giving him hassle. Lee Radford was spending money like it was going out of fashion.

One real bone of contention was that the committee was not happy about the £1,000 from P&D Engineering for tracksuits and polo shirts. We bought the gear and sold them to the lads for £25 each on the understanding that if they stayed with the club all season, we would give them the money back on presentation night. We wanted to ensure we did not lose them, as we did not have a big squad, but for some reason the open age people did not like this at all. It happened anyway, and when we finished, there was not another team to come up from the youth section into the open age, and we had about £600 left. It stayed in the bank until there was a team available to accept it, and when Lee Radford's youth team came through to under-18s he asked me if he could have the money. So I gave him it and I understand he blew it all on one bus to a game.

In 2004, my mother was taken into hospital after trying to commit suicide by taking a full bottle of paracetamol tablets. She was being visited by carers three times a day, which I think is the most humiliating thing that can happen to anyone who is not very mobile – to just sit there day after day waiting for someone to come in get you up, wash you, give you breakfast, then leave. All done as quickly as they can, because they are on a time limit with each patient. They then return at lunchtime to give you your food and get out as quickly as possible again, before returning in the evening to ensure you have an evening meal and get you to bed, even if you do not want to go. It must be the most demoralising existence for a human being. Having been a lively social animal, my mother had started to not wanting to go anywhere. She said she could not walk very far and everything had become a chore.

The carer had been in the morning and she said not to bother coming at lunchtime because she was going out – she had everything planned. We went to see her around teatime and, when we arrived, the carer, who was unable to get in, was waiting outside. My mother was in sheltered housing and the carer had contacted the housing control room, but could not get reply. This had only just happened, and fortunately we had a key and let ourselves in. The carer went in to her room and found the empty pill bottle on the side cabinet. She immediately called for ambulance which arrived within ten minutes. The paramedics took her to Hull Royal Infirmary, with us following the ambulance. We had to wait for a couple of hours while they pumped out her stomach and got her stable.

When we went in to see her she acted as if nothing had happened and was whinging about the nurses because she had a terrible headache and they would not give her any paracetamol. I told her she had taken enough to last a lifetime. They admitted her onto a ward, where she would not talk to anyone, including us. She just laid with her back to us, totally ignoring us, and Jacky used to say, "We are not leaving until you turn and talk to me." This went on for the full visiting time. She was really stubborn, but thinking back, I suppose she always did what she wanted to. She was the opposite to the old man, who was not a social person, and was just happy to be on his own at his allotment. Perhaps that is where I get it from. Being an only one, I spent a lot of time on my own – I love Jacky to bits, but I still need to be left alone at times. That is how I coped with working away so much – just doing my own thing and pleasing myself.

After a couple of weeks in hospital, my mother started to talk – not a lot at first, but she gradually started to become more like herself. The social services wanted her to go back home and live on her own again – they thought that she was working the system and that nothing was wrong with her. However, the ward sister disagreed with their assessment and would not let her out, saying she was not safe to live on her own. The social worker said there were no funds available for my mother to be put in a care home, so I asked him quietly if we could talk privately.

"No problem," he said, and we walked down the corridor in to a side room. I was fuming and gave him both barrels, mentioning that I had a friend at the *News of the World* and would give them the story. He was not happy, scurried off, and about half an hour later another social worker appeared, saying that her department had the funding to put my mother in the home. It is funny how things sometimes change when you mention newspapers. My mother moved into a care home on Hessle High Road. We had tried to talk her into coming up to Hedon, near us, but she wanted to be in West Hull, to be near my cousin Elaine.

My mother was quite happy in the home and quickly settled in, soon becoming known as 'the Queen.' At first, she shared a room upstairs, as her funding did not cover a private room. The system was complex then and I do not suppose it has changed. The more money you could put in, the better the room you could get. People were expected to sell their homes to help pay for their care, as well as having their pensions taken and just being given £15 a week 'pocket money.' I think people should spend their money and enjoy it while they can before it is taken off them. After a year or so, they moved her in to a smaller single room downstairs, and not long after that, a bigger room became available and she moved into that. But she soon moved back. Apparently the bigger room was too far out of the way and could not see anyone passing, but the smaller one was at the end of a long corridor and she could see everyone coming and going, so she was happy there.

I finished with East Hull when I got the opportunity of a job as projects estimator for Amec at the Corryton Refinery in Essex. It was unfortunate, but as I was away all week, it was impossible to commit time to rugby. When I started there, I found that the hotels in the Basildon area were very expensive – even the cheapest was still around £40 per night without breakfast. For about four months I stayed at Campanile, the cheapest I could find, whilst I looked for alternatives. I had never liked B&B's, which are basically just a room in someone's house – I like my own space. Then one of the guys told me he was living in a caravan on a site which only cost £60 a week including electric hook-up. This sounded good to me, so I went along to look at the site and found that there were vacancies. After discussing it with Jacky, I bought myself a Lunar fixed-bed four-berth for around £6,000. It was a lot, but I thought that if I was going to be there long-term I would get my money back when I sold it – and as it happened I was right.

The site was on a working farm and was not at all bad. The showers and toilets were always kept really clean and heated during winter, and it was very handy for the works and great value. Several of the other contractors were on the site, one of them from Hull, who was working on the high speed rail link to channel tunnel. He had been on the site for about three years – it was the nearest one to the rail site, but he still had quite a way away to commute every day. I joined the local gym in Basildon and was enjoying that until my knees started playing up and I started to get quite a lot of pain, so I started just doing upper body exercises. But I was already a 48" chest, and did not want to get any bigger, so I reluctantly packed it in. One of the guys from the site, Tom, who was also from Hull, used to join me whilst we did circuits on the machines, sometimes a swim in the outside pool, depending on the weather, then a couple of beers after in the bar. It was a pleasant way to spend an evening.

CHAPTER 19
GOOD AND BAD TIMES

Two close family members passed away during my time at Corryton. The first of these was Jacky's mother, Vera, who died on August 21st 2006, aged 85. She had been ill on and off with various ailments for a few years, but it was still a shock when she died. I got a phone call from Jacky to say that she had passed away during the night and that her dad, George, woke up to find her just lying there next to him. Apparently, she had tried to get up but collapsed on the bed. George took it very badly and was heartbroken. They had many arguments, but he loved her very much and was never the same man again after she went. He used to say that he did not want to be here anymore, and that he had lived too long. It surprised me how badly he took her death, because when they argued Vera could be quite nasty to him – she had really vicious tongue at times. What she said about others made me wonder what she said about me behind my back – but what you do not know cannot hurt you. The only one that was safe was her favourite son, Ian, who could do no wrong – whilst her son-in-law could do no right. I used to sit talking to George in his favourite chair in the corner next to fireplace and Vera would stand between us to interrupt and give her opinion on someone or other. George was a bit hard of hearing, but I always thought it was selective hearing.

I loved the job at Amec, the guys were great to work with, the work was interesting and the money was decent. I was the lead estimator for the projects group, covering all aspects of the site engineering. I really enjoyed getting up in a morning and going to work. Apart from being away from home again it was a great job, and quite a few of the lads had been there for several years. I had been there about 18 months when I had a phone call from an agency asking if I was interested in a job in Central London with a large EPC contracting company. They told me the gist of the position, which paid a lot more money, and suggested they put me forward for an interview. I agreed and an hour later got another call saying that the company was interested in me and asked if I could do a phone interview. By then, this practice was becoming increasingly common, as it saves the expense of having candidates travel for face-to-face meetings. I agreed and, within a couple of hours, I got a call from the company. I spoke with some bloke at length about what they were looking for, what they wanted from me, and what I could contribute to their company. But it was not long before he said, "Okay, I've heard enough. When can you start?" I was quite taken aback to be honest. He asked what money I wanted, which is rather unusual as money is usually agreed with the agent. When I pointed this out to him, he told me he did not work that way.

"I will tell them what we have agreed and that is final," he said, "You get what you are getting and they will get theirs on top." I told him I was quite happy where I was, but would consider his offer and get back to him as soon as possible. I was very tempted and after a lot of thought, being the mercenary that I am, I decided to leave. I gave my notice in to Jim Morrison, the project manager, and he asked me what could he do to make me stay. I told him I would be clearing £100 a week more than I was getting there and he told me he could not up my rate but asked what else would make me stay. I asked if I could work the 40 hours a week over four days. I used to travel down early on Monday and back on Friday evening – and it is no fun whatsoever being stuck in the M1 car park on Monday mornings and Friday afternoons.

Jim asked if I would give him a couple of days to try and sort something, so I agreed and left it at that. He came over to see me in my office the following morning, and said that my request had been agreed. He then told me to book three hours a week extra and that would compensate me for the hundred pounds I would be down. It was a hell of a result and I was over the moon. I rang the guy who had offered me the other job, to tell him I had decided to stay where I was, and he then offered me more money to leave. Apparently, I had exactly what they needed, someone with experience of site work, not an office based estimator, also I was working on a live refinery, which was what they were desperate to break into – but I had given my word to Jim, so I declined. The guy got rather angry and suggested I had messed him about, saying that I had gave him the impression I was going to join them, that he had organised with the agency for me to start, and so on. It was a load of rubbish and I started to realise that I had made the right decision.

"Whoa, hang on mate," I said, stopping him in his tracks, "Nothing was agreed – you have just offered me more money to join you, so how could you have agreed with the agency for me to start? But listening to you rant on, I think I have made the right choice – you could not pay me enough to work for you, or your company!" With that I put the phone down.

About an hour or so later the agency rang to give me a bollocking about how I had talked to their client and that I had been out of order. I told them a few home truths too. What they had said was nothing like the conversation I had with their client. In the end, I told the guy to fuck right off and not to ever ring me again – there was obviously no chance they would, but I enjoyed saying it.

I was with Amec about three years in all, but towards the end of that time the refinery was sold to a Swiss company, Petroplus. It was never the quite same after they took over – there was a difference in the atmosphere within the workforce somehow. About four years after I left, the new owners filed for bankruptcy and on May 28th 2012 it was announced that the refinery would close, as the administrators had failed to find a buyer, and on February 28th 2013 the gas supply to the site was shut off. Around twelve hours later the flare went out, bringing to an end over 60 years of operations at the refinery. A lot of good guys lost their jobs, and it is another example of a foreign company buggering up a British facility. It is now a diesel import terminal.

Whilst I was at Corryton, we went to the states a couple more times. In 2005, we went to California again, this time to Los Angeles and Palm Springs. LA was a bit of a disappointment to me. It was not what I expected, it lacked the glamour and glitter you see on TV, and it seemed rather run down to me. We went out to Venice Beach, Santa Monica, with its pier, and Muscle Beach, where the guys work out in the outside gymnasium – posing bastards and tits in more ways than one.

But, after a few days in LA, we went on to Palm Springs. Now this was something else. We had rented a great house and with a pool area surrounded by seven foot wall all the way round. It was owned by a very pleasant, if rather effeminate guy. As it was so private, I was able to spend the full week in the pool naked. Algeria had given me the taste for that and it was great.

On the first night there, we went to nice Italian restaurant on the main street in Palm Springs. There was a couple on the next table to us, who, by the look of them, were deeply in love, holding hands across the table gazing into each other's eyes – it was very romantic. I asked Jacky, "Have you noticed anything unusual?" When she said not, I pointed out that there were no women there, apart from her – they were all guys in twos. I had never seen anything like it. But we had a great meal with fantastic food and it was definitely an experience.

We went on the cable car that took you up the three levels of the so-called San Jacinto Mountain. It was really hot at the bottom, then there was a cooler area with green trees half way up, and at the top it was very cold and rocky – it was quite remarkable. Construction of the tramway itself was an engineering challenge that was labelled the 'eighth wonder of the world.' Helicopters were used in erecting four of the five supporting towers – only the first can be reached by road. They flew some 23,000 missions during over two years of construction work, hauling the men and materials needed for the four other towers and the 35,000 square foot mountain station. Twenty-years later, the tramway was designated as a historical civil engineering landmark. The cable car itself provided a bit of a hairy ride. As you came to each tower it dropped suddenly then climbed again, then dropped again as it went over the top of the tower.

Palm Springs may be another place that you would not think of going on holiday, but it is really worth a visit, believe me. After we left Palm Springs, we drove back to Las Vegas where we had booked in to the *MGM Grand*. Grand is an understatement – it took us twenty minutes to walk from the reception to our rooms and we never went outside. As you walk through the casino part there are two lions in a glass enclosure. It must have been boring for them but they were a couple of trainers with them, one of whom told me they there were in fact several of them at a ranch outside Vegas and they brought them 'into work' on a rotation basis. The rooms at the *Grand* were amazing. It was the first time I had ever seen a TV built in to the mirror in the bathroom, so you did not miss any of your favourite programmes whilst performing your ablutions. Jacky was ill for three of the days whilst we were there, and was confined to bed for a couple of them, but she improved and enjoyed the rest of the stay.

One thing we learned was that if in Vegas not to use the monorail. It stopped inside the *Grand*, which is great if you want to get on or off there, but it runs around the back of the strip about a mile away from the main road. It was a hell of a walk in the heat to get back on the strip, or to any of the other resorts.

We returned to the states in 2006, this time to Florida. The whole family went along, including Jason who had not been on holiday with us for over twenty years – since he was about 15. We had decided this would be our last holiday together as a family – sadly a prescient decision. We rented a house in Kissimmee in a gated community complex, complete with swimming pool. We did all the usual things, including all the parks and meeting Mickey Mouse again – he had not aged or changed much over the years, it must be the climate. The best thing we did was swimming with the dolphins. It has to be the best day ever, not cheap, but a great experience nonetheless. Jason did not go into the water due to the punctured ear drum he suffered as a kid, but the rest of us did.

The way they train these animals is fantastic. There is a compound away from the main lagoon where they are kept, and when they want them to come out to perform, the trainers go and call them by name. If a particular dolphin does not want to 'play' that day they do not force them. They try a few times, but if this does not succeed they ask another. Each trainer has about six to eight dolphins under his charge, but the senior trainer can call on ten or more. If you are not a very strong swimmer you can wear a lightweight life vest, which I did. You go through a series of games with the dolphin, when they pull you from one point to another between two trainers. You have to hold on to the top dorsal fin and its nearside flipper and off you go – it is the most amazing experience you will ever have. The trainers also ask you to put your hands together so that the dolphin can lay its head on them and they tell it to kiss you. Then, as you lean towards it, it spouts a mouthful of water into your face. I also loved the Sea World Orca show, *Orca Rocks the World*. We went at night time and the lighting effects were fantastic – they do know how to put on a show over there!

Our second bereavement around then was when my mother passed away on March 12th 2007. She was still in the home at Hessle and had given up the will to live again.

"You can live too long," she had often said – and this time she meant it. She had started not eating properly, and although we used to take her the things she loved every week, the carers told us they had to throw most of them away. I was still working at Corryton when I got the message to say that she had passed away with Jacky at her side. Jacky said that my mother looked up at her and made an unusual sound before laying down, closing her eyes and slipping away. It seemed that she had done it in her own way for one final time. It was very painful at first and I had a sense of having become an orphan, but time does heal. At the funeral, we had Sinatra singing, '*I did it my way*' as the service ended. It seemed an appropriate farewell.

Back at work, I was looking around for a change when an agency rang me to ask if I was interested in a job on the banks of the Humber – this was a bit of a surprise as not many jobs come up that are local. It was Conoco Phillips Humber Refinery, who were looking for an estimator. I knew a guy who worked there as Construction Manager, Colin Hodgson, who had been one of the business directors at Fabricom. I called him and asked if he had any information about the job and he made some enquires and called me back with some useful background. I was interviewed by the costing manager, Jim Waite, and Lee Cockburn, who was my contact when I was on site with SLP. It went quite well – you usually can tell when you have done ok. We did not talk about money, which is usual when you take a job as a freelance contractor, as you only discuss money with the agent.

I went back to Corryton on the following Monday, saying nothing to anyone, but hoping I had done enough to get my foot in the door at Conoco. Jacky was coming down for a long weekend in the caravan on the Thursday and I was at Stevenage station waiting for her train to arrive when I got a call from the agents. He told me that he had heard from Jim Waite, and they wanted me to join them. I asked him what rate had they offered, not thinking I would get the same or anywhere near what I was on down in Essex, but he said they had offered me a pound an hour more than I was currently on,

Keith Pollard

so I agreed there and then. When Jacky arrived I gave her the good news about the new job, saying that I would not need to be away all week any more. On reflection, I am not really sure of her reaction – she was used to her own space and not having me around to mess up the house.

One of my first jobs at Humber Refinery was to devise an estimating package based on Excel spreadsheets, as they only had the corporate system that was used in Houston, Texas, and was not really suitable for the UK market. By a stroke of luck, I had been working on a similar Excel estimating spreadsheet for Corryton, whose system had been inadequate, so I was able to use that.

I enjoyed being back home, even if Jacky had reservations! I did not try to get back into coaching, but just went down to East Hull to help out a bit. We had been away in the caravan to see if we liked that type of holiday, which we did, so we changed it for a newer model. We bought a German Geist from Wandahome near Hull, and started travelling around the UK with it. We still are caravaners, and it is one of the best things we have ever done – it beats airport lounges and flying delays anytime. You meet some great people and the camaraderie amongst campers is brilliant.

Also in 2007, we decided to go on *North Sea Ferries* from Hull to Rotterdam, having exchanged our time share for one in the Netherlands. We enjoyed that experience too, visiting Amsterdam, the tulip fields, and an emotional trip to Arnhem. We saw the 'bridge too far' that British troops in World War II held, whilst heavily outnumbered by the Germans in Operation Market Garden. There is a museum there which shows a film of the action in what was the largest airborne operation in history. There cannot be too much recognition for what those soldiers gave for us, and as they say, we must never forget. Jacky's father should have gone on that mission, he was a sergeant in the paratroopers who was based in Scotland, but there was a change of orders and someone went in his place and was, I believe, killed in action. There were some Dutch people in the museum when we visited and when they found out we were British they were thanking us for what the allied forces did for the Netherlands.

I stayed at Conoco until 2011. It was a really good job; my immediate gaffer, Jim, was great to work for and although we had a couple of disagreements there was nothing that threatened our relationship. In the bad winter of 2010 when the snow and ice lasted for weeks, I had a 'four-by-four' and so did not have a lot of bother getting back and forth to Immingham. But we had had a really heavy fall of snow one Friday, and I set off not realising how bad it had been until I got over the Humber Bridge and set off down the A15. I managed to get through, half-wishing that I had not set off, but for a contractor, no show means no pay, and as a proud

RED & WHITE PHOENIX

Yorkshireman, I do not like losing money. By the time I had got to the plant, I was about an hour and a half late, but as I was there I intended to put in a full day. To my surprise, I was one of only about five people that had managed to battle through the weather to get to work.

Jamie, one of the planners, had managed to get in, as had one of the office girls. The controls lead engineer arrived a bit later and was surprised that we had got in at all. Then, around lunchtime, the plant manager came around and told us to go home, as more bad weather was forecast. I said to Jamie that I was not going anywhere, as I intended to get my full shift in. He was a permanent staff member, so he got paid even if he was not there, as long as there was a good reason for absence. After a couple more hours, the sky was full of snow and the plant manager came round again and told us that we were not needed. He thanked us for taking the trouble to get in, and said we should leave without delay. I told to Jamie that was good enough for me, and handed him my timesheet, as he was authorised to sign it in Jim's absence. I had booked the full eight hours and he whinged about me not having a full day in. I pointed out that he was going to be paid for a full shift, the staff who never came in would get the full shift, and I was being sent home by the gaffer, so he duly signed it and off I went.

On the Monday, Jim came to see me.

"You booked eight hours on Friday but did not work them all," he said. I told him that I had been sent home by the plant manager but he said, "You can't book them, we only pay for hours worked."

"Look Jim, I struggled to get here, whilst you never even got your arse out of bed and tried to get to work," I said, quite annoyed by then. "I was here and quite willing to put the eight hours in, but the gaffer instructed us to go home. If you don't like it, sack me. I am not changing the sheet. You can shove your job up your arse as far as I am concerned if that is how you want to treat me." He did not say another word and went away rather red-faced.

Jamie had been trying to pretend he was not there and got up to walk away.

"Come back here you, I want a word," I said. "What has Jim had said to you?" He told me that Jim had said nothing, but one of the girls who was also a contractor had been whinging about me getting the eight hours. I was fuming and was going to say something to her, but decided better of it. Later that afternoon, Jim came back and apologised. He had spoken to his immediate manager, Lee, and had been told to pay me the eight hours. Lee said I had taken trouble to get in and been told to go home, it was only right that I should be paid. The episode really pissed me off and I never put myself out for Jim again. I believe in 'give and take' but it was all take from Jim – Lee was a different story though

323

Keith Pollard

and, all in all, I really enjoyed working at Conoco.

In 2009, we decided to take the caravan to Europe and travel down to the South of France for two weeks, including making the trip over to Perpignan, where Hull KR were playing the Catalans Dragons. We went over on the ferry from Hull to Zeebrugge and drove down through Belgium and France. It was a hell of a journey, all on the motorway, and the toll costs were exorbitant. We had one stop going south, at Lac De Lietz on the Ardennes, before reaching our destination, Avignon. That was a great place, with a camp site right on the river Rhone, nearly opposite the old bridge that is no more.

Avignon was the capital of Christendom in the Middle Ages and has kept a lot of its history and heritage. There are the Popes' Palace, with its square, the baroque facade of the Hotel of Currencies, the museum of the Petit Palais and the cathedral of Doms – as well as the famous Bridge of Avignon itself, with the ramparts up that lead up to it. According to legend, a young shepherd from Ardèche, Bénezet, heard voices telling him to build a bridge in Avignon. When it was completed, it was the only place to cross the Rhône between Lyon and the Mediterranean Sea. Today, all that remains of the original 900-meter structure are four arches and a chapel dedicated to Saint Nicolas.

We had a wonderful time there, wandering through the little back streets, nipping into some of the bars and cafés, and going on the little free ferry across the river – it was really well worth the visit. We left the van on the site when we drove across to Perpignan, a 320-mile round trip, to see the Rovers game. We stayed in a hotel just across the road from the square where all the Rovers supporters met in the bars and cafes. Rugby league supporters make the most of the annual weekend trip to Perpignan and it is a wonderful atmosphere no matter who you support. Before and afterwards, the locals make you very welcome, albeit not so much so at the stadium, where they are very partisan, playing the Catalan national anthem before each game. The atmosphere is more like being at a bull fight than a rugby match.

We booked our tickets for the game through a tour company and sat with the French supporters in the main sitting area, whilst the Rovers supporters were in the end stand behind the posts. Buses were put on to and from the square to the stadium – the organisation was brilliant. Sadly, some of the Rovers supporters proved that so many Brits just cannot take a drink abroad. I had a few before the game and even more after, and by midnight I'd had enough – but they were still at until the early hours, a lot of them legless. After that, we drove back to Avignon to finish off our eight days there, before heading back up to Zeebrugge. It was a hell of a trip in two weeks but well worth the journey.

RED & WHITE PHOENIX

On July 17th 2009, Jacky's dad passed away. I was at work and got a message that he had suddenly been taken ill. His health was not at all bad for a 90-year old. He had a few problems, mostly with his breathing, and when I rang Jacky, she said that the doctor was coming, but that there was no immediate concern. She asked if I would I pick her up from her dad's on my way home. When I turned into Anson Road where he lived, there was an ambulance and a responder outside the house, which obviously did not look good. When I walked in, Jacky was in tears and her brother Ian was in a bit of a state. I said the first thing that came into my head, "How's Dad?" Jacky then broke down and said, "He's dead, Keith. My dad's gone."

Apparently the doctor had been and given him a prescription, which Dena, her sister, had gone to the chemist to collect. Dad had said he was going up for a bath, so Jacky said she would hang on there, until I arrived to pick her up as arranged. About ten minutes later, Jacky heard a bang from upstairs and went up to see if he was ok. She told me he had collapsed and she found him holding onto the wall. She tried to hold him and get to the phone to call 999, but he died in her arms. The responder arrived within minutes, as he was in the vicinity, and worked on Dad straightaway. When the ambulance arrived they also worked on him for nearly half hour, but it was no good.

Whilst we waited for the police to come, Dena arrived back with the prescription and she too was in bits when she found out what had happened. The police arrived, asked a lot of questions, and interviewed the paramedics. When they were satisfied there was nothing untoward, they left, and we waited for the undertaker to arrive. I felt numb – just trying to think straight and mourning the loss of yet another loved one who had departed. Jacky handled the situation really well. She had already sorted out who needed contacting when her mother passed away – I would not have realised all that needed doing. But, at least, I think that doing something helped her to take her mind off what had happened.

We had to empty the house within two weeks. Jackie's parents had lived in that house for 40 years, but they could not wait to get someone else in to pay the rent. Councils are really sensitive aren't they? It was a heart-breaking process having to empty all the contents and talk about who wanted this and that, and what would end up being just thrown away. All our parents had now passed away – it was not shaping up to be a great start to the new century.

We went back to Australia in January 2010 for holiday with Tracy and Libby. We flew into Brisbane and rented an apartment in the city for a few days. Having never actually stayed in Brisbane before, I had not realised what a great city it was, and looking back we did not stay long enough. I would definitely go back for longer visit. We picked up a hire car and went up to Mooloolabah, a superb coastal resort just over sixty miles north of Brisbane. We rented a house with a pool, not far from the beach, for ten days. Daniel, Tracy's boyfriend at the time, had been somewhere in the Far East on business and stayed with us for a while. We went to Brisbane airport to pick him up and visited some friends nearby, Chris Draper and his wife Debbie, who had emigrated out there and had just moved in to their new home. Chris's father, Chris senior, a former Rovers director, and his wife Wendy, were out there at the time on holiday, so we all had the traditional barby and a few beers together. They were good enough to put us up for the night as we were picking Daniel up quite early the next morning before heading back up the coast to Mooloolabah.

We the continued down the east coast to Coffs Harbour, where we stayed in an apartment for a week. Whilst we were there we visited Kempsey for a day, where Judy and Debbie Cameron had organised a reunion at their place with the guys who played with me at the Kowboys in 1974/75. They are fantastic cooks and really did us proud – it was a great afternoon, lots of amber nectar was drunk, and old games were replayed. Tracy did not have a lot to drink and drove us back the 68 miles north to finish our few days in Coffs.

We then drove the 175 miles to Maitland, and our friends Alan and Gaye McNab's house in Tenambet on the east side of the town. We had arranged to stay with them for ten days or so over the Easter period. They had organised another reunion, and most of the 1973 Grand Final team turned up for a great night. Terry Pannowitz had a DVD of the game, so we had a good feed on some fantastic grub, then watched the game on the big screen. I relived every minute of it. Some people say you cannot remember what happened on the field, but this game was something very special and I could have almost done a commentary on the game. The beer was flowing in as quickly as the tries on the screen, and it was a fantastic night – another I will always remember, almost as well as the actual win against the Western Suburbs Rosellas itself! We visited all our friends in the area again, there were more barbys and even more beer was consumed. It seemed that every time we went back to Oz, I always seemed to have a can, or stubby as they call them there, in my hand.

After we left Maitland, we headed off to Sydney for the last part of our trip. I had really pushed the boat out for our final accommodation this time. I had booked a three-bedroom apartment in the Casino on Darling Harbour, a really upmarket place, and we did the usual tourist things. I got in touch with mate of mine from Maitland, Peter Sharp, who met us at the casino, where we had couple of beers before going for a meal in the buffet restaurant. As we were going in, we saw a man who was surrounded by people all trying to get his autograph. Sharpy told us that it was Danny 'The Green Machine' Green, a world ranking boxer. I must be honest and admit that I had never heard of the him but he was obviously quite handy. Peter said, "G'day mate, how's you? Come and meet some Pommie mates of mine." Green managed to get away from his admirers and came over to talk with us. Peter introduced him and we shook hands. He was really bouncing, and I thought hope no one rings a bell or we are in deep shit. Like a fool, I asked him what division he fought in. He looked at me in disbelief, as if I should know, and said middleweight.

"Oh, like Joe Calzaghe," I said.

"Yes, the bastard won't fight me," he replied. I thought if Calzaghe won't fight him I'd better not take the piss anymore. Sharpy was giving me a look that said 'stop winding him up.' Green then said to me, "You look as if you have had a few on that nose."

"Yes, I've had 101 fights and lost 103," which broke the ice a bit. Although I think he still thought I was taking the mickey until Sharpy followed up by telling him about me playing footy, and we ended up having a good yarn. Apparently, he was from Perth and stayed at the casino when he was training in Sydney. As he moved about he was bouncing on his toes like boxers do – a really fit-looking guy, but I suppose you have to be when you are going twelve rounds with the best in the world. Rather him than me. As we said our goodbyes and moved into the buffet, Peter said, "Are you wrong in the head? Taking the piss out of him!"

"No,' I said, "I had never heard of him until that moment you introduced us. He seemed like a nice guy."

"Jesus Pom, he's a facking animal! And you were winding him up!" We had a good night, even better when Peter footed the bill! To be fair he got a good discount because he was assistant coach at Parramatta and they had a sponsorship of with the hotel.

A few years later, I saw one of Green's world title fights on TV and Jacky said, "You were lucky Peter was with us that night in Sydney – otherwise I might have been a widow now". To be fair, it occurred to me that if Peter had not been with us, we would never had met the guy.

Sharpy had asked us what we were doing over the final few days of our trip, and asked us all to go to the club, have a look around and meet some of the players. Daniel, Tracy and Libby wanted to go to Bondi on one of the days if the weather was good, so we agreed that if the weather was a bit iffy, we would take the ferry out to Parra and visit the club. As it happened the following day was lovely, so we all got the bus at Circular Quay and headed down to Bondi Beach for the day. They went off for a few hours on

Keith Pollard

Jacky on holiday

Our first holiday in Florida, 1991

Daniel, Libby and Tracy, with Isla-Rose on her 3rd birthday

the beach, but we had seen it all before – just a load of sand and young Sheilas in skimpy bikinis.

"What on earth would we want to go there for?" Jacky had asked. Surprise, surprise – we went shopping and met them later. We met for lunch, a burger and a can of coke – the staple diet of the typical Ozzie surfer, a bit like fish and chips at the seaside here.

The following day was overcast, so we decided to go to go out to Parramatta. I rang Sharpy up to let him know and we went down to Circular Quay again to catch the ferry. The ferry system and public transport in Sydney is fantastic and to see the harbour in all its glory is one of the things you should do before you die. We went on the River Cat catamaran, which is an express non-stop service that takes you under the Sydney Harbour and Gladesville bridges, a pleasant 20km cruise from Circular Quay to Parramatta City. Sharpy met us at the ferry stop and took us to the ground where we met the Chairman and a few of the personnel. Darren Anderson, who was head coach at the time, got a bit of stick from Jacky as he used to be the St Helens coach and Rovers beat Saints on a couple of occasions whilst he was there – but it was all in good fun.

A few of the players came out for a yarn, and Nathan Cayless had announced his retirement that day, so there were a few reporters about too. What struck me more than anything was the size of the players. I cannot remember ever playing against guys as big. We had a few photos taken, and in one I am standing between Nathan Hindmarsh and Joel Reddy, who both towered over me and I am five feet eleven inches. Fui Fui Moi Moi is about as tall as me, but his arms are as thick as my legs – he is built like the proverbial brick out house. Another player who I never thought was so big was Jarred Hayne, who was only in his early twenties then. They are definitely a bigger size of athlete. When we went into the gym, two or three younger players were walking out and one of the coaches said to me, "How would you like to be 14 again?"

"Jesus," I said, "Is that all they are?" They were all towering over me. I sometimes see watch Parramatta on Premier Sports now and wonder how many of those young boys are now in the first team. For me the day was a great ending to another fantastic Australia trip.

Around this time, we booked a few days away in Kent at a time share resort with Sean and Jean O'Brien. I thought it would be a good idea to try to get in touch with George and Christine Kennedy again, whilst we were in their neck of the woods. So I found the number of a George Kennedy in the BT directory and left a message.

A few days later I got a call back – it had been the same George Kennedy. Apparently by then he was semi-retired and was now busy as chairman of his local cricket club and played a lot of golf.

Keith Pollard

The Queen Elizabeth in Circular Quay, Sydney

He had just got home after holidaying in South Africa. We arranged to meet at a pub on the Monday after our arrival. George had chosen a very pleasant old English type of establishment about a mile from the resort we were staying at, called the *Jackdaw*.

When they arrived we naturally got to chatting about what we had done in the intervening years. I knew George had done well for himself in the previous thirty years or so, but not just how well. He had been awarded the CBE for services to the health industry and was also a founder member of A.B.H.I, the British Health Care Industries Association, of which he was chairman for 38 years. The 'local cricket club' of which he was chairman was only Kent County Cricket Club!

George asked me if I played golf, so I told him that I used to play a bit but that I was ok now. Apparently he played 'a bit' and I asked him where.

"I play at Royal St Georges in Sandwich," he replied. I do not know much about golf but I do know you need a few quid to play there. You can imagine my reply when he told me it was £160 a round, but he could get it at reduced rate. I could not help saying, "Just think, if you had not come south and played for Rovers you would still be an electrician in Leith!"

"Give us a wee bit of credit, you bastard," he replied.

CHAPTER 20
IT SHOULD NOT HAPPEN

In July 2010, Jason had an offer from his old boss at Kimberley Clark to go and work at their plant in Singapore, and asked me what I thought about him going to live out in Asia. I told him I had no problem with him going, if it was what he really wanted. He did well. He got himself a great job and a fantastic apartment in Singapore, his girlfriend Maria moved in, and everything was going well.

Then, on February 24th 2011, I was sitting at my desk at work reading when I saw an email from him in Singapore. "I've got some bad news dad," it read, "I need to talk to you."

"I am at work if you want to talk right away," I replied, and gave him my number. He rang within minutes, and after the usual pleasantries I said, "Okay, what's up then?" I thought he had lost his job or something like that.

"I need a liver transplant," he said. I can't remember my exact words, but I think it was along the lines of, "Fucking hell why? What's wrong?" He went on to tell me that he had been to the doctors in Singapore as his legs and tummy were a bit swollen. They had done several tests and he had a CT scan, which showed he had a tumour the size of a cricket ball on his liver and also had sclerosis of the liver.

There are comes a point in most peoples' lives when they realize the stakes have suddenly changed. The carefree ride along life's highway suddenly hits a brick wall. All those years when you think nothing can go wrong, when everything more or less falls into place, abruptly ends. But these things happen to other people, not you. Well, now it was my turn.

Jason had been told that they could operate on him, but it would cost approximately $200,000, which was not covered by Kimberley Clark company insurance. I told him to get on a flight and get himself home. We would sort him out when he got here. I told him to email his medical records and any other relevant information that he could to me. I contacted his doctor in Anlaby, informed them of the situation, and they told me as soon as he knew when he would be arriving in UK, they would organise an immediate appointment.

I had to get home to tell his mother the news, and that was not going to be an easy job. I told Jim at work what was going on. I had tears in my eyes, but I had to keep strong for Jacky. I got home around lunchtime, and as I walked in Jacky, asked what was I doing home so early. I told her to sit down as we needed to talk. I said, "It's Jason, he is not very well." What an understatement. I told her that Jason had a problem with his liver and it looked as if he needed a transplant. She just burst into tears, which I had expected – she is susceptible to tears, a sentimental film sets her off, never mind this news. After all, Jason was still her baby boy and the worst thing in the world had just happened.

I had told Jason I would email him when I got home, so that we could Skype and talk face-to-face. We went upstairs and logged on. Jason came on looking awful, but, Jason being Jason, was still his usual smiling self. We discussed what had happened, he told us that his boss had agreed to get him home, and that they would cover the costs. We were in turmoil. We discussed with Jason selling our houses to get the money for an operation if necessary, but time was of the essence, and we did not have enough of it.

I should mention that in Singapore they will only carry out liver transplants from live donors, they will not take them from deceased people, which certainly complicates matters. For that reason too, he needed to get home to be here with his family. I have realised since, how difficult it would have been if we were still in Australia and someone back home had been taken ill, and it has really changed my opinion about being thousands of miles away from your loved ones. We let Tracy know the situation and did not hide anything from her. We knew this was going to be a battle, but we did not know just how much of a battle Jason faced.

We did not sleep that night. We both were in tears thinking about Jason and what he must be going through – it made it worse that we were not there to hold him and console him, tell him how much we loved him and what he meant to us. All things I never thought much about till then.

On March 14th, Tracy and I went over to Manchester to pick Jason up from the airport. As he walked out of the arrivals area he looked terrible, but once again he was still smiling. We hugged and held him tight. To have him home, even though in such terrible circumstances was wonderful. It had only been eight months, but now we had him with us and our battle to get him better could begin.

I took him straight to his doctors, where Dr Cassim examined him. He could not believe Jason had no pain, but said he would refer him to Castle Hill Hospital to see a surgeon. It took a week, but that was quick according to what we were told. Jacky and I went with Jason to see Mr Wedgwood, who examined him, along with a liver specialist, and again, he could not understand why Jason was not in pain. We were then given an appointment to see Mr G. Toogood, head of the transplant team, and his specialist registrar, Mr A. Aldouri, at St James's Hospital, Leeds on March

29th. Meanwhile, as Jason was stopping with us, his GP registration was transferred to Dr Ruth Driver in Hedon. Jason himself was, as usual, positive. He was going to beat this.

The doctors at St James's had all Jason's notes and the information he had brought from Singapore. The bad news was that, as Jason had sclerosis of the liver and also a tumour the size of a cricket ball on his liver, they could not do a transplant. I will never ever forget the look on Jason's face when he was hit with this bombshell. He was told that Singapore should never have told him he could have a transplant, as it was internationally known that the survival rate for people with such severe problems was very low. Mr Toogood said to Jason, "If livers grew on trees I would give you one, but they don't, and we can't afford to waste one."

He explained that the only course of action was to try and get the liver working better, so they could try to kill the tumour by injecting it with chemotherapy drugs. Once they had got rid of that, they could then manage the sclerosis, and give him an extended life – but they could not put a timeframe on that. They organised an appointment with a blood specialist, Dr Ruth Jones, who would try to get his liver working better, so that the chemo could be carried out.

Jason received a letter from St James's a week later explaining why they could not do the transplant. It basically said that the illness was due to the amount of alcohol he had consumed – in Mr Aldouri's opinion, Jason was more or less an alcoholic. He broke down on reading this. He had explained that he had not lived a healthy lifestyle over previous years due to his work and not eating properly.

Jason wrote a letter to Mr Toogood and handed it to Dr Jones when he went back on April 12th. She read the letter and looked quite shocked at what was in the one sent from Mr Aldouri, but did not comment. She undertook to give Mr Toogood a copy of the response and discuss it with him. She discussed what was need to try and get his liver functioning better – and changing his diet was the main thing. She asked for another CT scan, and Jason went to Leeds General on the 19th April.

At that point, it was decided to wait until the 10th May to see if the treatment worked. Dr Jones also asked for a test for Alpha 1 Antitrypsin Deficiency, as she could not understand why Jason had got sclerosis of the liver. When we returned to see Dr Jones, the results of the tests showed that Jason was suffering from AATD, which was the reason he had got sclerosis. It was not through alcohol abuse but a genetic disease.

Everyone has two genes, either M or Z, which affect Antitrypsin levels. It is the Z gene which causes the problem, and whilst people who are MZ are themselves not at risk, they are

Keith Pollard

Jason in 2011

Only Jason was in fancy dress

Jason in Singapore 2010

Jason and Ken, his best school pal

carriers. Both Jacky and I are MZ, and, unknown to us, had both passed down the Z gene to Jason, who was therefore ZZ and had developed AATD, which can lead to lung and liver disease.

Tracy had to have blood tests, and she too was found to be ZZ. She had an x-ray and tests and her lungs and liver were clear. There is no cure for AATD but it can be managed, in particular by maintaining a healthy lifestyle and certainly never smoking. In my own case, as I have said, I always get a bad chest whenever I get the colds and flu – and I now knew why. As a carrier you are susceptible to the same infections as someone who had AATD, but you do have some immunity and there should not be the same risk.

Jason had been having weekly blood tests at his GPs, but there was no improvement. On May 16th, Dr Driver told him that there was nothing they could do. Jason was terminally ill. No-one could give him a timescale, but there would be no recovery.

Throughout all this, Jason had been unbelievable. He went to see all his mates, answering them when they asked how he was with, "Well considering that I am dying, I'm not too bad." It was other people rather than Jason himself who found the situation so hard to deal with. His best mate, Ken, could not handle it at all, and it was Jason that was having to console him.

One night, Jason asked what would happen when he died, and I asked if he wanted cremation or a burial. Typically, and like his mother, he said, "Whatever is the cheapest." When we agreed on cremation, I asked about the ashes.

"Do you want to go in the river with Grandma and Granddad's ashes?" I asked.

"Fuck off! You know I can't stand water!" he replied, and we all laughed. It was surreal.

Jason had been going through his affairs trying to sort everything out in readiness, but one thing he had not done was to explain to Maria how bad things were. She was under the impression he was going to get better, and at least be able to go back to Singapore. There was talk of her coming over for holiday whilst Jason was here. When he was told that the illness was terminal, he stopped skyping her and after a few days she started to get worried and sent texts for him to contact her. In fact, he did not call her for a few days, and she was obviously getting worried.

After some persuasion from us, he organised a Skype session. He talked to her about trying to organise a visa for her to come here, but she is a Philippine and knew she would find it hard to get a visa from Singapore. It became all too much for Jason at that point, so he put Jacky on cam and he went in to the kitchen. I followed him and he broke down. I put my arms around him and hugged him as he sobbed on my shoulder, "Why me?" I just did not know what to say. He pulled himself together, his inner strength

Keith Pollard

Jason meeting up with some old friends just before he died

was amazing, and he went back on the webcam to talk to her. He said he would contact her later about the visa application, and they said their goodbyes. I felt so sorry for him. I cannot describe the hurt and helplessness I felt. This should not have been happening – it was a nightmare from which I would not wake.

The following day, Dr Driver visited the house to say that that the cancer had now spread, and when I got home Jason and Jacky told me the bad news. Jason broke down for only the third time. He was just sobbing and asking that question again – 'why me?' I went over and took him in my arms again, feeling more helpless than ever. What can you say when you know your son is dying in front of you – it is not supposed to happen, you are supposed to go first. I told him we loved him and that we were always going to be there for him. He stopped crying, took a deep breath and said, "Ok, dad, I'm ok." Again I felt so proud of his strength and the way he had dealt with the whole thing.

I have heard it said that it is easier for those that are going to die, who know it is going to happen, than it is for the family and friends, when there is nothing that they can say or do to make it easier. In his book, '*It's not about the bike*,' Lance Armstrong said, "It is not the individual that beats cancer, it is the doctors and surgeons, the specialists, who beat the disease; you survive it."

Jason fought but to no avail, he tried his best, but he could not beat it alone. Cancer has no favourites, money cannot save you, you can be the richest person in the world but if cancer strikes and the known treatments do not work, that is the end.

On 20th May, we had a visit from the McMillan nurses. Jason asked them to be open and frank with him. When he had been to see the doctors previously, he had a list of questions for them, and when they answered one, he ticked it off, and went onto the next. It was the same scenario that day.

"How will I die? What will happen?" was his first question. The nurse told him she had never been asked that question before so openly, and said he would gradually get more and more tired, and as time went on he would not want to do much. When she asked if he wanted a wheelchair he said, "If I can't walk, I won't be going out."

Did he want a hospital-type bed bringing to the house, she asked? We suggested putting it in the living room but he said he would consider that one and get back to them on it. I was in tears as they were discussing these things and he looked at me and said to the nurse, "I'm more worried about him than me, look at him!" Just the memory brings tears to my eyes now.

She went on to describe how, in his final days, he would go in to a coma, how his body would eventually shut down and how he would pass away in his sleep. His main concern was would he suffer any pain – he never could stand pain. They said that there need not be any pain, which could be handled with medication. He was happy with that and thanked her for coming and being so frank with her answers. She told him again that no one had ever asked her these questions in such detail before and that she thought he was very brave.

Jason had his 41st birthday on May 22nd and we had a barby. One of his mates, Chris, had organised the meat, which was donated by a high class butchers in Anlaby. By now, he had lost a lot more weight and was looking much worse. He had started to put on weight at one point during his weeks at home, but since the cancer took hold, he had started to go downhill.

May 26th was a Thursday and I had woken up as usual, about 6am. Jacky was complaining about her back, which had gone into a spasm and said she could not move. I helped her up, and when it eased a bit she said, "It's okay – get off to work." Around 9.30, I was at my desk when I got a phone call from Jean O'Brien, a friend of ours. She said, "You had better get home – an ambulance is on the way."

I just said, "I'm on my way," and drove as fast as I could from Immingham. It usually took about three-quarters of an hour on a good run, but I did it in record time. As I turned into Acklam Road, where we lived, there was an ambulance outside the house. It then dawned on me that in my alarm I had not asked if it was for Jacky or Jason. As I opened the front door and entered the living room I saw a wheelchair-type stretcher but with no one in it. I then saw Jason and he looked terrible; his colour was the worst it had been and his eyes, which I will never forget, were bright yellow and flaky-looking. He had woken up in terrible pain with a very bloated stomach. He was already booked in to have a drain fitted to take away the fluid that had built up – a feature of liver disease, because the body tries to protect it by surrounding it with fluid. Jacky had called Jean, who was formerly a nurse, to ask if she could come round and help, and she had called our GP.

There was the usual inquest about whether it was an emergency, but Jean obviously knew what to say because Doctor Innes came straightaway, gave Jason a shot of morphine to kill the pain and sent for the ambulance. The paramedic asked him to get in the wheelchair but he said, "No – I will walk out, thanks." I took his arm and walked him in his dressing gown to the ambulance, with him saying, "Stop worrying – I'm okay," every time I asked if he was alright.

Jacky got in with him and I set off to Hull Royal Infirmary. By the time I got parked up and into A&E, Jason had not arrived in the Acute Assessment Unit and I was sitting waiting when they arrived and took him in. We were allowed in after about half an hour, and a young doctor came to take some blood samples. Jason hated this, in fact he was like me and hated hospital full stop. We sat there at the side of his bed, waiting to see when they were going to do the drain on his stomach.

They came back a couple of hours later saying they were going to move him in to a more comfortable bed in a side ward, still in the AAU. The pain was starting to get a bit worse again as the morphine wore off, and the nurse said she would go and get some more for him. After a while he said to his mum, "Where's that fucking morphine?"

"A few weeks ago, you would not even take paracetamol and now you've a craving for morphine!" Jacky replied, and we all had a laugh. Then Jason turned to his mum and said, "Is this it, then? Am I going to die today?"

"Not today, Jason, not today," she said. He just smiled and laid his head back on the pillow, quite content that his mother had told him he was not going to die that day. When he was transferred up to the ward we went up with him, and they asked if he could get into a wheelchair to go to X-ray. We told them there was no chance of him sitting in a wheelchair as the pressure on his stomach was unbearable. They were not entirely happy, but in the end he was taken away in the bed. When he came back he had a cross marked on his side where they were going to put the drain tube. Jason explained to us what the procedure was, and how it was going to work to ease the pressure on his stomach. It all sounded perfectly simple. I wondered why had it not been done already and whether there was something we were not being told. Jason had not had much sleep the previous night and was getting very tired by this time, so we decided to leave him to rest and he would see us in the morning.

Neither of us got much sleep that night, and we were up early when we got a phone call from a McMillan nurse at Castle Hill Hospital, who said they were going to organise for Jason to be transferred to their palliative care unit after the operation. She said that a nurse would meet us at Hull Royal Infirmary to tell us what had been arranged. Around 8am, I called the hospital to ask how Jason was. I was told that he had a restless night but was then sleeping. They asked us to see Dr Ali when we came in and said that we could go in anytime.

Our friends, Jean and Shaun O'Brien, called round to see how Jason was before we left, and whilst they were at the house Hull Royal rang again, asking us to come in as soon as possible. Shaun had a car park pass and insisted on taking us, so we left straightaway with his pyjamas and a few other things. When we got there, we walked past the side ward where Jason was and I glanced in. He was sitting up with his hand behind his head and did not look too bad, but the doctor took us into an office and told us that his blood pressure had dropped a lot, and they had to get it back up before they could carry out the drain operation. Shaun was waiting outside, so I rang him and asked him to do us a favour and go and pick up Tracy, without telling her how serious the situation was.

Whilst we were talking to the doctor, a nurse rushed in to tell him that Jason was getting weaker and that his body was starting to shut down. We rushed into his room, where he was half sitting up with his eyes open, but he had gone into a coma. The machine monitoring his blood pressure and heartbeat was blipping more slowly as his heart slowed down. The nurse turned off the sound and I sat at one side holding his hand, with Jacky at the other. She was crying and talking to him, telling him he was going to be ok, but there was no response. He just laid there staring as we sat with him for about fifteen minutes.

I had read somewhere that when someone dies, the last sense to stop working is hearing, even after the heart has stopped pumping, apparently people continue to hear briefly. Jason was breathing slower and slower as it became longer between each breath. He then took one long deep breath and there was silence. I looked at the nurse and said, "Has he gone?" The nurse leant over and felt Jason's pulse and shook his head. "Yes, I think so."

Jason's work colleagues, Crichton Waddle and Esther Neo

Jason's work colleagues at Kimberley Clark, Singapore

RED & WHITE PHOENIX

Jacky just broke down. She lay across his body sobbing, "My baby has gone – why, why, why?" I got up and went to kiss Jason on the forehead and said, "See ya' kid – love you." I put my two fingers on his eye lids and closed his eyes, as they were still staring open. I had seen John Wayne do that numerous times in cowboy films, but could never have imagined I would ever do it to my own son. He lay there at peace – he had left us. Then his eyes opened again and I could not help myself, "Fucking hell!" I said. But the nurse closed them again and said, "That often happens. He has gone, Keith."

Jacky was still holding Jason in her arms, and as more nurses came in, I told her gently that we had to go.

"I am not leaving him. I won't leave him alone," she cried out in anguish. I physically had to pull her off him and took her back to the office. As we went into the office, Tracy arrived. I think she knew what had happened by the state of us, and we took her into a room to tell her that she was too late, and that Jason had just passed away. I asked her if she wanted to see him, and after she broke down and cried, she said 'No.'

She wanted to remember him as he was. The three of us just stood there hugging each other and crying uncontrollably. It was the worst day of our lives. Jason's favourite saying was, 'shit happens,' and it had, in bucket loads.

I called Shaun, who was sitting in the car park waiting for us and he said he would wait, no matter how long we were. He was brilliant for us. Then there were the calls to the family, to my work, and to Jason's solicitor, who was coming to the hospital to talk to him about his will, which he had been putting off.

We waited for the death certificate, which had to be completed by the duty doctor, and I stood waiting at the desk until they could give me the official notice that my son was dead. People were getting on with their business, nurses running around, patients walking about pushing drips on stands, all the usual hospital activity continued as normal. One guy walked past who was the same jaundiced colour as Jason, in fact Jason looked healthier than this poor soul. He nodded at me, smiled said, "Hi." I could not help wondering how long he had left. At that moment, I honestly believed that Jason dying meant nothing to anyone but us. It was our grief to take away from that hospital. To everyone else our son was just another body going to the mortuary. The little nurse who had rushed in to tell us Jason was going downhill came up and passed her condolences, and I thought she had a tear in her eye as she gave me a hug, but apart from her, it just seemed his passing was simply an everyday occurrence.

As I stood waiting, it took me back to when I was at school, stood alongside the teacher as they were analysing your work, and

Keith Pollard

The Memorial bench at Kimberley Clark in Singapore

you waiting for either a praise or a bollocking. The doctor was chatting to other people as she was writing, and actually giggled about something that was said. I could not believe it, she was actually laughing, and I had just lost my son. I felt like grabbing her and giving her a good slap. Looking back, I was out of order and I feel a little ashamed of myself – they have to be able to cope with seeing death every day.

We left the hospital, taking Jason's possessions with us to where Shaun was waiting. He did not know what to say, what can you say in those circumstances? Back at home the house seemed empty, and Jacky started to talk about what we had to do about the funeral and letting people know. I was just numb and I broke down in the kitchen. My son had gone, and there was nothing I could do to help him, nothing. I felt I had let him down, I felt so angry with that disease that had killed him.

Ian, Jacky's younger brother, Angela, his wife, Ian and Dena, Jacky's younger sister, and Stewart, Jacky's eldest brother, all came round to see us and we sat there not knowing what to say. We talked about Jason of course, you always recall things the deceased had done in their lives, which I suppose is the first part of the grieving process.

We now had the job of telling Maria that she would never see

Jason again, that he would not be coming back to Singapore. The time difference between the UK and Singapore is about seven hours. Maria worked at the airport as a sales manager for one of the jewellery outlets, and we did not know what shift she was working so we were not sure if she would be at work, at home or in bed asleep, so we left it until it was about 10 o'clock their time.

We went to my PC and turned on Skype and called her. When she answered she looked tired and drawn. I think she hoped we were going to say Jason was okay, but when she looked at us I think she could tell by the look on our faces. When we told her that Jason had passed that morning she just screamed and collapsed into sobbing. We tried to console her, but how can you do that from thousands of miles away? We asked if any of her friends were nearby to come round and see her, but we could not get through to her, she was in hysterics. I kept talking to her and trying to calm her down, but it was not working. We could not just turn off the PC, but we had our own grief to contend with and this was the last thing we needed. She was really a stranger to us and at that moment Jacky particularly could not handle Maria's pain as well as her own. Eventually she calmed down a bit and she called a friend as we spoke. I explained what had happened to Jason, who had never told her how ill he really was. It was typical of him to try to spare her feelings, but this time it had done her no favours. it was so sad seeing her the way she was, and not being able to console her. We told her we would talk again tomorrow and set a time.

When we went back downstairs, Dena, Ian and Stewart were still there. Ian and Angela had gone – the sound of Maria's screaming and crying was too painful for them to bear. I sent an email to Jason's boss Crichton, asking him to call us when he got the message. He rang us later on and we gave him the sad news his voice broke. He said he would be in touch in a couple of days, once we had time to make the necessary arrangements.

The process began to tie up Jason's affairs, as he never got to make a will, and we had to go and see a solicitor to get probate. I would say to anyone that you must make a will. I know it is not the nicest thing to do, but two things are certain in this life, one is being taxed and the other is dying. You just do not know when the latter will happen, so just do it straightaway – it saves a lot of grief for your relatives, when you are in your box with no more worries.

We had to organise his affairs, not only here in the UK but also in Singapore, which was really difficult both emotionally and practically. It was a nightmare trying to organise everything that needed doing, even though Jason had attempted to go through his paperwork during the last twelve weeks. I cannot imagine what was going through his head as he sorted everything out with Jacky, particularly as the weeks went on and every time he saw the

Keith Pollard

doctors there was no good news.

We had a phone call from one of Jason's mates, someone we had never even met, Barry Dixon, who called to pass on his condolences, after reading in the paper that Jason had passed away. He asked if he and some other friends could come and see us over the weekend. We agreed and they came on the following Sunday. We could not believe some of the things they told us. You think you know your kids, but deep down you really do not. We learnt so much about Jason, but sometimes it seemed that they were telling us stories about a stranger.

We had booked the small chapel at crematorium but, when we told Barry and his pals about it, they suggested trying for the big chapel. They thought there would be quite a few people who would want to come and pay their respects. We also met some of Jason's old workmates from the KC factory, just over the Humber Bridge at Barton; they told us they were going to put a bus on to bring people to the service. It was overwhelming.

When the day came, we followed the cortege into the chapel as usual. The Bob Marley song *'Three Little Birds,'* better known as *'Don't Worry About A Thing'*, one of Jason's favourite songs, was playing. We had asked people not to wear ties but to come casually dressed – football shirts would be great – he would not have wanted people to be morbid or unhappy at his passing. We had a Humanist to carry out the service as we are not practicing Christians. Jacky is a believer, but to be honest I am not. I think if there was a God, there would not be so much suffering in this world. The celebrant went through Jason's life using information she had gathered from us and Jason's friends. In the middle of the service, we played Elvis singing the old Tom Jones song *'Green Green Grass of Home.'*

One of Jason's mates was going to say a few words but in the event he just could not do it. Jacky said to me, "We will have to say something," and she pushed me up to thank everyone for turning up to say good bye to Jason. When we stood and turned to face the gathering, I could not believe how many where packed in to the room, they were literally hanging from the rafters, they all could not get in. It was estimated that about three hundred people had come. I was dumbstruck. I started to say something, but then the words would just not come out – I was so close to breaking down. Jacky took over and being the trooper she is she thanked everyone.

The celebrant closed the service and said that if anyone wanted to say goodbye they could come forward. Jason had followed Liverpool from being a kid, and the club anthem *'You'll never Walk Alone'* then started playing. I shouted, "If you know the words sing them!" So everyone started singing and I was in tears. As people started to leave the chapel, we stood in the porch to thank everyone individually and the line just went on and on and on. There were people we have never met in tears as they passed – it was one of the most moving things that has ever happened to me. It was just so sad that my son had to die for it to happen.

The realisation that I did not really know my son, really hurt. I have never been a 'lovey-dovey' type of person. I hear other people on the phones to their kids and at the end it is always, "Bye bye, love you." I do not understand that. If they do not know you love them, they should, you are their parents for heaven's sake, why do you have to keep reminding them? I was never brought up with that happening to me, so maybe that is why I think that way. My parents rarely expressed their feelings – they did not do it to each other never mind anyone else. I remember reading some old letters my father sent my mother from Africa and Italy during the Second World War. He used to address them 'Dear Wife,' and to me they did not have any real love in them. But we are what we are, nothing can change that, but you can learn from your mistakes.

I know Jason was a bit of a loner; he could be hard to talk to and often spoke in monosyllables. When you asked him a question, he often just said 'yes' or 'no.' He never really opened up, even as a kid he was not a talkative one. But was it just me that he could not converse with? I do regret that we did not get to know each other better and I tell people now to make sure you know your kids before it is too late. You do not have to live in their pockets, see them every day, or call them every day – to me that is not right. They should live their own lives and make their own mistakes, as we have, whilst we will always be there to help them.

We were not expecting him to go so quickly, from him landing at Manchester airport to that final day had been only twelve weeks. He passed away just a week after his 41st birthday. It is so very hard to lose a child; I do not think we will ever fully get over it. We can only be thankful that we had him at home to be with us when he died. We are so glad he did manage to get home from Singapore – I just do not know how we would have handled it if he had not.

Those final weeks he was with us are so precious. I would have missed seeing that stupid grin and hearing him saying, 'Goodnight Father,' as he went through the door to bed. We all miss him so much, and quoting the words from a Kristofferson song, '*I would trade all my tomorrows for one single yesterday.*'

Not a single day goes by without him coming into my head. I think about the things we did, and the things we never did. As I have written this chapter, the tears have flowed regularly and sometimes I could hardly see the screen. But I had to put it down on paper. It helps to talk about him and I also hope my words may help anyone who one day loses a loved one. I only hope that it is not a child, for that really should not happen.

CHAPTER 21
RETIREMENT

I retired from Conoco Philips in January 2012. Then, after the worst year in our lives, we went back to Australia again for a twelve-week holiday. This time we went via Singapore and visited Kimberley Clark, where we had hoped to scatter some of Jason's ashes. This was not possible for a couple of reasons, but we had a memorial bench put in the grounds of the plant in Jason's memory, hoping that people would use it when they went outside for breaks.

We met up with Jason's girlfriend, Maria, who took a few days off work to see us during the daytime. We told her that Jason would want her to move on, she was only a young girl and should not be in mourning for too long. She told us that she could not think about other men, all she wanted was Jason back. It had been eight months since he passed away but she was still taking it very hard.

We met some of Jason's old work colleagues including his boss, Crichton, and his PA, Esther, who had been such a help. We went round the plant and were introduced to the guys who worked with him on his shift. It was very harrowing having to explain over and over again how he had passed away so suddenly. It must have been as hard for them to talk about Jason as it was for us, and the suddenness had hit them very hard too. One of the guys, a Texan called Carlos Young, had known Jason from his time in training in Paris, Texas, and had been very close to him. He had been devastated by Jason's passing and I really felt sorry for him. Most of the others were from Singapore or Malaysia and they were very nervous about talking to us, until Carlos broke the ice. Then there were lots of tales told about Jason both and it was a real eye opener talking to all his work mates. Even though he was their supervisor they all spoke very highly about Jason and were truly upset about our loss.

Everyone was very kind to us and Kimberley Clark could not have done anymore for Jason – if ever a company went beyond the call of duty they did. We still converse with Esther but Crichton was transferred to plant in Malaysia and I believe is now back in the UK. I am sorry to say that we have lost touch with Carlos since he left Singapore.

We had a great week in Singapore, also meeting up with relation of mine, Dave Betts, who now lives in the Philippines and flew over to meet us with his partner Gina. Dave used to live in Singapore before his wife Leslie passed away and he moved to the Philippines. His job as a Salvage Master took him all over the world and it did not really matter where he lived. They booked in same hotel as us, took us around some of the sights in the city, and we had a few beers with them. Alcohol is very expensive, the cheapest we had was $15 a pint and it was $19 in the hotel bar – about £8. We went to a local market for lunch; it was great food and a third of the price as you would pay in the tourist restaurants.

Whilst it was a sad and difficult trip, we also had a great time there, and I could understand why Jason loved it so much. After that, we went on to Australia where we visited Melbourne, a city we had not been to before. We met up with Jacky's younger brother, Ian, and his wife, Angela, who were to spend our first four weeks in Australia with us.

We enjoyed Melbourne, where we stayed four nights, taking in the sights. Like Sydney, there is a free tram that goes around the city centre and you can get on and off at your convenience. It is ideal for tourists and would be a good idea for some of our major cities. All the main sporting arenas are in the same area, with the cricket ground the big attraction. It is quite some place, with its statues around the ground of some of the Aussie greats, like Don Bradman and Shane Warne, and some from Australian Rules Football.

I was nearly run over when I got off a tram that I had boarded by mistake. I got off onto what I thought was the pavement, but was actually the road, as the tram was in the middle of the two carriageways. I heard a screeching behind me and turned to see a blue sports car heading straight for me. The driver braked hard to a stop and I tried to take evasive action, and somehow it missed me. The lady driver, lady being a loose description, gave me a hell of a mouthful, only to get one back from the tram driver for speeding. I was a bit shaken and very lucky.

After leaving Melbourne we headed to Lakes Entrance. This is a coastal town in eastern Victoria, known mainly for the Gippsland Lakes, a vast system of inland waterways. It is an old-fashioned town but is well equipped with accommodation, services and facilities for people enjoying a coastal getaway. Across a footbridge from the promenade is one of the most popular beaches in Victoria, Ninety Mile Beach, which is a pristine surf beach patrolled by lifeguards during the summer months. You can explore the lakes in a kayak, join a boat cruise or hire a paddleboat and enjoy the sparkling waters. The Victorians go in their thousands to join the boating and fishing enthusiasts all year round. It is a really popular place, with a wide range of camping spots that surround the calm lake waters and line the shore. Lakes Entrance is renowned as a seafood capital due to the large number of fishing trawlers operating in the area. You can catch your own fish or savour the catches from fresh seafood shops around town.

Keith Pollard

Jacky, my wonderful wife

Tracy, wait til she sees this!

Tracy, Isla-Rose and Baxter

Daniel, Libby, Tracy and Baxter

RED & WHITE PHOENIX

The house we rented was called *Lakes on View*. It was a bit old fashioned and needed some TLC, but it had a decent-sized swimming pool that was clean. It was a bit too far to walk to the beach for us, although Ian and Angela used to walk everywhere.

After Victoria, we headed up the coast to Batemans Bay, on the south coast of New South Wales. This part of the state is really beautiful and it has a spectacular coastline. We rented a house for eight days called *Lochinvar at the Beach,* which was on its own private bay and had a little village within walking distance with a small bar and shop. It was on sale for one million Australian dollars and cost us the earth – we could only afford to rent it because there were the two families sharing the bill. It was a case of, 'how the other half live'. I could have got the taste for it, and I wondered what might have happened if we had stayed in Oz all those years before – but that was water under the bridge.

I do regret coming back to England at times, but what has happened made me realise that it was for the best. I also realise that it would have been very difficult for Jacky and her family. As an only child, I tend to be a bit self-centred and selfish. Although I am a social animal, I have always liked being alone and love my 'own space.' But I think this is still difficult for Jacky to understand, as, with two brothers and a sister she is very family orientated.

When I worked away from home, I really missed her and the kids, but deep down I enjoyed I being alone in my own world, doing what I wanted to do, and not having to take others into consideration. I think that experience also made me realise the need to make my own decisions, and as a result I became a stronger person.

After Batemans Bay, we headed up the coast towards Wollongong and stayed at a small town called Gerringong. Six famous people have come from this area and four of them are rugby league players, with Mick Cronin being the most famous. Our visit did not start off well. The house we had rented was, for want of a better description, a 'shit hole.' I contacted the owner and asked for our money back, which she gave us without any argument. We went to the only motel in town, told them what had happened, and they gave us two rooms for the time we were staying in area for what it would have cost us in the house – which was a lot less than their standard rates. I think they must have felt sorry for us!

By this time, I was starting to feel the need for my own company, so when the others decided they wanted to go to the beach, I decided to go off on my own to *Cronin's Pub*. I went into the pub and was looking at the photographs around the walls and chatting to one or two locals when Mick Cronin himself came in. Mick was an idol in Gerringong – having played for Australia

Keith Pollard

The second Maitland Reunion

More friends in Maitland

whilst still playing for his local team, which would be unthinkable now, before going to play in Sydney and winning 33 Australian caps. I introduced myself to him and told him a bit about my background, and he called across to a bloke nearby.

"Hey Barry, you played for one of the Hull mobs didn't you?"

"Yeah, mate," this guy replied, and I asked which one.

He said he had played for Rovers, and I did not know if he was bullshitting, as I did not recognise him, and I asked his name.

"Barry Andrews," was the reply. Now I recognised that name – he had played for Cronulla in the 70s before finishing his career at Eastern Suburbs – but I never knew he had a spell in the UK. Barry said that he came to Rovers when Harry Poole was coach in 1976. He was a half-back, but Steve Hartley and Roger Millward were embedded in those positions at Rovers, so Harry gave him his first-team debut at full-back against St Helens. Rovers got beaten, he did not have a great game, and after a couple of substitute appearances, he left to join York. He never enjoyed it there so, as young Aussies do, went off to tour Europe before returning home. He was quite a prolific goal-kicker at Cronulla.

Whilst I was chatting away to Mick, Barry got on his phone, and after a couple of minutes handed it to me saying, "It's a mate of yours!" I thought who the hell does he know that I know?

"Hello," I said, before a well-known Brummie voice said, "Hello Keith, when are you coming to see me?" It was Cliff Watson, the legendary St Helens and Great Britain prop-forward who emigrated to play for Cronulla. I knew Cliff as an opponent from when I played against him in that memorable game back in 1965, and had met him once socially when I lived out in Oz. We once went out with Cliff and his wife for a meal and finished up at his house for a bit of a party, but I had not been in touch with him since. However, he said he hoped I would go and see him whilst he was there. As it happened, were going back to Sydney to pick up my daughter and grand-daughter a couple of weeks later, so I took his number and said I'd call him. As it happened, I did not have time to arrange anything, and I have just heard that Cliff has sadly passed away. He was a gentleman and a true great of the game.

It had been a super afternoon, I'd had a few beers, met one of Australia's greats, met Barry Andrews, and had a very pleasant surprise talking with Cliff. Barry gave me his business card and email, asked me to keep in touch, and asked me to give my regards to anyone who could remember his stay at Craven Park. When I got back, I sent Barry's details to Marjory Hutton, Colin's wife, because like most of the single Aussies that came to play for Rovers, he stayed with the Huttons at their pub 'The Zetland Arms' whilst he was there. Marjory liked to keep in touch with all 'her boys,' as she puts it, and had lost touch with Barry. If you are ever

Keith Pollard

The Maitland reunion 2017

Terry Pannowitz and Brian Burke

RED & WHITE PHOENIX

in Gerringong, you should visit '*Cronin's Pub*' and the Bowling Club on the beach, where they make you make you really welcome and have an excellent Chinese restaurant and bar meals.

After Gerringong, we went to Sydney for Ian and Angela's last few days with us. We were advised by our travel agent to stay at the *Breakfree* on George Street. I will not bore you with the details, but it was worse than the house in Gerringong – we stayed one night and I was itching from the minute we walked in to the room. Our contact at Trailfinders in the UK got us a special rate at the Mercure Hotel in George Street near the Central Railway Station – it was a four-star hotel and it was spot on. Whilst we were there we went in the NSW Leagues Club for a few beers and as the restaurant looked ok, we decided to eat there on the night. We ended up eating there on each of the nights we were there – the food was brilliant and they would anything we wanted. Added to which, of course, as it was a club, the beer was cheap.

After those few days, our two travelling companions went home but we had another two months in Australia. We had one more night on our own at the hotel and then set off on our travels to some friends at Shoal Haven, south of Wollongong, Graham and Julie Rollinson. Graham played with me at Maitland and we remained good friends. He joined the Pickers as a scrum half from the Maitland Blacks Rugby Union but suffered a horrendous injury that more or less finished his career. He broke and dislocated an ankle, and the sight of his foot pointing in an unnatural angle as they carried him off made me feel quite sick. He made a comeback a few years later whilst living in Wollongong, where he had moved with his job as a town planner, but was never the same player again.

We stopped at Rollo's for a few days. His wife Julie had always been very arty. She was Head of Art at Wollongong College but had retired and started her own business, '*Drab to Fab*' she called it but then changed it to '*That Travel Chick.*' I am no expert in this field, but to put it in layman's language, she is an image consultant who helps ladies purchase clothes for travelling. Her motto is, 'Style it, Pack it, Wear it' – and that is all the free advertising you get, Julie! We had great time with them and met up with some St George supporters in the local pub. I wound them up about how poor their team was – in particular their so-called great player, Jamie 'the Coward' Soward – I enjoyed telling them that I did not know how he even got a game!

We then set off for Taree, where we stayed at Diamond Beach for eight nights in a lodge. It was a good spot to walk through the grounds straight onto the beach and there were other beaches nearby. Johnny and Lynn Mayhew, our closest friends from Kempsey, came to stay with us for the week. I also got in touch with an old friend from Widnes, Brian Atherton, who lives in Taree

Keith Pollard

Mick Finch, his dad Bob, Ron Clark, Me, Robert Finch, Tommy
Driffield, Terry Pannowitz and Alan Mc Nab

Chatting with Luke Dorn

Back: Jacky with Michael Zysek
and Merv Wright's partner
Suzanne Margetts. Front: Phil
Eulo, Gary Oldfield and me

and is President of the Mid North Coast Men of League organisation. Men of League is a society run by ex-players to help those less unfortunate than themselves who have been involved in the game as players or administrators of any standard – in fact, anyone can join for $20. Former South Sydney and Australian captain, Ron Coote, is the president, and because Australia is so large, the organisation is split up into areas. They hold meetings and events, and there is an informative quarterly magazine about what they are doing – including, unfortunately, an obituaries section. It is a really great organisation though. Brian and his wife Carol joined us and we all had bit of a barby and few drinks. Once again it was great to catch up with old friends.

After Diamond Beach, we went up to Kempsey for a few days. We went to visit Judy Cameron, whose husband Max had been the strapper at Kempsey, and her daughter Debbie – we had always got on really well with the family. We did not know it then, but we would not see Judy again because she passed away last year. She was a real trooper, very sharp tongued, but had a heart of gold – wherever she is now, old Max will be getting an ear bashing!

We stayed with Johnny and Lynn and, of course, went into the Kempsey Heights Bowling Club, just down the road from them, and met some of my old team-mates there and caught up on news, including some old teammates who had sadly passed away. We all went to meet Ian Martin, who I had played with in North Coast team, at his place out in the bush near Sherwood, and had a couple beers with him and his wife, Julie. Julie comes from Nottingham, so it is a bit of a coincidence that she now lives in Sherwood. Ian works for the council looking for damaged roads, logging them into his computer with map co-ordinates so that they can be included in repair programmes. When they have enough in a particular area they send work crews out to repair them. It is a pity our councils do not have the same system – and they have no-where near the size of area to cover.

Ian is a real outdoor man, always fishing, hunting or shooting out in the bush – what a life! He had a couple of dogs running around the property, both very friendly and playful, but I saw another dog, a very large one in a type of cage, and as I approached, Ian shouted, "Don't go near him, Pom! He's facking crackers!"

I could not resist having a closer look, but this beast launched himself into the side of the cage and the look on his face caused my bowels to loosen. Thankfully, it was only ever allowed out with a muzzle and a lead.

When we said our goodbyes to Ian and Julie it was a bit emotional – I hate saying farewell and I thought it would probably be the last time we would meet. We are so far away from Australia and their living so far off the beaten track makes it seem so much

Keith Pollard

Tommy and Kate Ball in Florida

Ex-Kowboys' scrum-half,
Johnny Mayhew

On holiday with Jacky's brother
Ian and his wife Angela

RED & WHITE PHOENIX

further – it is not as if you can just nip round for a beer or a coffee. My relative, Dave Betts, follows the old fisherman's superstition and never says goodbye – the fishermen thought if you say it you are tempting fate, and considering the number of colleagues they have lost, it is no wonder they had superstitions.

On the way back, John was showing us around the new areas of Kempsey area that had shot up over the years since we left. There were some wonderful houses on great big blocks of land. Passing one of these houses, I spotted Geoff 'Gully' Trees, who I had worked with at HF Hands. He was just coming out of his house to go into the back yard, which, typically of Geoff, was full of old machinery and trucks. We stopped so that I could jump out, and as he saw me he said, "G'day mate, can I help you?"

"How are you mate? Do you remember me?" I replied.

"You old Pommie bastard," he said, "How the fack are you mate? Been a while between drinks!" We had not met for not far off 40 years, but after we chatted for a few minutes and I left him to work on his trailer, it was just as if the years had never been and gone. I like that about the Australian lifestyle – it always seems so easy, perhaps more so in the smaller towns like Kempsey, and even Maitland, although that has grown out of recognition due to the coal industry, and still is.

We left John and Lynn's to head down to Maitland and the McNabs. They are our closest friends out of a group of about ten couples, whom we first met when we went to Maitland and who welcomed us in to their midst with open arms, making settling into a new life in a new country so much easier. One or two have since passed away, and one couple have split up – but they still hold a place in our hearts and we try keep in touch with them either by a letter or card every Christmas and on Facebook. I know that Facebook is not everyone's cup of tea, and it irritates me when people post about what they had for breakfast or that they have taken the dog for a walk, but it is such a great way of keeping in touch with friends on the other side of the world. For me, it is the greatest thing invented since the telephone.

We had arranged to stop with the McNab's for three weeks, with a week in the middle at Nelsons Bay, where we had rented a house for when Tracy and Libby joined us. Once again we were in Maitland over the Easter period – we tend to go back at that time of year to get away from our bad winter months in January to March. We had our usual reunion, getting all our friends and former team-mates and partners together. There were Kevin & Rhonda Cousins, Brian & Peggy Burke, Ronnie & Betty Clark, Merv Wright and Suzanne, his partner of so many years, Ray & Rae Waskovtiz, and I apologise to any I have missed. Without doubt this was the best group that I ever played with. They may not

Keith Pollard

Kevin and Rhonda Cousins, friends in Maitland

Alan and Gaye McNab

My mate Alan McNab wearing his favourite pommie team's colours

358

all have been the best players, but they were a really close-knit group. As I have said before, the Newcastle competition was in those days the next strongest to 'the big league' in Sydney. How it would have compared to today's Super League in the UK I do not know, but I have discussed this with several knowledgeable people that have been involved in both eras in Australia and the UK and they reckon that some of the players who think they are 'stars' here, would not have got a game in the Newcastle competition when we played there.

We had a great stay with all our friends in Maitland and the surrounding area, as well as in Nelsons Bay with Tracy and Libby. That was a nice big modern house in a complex with a communal swimming pool that no-one seemed to use. It was a waste, but the beach was so close and the Aussie always prefer the beach. After we returned to Maitland, Tracy and Libby stayed on their own for a bit. Then they joined us for the scattering of some of Jason's ashes on the Maitland Sports Ground, up on the hill where he had learned to walk and spent so much time in his early years. We had a little private ceremony; the four of us along with Alan and Gaye and Tommy and Carol Driffield. Jacky had got some red white and blue balloons to release as we spread his ashes. It was a difficult moment for us. They were the first we had placed anywhere after not being allowed to do so in Singapore. We opened the box and as I undid the plastic bag, Jacky, Tracy and Libby released the balloons. As with my old man's ashes on the Bull Nose off St Andrews Quay, once again the wind suddenly got up and the ashes went everywhere.

I then walked out to the centre of the pitch on my own, to reflect on days gone by. Tears were rolling down my face as I thought of the great times we had as a family in Australia; what might have happened if we had not gone back to the UK, and whether Jason's life would have panned out differently if we had stayed. All this was going through my head as I stood there alone, and not for the first time. I miss him so much and the tears still come. We never had a close father and son relationship, which I suppose was my fault and that of my upbringing. I often now lament on the fact that we were not closer and how I would change if I had him back. Whether that would have changed the way he was, I will never know. Was he so deep and hard to talk to, or was that because of me? We never discussed things deeply, even at the end. I told him then that I loved him and that I always would – but I cannot remember ever saying that to him previously. Even now, I do not say 'love you,' when I leave Tracy or the grand kids – they would think there was something wrong with me if I started doing it now. Maybe I should.

After that, we left Maitland and went to Sydney for the last few

Keith Pollard

The family with the McNabs in Australia, 2010

Our dream fulfilled, a Burstner Solano

days of our three-month trip.

Whilst writing this last chapter, I have just learned from our friends in Maitland that one of my old team mates from the Pickers, legendary winger Merv Wright, has sadly passed away, He was an aboriginal guy, a great player and a great person, who will be sadly missed. He had recently been voted Maitland's favourite player of all time in a poll carried out to name the top 20 club legends. He had been suffering from Alzheimer's disease and passed away in his sleep. 1,000 people attended his funeral at the Maitland Sportsground.

Sad news like this reminds you that you are not immortal. Since I started to write these memoirs, several former team-mates have passed away, people at Hull KR like the great Roger Millward, Terry Major, Johnny Moore, Brian Wrigglesworth and John Hickson, just to name a few. Cliff Watson, the old pommie front rower also passed away a few weeks ago in Australia, now he was a legend.

Recently I also sadly lost some good friends that we have made along the way. I would just like to acknowledge these people for they all in some way influenced my, or should I say our lives.

First of all, one of our dearest friends Nev Lucas, who was one of the most friendly and honest of men you could ever wish to meet, he went in his sleep, doing what he loved most in this world, watching golf.

Another one to leave us was Shaun O'Brien, a guy who I had known since our Constable Youth Club days back in the 60s. He left us after a long illness, in fact you name it he had it. I used to say to him you have had everything but distemper. What a fantastic person he was, he was simply 'one of the best' and will be sadly missed by everyone who knew him.

John McLane was another to leave this world, once again after a long illness. He was another guy who was involved with both professional Hull rugby clubs over the years, finishing up as 'kit man' at Rovers.

There are others who have passed on all of them either ex players I played alongside or against who were great friends during my lifetime.

Terry Ramshaw had more clubs than Jack Nicklaus, but always said Rovers was his favourite.

Keith Barnwell - Constable Street and Hull FC, one of the first black men I ever met during the days when there wasn't that many in Hull. A real extrovert and larger than life character.

Laurie Rawlings, another Constable Street lad who became one of the most prominent amateur Rugby League coaches in the game, hard as nails on the field but a real gent off it.

Tommy Smith, yet another ex-Constable Street lad, heart as big as a dustbin lid, would run through a brick wall, a real character off Hessle Road.

Another character to go was Jimmy Hicks. If you were down in the dumps and feeling low and you bumped into Jimmy, he lifted you up. He just had this aura about him, always on his bike wherever he went, played for lots of amateur clubs and finished up playing Union, to everyone's amazement, a great guy.

Dave Worthy - Keighley, one of my front row partners during my time at the club, a great, hard as nails prop forward, as well as a wonderful human being.

Most lately, Jeff 'Clanger' Bell passed away. He played for Constable Street with me when we were both 15. I didn't see him for years, then we got back in touch. He had moved to the West Riding and lived in Kippax near Castleford and had been in the licensing trade for many years, another great lad, who like them all will be sadly missed.

I hope I have not missed anyone out but I just had to put a few words together, as after all this story is about my life and they played a big part in it.

Today as I look back and remember them, I cannot help but think how much the game has changed since we played. As we all know, it is now a full time professional sport, which people think only started when Super League was introduced. But I remember reading back in 1973, when I was playing in Australia, that Eastern Suburbs, now the Sydney City Roosters, were planning to go full time within two to three seasons as they were trying to beat the NSW Leagues ceiling figures of $2,000 signing on fee and $200 a game match payment. Their intention was to employ 18 players who would be fully employed by the Leagues Club. At the time, they were building a new Leagues Club, which was costing $3m and was envisaged to employ 900 people – to lose 18 amongst them would be nothing. They were ambitious plans and I do not know how long it was before they came to fruition, but they still are one of the richest clubs in the NRL.

The players of today are bigger and fitter than in my day, but I do not believe that they are as skilful. Perhaps I am an old fogey, but in my humble opinion most of the players now do not actually play rugby. The accent now is on making yards and defensive patterns. As long as they can run and make yards that is all that matters. Statistics now focus on the number of carries and yards gained, tackles made and errors. Players do not need to know how to pass a ball or put a man through a gap, yardage is the aim of the game.

Substitutes were first allowed in 1964, but only for players injured before half-time, and have developed from there to the extent that today players only play in spells like American football.

RED & WHITE PHOENIX

Like many an old forward, I wish I had the advantages of being able to train full time, play on better grounds, and only play half of the game – and think what a great player I could have been!

It would have been fascinating to see the likes of Billy Boston, Vince Karalius, Eric Ashton, Alex Murphy and Roger Millward – all time-greats of the game – if they could have the advantages of being full-time players and hard fast grounds like the players of today. They could all really play rugby – they could play 'off the cuff.' I hanker after the old days when the game was the game I loved, when players were encouraged to show their skills, when individual talents were appreciated. I enjoy reminiscing about the old days, like *'For fans who don't want to forget'* in the *Rugby League Journal*, and walking down memory lane at the Rovers Heritage nights.

My old club, Hull KR, has endured some 'ups and downs' over recent seasons. We all have our opinions about the reasons for their problems – poor recruitment, bad luck with injuries, inconsistency, failure to get the basics right – I could go on – they have all played their part. Like all supporters, you just hope! There are some bright prospects at the club, players like Robbie Mulhern, Chris Atkin and Will Oakes, and there are good experienced players in what they now call the 'spine of the team' in Danny McGuire and Shaun Lunt. But they do need to recruit a bit more quality and strength if they are to be a force again.

I hope that you do not think I sound negative. I truly believe we had a great game, but I am sad that we have lost so much of what made it so great.

In 2017 we visited Australia and New Zealand, for what could be our last trip 'down under'. We had a fantastic time in New Zealand touring from Paihia, which is an excellent base from which to explore the Bay of Islands in the North, down to Wellington on the North Island. Then across the Tasman, which must be one of the most beautiful ferry trips in the World, and down to Queenstown in the South Island. We were there just after the earthquake around Kaikoura on the eastern coast, which had been cut off by road and rail. This had made us re-route our trip down the west coast, something we would not have done, but now allowed us to see some great places and met some new friends along the way.

Of all the places we have visited and would love to live, this country must rank amongst the most beautiful. If you ever get the chance you must go there, do it, never mind Spain, Portugal and Florida, anyone can go there. Save your pennies for a few years, miss out on your annual holidays and go to places you only dream of and look at in brochures, you won't regret it, I promise you.

Keith Pollard

Then we travelled across to Australia for a month, meeting up with a lot of the people I've mentioned in the book, as well as an old friend, John Shackleton and his wife Bridget in Manly. His daughter emigrated to Sydney a few years ago and they make quite a few trips there to visit her. John was working at Fulworth Engineering in Keighley as a junior draughtsman when we first met he also played down at Lawkholme. It's funny how things work out, he actually took over at Fulworth after I had left - and then we met up again on the other side of the world.

In Australia we enjoyed lots of the usual stuff: barbeques and stubbies, talking about old times and playing old games again and again. We stayed with our old friends Alan and Gaye McNab, who once again opened up their home to us. We can't thank them enough. All of our friends will stay long in our hearts. For times like these can't be bought, they only come from lifelong friendships that have to be earned.

I am 70 now and my mother and father both lived into their nineties, so I may be lucky – but that is only twenty years away, and it is 47 years since I left these shores to go to Australia. I can remember it as if it were yesterday.

It all reminds me of the well-known quote, 'You only live once – it is not a dress rehearsal.' So live every day as if it was your last, for one day it will be. Do not end up regretting that you did not do something when you could have done it.

Well that's just about it. I hope you have enjoyed our journey together through the paths of my life. It has been great looking back through my memory box at the past 70 years or so, it has been a full life, there are things that I would like to have done and may well still do. I would love to visit China and Japan, to do the Route 66 Chicago to Los Angeles; and to go to Brazil for the carnival. The world is such a small place nowadays, dangerous, yes, but with jet flight, almost anywhere is accessible.

If you have enjoyed my story, please tell your friends so that they can read it; if you have not, recommend it to the people you dislike.

Good luck – and have fun!

Keith Pollard
October 2018

WHAT IS ALPHA-1 ANTITRYPSIN DEFICIENCY?

Alpha-1 Antitrypsin Deficiency also known as Alpha-1, A1AD or AATD is an inherited, genetic condition, which may lead to lung or liver problems that can significantly affect your health. Alpha-1 antitrypsin (AAT) is a protein that is produced in the liver and, in healthy people, it is released into the blood circulation so that it can protect the body, from the damaging effects of inflammation.

The protein that is produced by AATD patients does not function properly and gets trapped in the liver. This can cause damage to the liver and, because the protein can't reach the circulation, the lungs lack the protection they need from the damaging effects of pollutants (particularly cigarette smoke) and infections.

Although the lungs and, to a lesser extent, the liver are the most commonly affected organs in AATD, there are some rarer complications that can lead to problems with the skin, kidneys and pancreas.

WHAT ARE OUR OBJECTIVES?

To relieve the needs of individuals suffering from the genetic condition Alpha-1 Antitrypsin Deficiency (AATD), their families, carers and friends, in particular, but not exclusively by:

a) Providing advice, support and equipment with a view to improve the quality of life of those suffering with AATD, their families, carers and friends;

b) Advancing awareness and knowledge of AATD, in particular among affected patients and medical professions and healthcare provider organisations;

c) Fostering improvements in access and equality of access to clinical expertise and optimal disease management and treatments for AATD;

d) Supporting initiatives aimed at development, introduction and widespread adoption of novel therapies for AATD, including research.

e) Working collaboratively with our members and relevant external individuals, groups of individuals, organisations and institutions in order to achieve a) - d).

All proceeds from the sales of 'Red & White Phoenix' will be donated to the Alpha-1 UK Support Group.

Lightning Source UK Ltd.
Milton Keynes UK
UKHW011144020721
386521UK00002B/623